A
MARVEL COMICS
PRESENTATION

CIVIL WAR
BLACK PANTHER

WRITER
REGINALD HUDLIN

ISSUE #19
PENCILER: SCOT EATON
INKER: ANDREW HENNESSY
COLORIST: DEAN WHITE
COVER ART: TREVOR HAIRSINE
& DEAN WHITE

ISSUES #20-22
PENCILER: MANUEL GARCIA
INKERS: MARK MORALES (#20),
SANDU FLOREA (#20) &
JAY LEISTEN (#21-22)
WITH SEAN PARSONS (#22)
COLORIST: MATT MILLA
COVER ART: ESAD RIBIC (#20),
GARY FRANK & DEAN WHITE (#21)
AND MIKE DEODATO JR.
& DEAN WHITE (#22)

ISSUES #23-25
PENCILERS:
KOI TURNBULL (#23-24) &
MARCUS TO (#24-25)
INKERS: DON HO (#23-25),
JEFF DE LOS SANTOS (#23-25),
SAL REGLA (#23-24)
& NICK NIX (#24)
COLORIST: J.D. SMITH
COVER ART: MICHAEL TURNER &
PETER STEIGERWALD
WITH MARK ROSLAN (#23-24)

LETTERER: VC'S RANDY GENTILE
ASSISTANT EDITOR:
DANIEL KETCHUM
EDITOR: AXEL ALONSO

COLLECTION EDITOR
JENNIFER GRÜNWALD

ASSOCIATE EDITOR
SARAH BRUNSTAD

ASSOCIATE MANAGING EDITOR
ALEX STARBUCK

EDITOR, SPECIAL PROJECTS
MARK D. BEAZLEY

VP, PRODUCTION & SPECIAL PROJECTS
JEFF YOUNGQUIST

SVP PRINT, SALES & MARKETING
DAVID GABRIEL

EDITOR IN CHIEF
AXEL ALONSO

CHIEF CREATIVE OFFICER
JOE QUESADA

PUBLISHER
DAN BUCKLEY

EXECUTIVE PRODUCER
ALAN FINE

BLACK PANTHER CREATED BY STAN LEE & JACK KIRBY

PREVIOUSLY:

THERE ARE SOME PLACES YOU JUST DON'T MESS WITH. WAKANDA IS ONE OF THEM. SINCE THE DAWN OF TIME, THAT AFRICAN WARRIOR NATION HAS BEEN SENDING WOULD-BE CONQUERORS HOME IN BODY BAGS. WHILE THE REST OF AFRICA GOT CARVED UP LIKE A CHRISTMAS TURKEY BY THE REST OF THE WORLD, WAKANDA'S CULTURAL EVOLUTION HAS GONE UNCHECKED FOR CENTURIES, UNFETTERED BY THE YOKE OF COLONIZATION. THE RESULT: A HIGH-TECH, RESOURCE-RICH, ECOLOGICALLY-SOUND PARADISE THAT MAKES THE REST OF THE WORLD SEEM PRIMITIVE BY COMPARISON.

RULING OVER ALL OF THIS IS THE BLACK PANTHER. THE BLACK PANTHER IS MORE THAN JUST THE EMBODIMENT OF A WARRIOR CULT THAT'S SERVED AS WAKANDA'S RELIGIOUS, POLITICAL AND MILITARY HEAD SINCE ITS INCEPTION. THE BLACK PANTHER IS THE EMBODIMENT OF THE IDEALS OF A PEOPLE. ANYONE WHO'D DARE TO MAKE A MOVE ON WAKANDA MUST GO THROUGH HIM.

DESPITE CONFLICT AMONGST HIS ALLIES IN AMERICA, THE BLACK PANTHER WAS ABLE TO ENJOY HIS MARRIAGE TO STORM OF THE X-MEN. YET, AS SOON AS THE CELEBRATION CONCLUDED, T'CHALLA AND HIS QUEEN WERE THRUST INTO THE NEW REALITY OF THEIR WORLD — ONE WHERE WAKANDA IS IN THE PRECARIOUS POSITION OF NAVIGATING A POLITICAL MINEFIELD. AND TO FURTHER COMPLICATE MATTERS, THE COUPLE WAS APPROACHED WITH A STARTLING PROPOSITION: AN ALLIANCE WITH THEIR ADVERSARY, DOCTOR DOOM!

CIVIL WAR: BLACK PANTHER. Contains material originally published in magazine form as BLACK PANTHER #19-25. Second edition. First printing 2016. ISBN# 978-0-7851-9562-7. Published by MARVEL WORLDWIDE, INC., a subsidiary of MARVEL ENTERTAINMENT, LLC. OFFICE OF PUBLICATION: 135 West 50th Street, New York, NY 10020. Copyright © 2016 MARVEL No similarity between any of the names, characters, persons, and/or institutions in this magazine with those of any living or dead person or institution is intended, and any such similarity which may exist is purely coincidental. Printed in the U.S.A. ALAN FINE, President, Marvel Entertainment; DAN BUCKLEY, President, TV, Publishing and Brand Management; JOE QUESADA, Chief Creative Officer; TOM BREVOORT, SVP of Publishing; DAVID BOGART, SVP of Operations & Procurement, Publishing; C.B. CEBULSKI, VP of International Development & Brand Management; DAVID GABRIEL, SVP Print, Sales & Marketing; JIM O'KEEFE, VP of Operations & Logistics; DAN CARR, Executive Director of Publishing Technology; SUSAN CRESPI, Editorial Operations Manager; ALEX MORALES, Publishing Operations Manager; STAN LEE, Chairman Emeritus. For information regarding advertising in Marvel Comics or on Marvel.com, please contact Jonathan Rheingold, VP of Custom Solutions & Ad Sales, at jrheingold@marvel.com. For Marvel subscription inquiries, please call 888-511-5480. Manufactured between 1/15/2016 and 2/22/2016 by R.R. DONNELLEY, INC., SALEM, VA, USA.

10 9 8 7 6 5 4 3 2 1

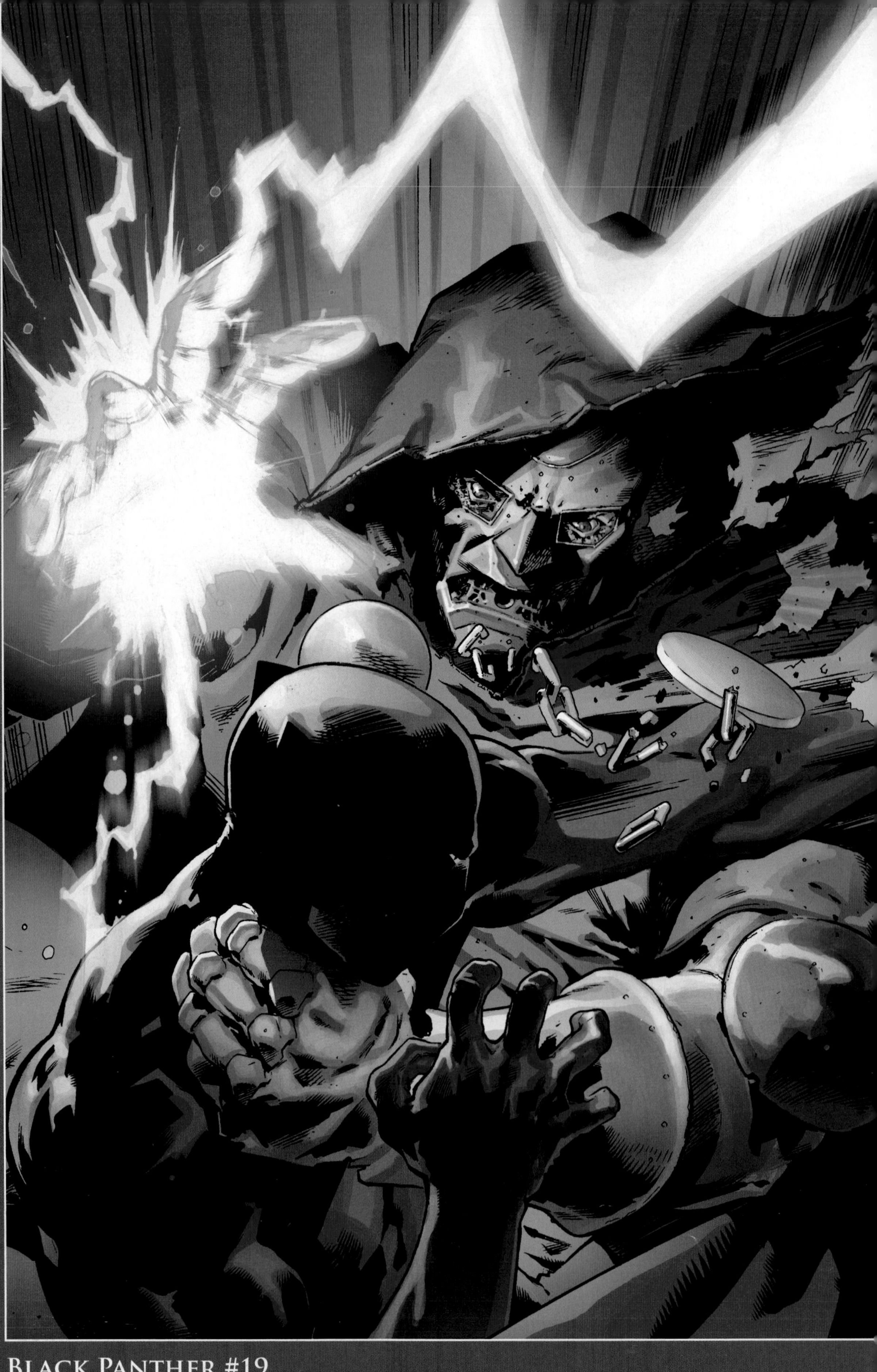

BLACK PANTHER #19

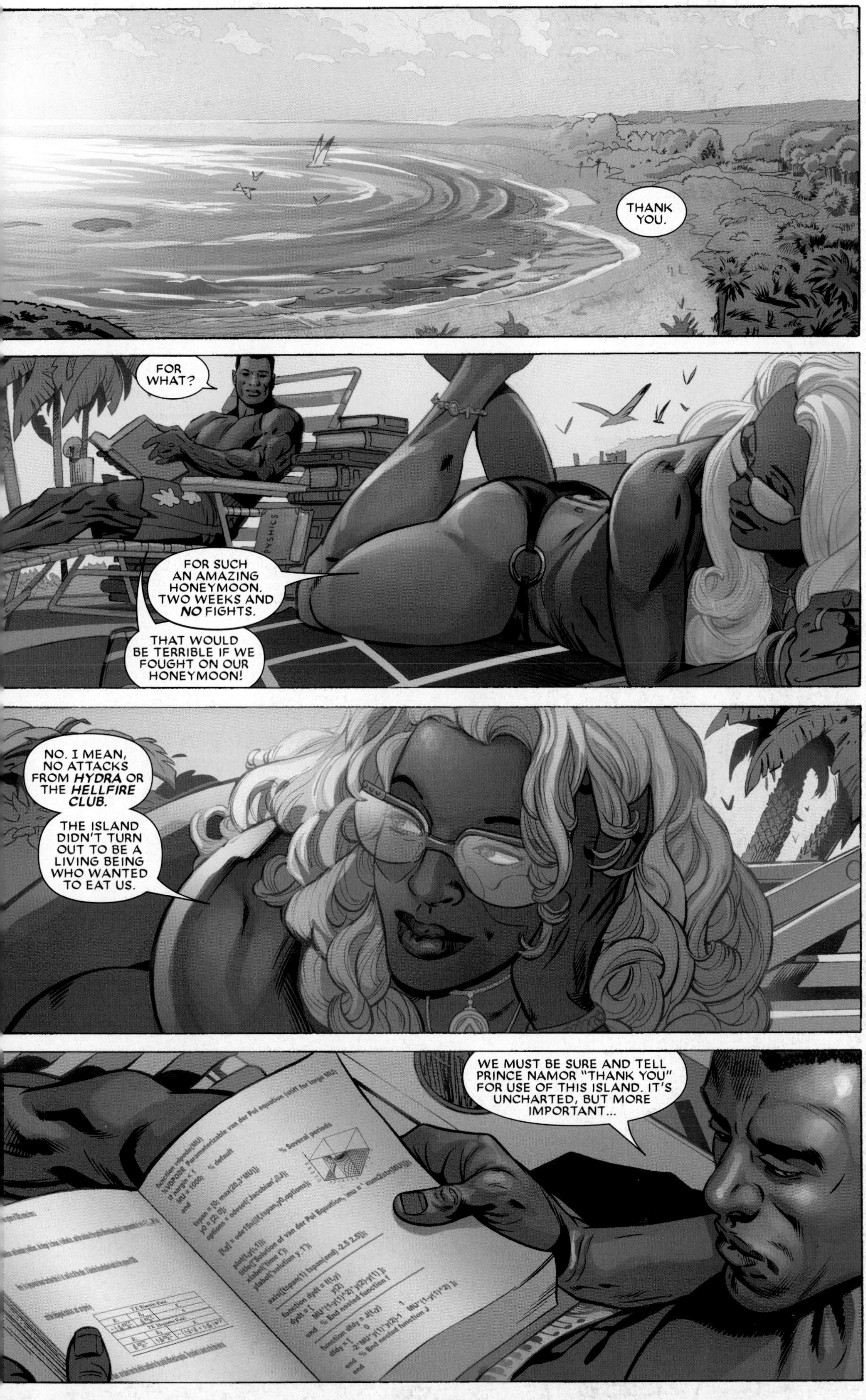
THANK YOU.
FOR WHAT?
PYSHICS
FOR SUCH AN AMAZING HONEYMOON. TWO WEEKS AND NO FIGHTS.
THAT WOULD BE TERRIBLE IF WE FOUGHT ON OUR HONEYMOON!
NO. I MEAN, NO ATTACKS FROM HYDRA OR THE HELLFIRE CLUB.
THE ISLAND DIDN'T TURN OUT TO BE A LIVING BEING WHO WANTED TO EAT US.
WE MUST BE SURE AND TELL PRINCE NAMOR "THANK YOU" FOR USE OF THIS ISLAND. IT'S UNCHARTED, BUT MORE IMPORTANT...

"...HE'S GOT THE MOST DANGEROUS SEA CREATURES ON EARTH PATROLLING THE WATERS AROUND THE ISLAND FOR MILES."

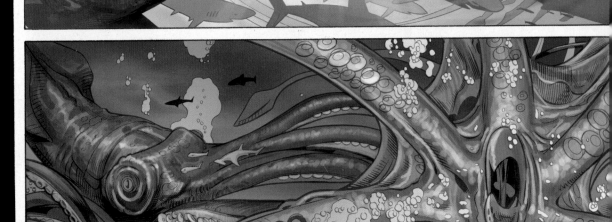

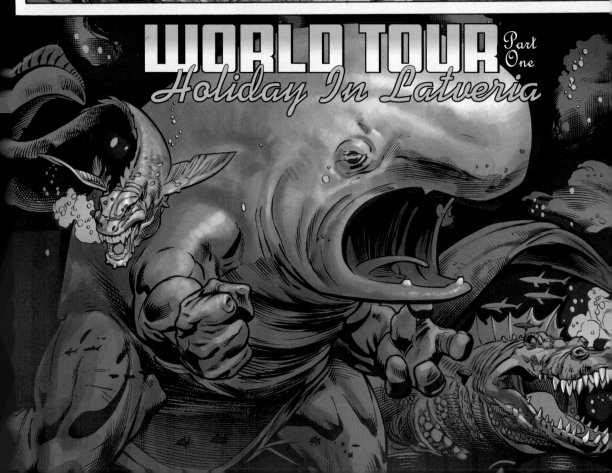

WORLD TOUR Part One
Holiday In Latveria

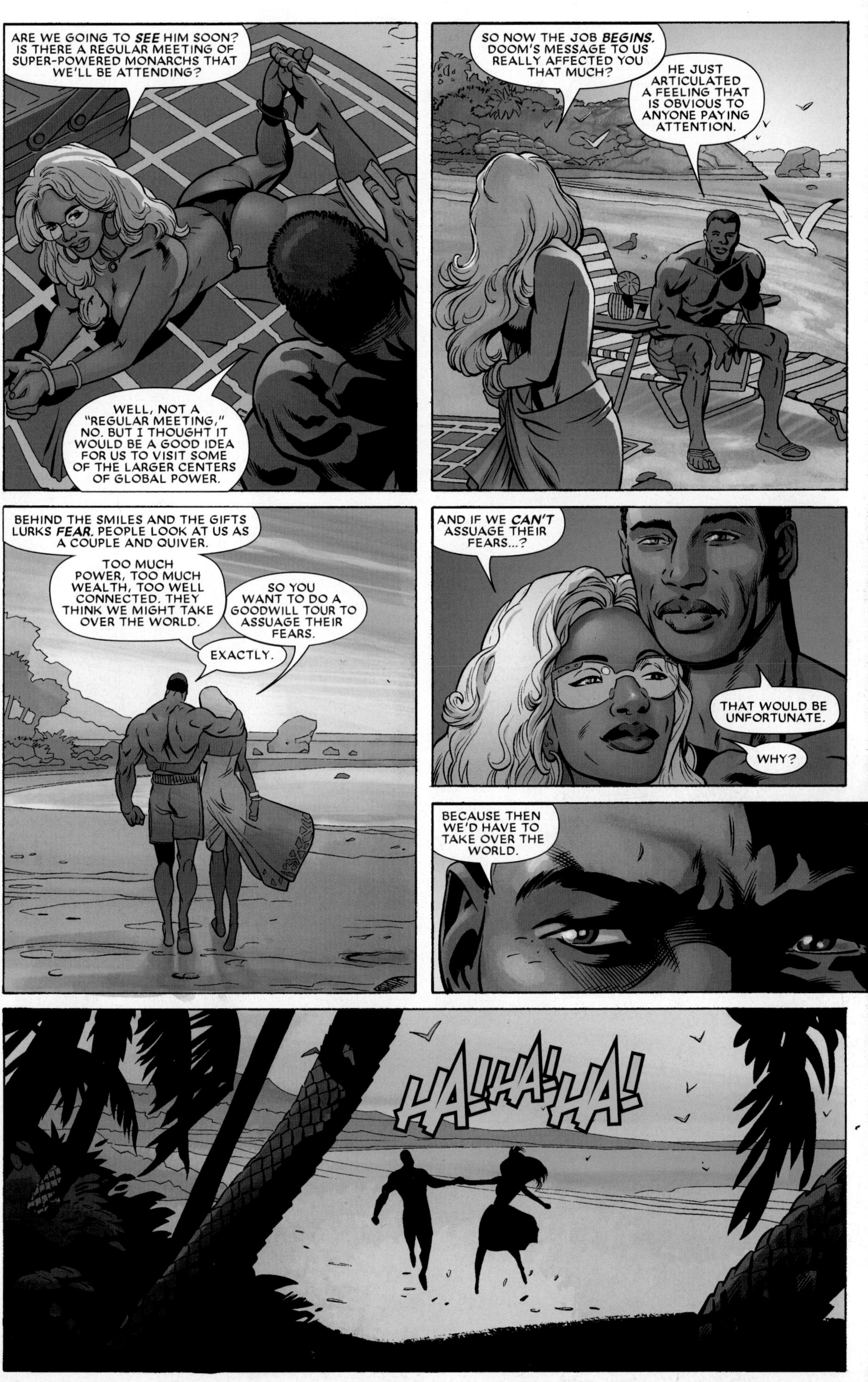
ARE WE GOING TO SEE HIM SOON? IS THERE A REGULAR MEETING OF SUPER-POWERED MONARCHS THAT WE'LL BE ATTENDING?
WELL, NOT A "REGULAR MEETING," NO. BUT I THOUGHT IT WOULD BE A GOOD IDEA FOR US TO VISIT SOME OF THE LARGER CENTERS OF GLOBAL POWER.
SO NOW THE JOB BEGINS. DOOM'S MESSAGE TO US REALLY AFFECTED YOU THAT MUCH?
HE JUST ARTICULATED A FEELING THAT IS OBVIOUS TO ANYONE PAYING ATTENTION.
BEHIND THE SMILES AND THE GIFTS LURKS FEAR. PEOPLE LOOK AT US AS A COUPLE AND QUIVER.
TOO MUCH POWER, TOO MUCH WEALTH, TOO WELL CONNECTED. THEY THINK WE MIGHT TAKE OVER THE WORLD.
SO YOU WANT TO DO A GOODWILL TOUR TO ASSUAGE THEIR FEARS.
EXACTLY.
AND IF WE CAN'T ASSUAGE THEIR FEARS...?
THAT WOULD BE UNFORTUNATE.
WHY?
BECAUSE THEN WE'D HAVE TO TAKE OVER THE WORLD.
HA! HA! HA!

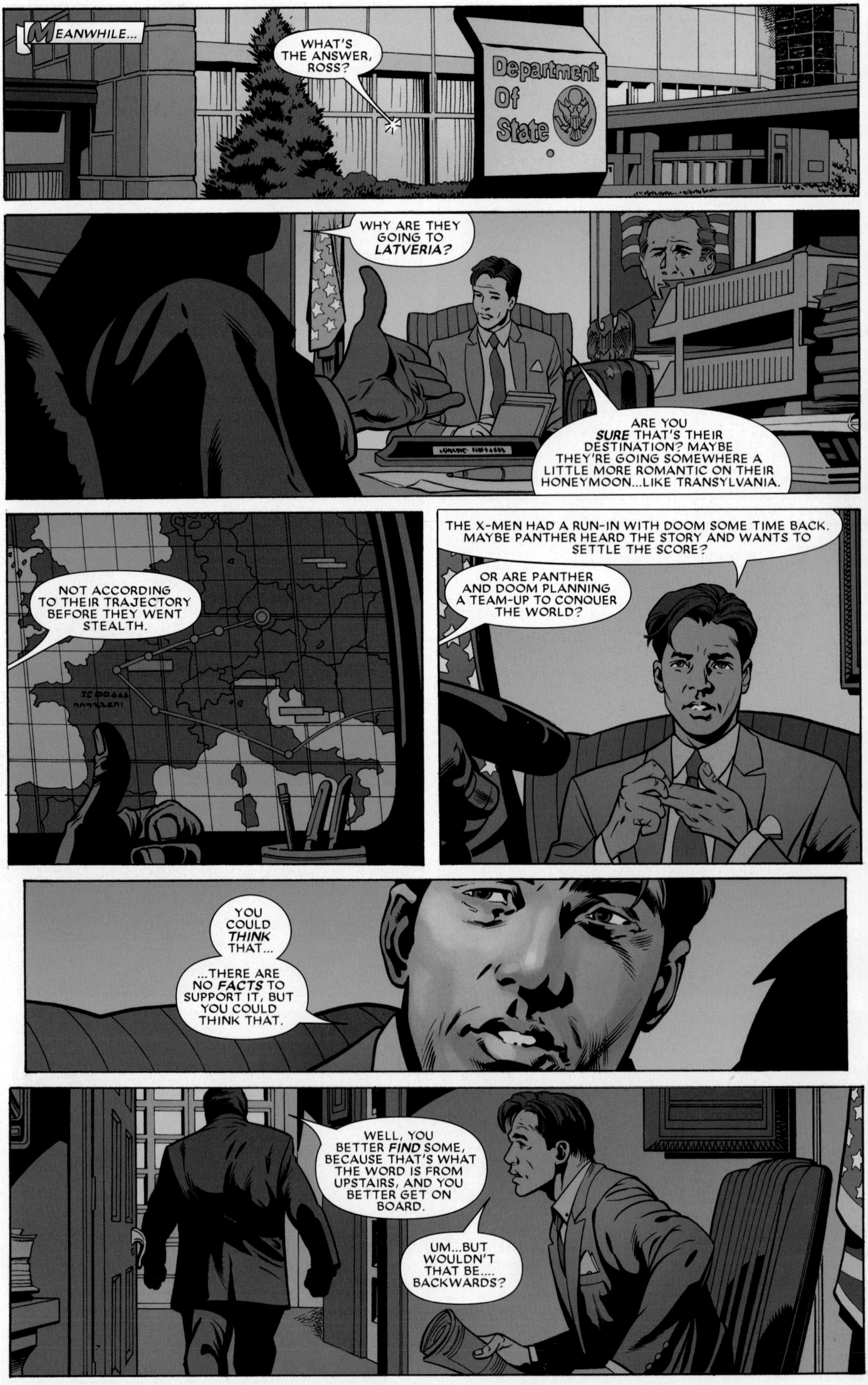
MEANWHILE...
WHAT'S THE ANSWER, ROSS?
Department Of State
WHY ARE THEY GOING TO LATVERIA?
ARE YOU SURE THAT'S THEIR DESTINATION? MAYBE THEY'RE GOING SOMEWHERE A LITTLE MORE ROMANTIC ON THEIR HONEYMOON...LIKE TRANSYLVANIA.
NOT ACCORDING TO THEIR TRAJECTORY BEFORE THEY WENT STEALTH.
THE X-MEN HAD A RUN-IN WITH DOOM SOME TIME BACK. MAYBE PANTHER HEARD THE STORY AND WANTS TO SETTLE THE SCORE?
OR ARE PANTHER AND DOOM PLANNING A TEAM-UP TO CONQUER THE WORLD?
YOU COULD THINK THAT...
...THERE ARE NO FACTS TO SUPPORT IT, BUT YOU COULD THINK THAT.
WELL, YOU BETTER FIND SOME, BECAUSE THAT'S WHAT THE WORD IS FROM UPSTAIRS, AND YOU BETTER GET ON BOARD.
UM...BUT WOULDN'T THAT BE.... BACKWARDS?

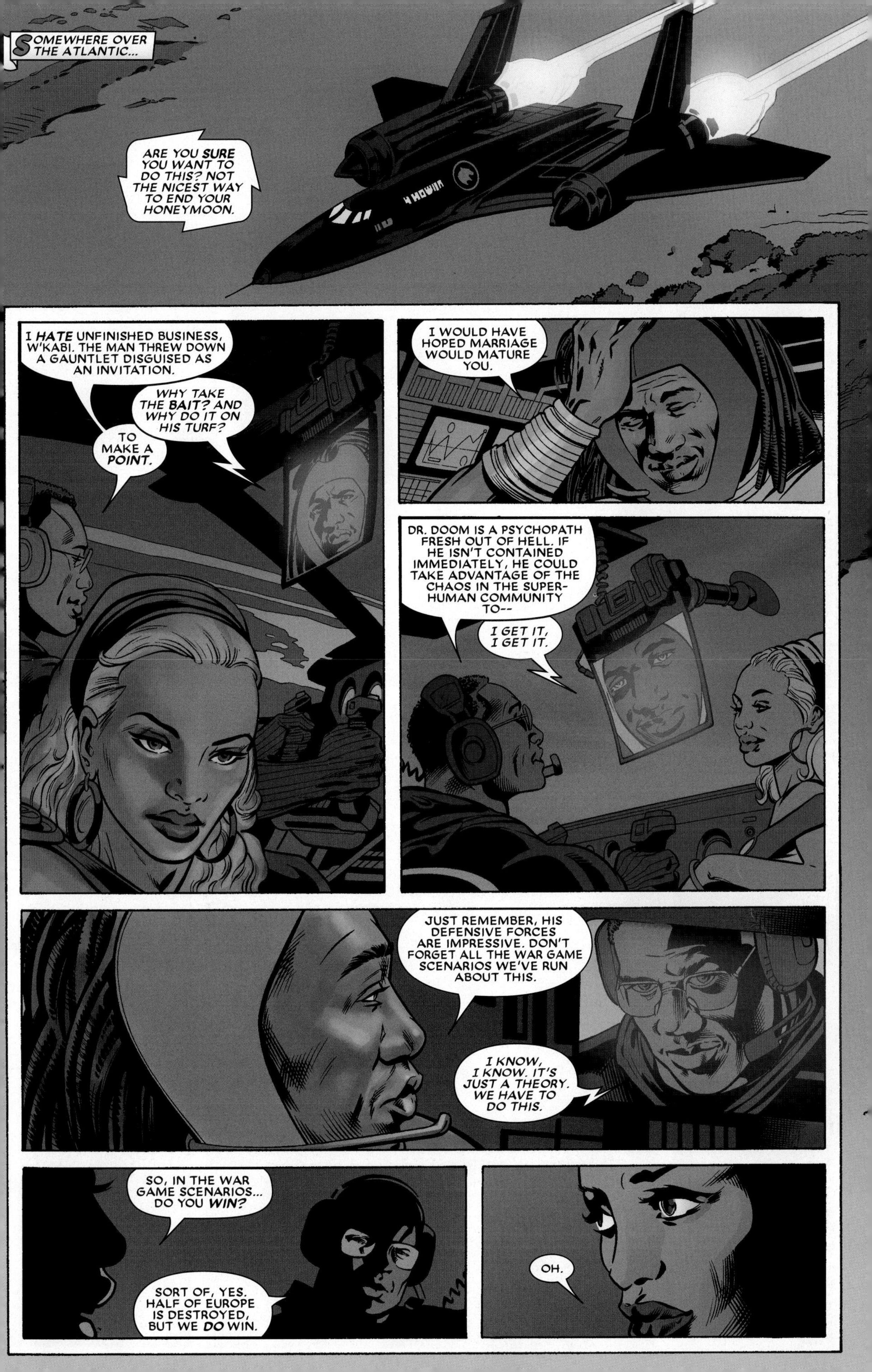
SOMEWHERE OVER THE ATLANTIC...
ARE YOU SURE YOU WANT TO DO THIS? NOT THE NICEST WAY TO END YOUR HONEYMOON.
I HATE UNFINISHED BUSINESS, W'KABI. THE MAN THREW DOWN A GAUNTLET DISGUISED AS AN INVITATION.
WHY TAKE THE BAIT? AND WHY DO IT ON HIS TURF?
TO MAKE A POINT.
I WOULD HAVE HOPED MARRIAGE WOULD MATURE YOU.
DR. DOOM IS A PSYCHOPATH FRESH OUT OF HELL. IF HE ISN'T CONTAINED IMMEDIATELY, HE COULD TAKE ADVANTAGE OF THE CHAOS IN THE SUPER-HUMAN COMMUNITY TO--
I GET IT, I GET IT.
JUST REMEMBER, HIS DEFENSIVE FORCES ARE IMPRESSIVE. DON'T FORGET ALL THE WAR GAME SCENARIOS WE'VE RUN ABOUT THIS.
I KNOW, I KNOW. IT'S JUST A THEORY. WE HAVE TO DO THIS.
SO, IN THE WAR GAME SCENARIOS... DO YOU WIN?
SORT OF, YES. HALF OF EUROPE IS DESTROYED, BUT WE DO WIN.
OH.

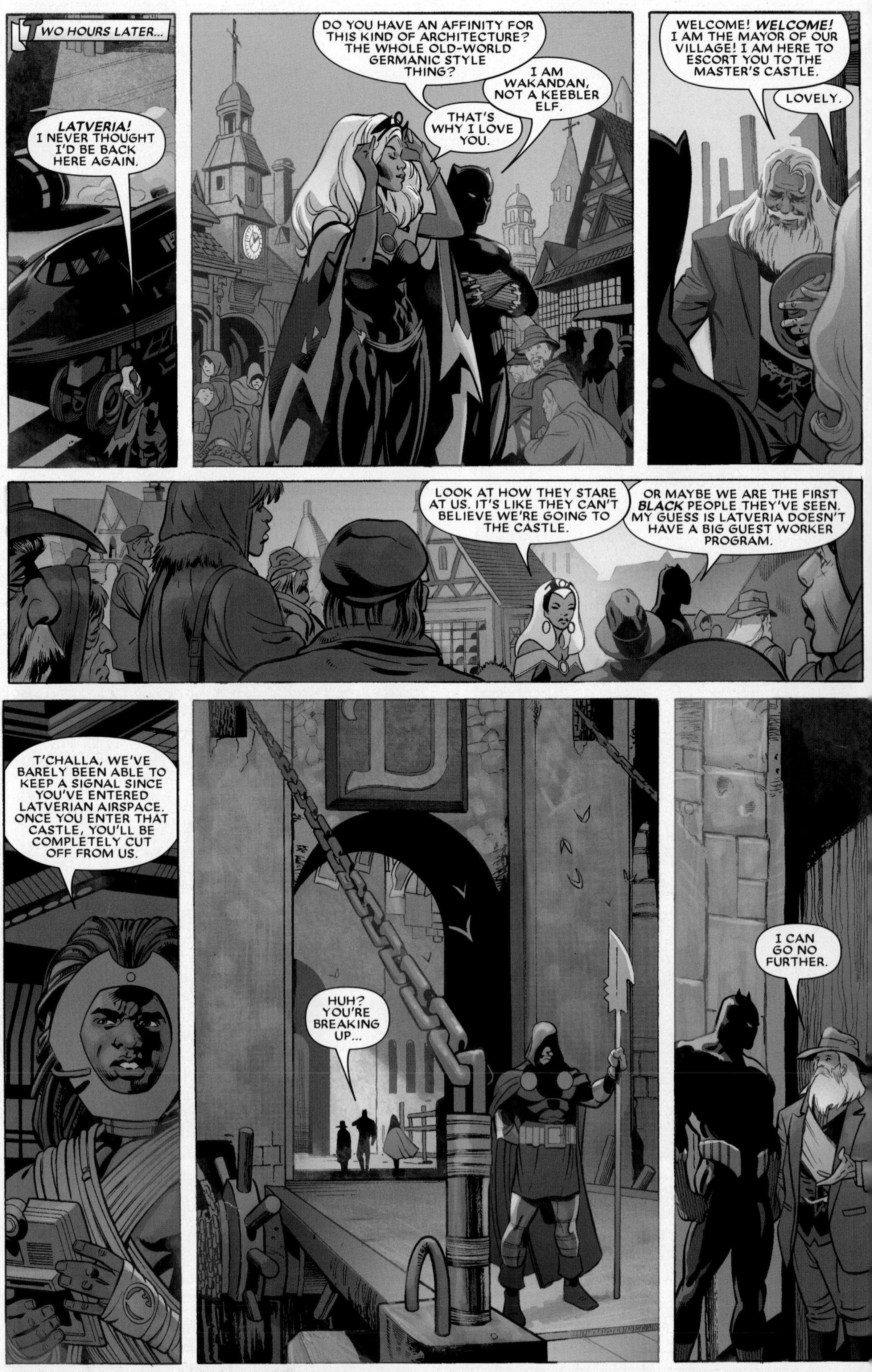

TWO HOURS LATER...
LATVERIA! I NEVER THOUGHT I'D BE BACK HERE AGAIN.
DO YOU HAVE AN AFFINITY FOR THIS KIND OF ARCHITECTURE? THE WHOLE OLD-WORLD GERMANIC STYLE THING?
I AM WAKANDAN, NOT A KEEBLER ELF.
THAT'S WHY I LOVE YOU.
WELCOME! WELCOME! I AM THE MAYOR OF OUR VILLAGE! I AM HERE TO ESCORT YOU TO THE MASTER'S CASTLE.
LOVELY.
LOOK AT HOW THEY STARE AT US. IT'S LIKE THEY CAN'T BELIEVE WE'RE GOING TO THE CASTLE.
OR MAYBE WE ARE THE FIRST BLACK PEOPLE THEY'VE SEEN. MY GUESS IS LATVERIA DOESN'T HAVE A BIG GUEST WORKER PROGRAM.
T'CHALLA, WE'VE BARELY BEEN ABLE TO KEEP A SIGNAL SINCE YOU'VE ENTERED LATVERIAN AIRSPACE. ONCE YOU ENTER THAT CASTLE, YOU'LL BE COMPLETELY CUT OFF FROM US.
HUH? YOU'RE BREAKING UP...
I CAN GO NO FURTHER.

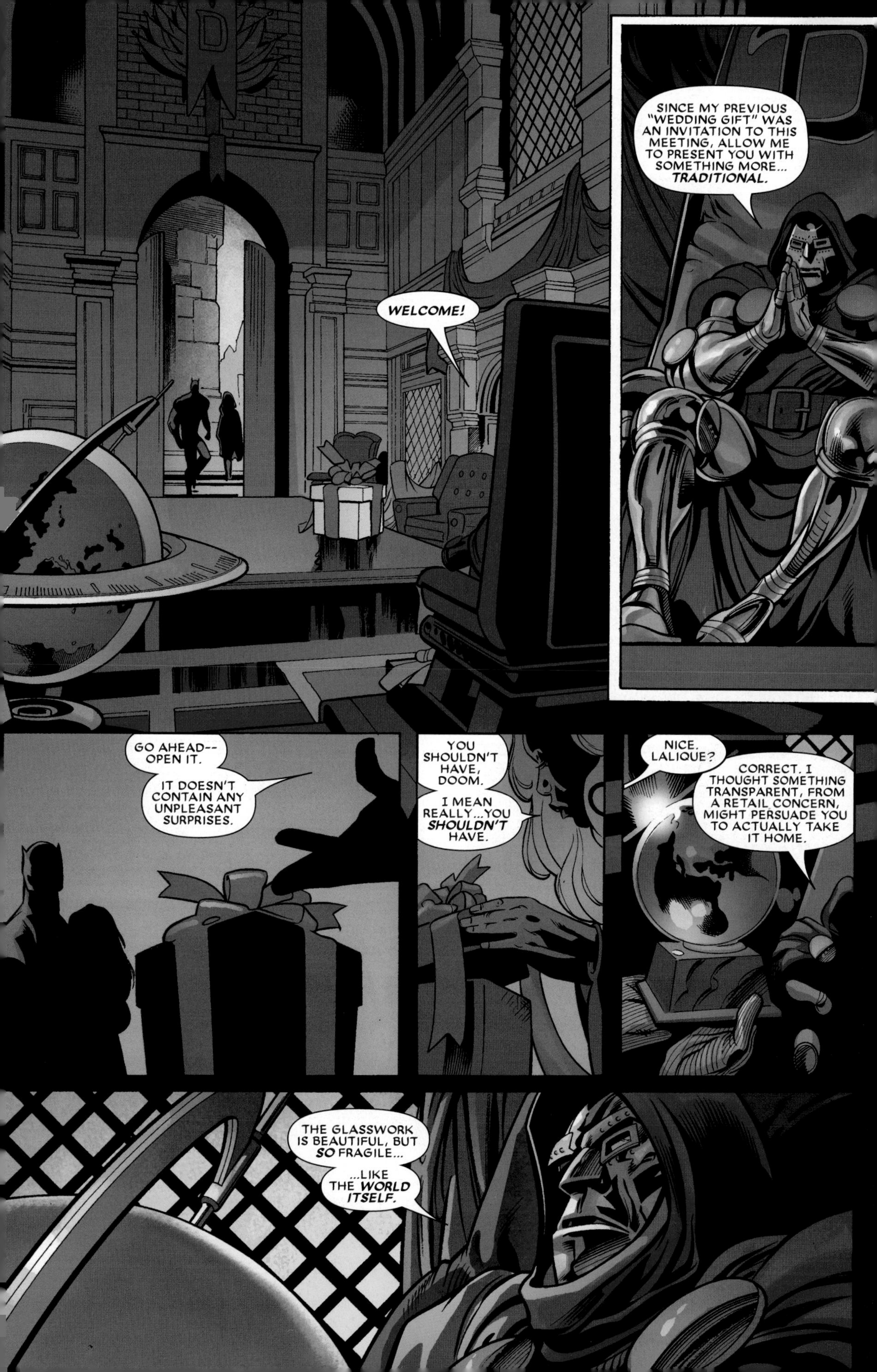

WELCOME!
SINCE MY PREVIOUS "WEDDING GIFT" WAS AN INVITATION TO THIS MEETING, ALLOW ME TO PRESENT YOU WITH SOMETHING MORE... TRADITIONAL.
GO AHEAD-- OPEN IT.
IT DOESN'T CONTAIN ANY UNPLEASANT SURPRISES.
YOU SHOULDN'T HAVE, DOOM.
I MEAN REALLY...YOU SHOULDN'T HAVE.
NICE. LALIQUE?
CORRECT. I THOUGHT SOMETHING TRANSPARENT, FROM A RETAIL CONCERN, MIGHT PERSUADE YOU TO ACTUALLY TAKE IT HOME.
THE GLASSWORK IS BEAUTIFUL, BUT SO FRAGILE...
...LIKE THE WORLD ITSELF.

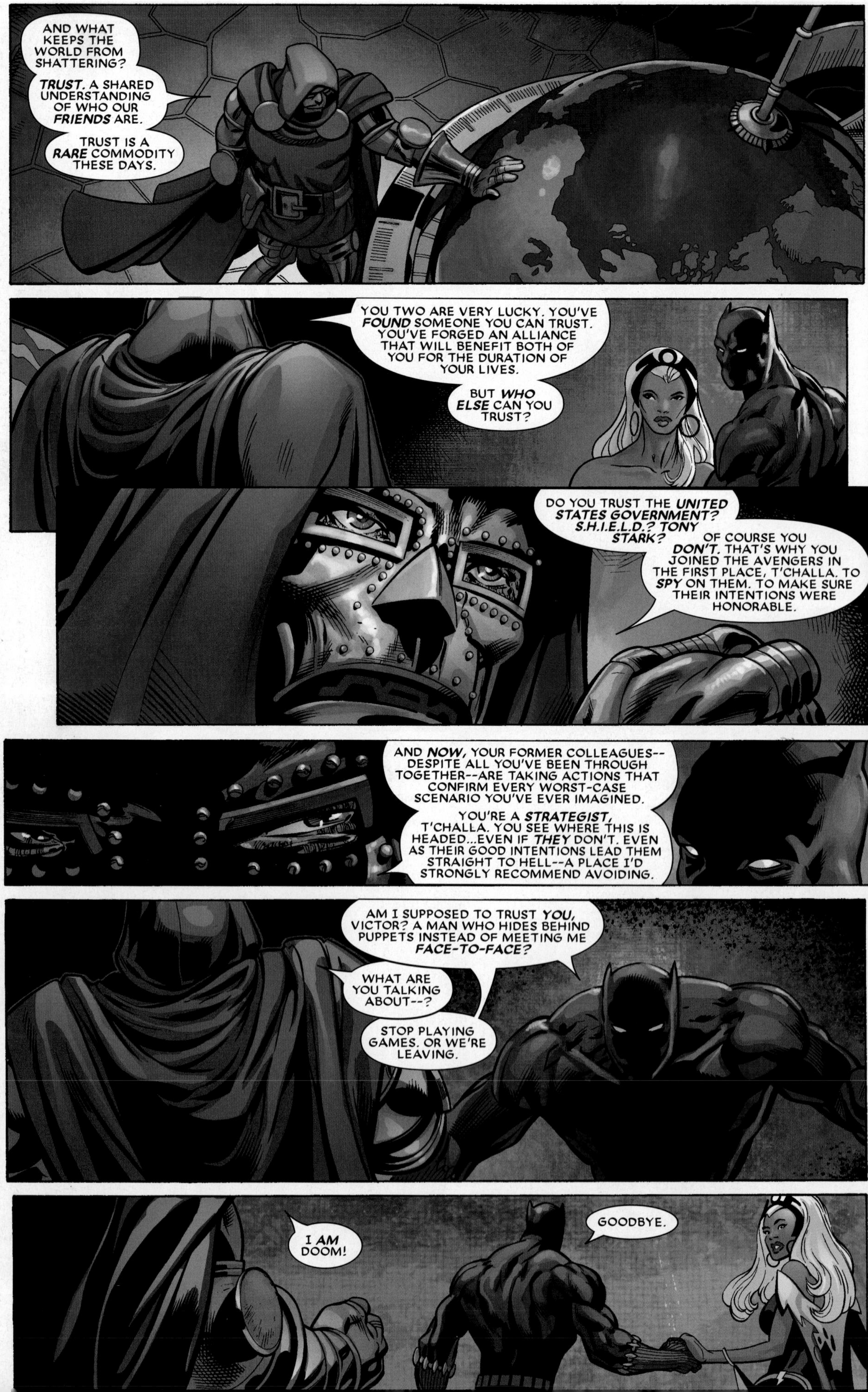
AND WHAT KEEPS THE WORLD FROM SHATTERING?
TRUST. A SHARED UNDERSTANDING OF WHO OUR FRIENDS ARE.
TRUST IS A RARE COMMODITY THESE DAYS.
YOU TWO ARE VERY LUCKY. YOU'VE FOUND SOMEONE YOU CAN TRUST. YOU'VE FORGED AN ALLIANCE THAT WILL BENEFIT BOTH OF YOU FOR THE DURATION OF YOUR LIVES.
BUT WHO ELSE CAN YOU TRUST?
DO YOU TRUST THE UNITED STATES GOVERNMENT? S.H.I.E.L.D.? TONY STARK?
OF COURSE YOU DON'T. THAT'S WHY YOU JOINED THE AVENGERS IN THE FIRST PLACE, T'CHALLA. TO SPY ON THEM. TO MAKE SURE THEIR INTENTIONS WERE HONORABLE.
AND NOW, YOUR FORMER COLLEAGUES--DESPITE ALL YOU'VE BEEN THROUGH TOGETHER--ARE TAKING ACTIONS THAT CONFIRM EVERY WORST-CASE SCENARIO YOU'VE EVER IMAGINED.
YOU'RE A STRATEGIST, T'CHALLA. YOU SEE WHERE THIS IS HEADED...EVEN IF THEY DON'T. EVEN AS THEIR GOOD INTENTIONS LEAD THEM STRAIGHT TO HELL--A PLACE I'D STRONGLY RECOMMEND AVOIDING.
AM I SUPPOSED TO TRUST YOU, VICTOR? A MAN WHO HIDES BEHIND PUPPETS INSTEAD OF MEETING ME FACE-TO-FACE?
WHAT ARE YOU TALKING ABOUT--?
STOP PLAYING GAMES. OR WE'RE LEAVING.
I AM DOOM!
GOODBYE.

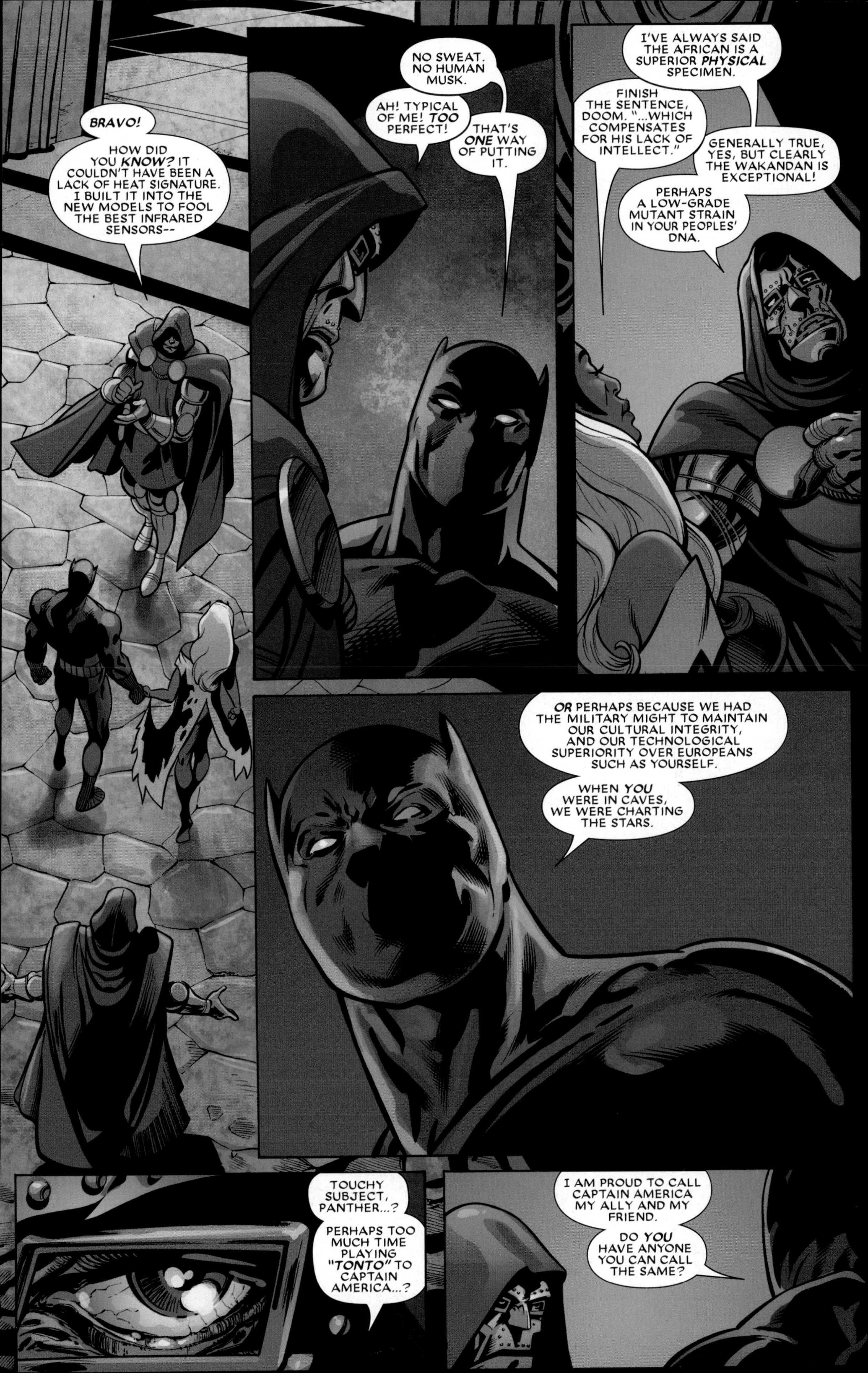
BRAVO!
HOW DID YOU KNOW? IT COULDN'T HAVE BEEN A LACK OF HEAT SIGNATURE. I BUILT IT INTO THE NEW MODELS TO FOOL THE BEST INFRARED SENSORS--
NO SWEAT. NO HUMAN MUSK.
AH! TYPICAL OF ME! TOO PERFECT!
THAT'S ONE WAY OF PUTTING IT.
I'VE ALWAYS SAID THE AFRICAN IS A SUPERIOR PHYSICAL SPECIMEN.
FINISH THE SENTENCE, DOOM. "...WHICH COMPENSATES FOR HIS LACK OF INTELLECT."
GENERALLY TRUE, YES, BUT CLEARLY THE WAKANDAN IS EXCEPTIONAL!
PERHAPS A LOW-GRADE MUTANT STRAIN IN YOUR PEOPLES' DNA.
OR PERHAPS BECAUSE WE HAD THE MILITARY MIGHT TO MAINTAIN OUR CULTURAL INTEGRITY, AND OUR TECHNOLOGICAL SUPERIORITY OVER EUROPEANS SUCH AS YOURSELF.
WHEN YOU WERE IN CAVES, WE WERE CHARTING THE STARS.
TOUCHY SUBJECT, PANTHER...?
PERHAPS TOO MUCH TIME PLAYING "TONTO" TO CAPTAIN AMERICA...?
I AM PROUD TO CALL CAPTAIN AMERICA MY ALLY AND MY FRIEND.
DO YOU HAVE ANYONE YOU CAN CALL THE SAME?

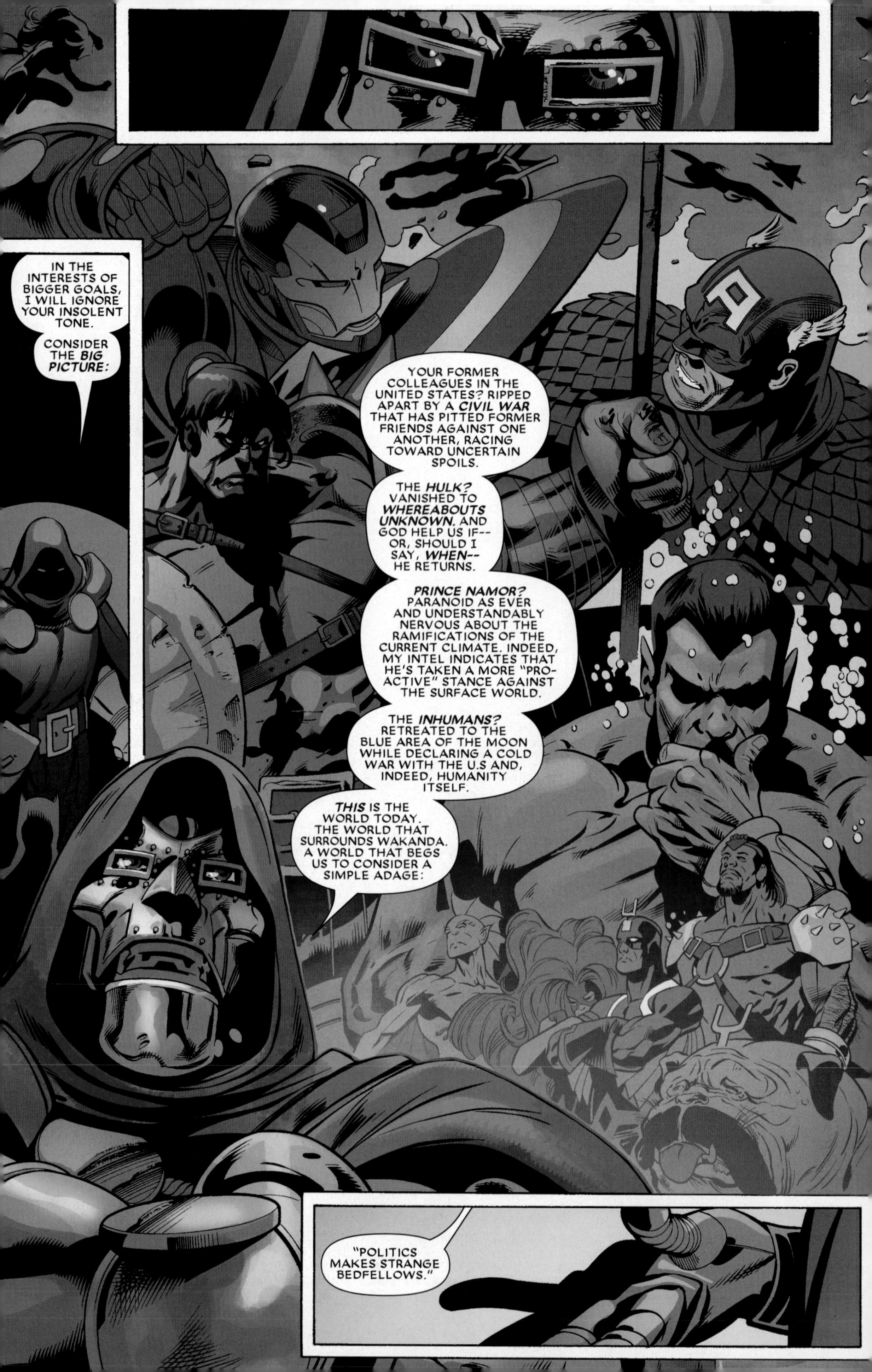
IN THE INTERESTS OF BIGGER GOALS, I WILL IGNORE YOUR INSOLENT TONE.
CONSIDER THE BIG PICTURE:
YOUR FORMER COLLEAGUES IN THE UNITED STATES? RIPPED APART BY A CIVIL WAR THAT HAS PITTED FORMER FRIENDS AGAINST ONE ANOTHER, RACING TOWARD UNCERTAIN SPOILS.
THE HULK? VANISHED TO WHEREABOUTS UNKNOWN. AND GOD HELP US IF-- OR, SHOULD I SAY, WHEN-- HE RETURNS.
PRINCE NAMOR? PARANOID AS EVER AND UNDERSTANDABLY NERVOUS ABOUT THE RAMIFICATIONS OF THE CURRENT CLIMATE. INDEED, MY INTEL INDICATES THAT HE'S TAKEN A MORE "PRO-ACTIVE" STANCE AGAINST THE SURFACE WORLD.
THE INHUMANS? RETREATED TO THE BLUE AREA OF THE MOON WHILE DECLARING A COLD WAR WITH THE U.S AND, INDEED, HUMANITY ITSELF.
THIS IS THE WORLD TODAY. THE WORLD THAT SURROUNDS WAKANDA. A WORLD THAT BEGS US TO CONSIDER A SIMPLE ADAGE:
"POLITICS MAKES STRANGE BEDFELLOWS."

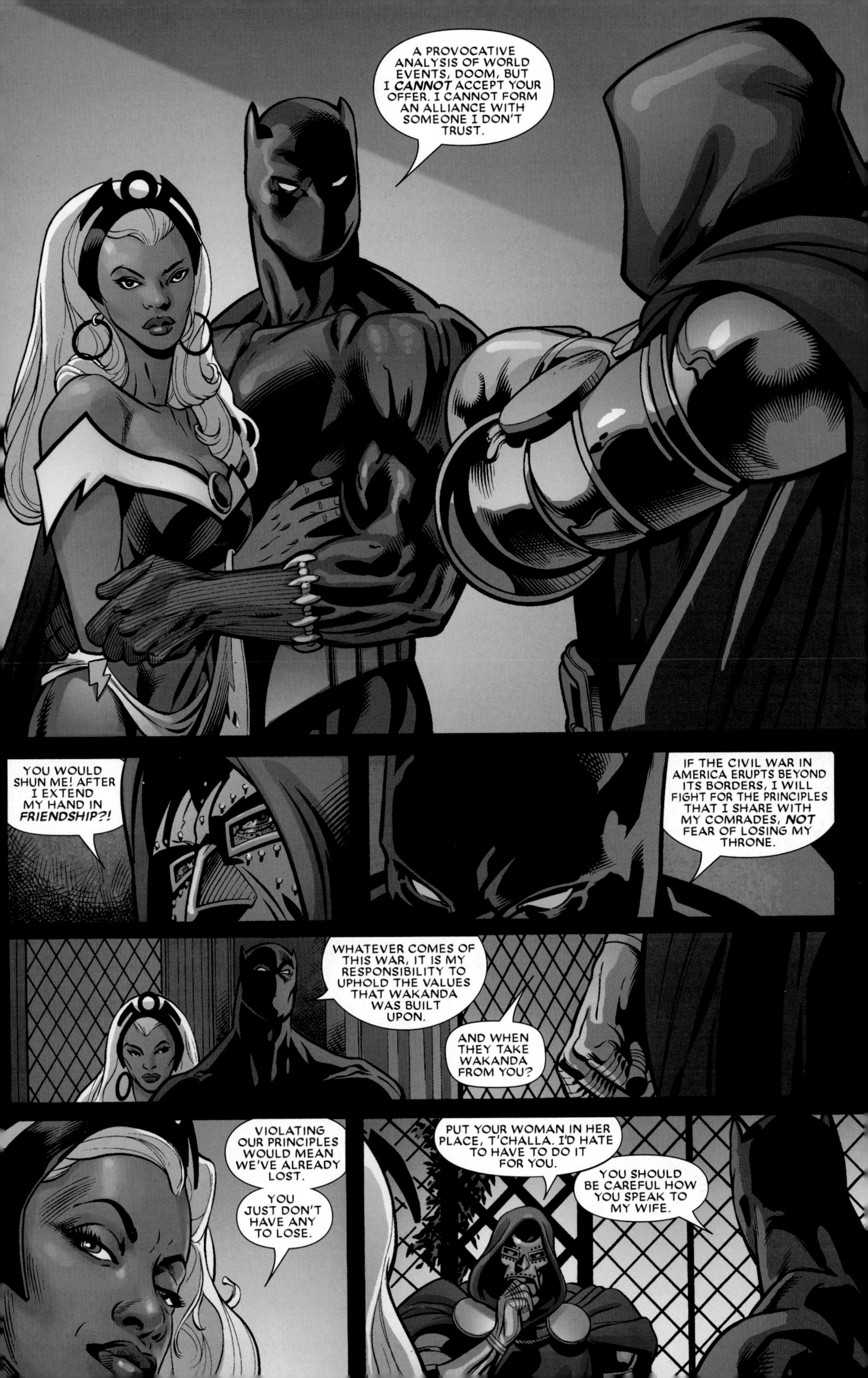
A PROVOCATIVE ANALYSIS OF WORLD EVENTS, DOOM, BUT I *CANNOT* ACCEPT YOUR OFFER. I CANNOT FORM AN ALLIANCE WITH SOMEONE I DON'T TRUST.
YOU WOULD SHUN ME! AFTER I EXTEND MY HAND IN *FRIENDSHIP?!*
IF THE CIVIL WAR IN AMERICA ERUPTS BEYOND ITS BORDERS, I WILL FIGHT FOR THE PRINCIPLES THAT I SHARE WITH MY COMRADES, *NOT* FEAR OF LOSING MY THRONE.
WHATEVER COMES OF THIS WAR, IT IS MY RESPONSIBILITY TO UPHOLD THE VALUES THAT WAKANDA WAS BUILT UPON.
AND WHEN THEY TAKE WAKANDA FROM YOU?
VIOLATING OUR PRINCIPLES WOULD MEAN WE'VE ALREADY LOST.
YOU JUST DON'T HAVE ANY TO LOSE.
PUT YOUR WOMAN IN HER PLACE, T'CHALLA. I'D HATE TO HAVE TO DO IT FOR YOU.
YOU SHOULD BE CAREFUL HOW YOU SPEAK TO MY WIFE.

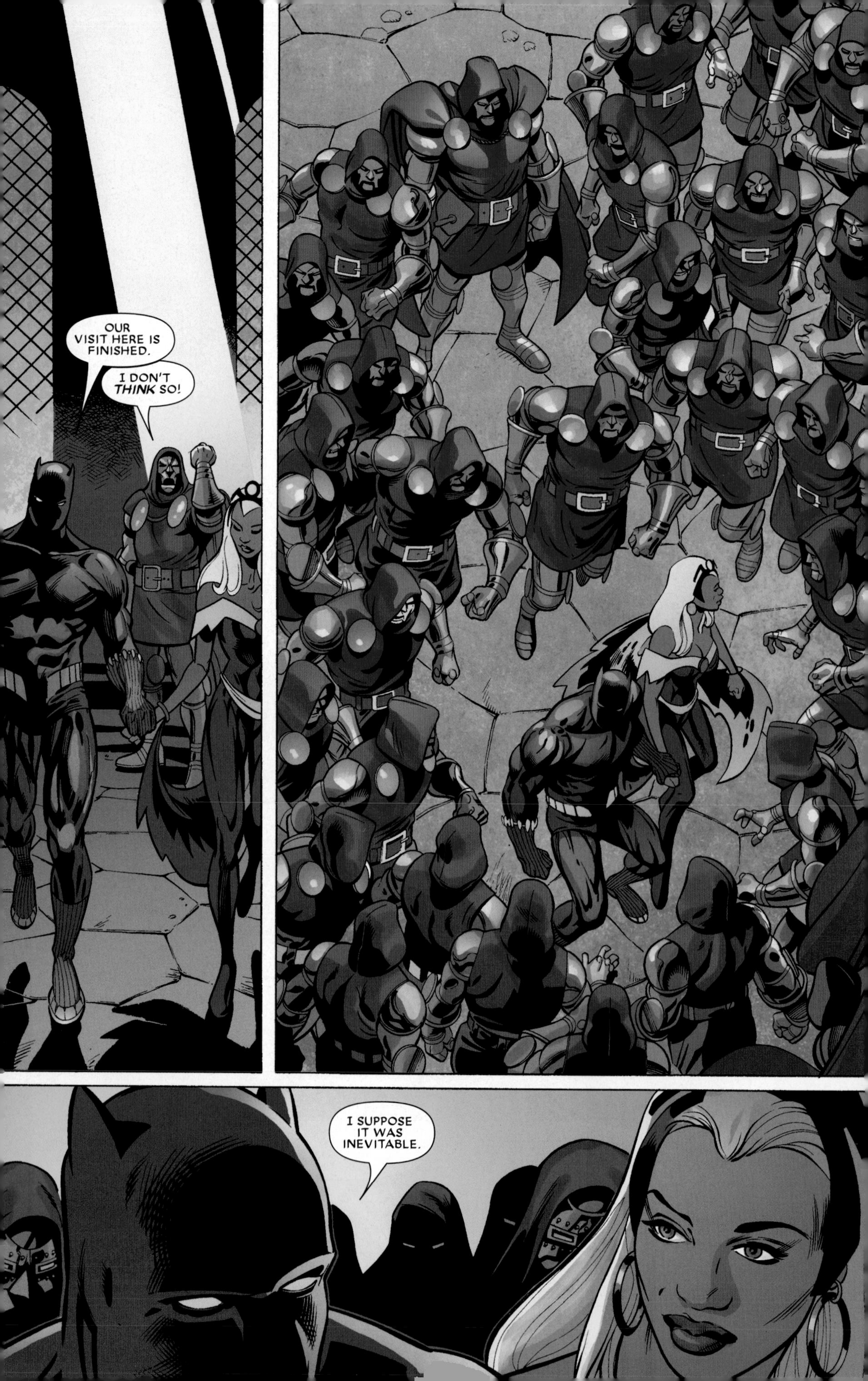
OUR VISIT HERE IS FINISHED.
I DON'T *THINK* SO!
I SUPPOSE IT WAS INEVITABLE.

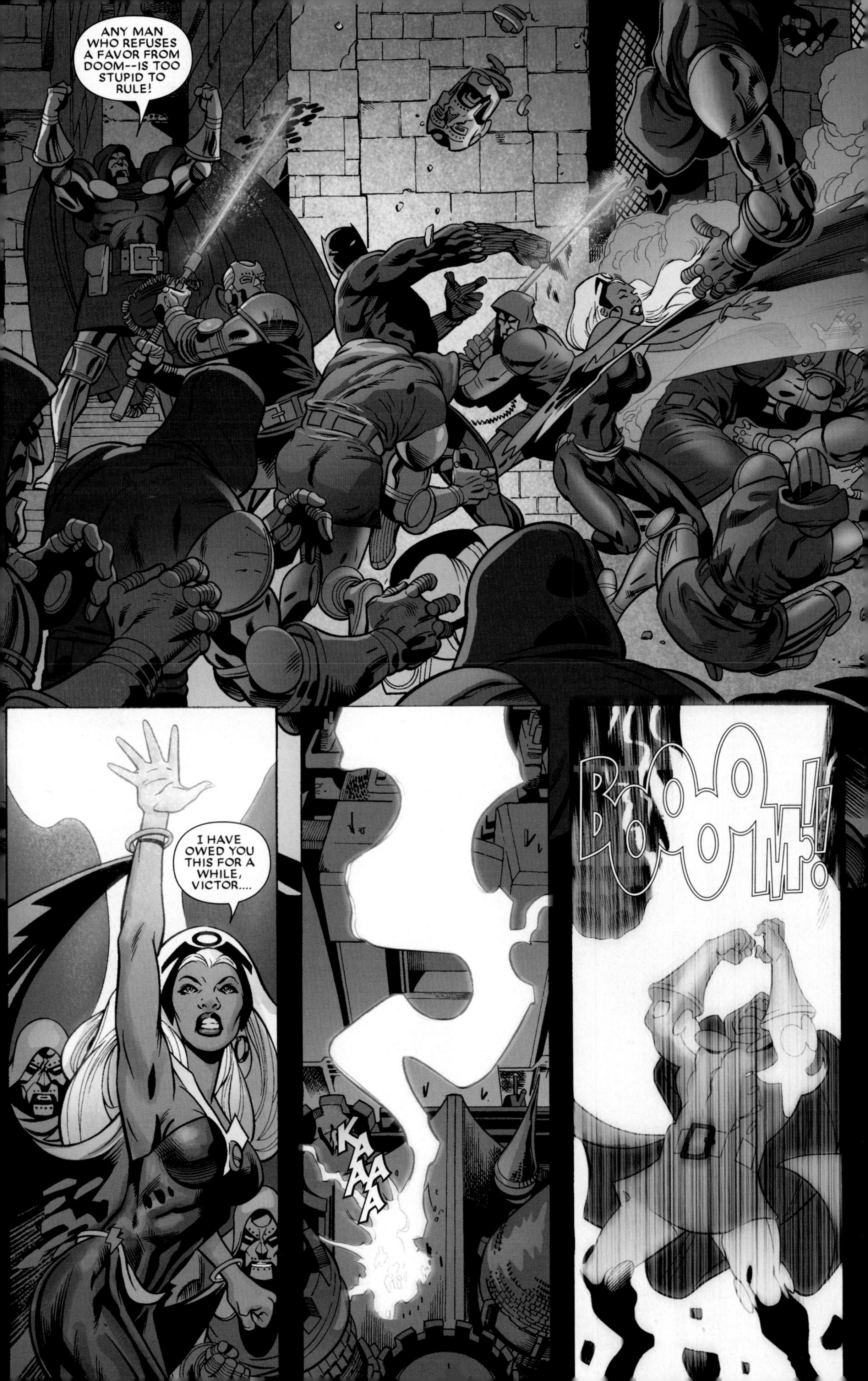
ANY MAN WHO REFUSES A FAVOR FROM DOOM--IS TOO STUPID TO RULE!
I HAVE OWED YOU THIS FOR A WHILE, VICTOR....
KAAAA
BOOOOOMB!!

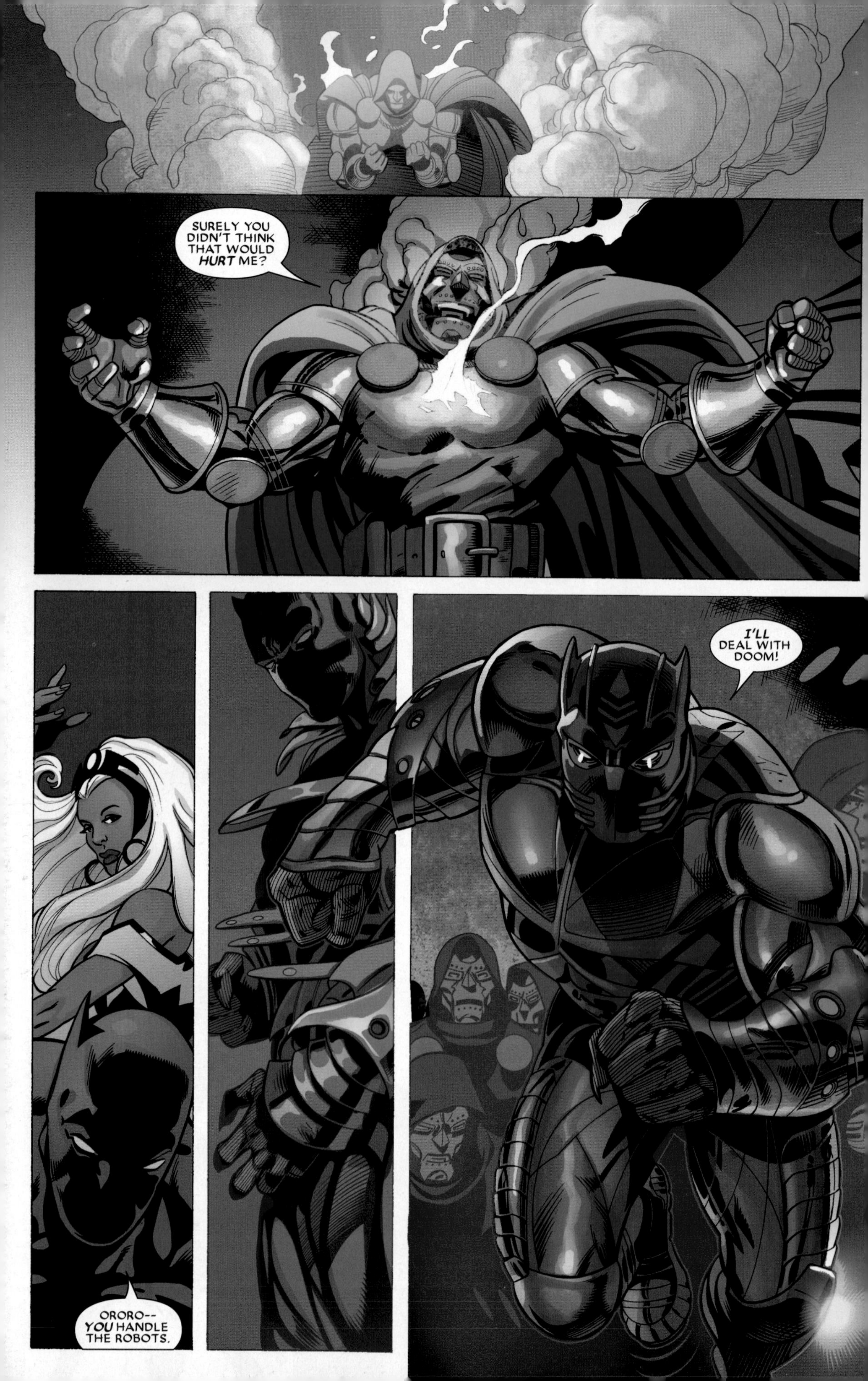
SURELY YOU DIDN'T THINK THAT WOULD *HURT* ME?
ORORO-- *YOU* HANDLE THE ROBOTS.
I'LL DEAL WITH DOOM!

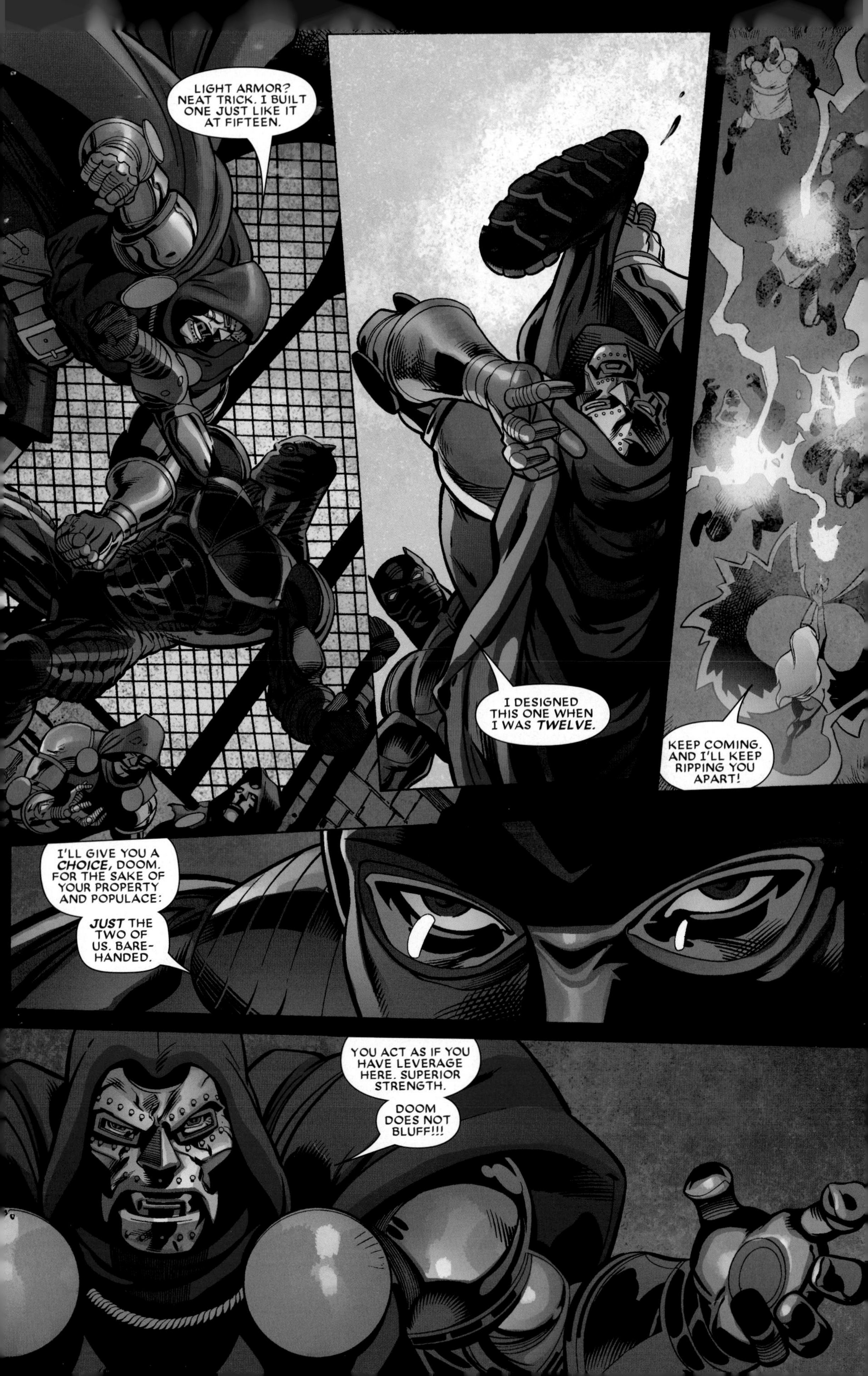
LIGHT ARMOR? NEAT TRICK. I BUILT ONE JUST LIKE IT AT FIFTEEN.
I DESIGNED THIS ONE WHEN I WAS *TWELVE.*
KEEP COMING. AND I'LL KEEP RIPPING YOU APART!
I'LL GIVE YOU A *CHOICE,* DOOM. FOR THE SAKE OF YOUR PROPERTY AND POPULACE:
JUST THE TWO OF US. BARE-HANDED.
YOU ACT AS IF YOU HAVE LEVERAGE HERE. SUPERIOR STRENGTH.
DOOM DOES NOT BLUFF!!!

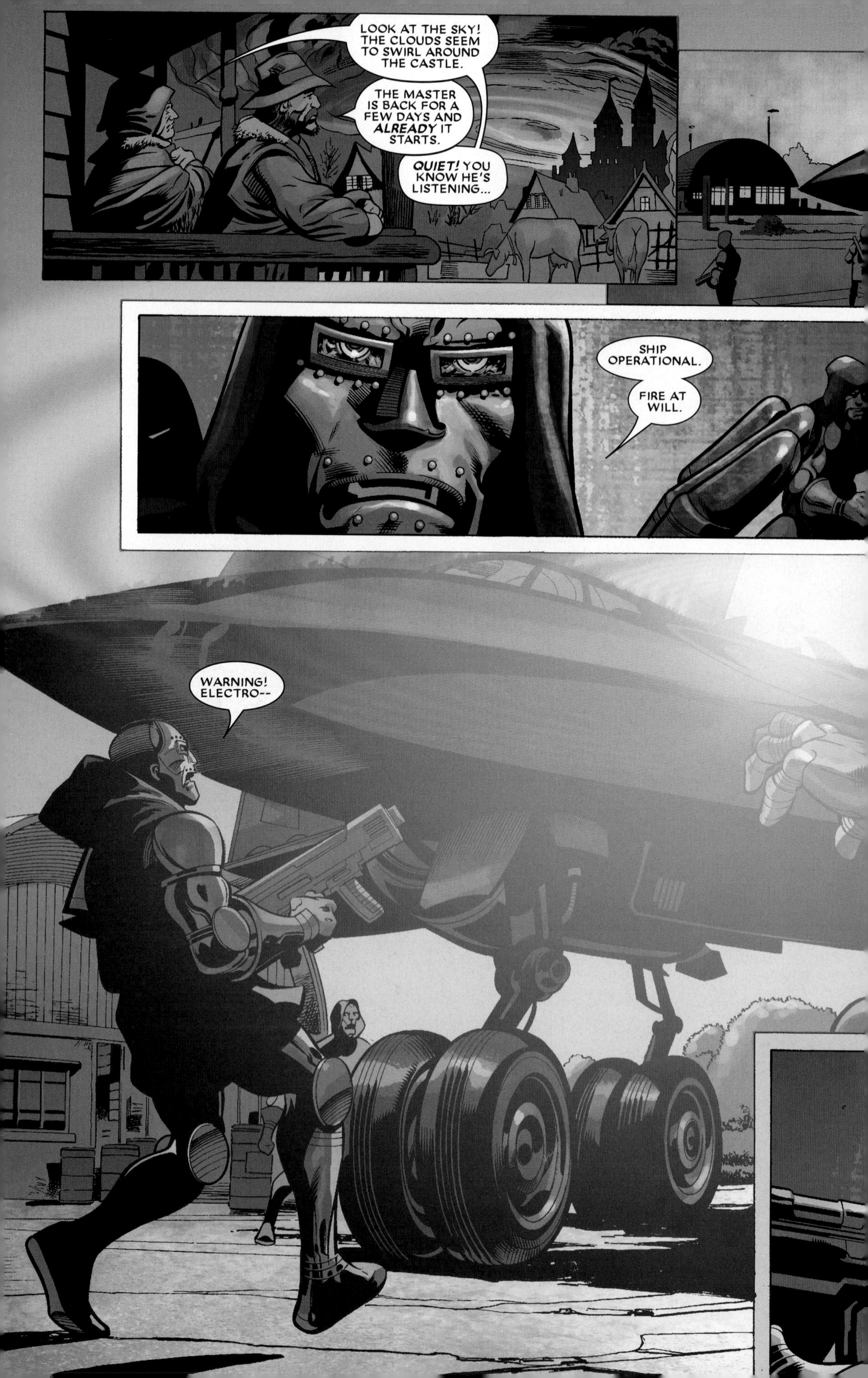
LOOK AT THE SKY! THE CLOUDS SEEM TO SWIRL AROUND THE CASTLE.
THE MASTER IS BACK FOR A FEW DAYS AND ALREADY IT STARTS.
QUIET! YOU KNOW HE'S LISTENING...
SHIP OPERATIONAL.
FIRE AT WILL.
WARNING! ELECTRO--

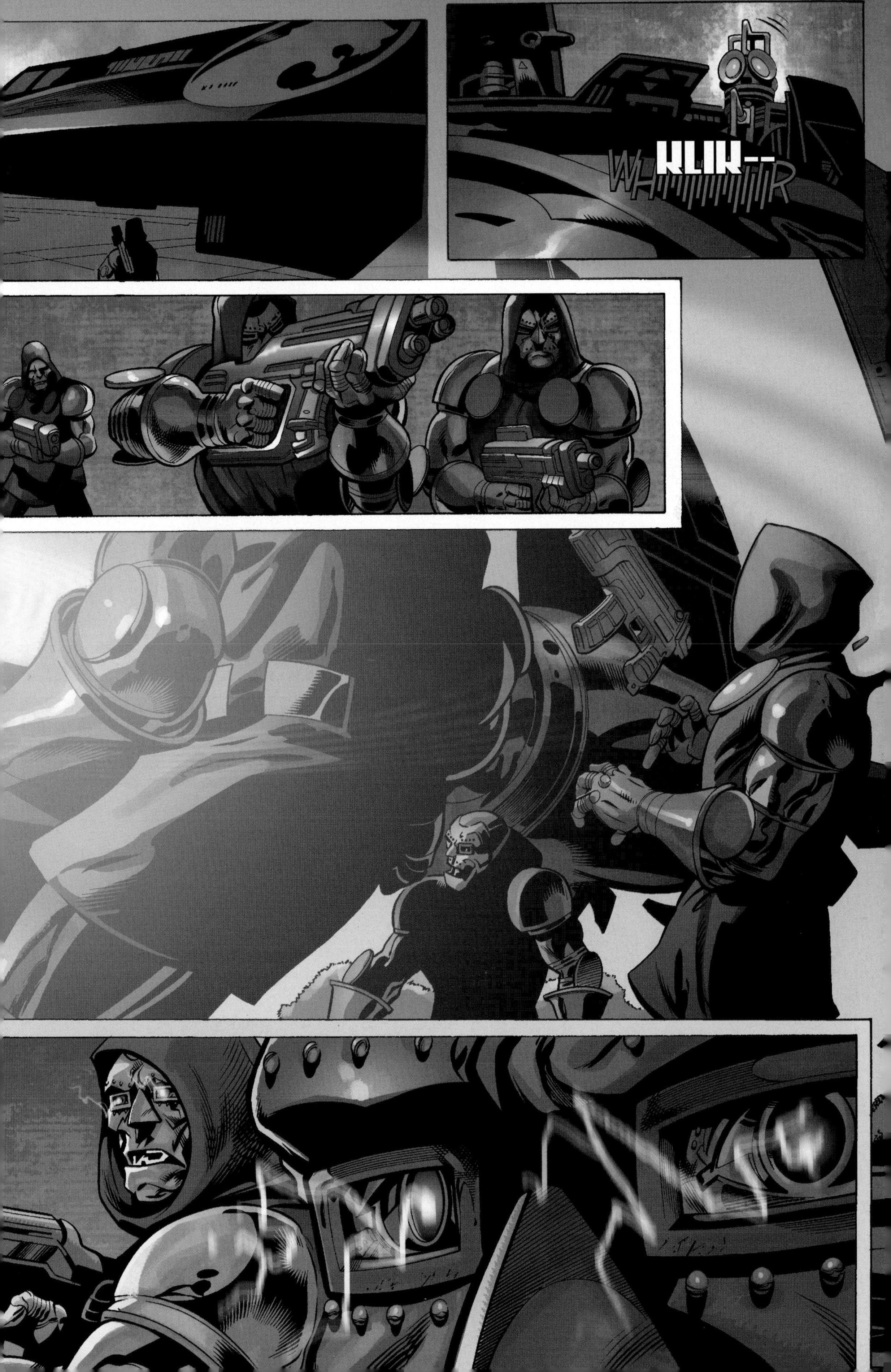
KLIK--
WHRRRRRRRR

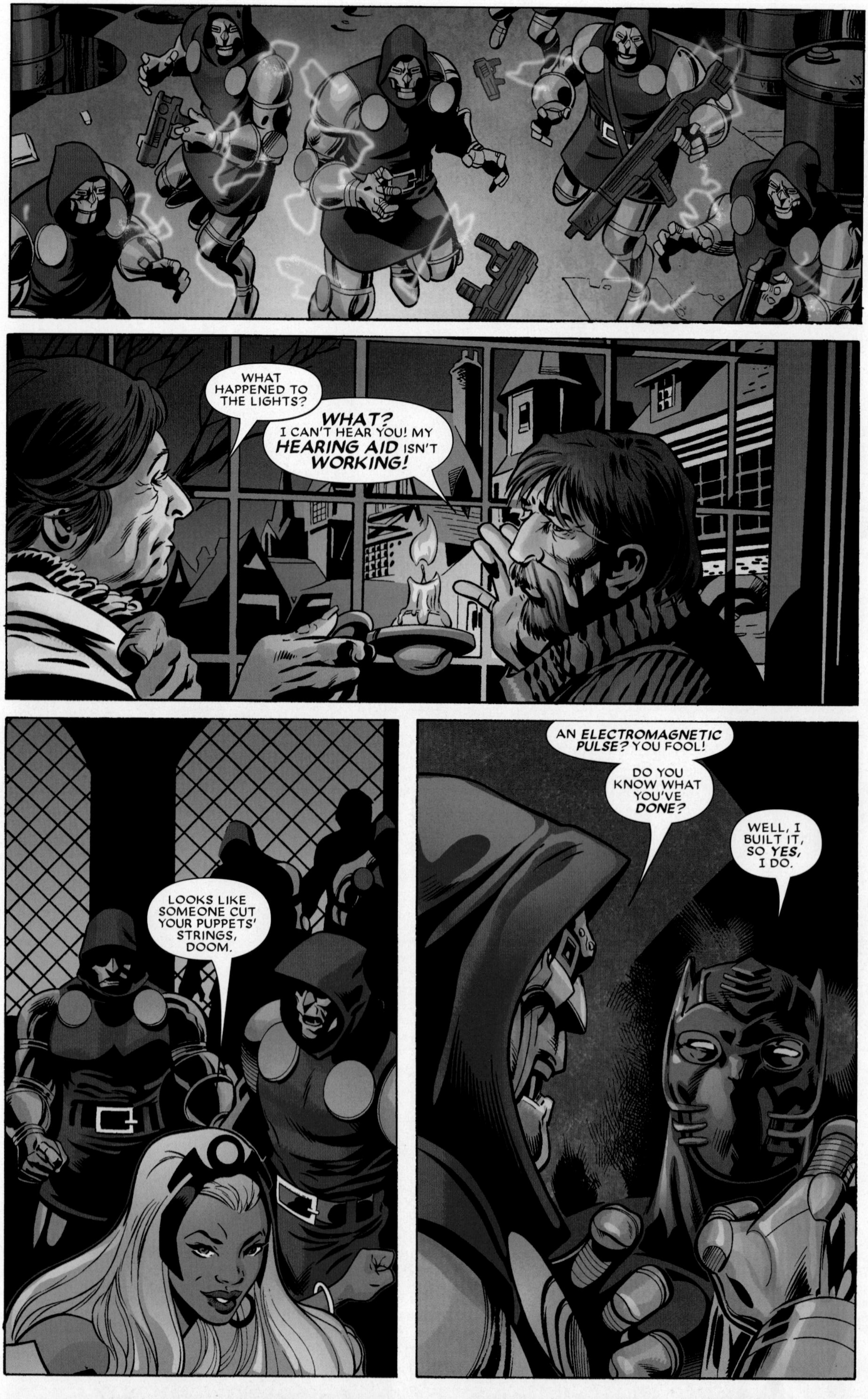
WHAT HAPPENED TO THE LIGHTS?
WHAT? I CAN'T HEAR YOU! MY HEARING AID ISN'T WORKING!
LOOKS LIKE SOMEONE CUT YOUR PUPPETS' STRINGS, DOOM.
AN ELECTROMAGNETIC PULSE? YOU FOOL!
DO YOU KNOW WHAT YOU'VE DONE?
WELL, I BUILT IT, SO YES, I DO.

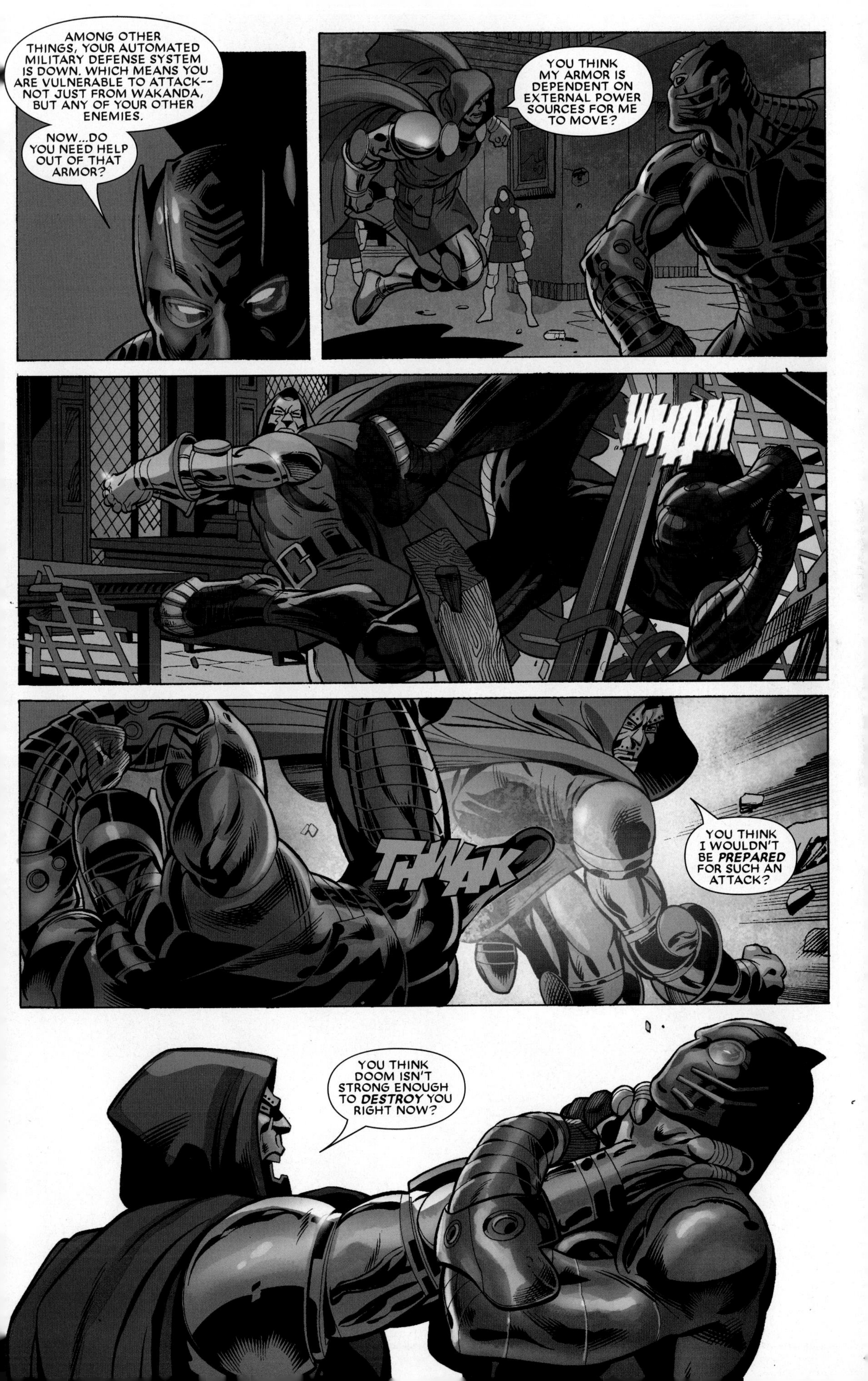
AMONG OTHER THINGS, YOUR AUTOMATED MILITARY DEFENSE SYSTEM IS DOWN. WHICH MEANS YOU ARE VULNERABLE TO ATTACK-- NOT JUST FROM WAKANDA, BUT ANY OF YOUR OTHER ENEMIES.
NOW...DO YOU NEED HELP OUT OF THAT ARMOR?
YOU THINK MY ARMOR IS DEPENDENT ON EXTERNAL POWER SOURCES FOR ME TO MOVE?
WHOM
THWAK
YOU THINK I WOULDN'T BE *PREPARED* FOR SUCH AN ATTACK?
YOU THINK DOOM ISN'T STRONG ENOUGH TO *DESTROY* YOU RIGHT NOW?

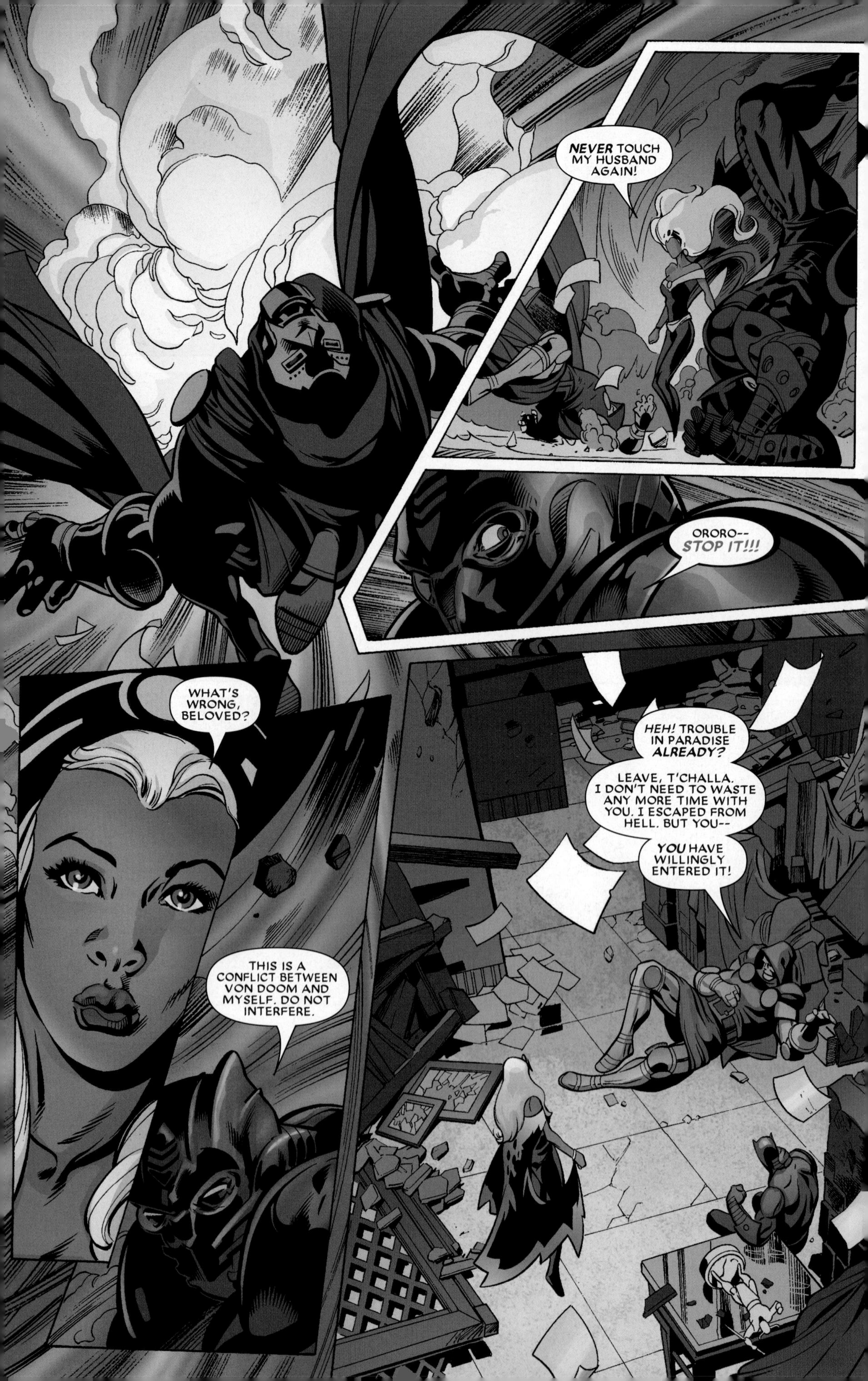
NEVER TOUCH MY HUSBAND AGAIN!
ORORO-- STOP IT!!!
WHAT'S WRONG, BELOVED?
THIS IS A CONFLICT BETWEEN VON DOOM AND MYSELF. DO NOT INTERFERE.
HEH! TROUBLE IN PARADISE ALREADY?
LEAVE, T'CHALLA. I DON'T NEED TO WASTE ANY MORE TIME WITH YOU. I ESCAPED FROM HELL. BUT YOU--
YOU HAVE WILLINGLY ENTERED IT!

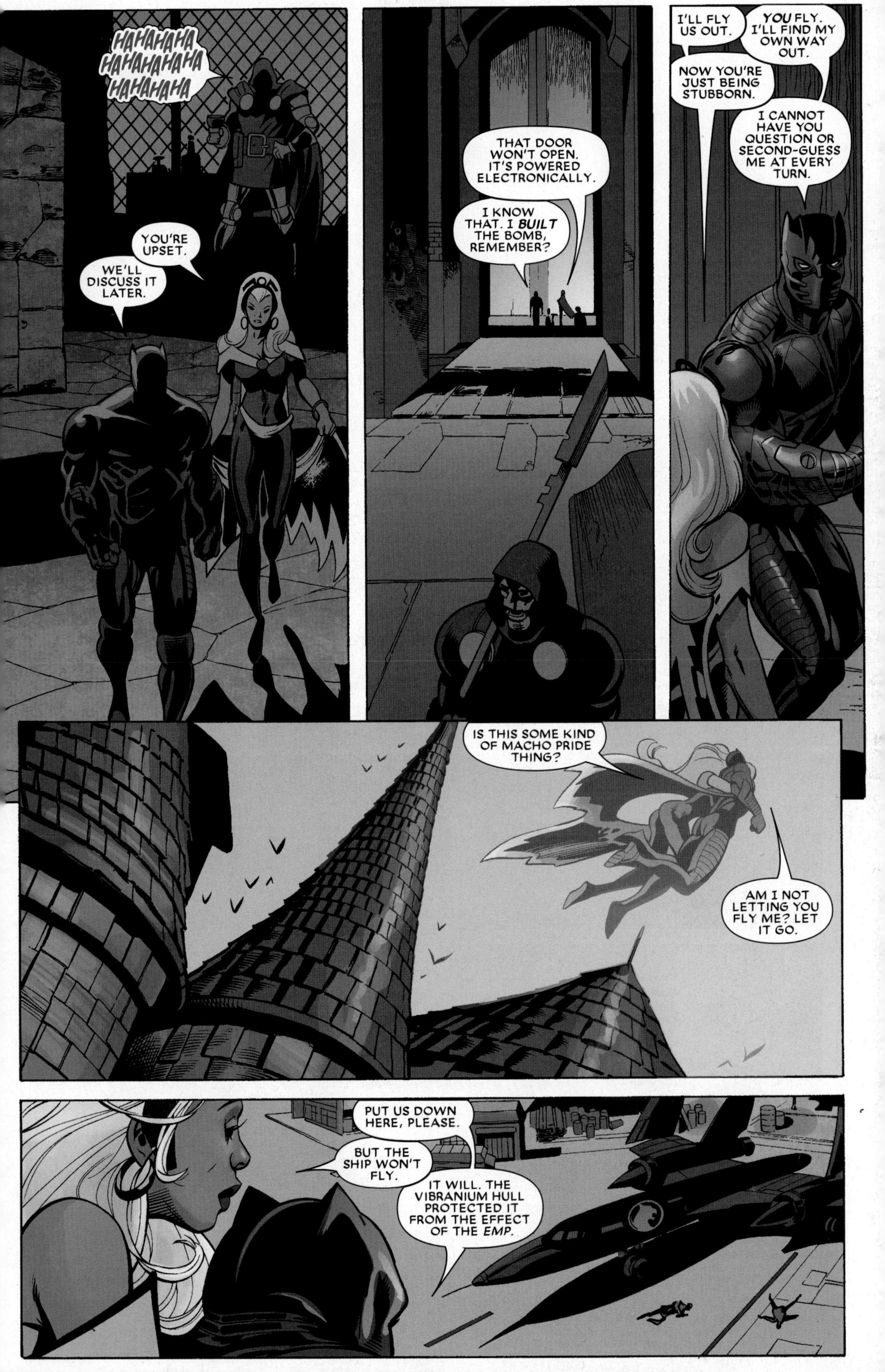
HAHAHAHA HAHAHAHAHA HAHAHAHA
YOU'RE UPSET.
WE'LL DISCUSS IT LATER.
THAT DOOR WON'T OPEN. IT'S POWERED ELECTRONICALLY.
I KNOW THAT. I *BUILT* THE BOMB, REMEMBER?
I'LL FLY US OUT.
YOU FLY. I'LL FIND MY OWN WAY OUT.
NOW YOU'RE JUST BEING STUBBORN.
I CANNOT HAVE YOU QUESTION OR SECOND-GUESS ME AT EVERY TURN.
IS THIS SOME KIND OF MACHO PRIDE THING?
AM I NOT LETTING YOU FLY ME? LET IT GO.
PUT US DOWN HERE, PLEASE.
BUT THE SHIP WON'T FLY.
IT WILL. THE VIBRANIUM HULL PROTECTED IT FROM THE EFFECT OF THE *EMP*.

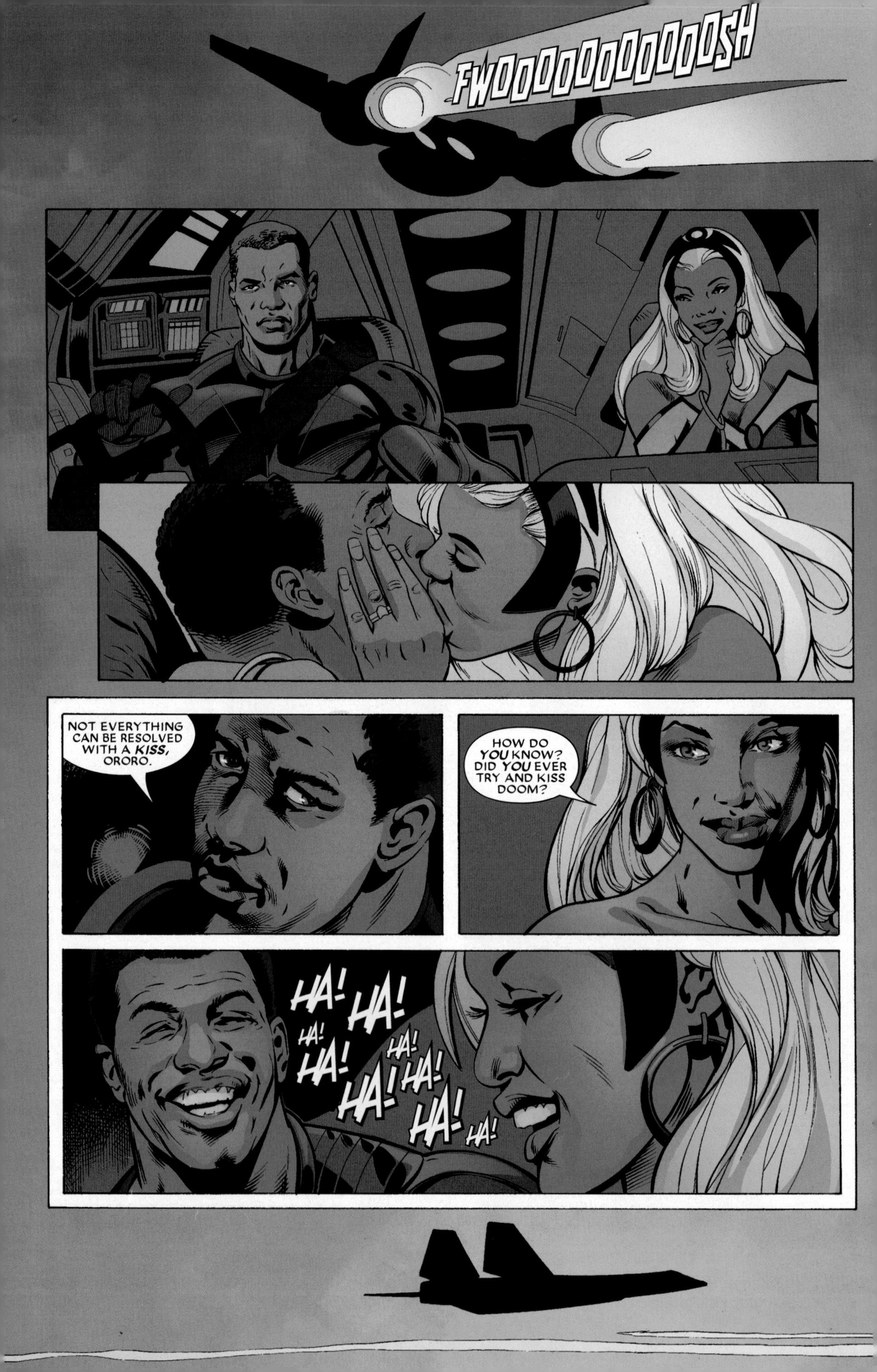
FWOOOOOOOOOOOOSH
NOT EVERYTHING CAN BE RESOLVED WITH A KISS, ORORO.
HOW DO YOU KNOW? DID YOU EVER TRY AND KISS DOOM?
HA! HA! HA! HA! HA! HA! HA! HA! HA!

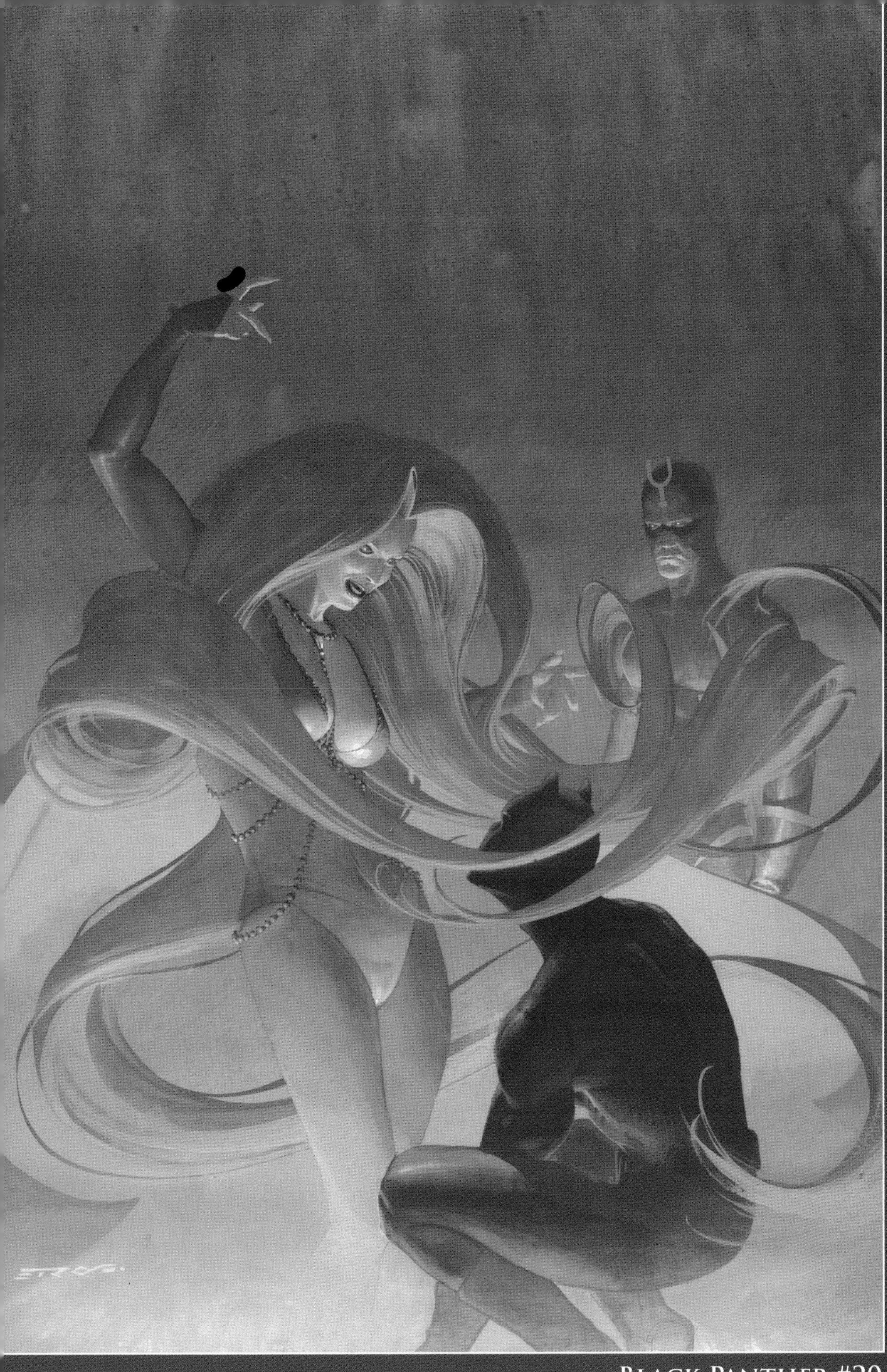

BLACK PANTHER #20

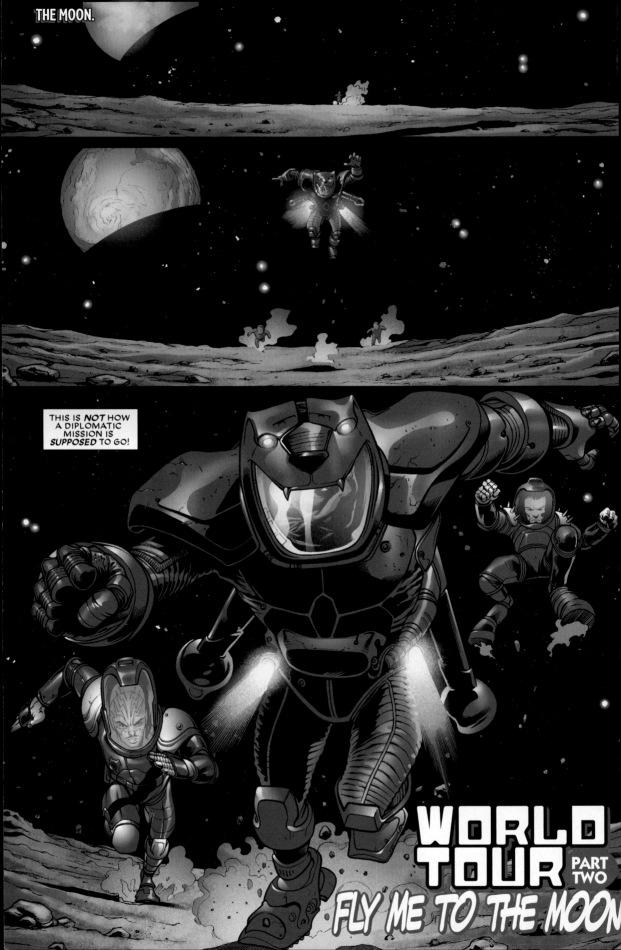

THE MOON.

THIS IS *NOT* HOW A DIPLOMATIC MISSION IS *SUPPOSED* TO GO!

WORLD TOUR PART TWO
FLY ME TO THE MOON

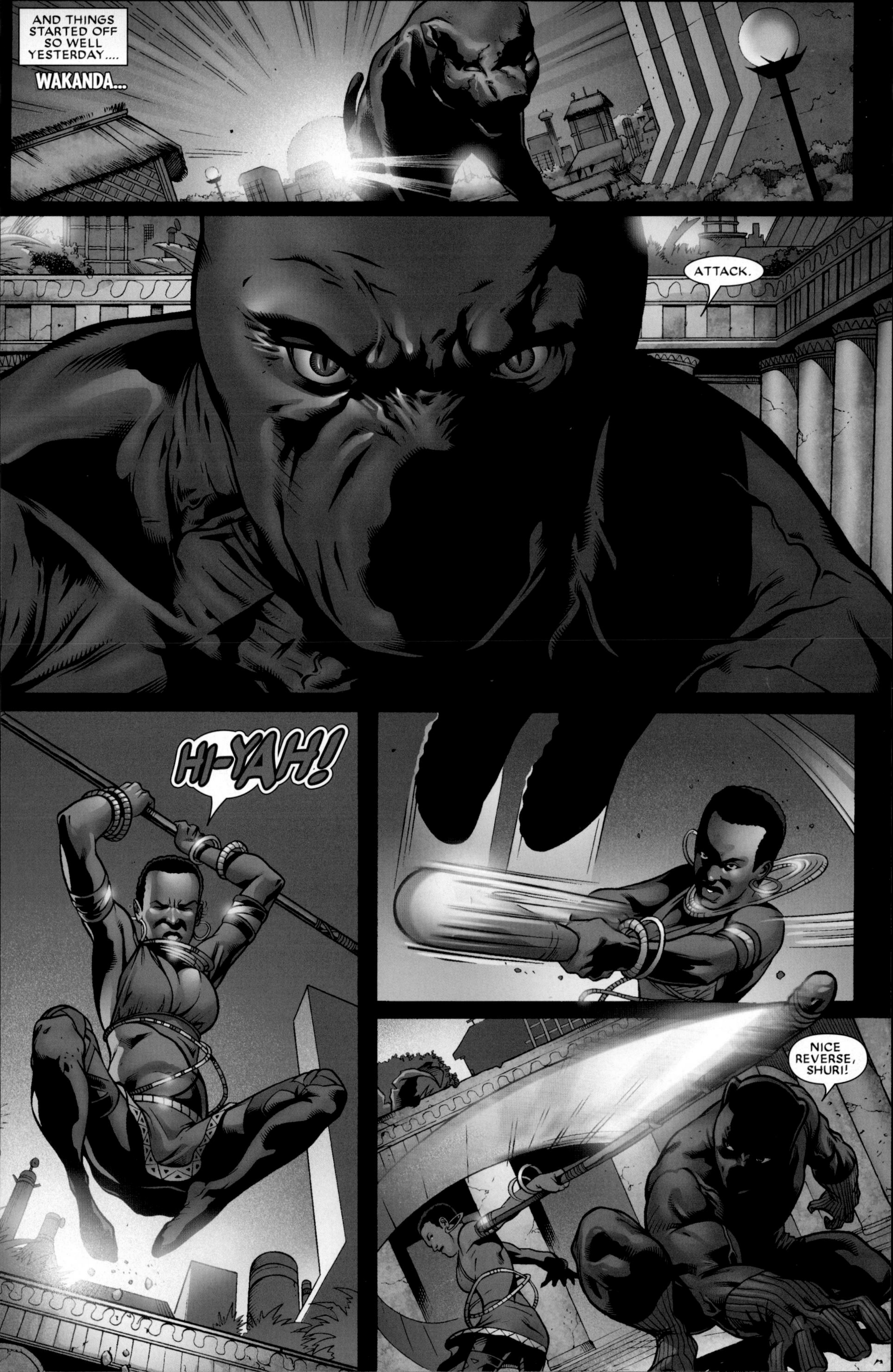
AND THINGS STARTED OFF SO WELL YESTERDAY....
WAKANDA...
ATTACK.
HI-YAH!
NICE REVERSE, SHURI!

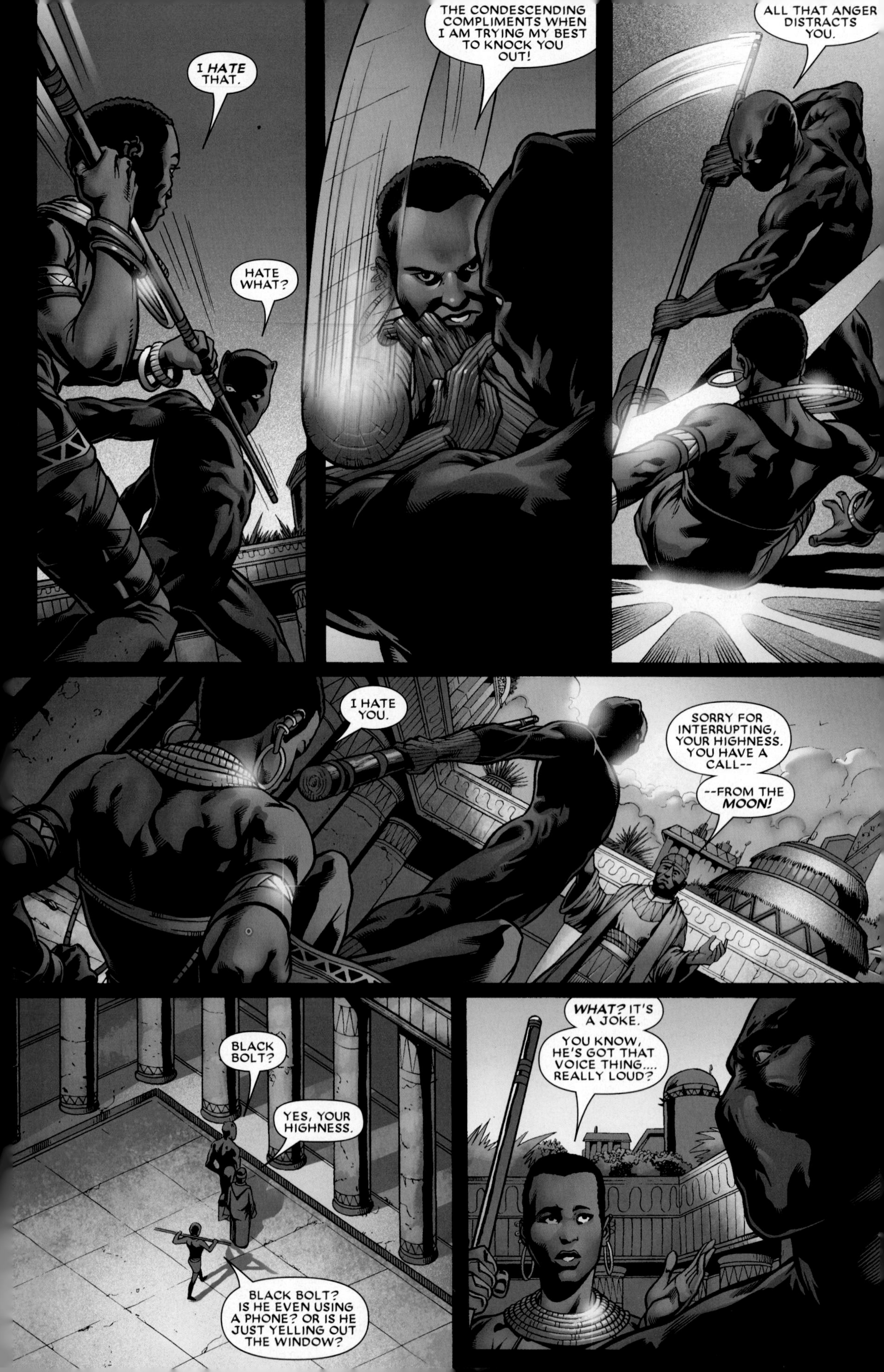
I *HATE* THAT.
HATE WHAT?
THE CONDESCENDING COMPLIMENTS WHEN I AM TRYING MY BEST TO KNOCK YOU OUT!
ALL THAT ANGER DISTRACTS YOU.
I HATE YOU.
SORRY FOR INTERRUPTING, YOUR HIGHNESS. YOU HAVE A CALL--
--FROM THE *MOON!*
BLACK BOLT?
YES, YOUR HIGHNESS.
BLACK BOLT? IS HE EVEN USING A PHONE? OR IS HE JUST YELLING OUT THE WINDOW?
WHAT? IT'S A JOKE.
YOU KNOW, HE'S GOT THAT VOICE THING.... REALLY LOUD?

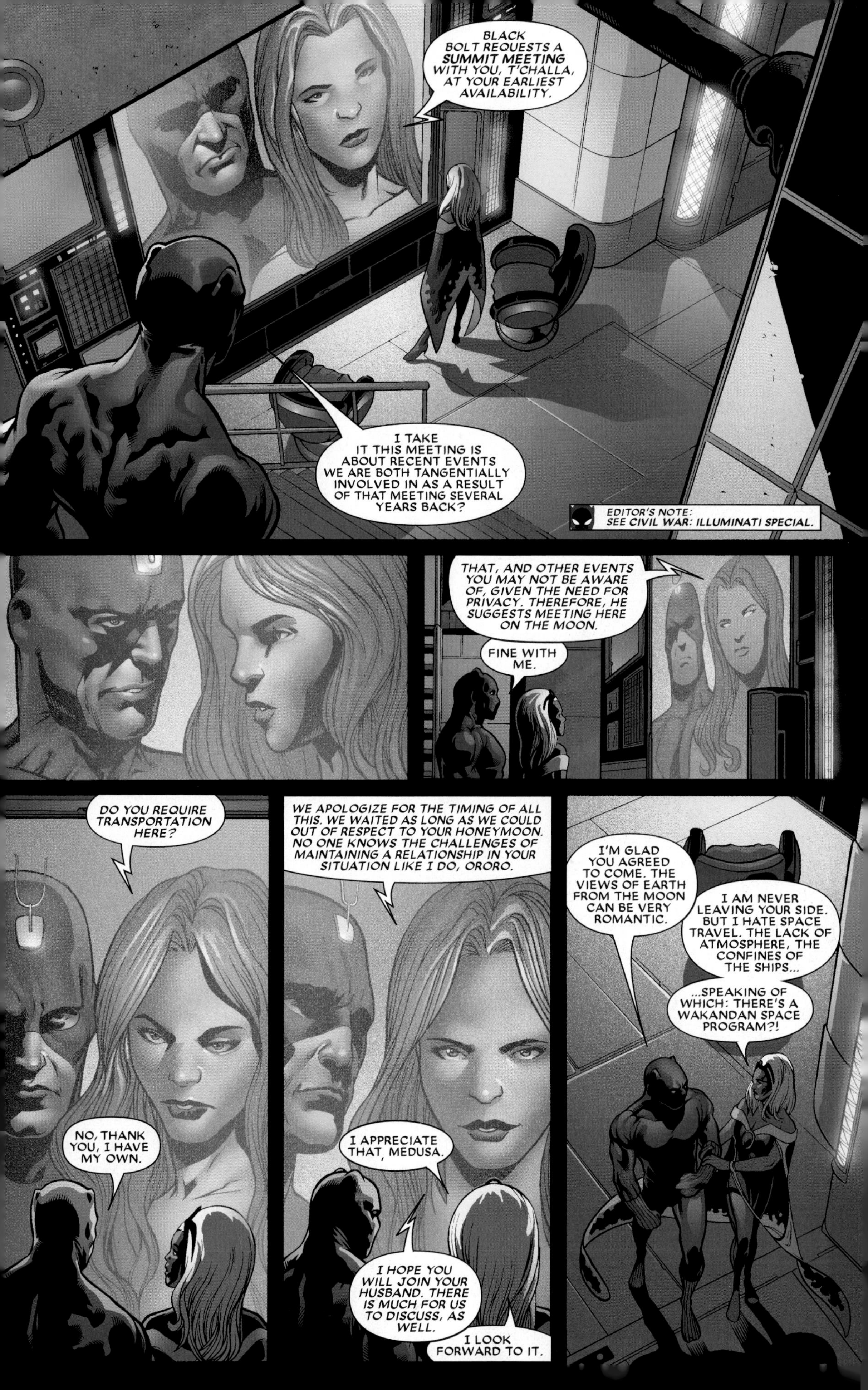
BLACK BOLT REQUESTS A **SUMMIT MEETING** WITH YOU, T'CHALLA, AT YOUR EARLIEST AVAILABILITY.
I TAKE IT THIS MEETING IS ABOUT RECENT EVENTS WE ARE BOTH TANGENTIALLY INVOLVED IN AS A RESULT OF THAT MEETING SEVERAL YEARS BACK?
EDITOR'S NOTE: SEE **CIVIL WAR: ILLUMINATI SPECIAL.**
THAT, AND OTHER EVENTS YOU MAY NOT BE AWARE OF, GIVEN THE NEED FOR PRIVACY. THEREFORE, HE SUGGESTS MEETING HERE ON THE MOON.
FINE WITH ME.
DO YOU REQUIRE TRANSPORTATION HERE?
NO, THANK YOU, I HAVE MY OWN.
WE APOLOGIZE FOR THE TIMING OF ALL THIS. WE WAITED AS LONG AS WE COULD OUT OF RESPECT TO YOUR HONEYMOON. NO ONE KNOWS THE CHALLENGES OF MAINTAINING A RELATIONSHIP IN YOUR SITUATION LIKE I DO, ORORO.
I APPRECIATE THAT, MEDUSA.
I HOPE YOU WILL JOIN YOUR HUSBAND. THERE IS MUCH FOR US TO DISCUSS, AS WELL.
I LOOK FORWARD TO IT.
I'M GLAD YOU AGREED TO COME. THE VIEWS OF EARTH FROM THE MOON CAN BE VERY ROMANTIC.
I AM NEVER LEAVING YOUR SIDE. BUT I HATE SPACE TRAVEL. THE LACK OF ATMOSPHERE, THE CONFINES OF THE SHIPS...
...SPEAKING OF WHICH: THERE'S A WAKANDAN SPACE PROGRAM?!

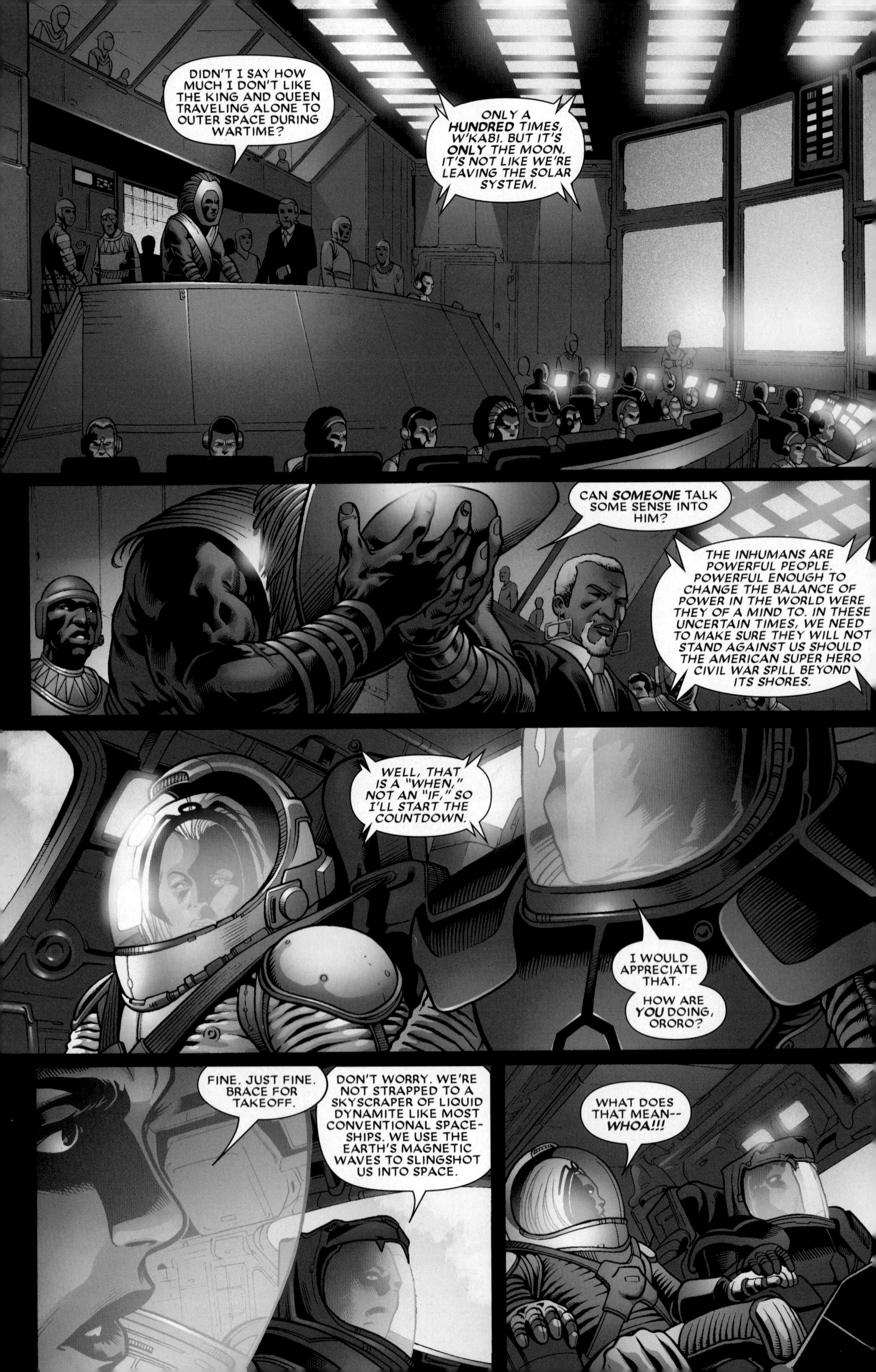
DIDN'T I SAY HOW MUCH I DON'T LIKE THE KING AND QUEEN TRAVELING ALONE TO OUTER SPACE DURING WARTIME?
ONLY A HUNDRED TIMES, W'KABI. BUT IT'S ONLY THE MOON. IT'S NOT LIKE WE'RE LEAVING THE SOLAR SYSTEM.
CAN SOMEONE TALK SOME SENSE INTO HIM?
THE INHUMANS ARE POWERFUL PEOPLE. POWERFUL ENOUGH TO CHANGE THE BALANCE OF POWER IN THE WORLD WERE THEY OF A MIND TO. IN THESE UNCERTAIN TIMES, WE NEED TO MAKE SURE THEY WILL NOT STAND AGAINST US SHOULD THE AMERICAN SUPER HERO CIVIL WAR SPILL BEYOND ITS SHORES.
WELL, THAT IS A "WHEN," NOT AN "IF," SO I'LL START THE COUNTDOWN.
I WOULD APPRECIATE THAT.
HOW ARE YOU DOING, ORORO?
FINE. JUST FINE. BRACE FOR TAKEOFF.
DON'T WORRY. WE'RE NOT STRAPPED TO A SKYSCRAPER OF LIQUID DYNAMITE LIKE MOST CONVENTIONAL SPACE-SHIPS. WE USE THE EARTH'S MAGNETIC WAVES TO SLINGSHOT US INTO SPACE.
WHAT DOES THAT MEAN-- WHOA!!!

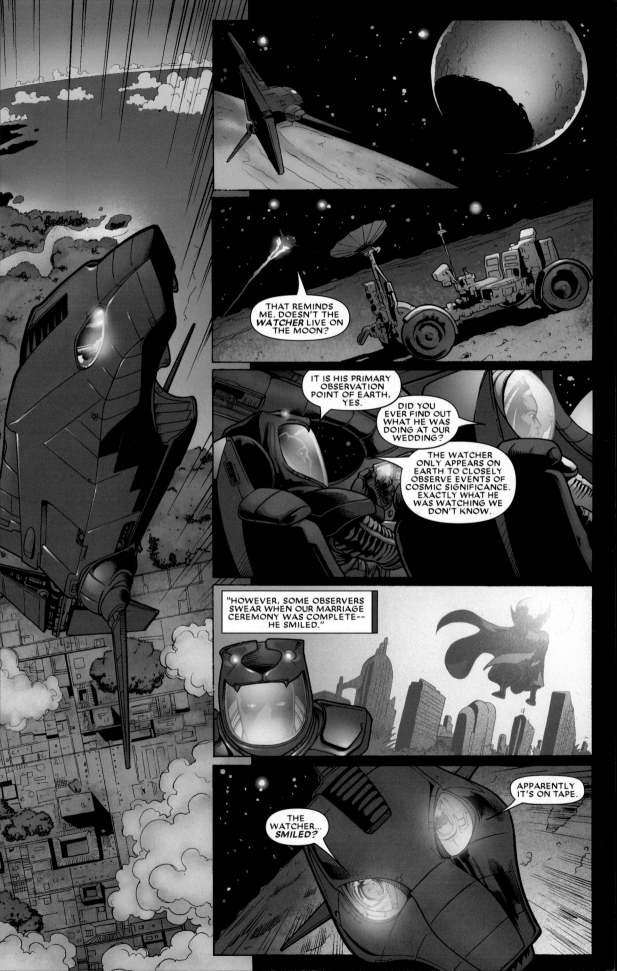

THAT REMINDS ME. DOESN'T THE *WATCHER* LIVE ON THE MOON?

IT IS HIS PRIMARY OBSERVATION POINT OF EARTH, YES.

DID YOU EVER FIND OUT WHAT HE WAS DOING AT OUR WEDDING?

THE WATCHER ONLY APPEARS ON EARTH TO CLOSELY OBSERVE EVENTS OF COSMIC SIGNIFICANCE. EXACTLY WHAT HE WAS WATCHING WE DON'T KNOW.

"HOWEVER, SOME OBSERVERS SWEAR WHEN OUR MARRIAGE CEREMONY WAS COMPLETE-- HE SMILED."

THE WATCHER... *SMILED?*

APPARENTLY IT'S ON TAPE.

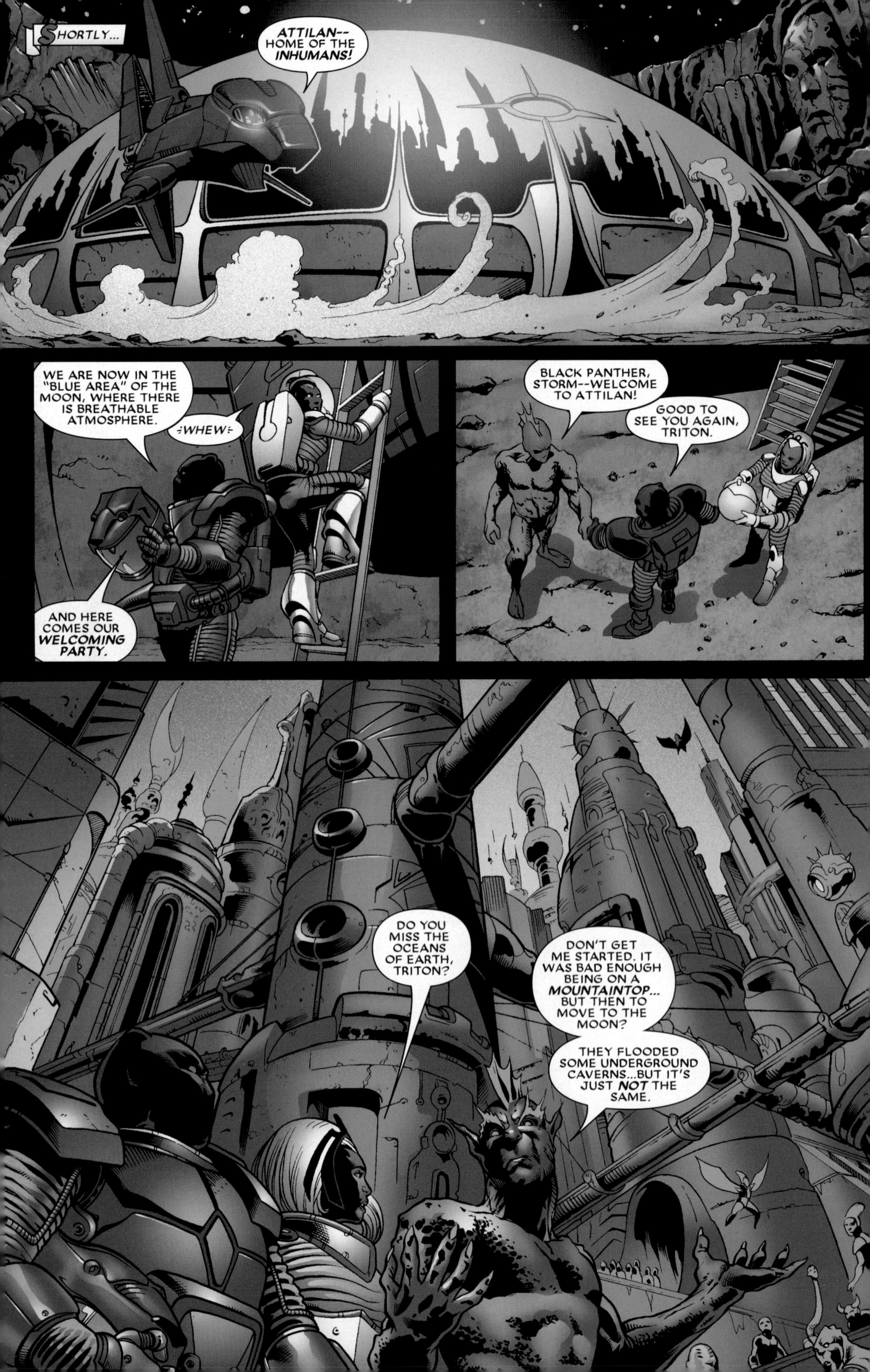
SHORTLY...
ATTILAN-- HOME OF THE INHUMANS!
WE ARE NOW IN THE "BLUE AREA" OF THE MOON, WHERE THERE IS BREATHABLE ATMOSPHERE.
WHEW
AND HERE COMES OUR WELCOMING PARTY.
BLACK PANTHER, STORM--WELCOME TO ATTILAN!
GOOD TO SEE YOU AGAIN, TRITON.
DO YOU MISS THE OCEANS OF EARTH, TRITON?
DON'T GET ME STARTED. IT WAS BAD ENOUGH BEING ON A MOUNTAINTOP... BUT THEN TO MOVE TO THE MOON?
THEY FLOODED SOME UNDERGROUND CAVERNS...BUT IT'S JUST NOT THE SAME.

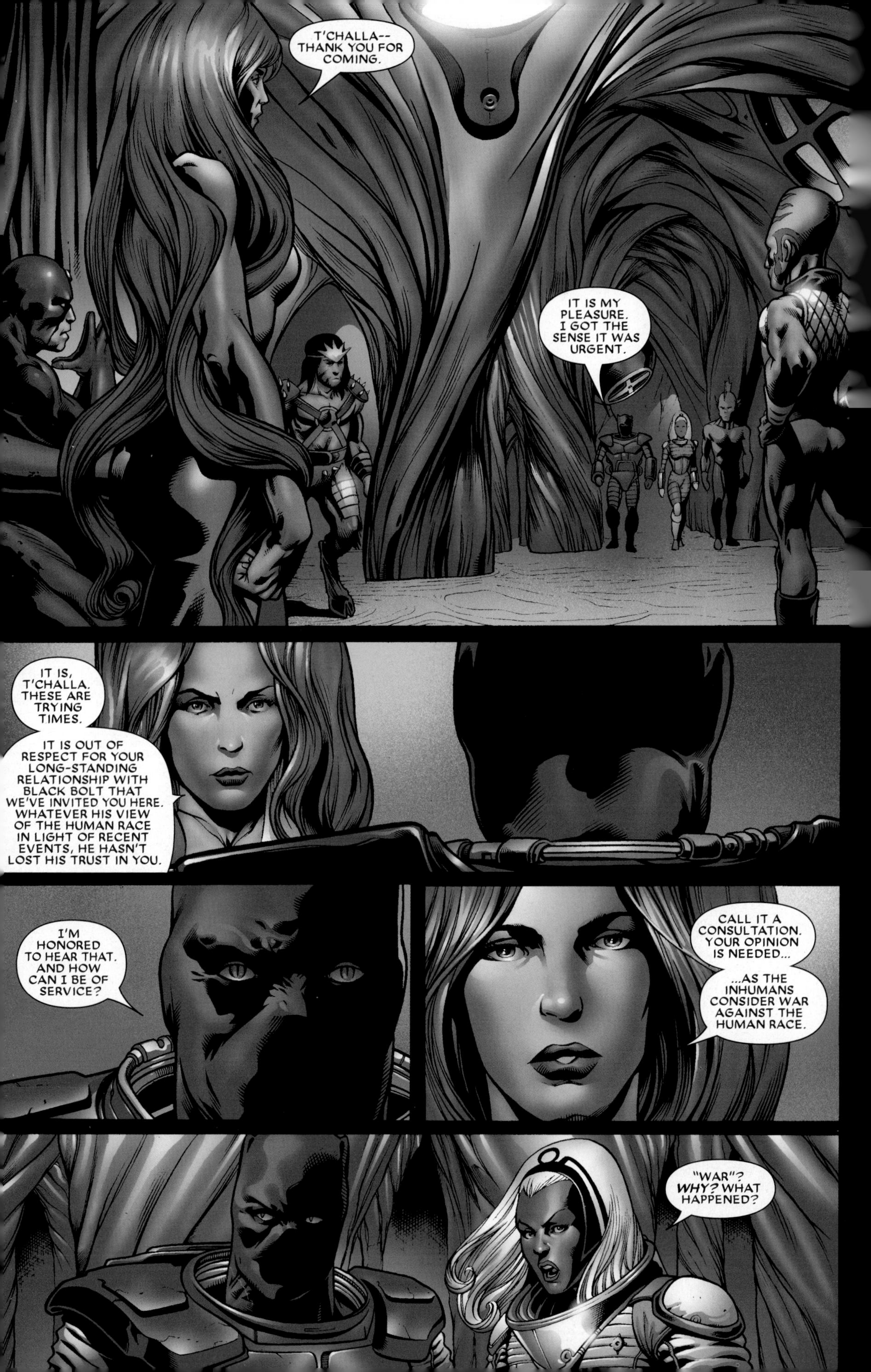
T'CHALLA-- THANK YOU FOR COMING.
IT IS MY PLEASURE. I GOT THE SENSE IT WAS URGENT.
IT IS, T'CHALLA. THESE ARE TRYING TIMES.
IT IS OUT OF RESPECT FOR YOUR LONG-STANDING RELATIONSHIP WITH BLACK BOLT THAT WE'VE INVITED YOU HERE. WHATEVER HIS VIEW OF THE HUMAN RACE IN LIGHT OF RECENT EVENTS, HE HASN'T LOST HIS TRUST IN YOU.
I'M HONORED TO HEAR THAT. AND HOW CAN I BE OF SERVICE?
CALL IT A CONSULTATION. YOUR OPINION IS NEEDED...
...AS THE INHUMANS CONSIDER WAR AGAINST THE HUMAN RACE.
"WAR"? *WHY?* WHAT HAPPENED?

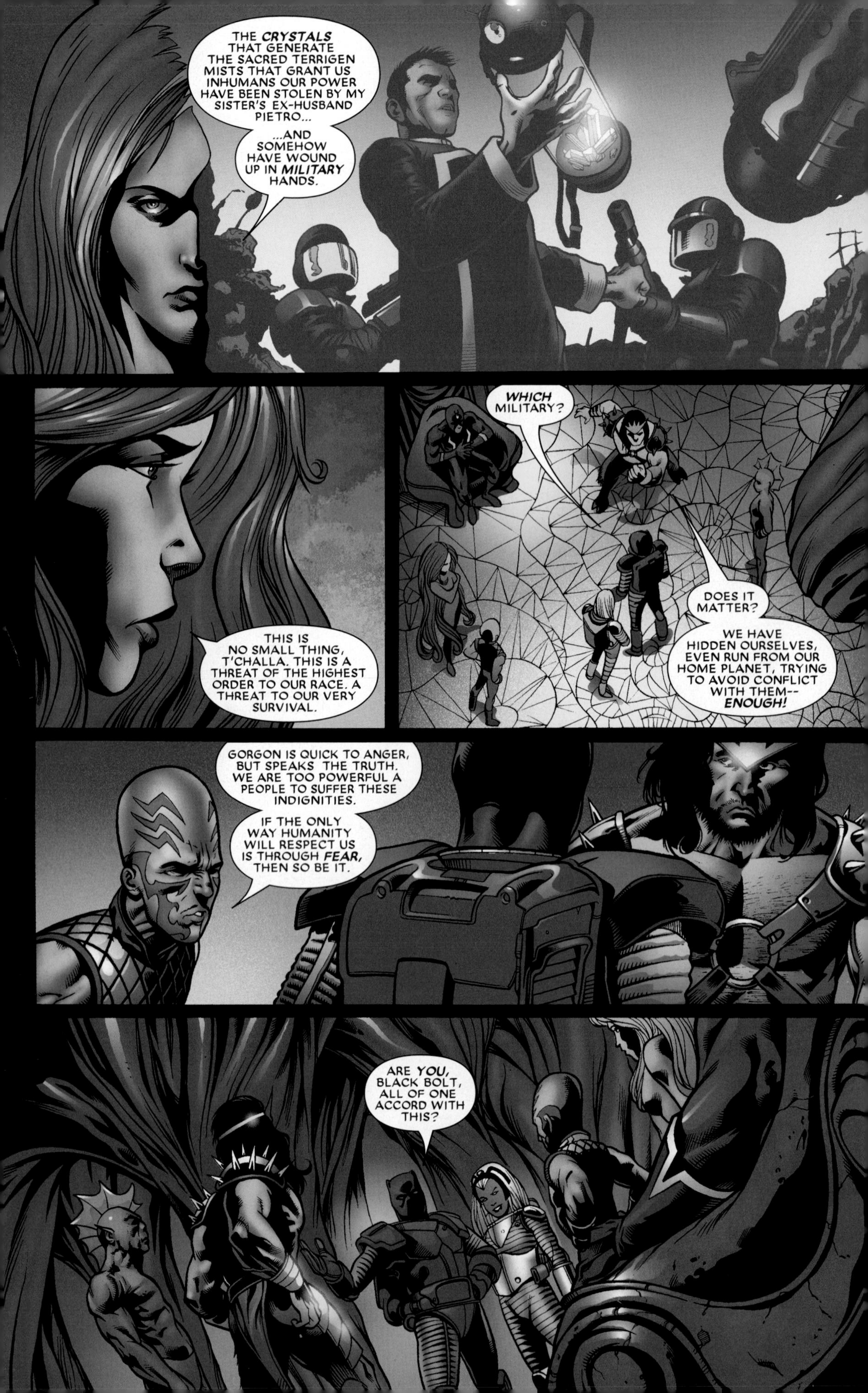
THE CRYSTALS THAT GENERATE THE SACRED TERRIGEN MISTS THAT GRANT US INHUMANS OUR POWER HAVE BEEN STOLEN BY MY SISTER'S EX-HUSBAND PIETRO...
...AND SOMEHOW HAVE WOUND UP IN MILITARY HANDS.
THIS IS NO SMALL THING, T'CHALLA. THIS IS A THREAT OF THE HIGHEST ORDER TO OUR RACE. A THREAT TO OUR VERY SURVIVAL.
WHICH MILITARY?
DOES IT MATTER?
WE HAVE HIDDEN OURSELVES, EVEN RUN FROM OUR HOME PLANET, TRYING TO AVOID CONFLICT WITH THEM-- ENOUGH!
GORGON IS QUICK TO ANGER, BUT SPEAKS THE TRUTH. WE ARE TOO POWERFUL A PEOPLE TO SUFFER THESE INDIGNITIES.
IF THE ONLY WAY HUMANITY WILL RESPECT US IS THROUGH FEAR, THEN SO BE IT.
ARE YOU, BLACK BOLT, ALL OF ONE ACCORD WITH THIS?

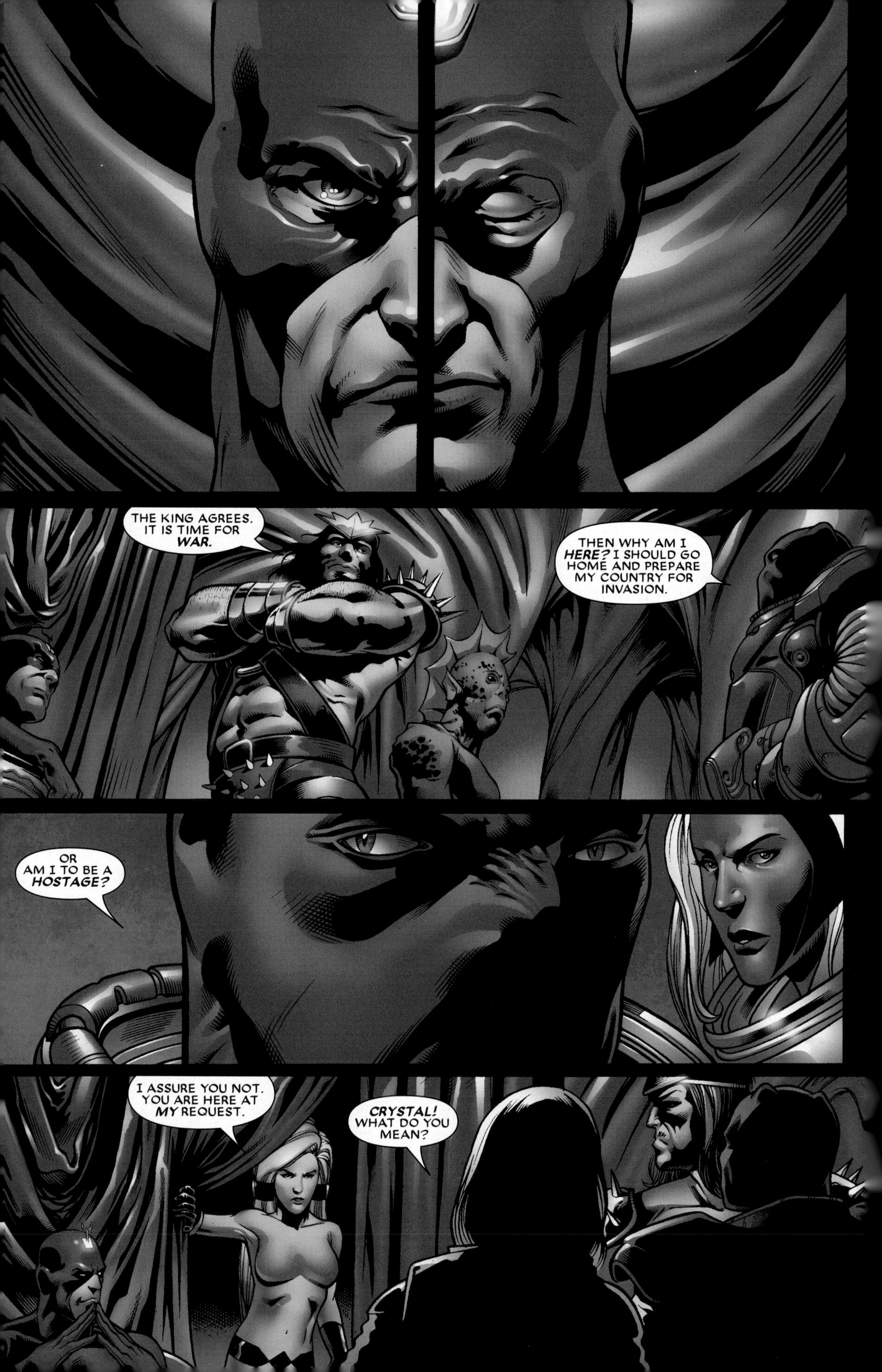
THE KING AGREES. IT IS TIME FOR WAR.
THEN WHY AM I HERE? I SHOULD GO HOME AND PREPARE MY COUNTRY FOR INVASION.
OR AM I TO BE A HOSTAGE?
I ASSURE YOU NOT. YOU ARE HERE AT MY REQUEST.
CRYSTAL! WHAT DO YOU MEAN?

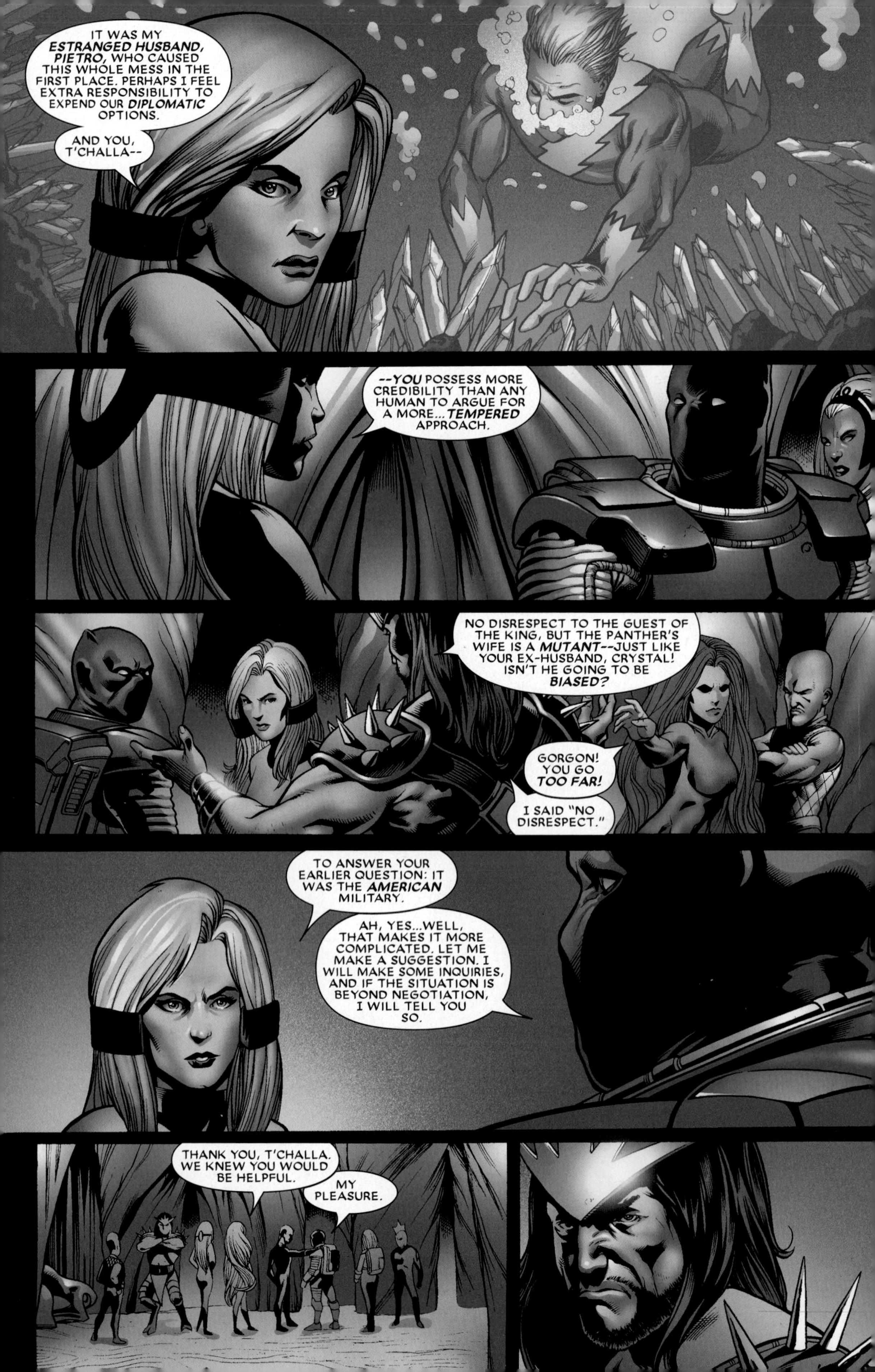
IT WAS MY ESTRANGED HUSBAND, PIETRO, WHO CAUSED THIS WHOLE MESS IN THE FIRST PLACE. PERHAPS I FEEL EXTRA RESPONSIBILITY TO EXPEND OUR DIPLOMATIC OPTIONS.
AND YOU, T'CHALLA--
--YOU POSSESS MORE CREDIBILITY THAN ANY HUMAN TO ARGUE FOR A MORE... TEMPERED APPROACH.
NO DISRESPECT TO THE GUEST OF THE KING, BUT THE PANTHER'S WIFE IS A MUTANT--JUST LIKE YOUR EX-HUSBAND, CRYSTAL! ISN'T HE GOING TO BE BIASED?
GORGON! YOU GO TOO FAR!
I SAID "NO DISRESPECT."
TO ANSWER YOUR EARLIER QUESTION: IT WAS THE AMERICAN MILITARY.
AH, YES...WELL, THAT MAKES IT MORE COMPLICATED. LET ME MAKE A SUGGESTION. I WILL MAKE SOME INQUIRIES, AND IF THE SITUATION IS BEYOND NEGOTIATION, I WILL TELL YOU SO.
THANK YOU, T'CHALLA. WE KNEW YOU WOULD BE HELPFUL.
MY PLEASURE.

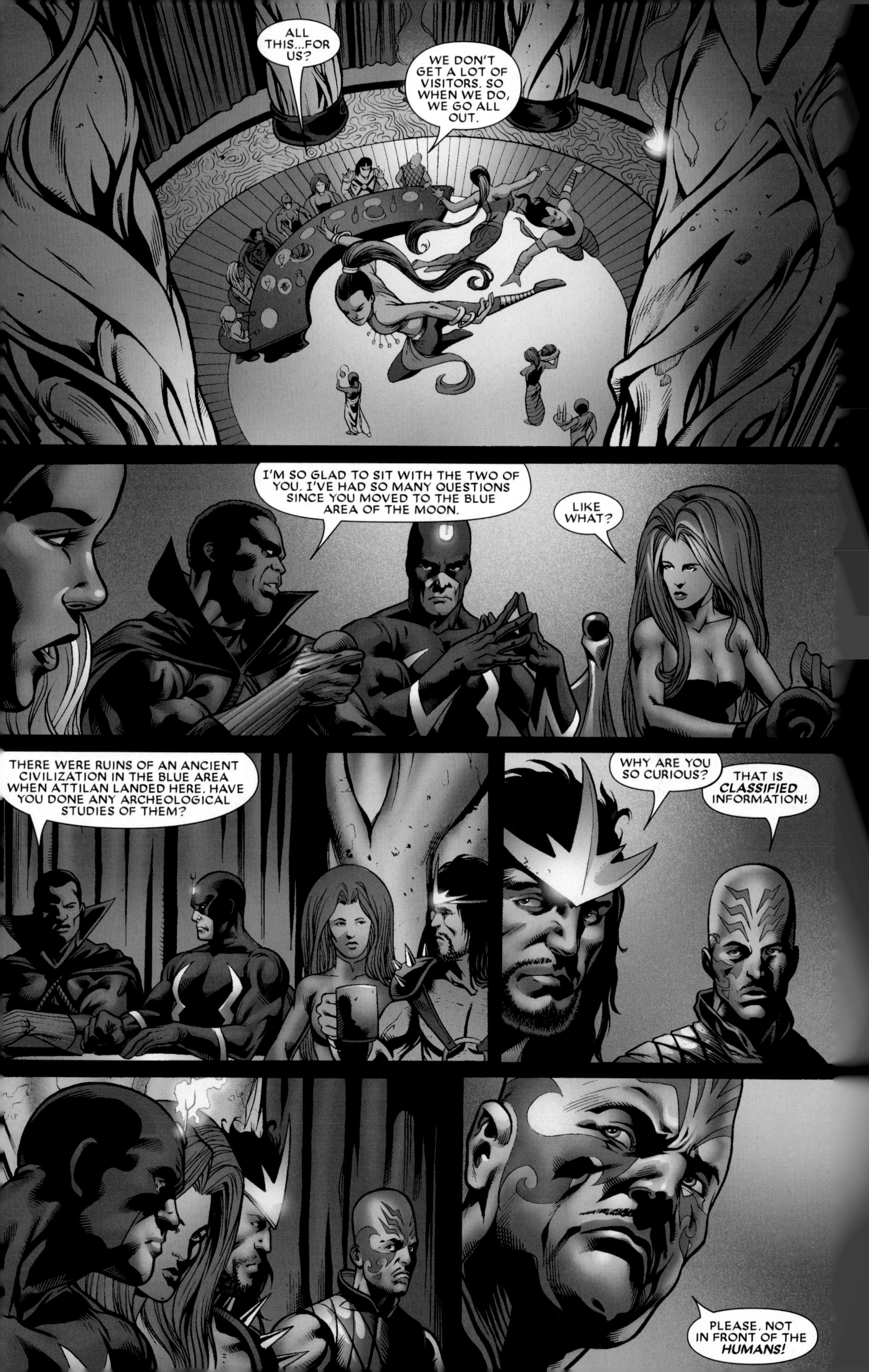
ALL THIS...FOR US?
WE DON'T GET A LOT OF VISITORS. SO WHEN WE DO, WE GO ALL OUT.
I'M SO GLAD TO SIT WITH THE TWO OF YOU. I'VE HAD SO MANY QUESTIONS SINCE YOU MOVED TO THE BLUE AREA OF THE MOON.
LIKE WHAT?
THERE WERE RUINS OF AN ANCIENT CIVILIZATION IN THE BLUE AREA WHEN ATTILAN LANDED HERE. HAVE YOU DONE ANY ARCHEOLOGICAL STUDIES OF THEM?
WHY ARE YOU SO CURIOUS?
THAT IS *CLASSIFIED* INFORMATION!
PLEASE. NOT IN FRONT OF THE *HUMANS!*

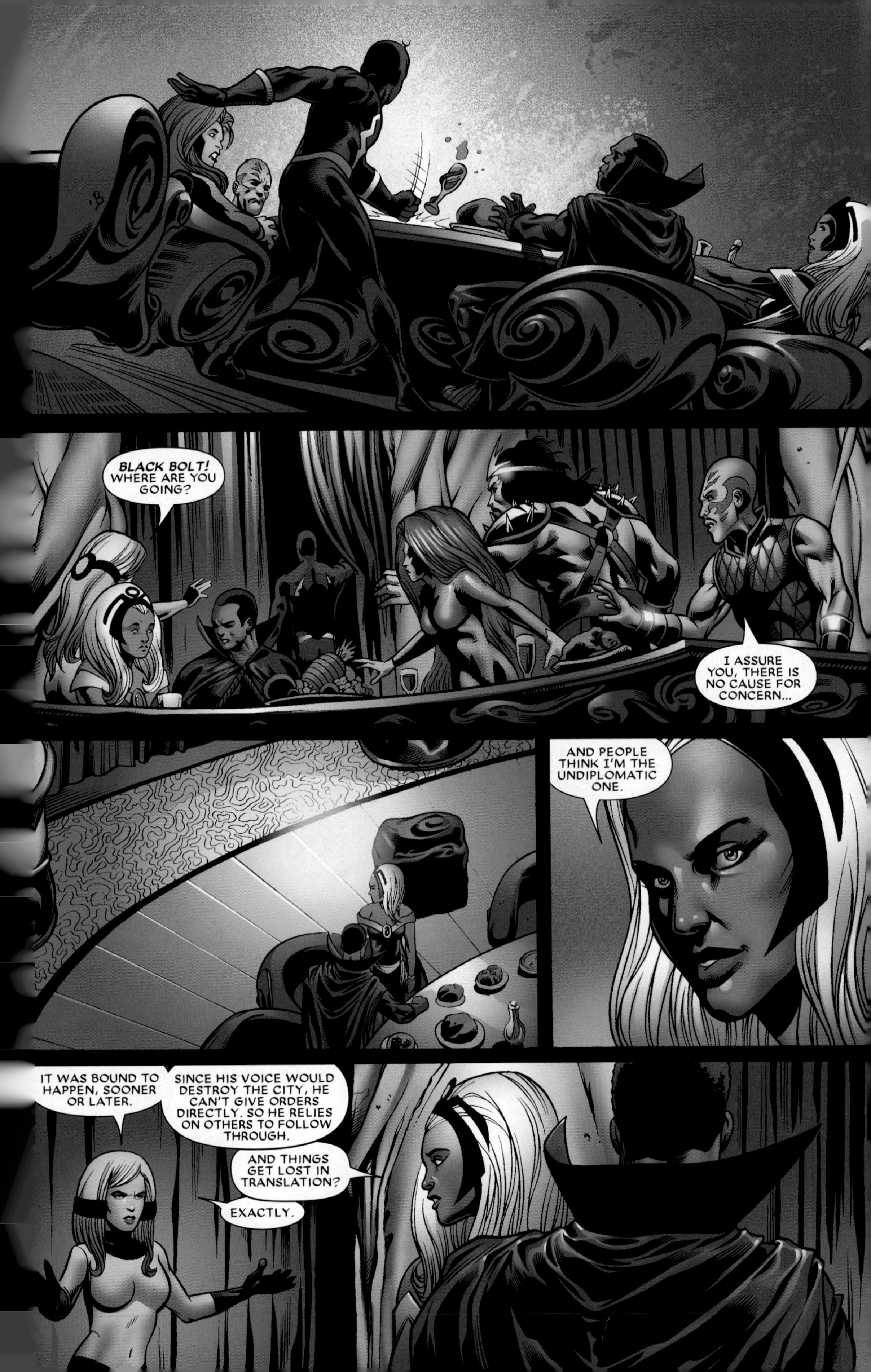
BLACK BOLT! WHERE ARE YOU GOING?
I ASSURE YOU, THERE IS NO CAUSE FOR CONCERN...
AND PEOPLE THINK I'M THE UNDIPLOMATIC ONE.
IT WAS BOUND TO HAPPEN, SOONER OR LATER.
SINCE HIS VOICE WOULD DESTROY THE CITY, HE CAN'T GIVE ORDERS DIRECTLY. SO HE RELIES ON OTHERS TO FOLLOW THROUGH.
AND THINGS GET LOST IN TRANSLATION?
EXACTLY.

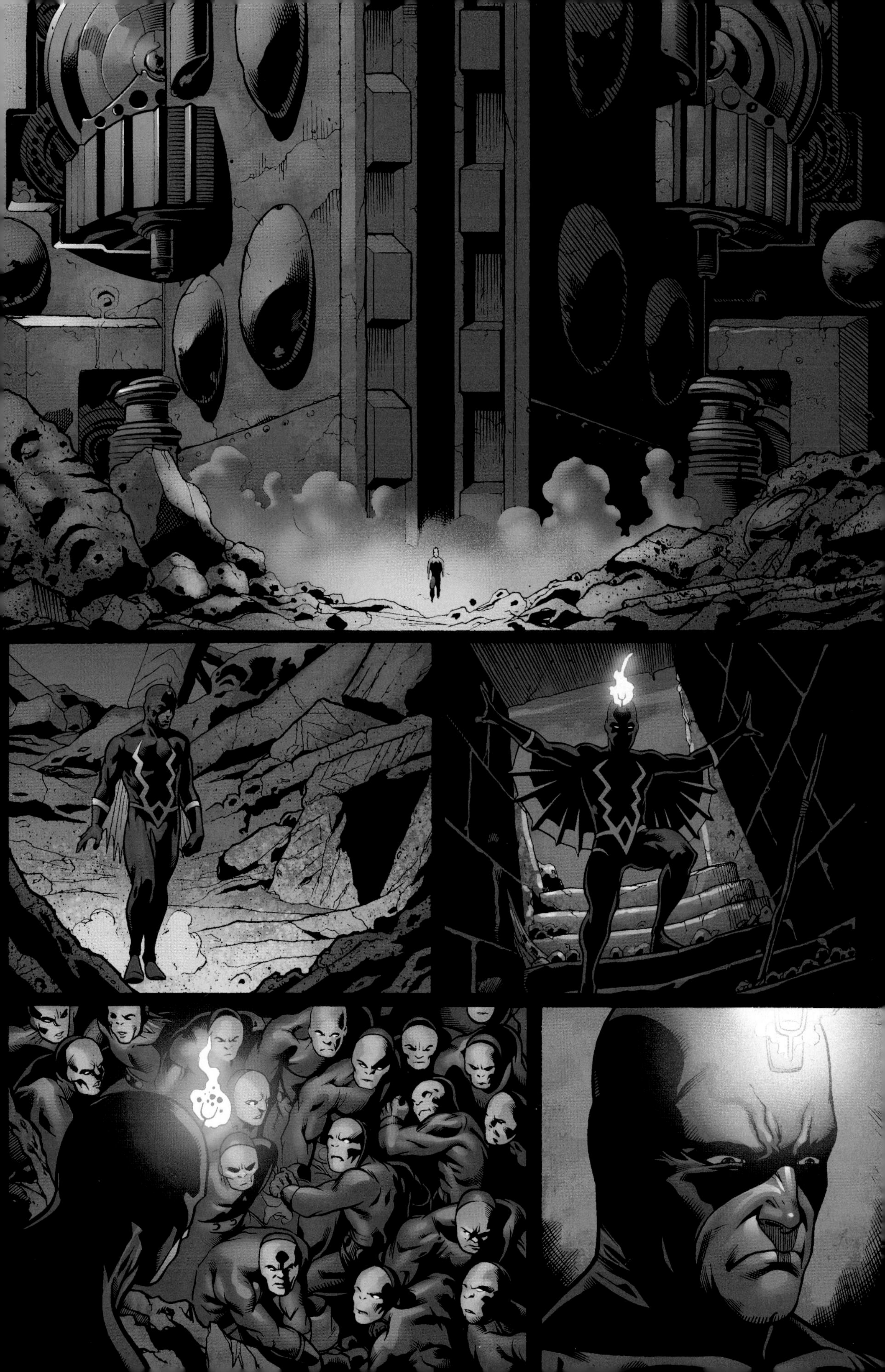

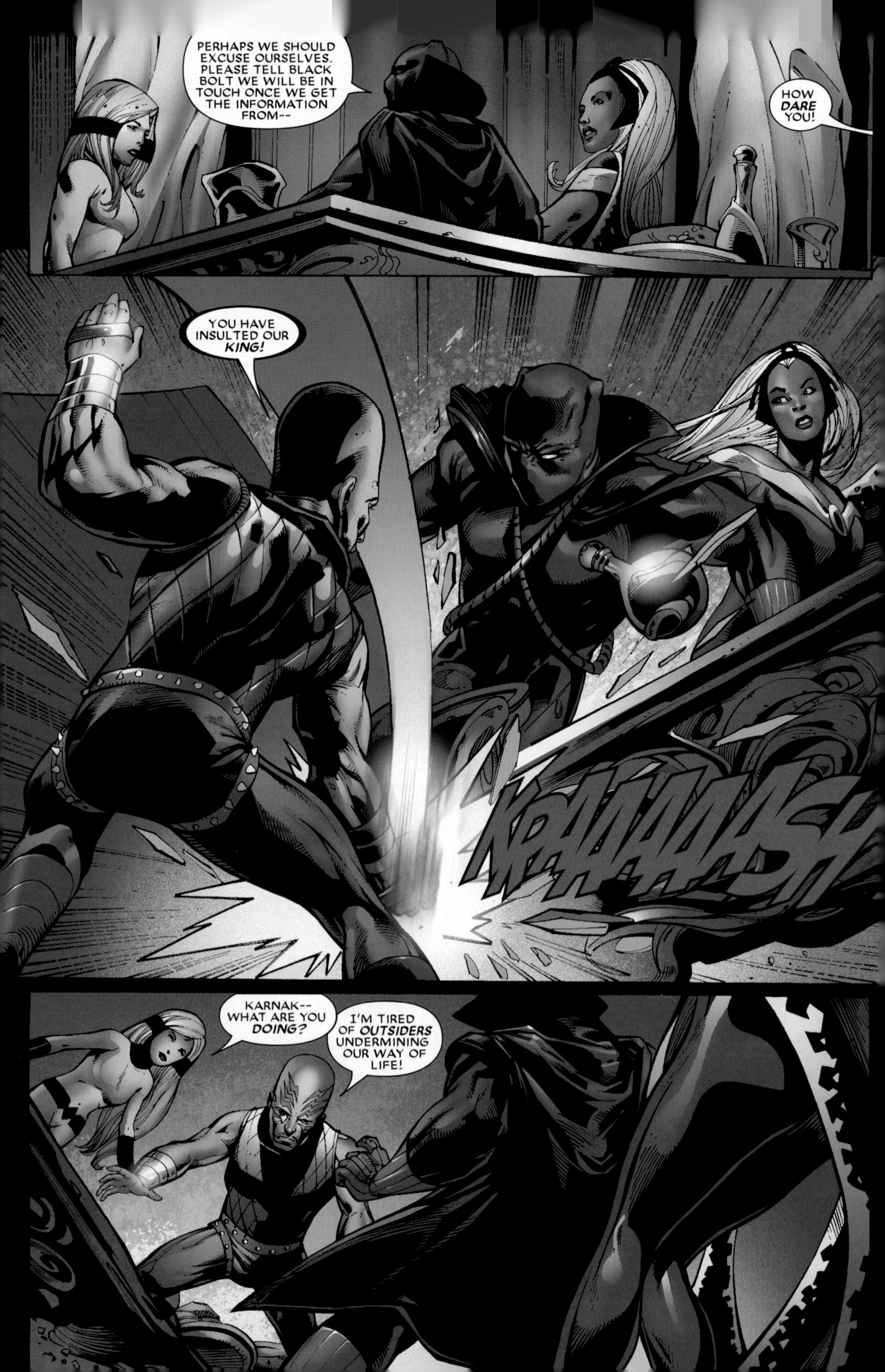
PERHAPS WE SHOULD EXCUSE OURSELVES. PLEASE TELL BLACK BOLT WE WILL BE IN TOUCH ONCE WE GET THE INFORMATION FROM--
HOW DARE YOU!
YOU HAVE INSULTED OUR KING!
KRAAAAASH
KARNAK-- WHAT ARE YOU DOING?
I'M TIRED OF OUTSIDERS UNDERMINING OUR WAY OF LIFE!

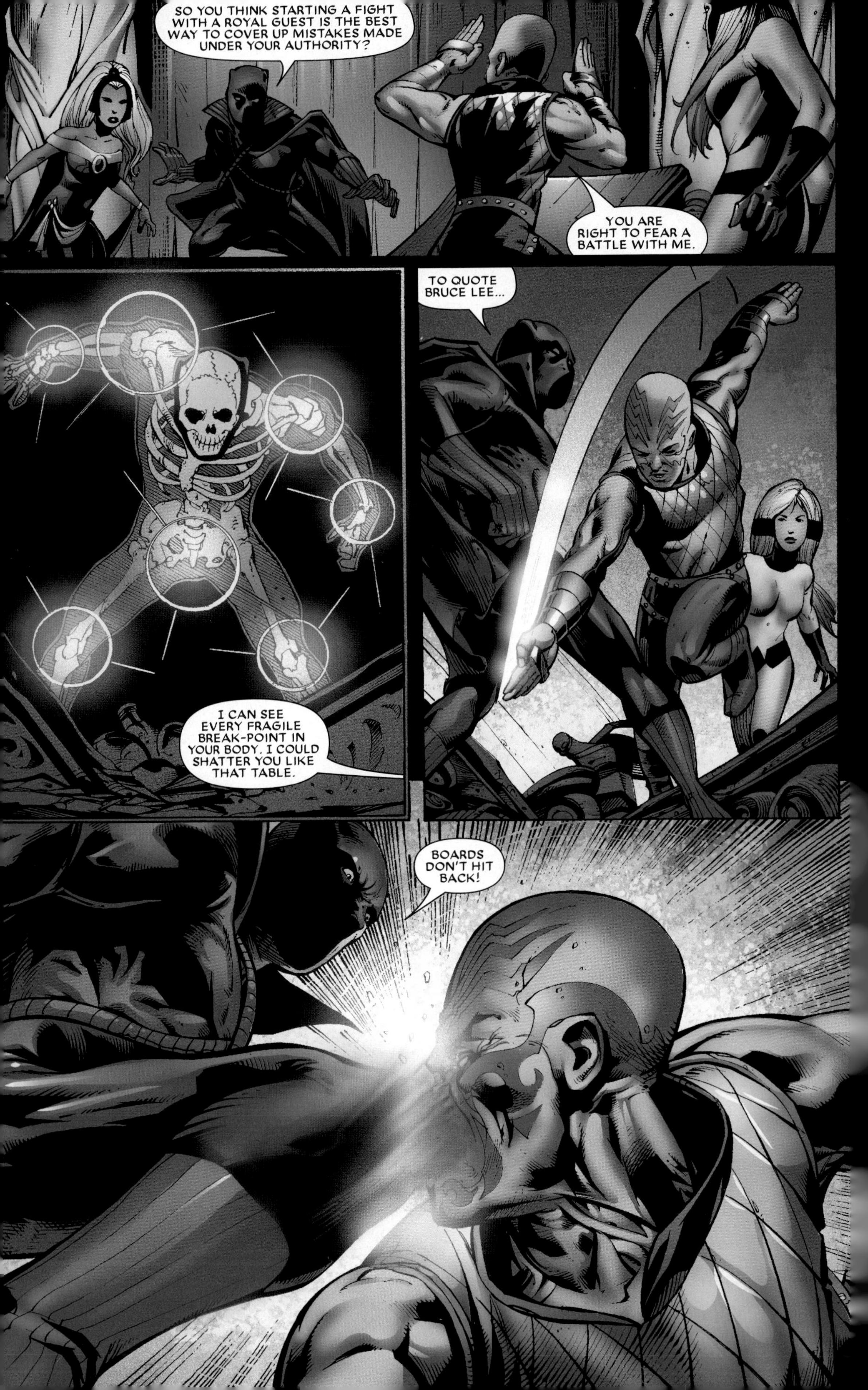
SO YOU THINK STARTING A FIGHT WITH A ROYAL GUEST IS THE BEST WAY TO COVER UP MISTAKES MADE UNDER YOUR AUTHORITY?
YOU ARE RIGHT TO FEAR A BATTLE WITH ME.
I CAN SEE EVERY FRAGILE BREAK-POINT IN YOUR BODY. I COULD SHATTER YOU LIKE THAT TABLE.
TO QUOTE BRUCE LEE...
BOARDS DON'T HIT BACK!

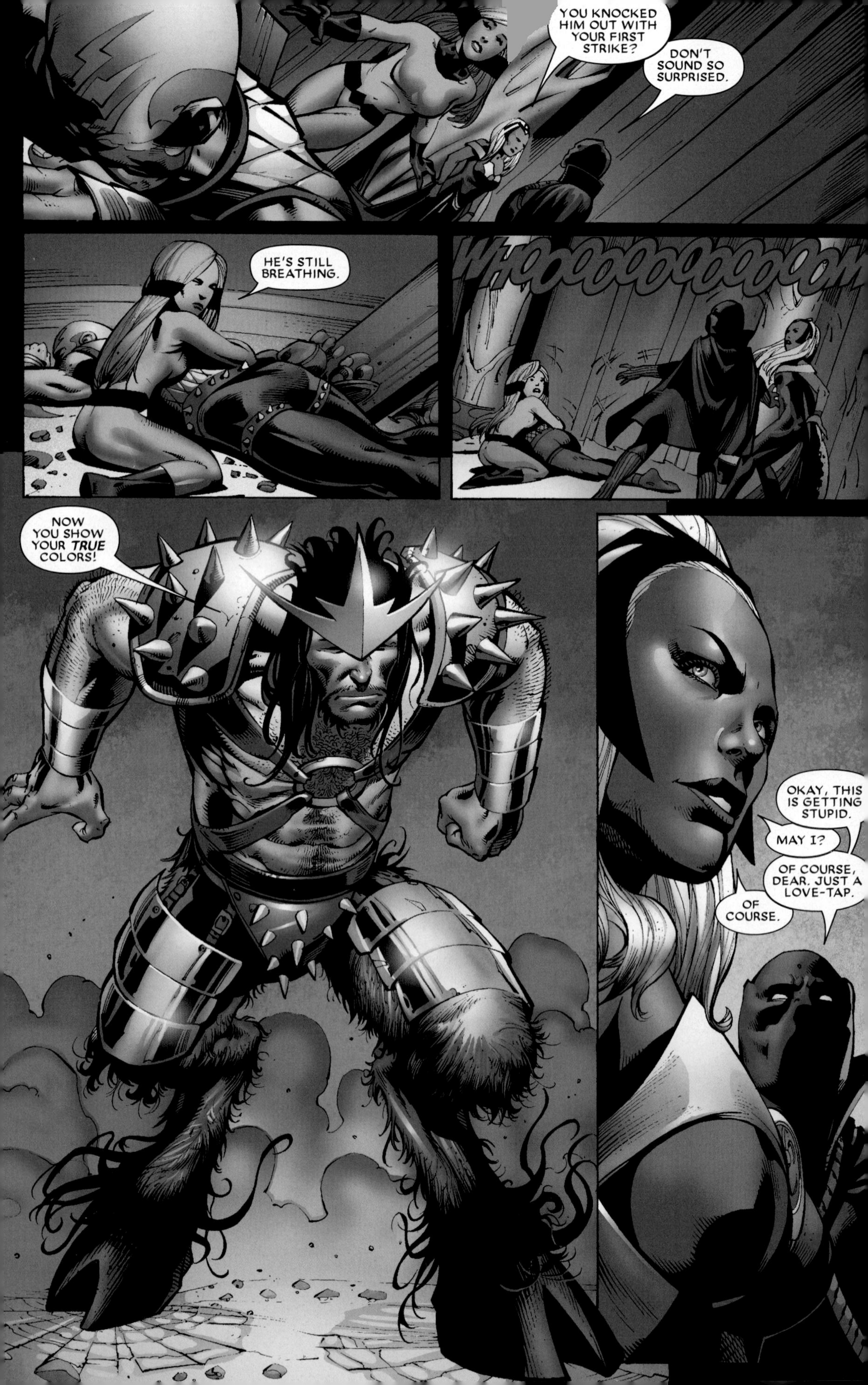
YOU KNOCKED HIM OUT WITH YOUR FIRST STRIKE?
DON'T SOUND SO SURPRISED.
HE'S STILL BREATHING.
WHOOOOOOOOOOOOOM
NOW YOU SHOW YOUR *TRUE* COLORS!
OKAY, THIS IS GETTING STUPID.
MAY I?
OF COURSE, DEAR. JUST A LOVE-TAP.
OF COURSE.

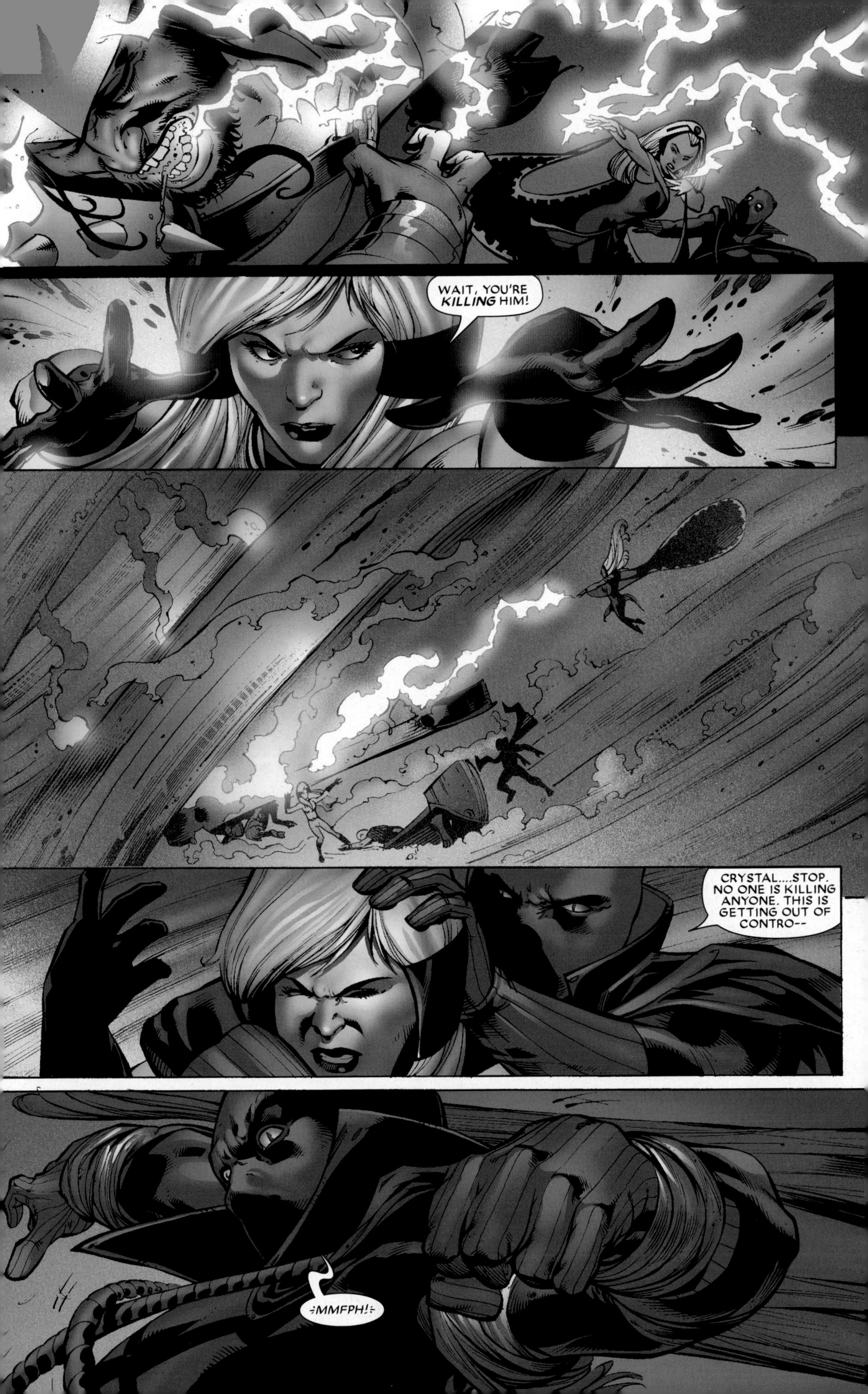
WAIT, YOU'RE *KILLING* HIM!
CRYSTAL....STOP. NO ONE IS KILLING ANYONE. THIS IS GETTING OUT OF CONTRO--
MMFPH!

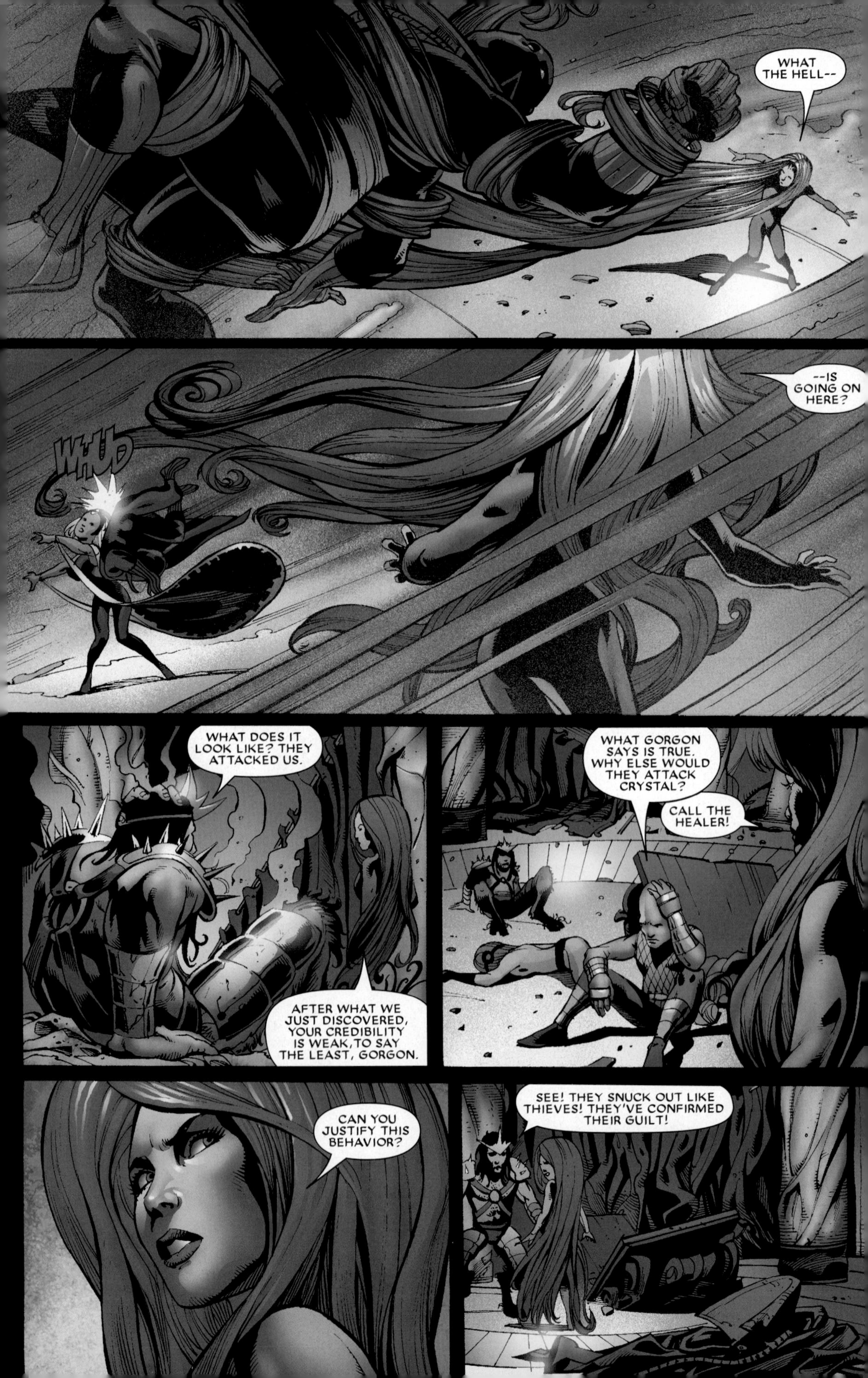
WHAT THE HELL--
--IS GOING ON HERE?
WHUD
WHAT DOES IT LOOK LIKE? THEY ATTACKED US.
AFTER WHAT WE JUST DISCOVERED, YOUR CREDIBILITY IS WEAK, TO SAY THE LEAST, GORGON.
WHAT GORGON SAYS IS TRUE. WHY ELSE WOULD THEY ATTACK CRYSTAL?
CALL THE HEALER!
CAN YOU JUSTIFY THIS BEHAVIOR?
SEE! THEY SNUCK OUT LIKE THIEVES! THEY'VE CONFIRMED THEIR GUILT!

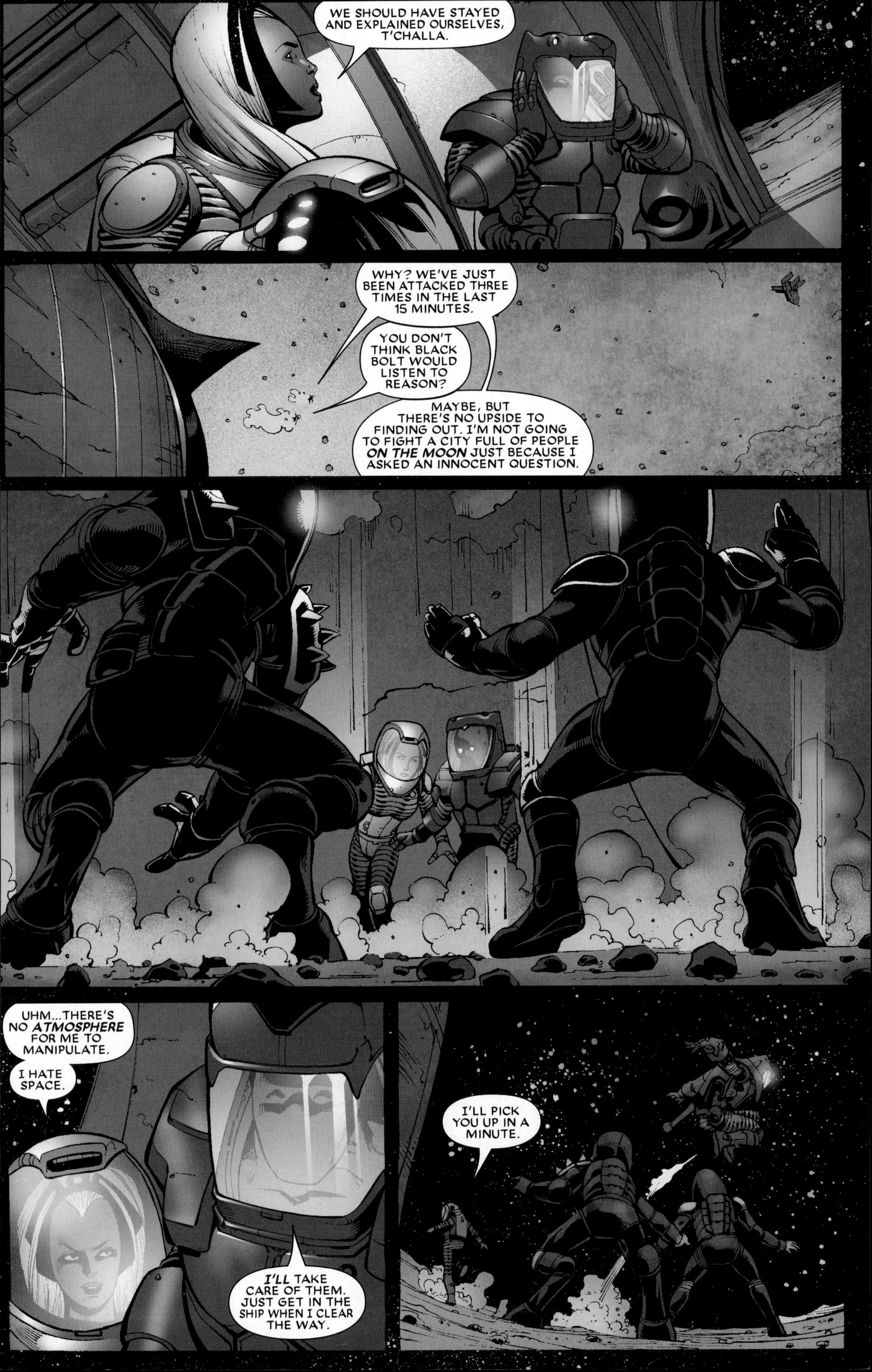
WE SHOULD HAVE STAYED AND EXPLAINED OURSELVES, T'CHALLA.
WHY? WE'VE JUST BEEN ATTACKED THREE TIMES IN THE LAST 15 MINUTES.
YOU DON'T THINK BLACK BOLT WOULD LISTEN TO REASON?
MAYBE, BUT THERE'S NO UPSIDE TO FINDING OUT. I'M NOT GOING TO FIGHT A CITY FULL OF PEOPLE ON THE MOON JUST BECAUSE I ASKED AN INNOCENT QUESTION.
UHM...THERE'S NO ATMOSPHERE FOR ME TO MANIPULATE.
I HATE SPACE.
I'LL TAKE CARE OF THEM. JUST GET IN THE SHIP WHEN I CLEAR THE WAY.
I'LL PICK YOU UP IN A MINUTE.

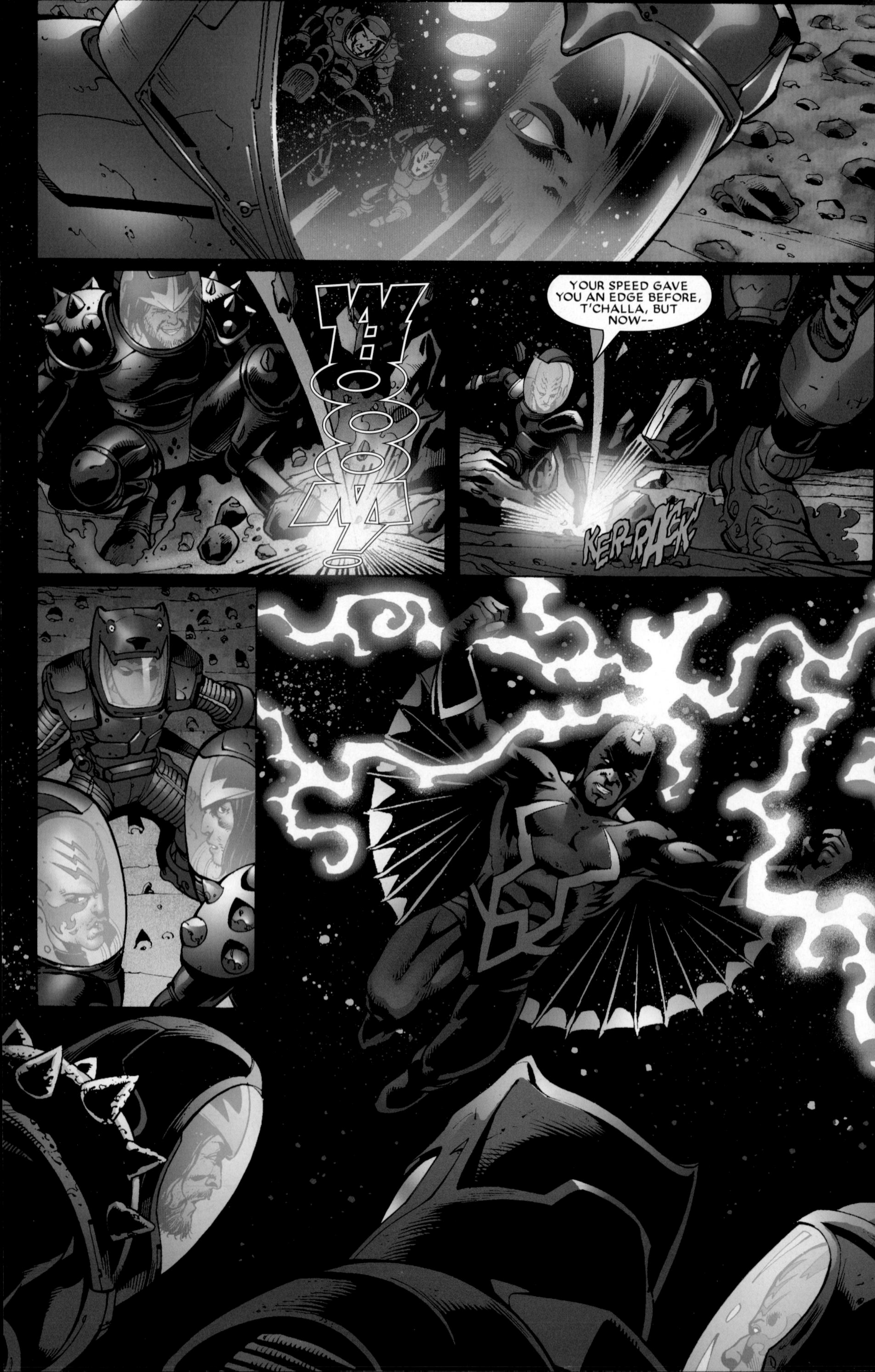
WOOOOM!
YOUR SPEED GAVE YOU AN EDGE BEFORE, T'CHALLA, BUT NOW--
KER-RACK!

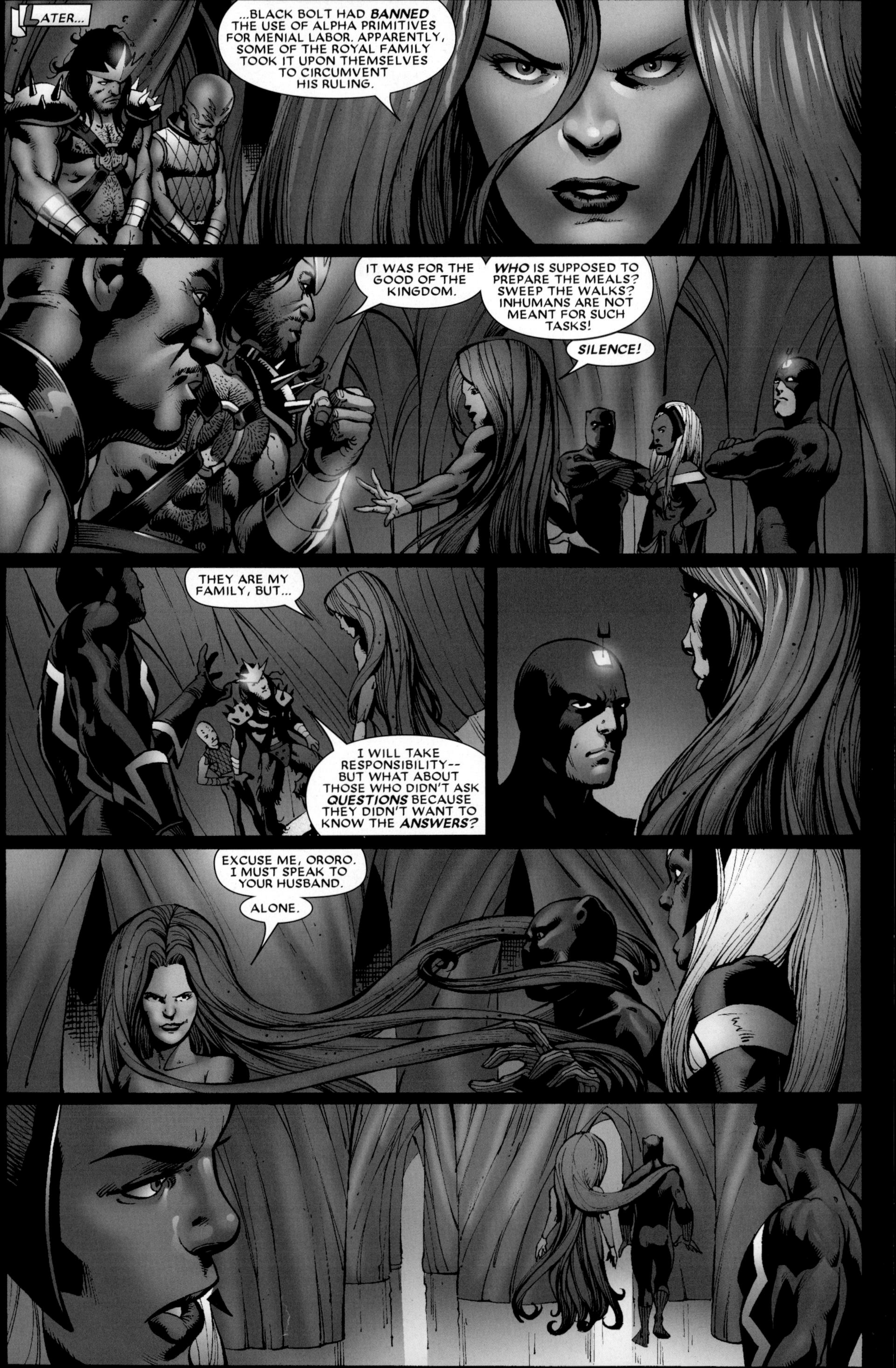
LATER...
...BLACK BOLT HAD BANNED THE USE OF ALPHA PRIMITIVES FOR MENIAL LABOR. APPARENTLY, SOME OF THE ROYAL FAMILY TOOK IT UPON THEMSELVES TO CIRCUMVENT HIS RULING.
IT WAS FOR THE GOOD OF THE KINGDOM.
WHO IS SUPPOSED TO PREPARE THE MEALS? SWEEP THE WALKS? INHUMANS ARE NOT MEANT FOR SUCH TASKS!
SILENCE!
THEY ARE MY FAMILY, BUT...
I WILL TAKE RESPONSIBILITY-- BUT WHAT ABOUT THOSE WHO DIDN'T ASK QUESTIONS BECAUSE THEY DIDN'T WANT TO KNOW THE ANSWERS?
EXCUSE ME, ORORO. I MUST SPEAK TO YOUR HUSBAND.
ALONE.

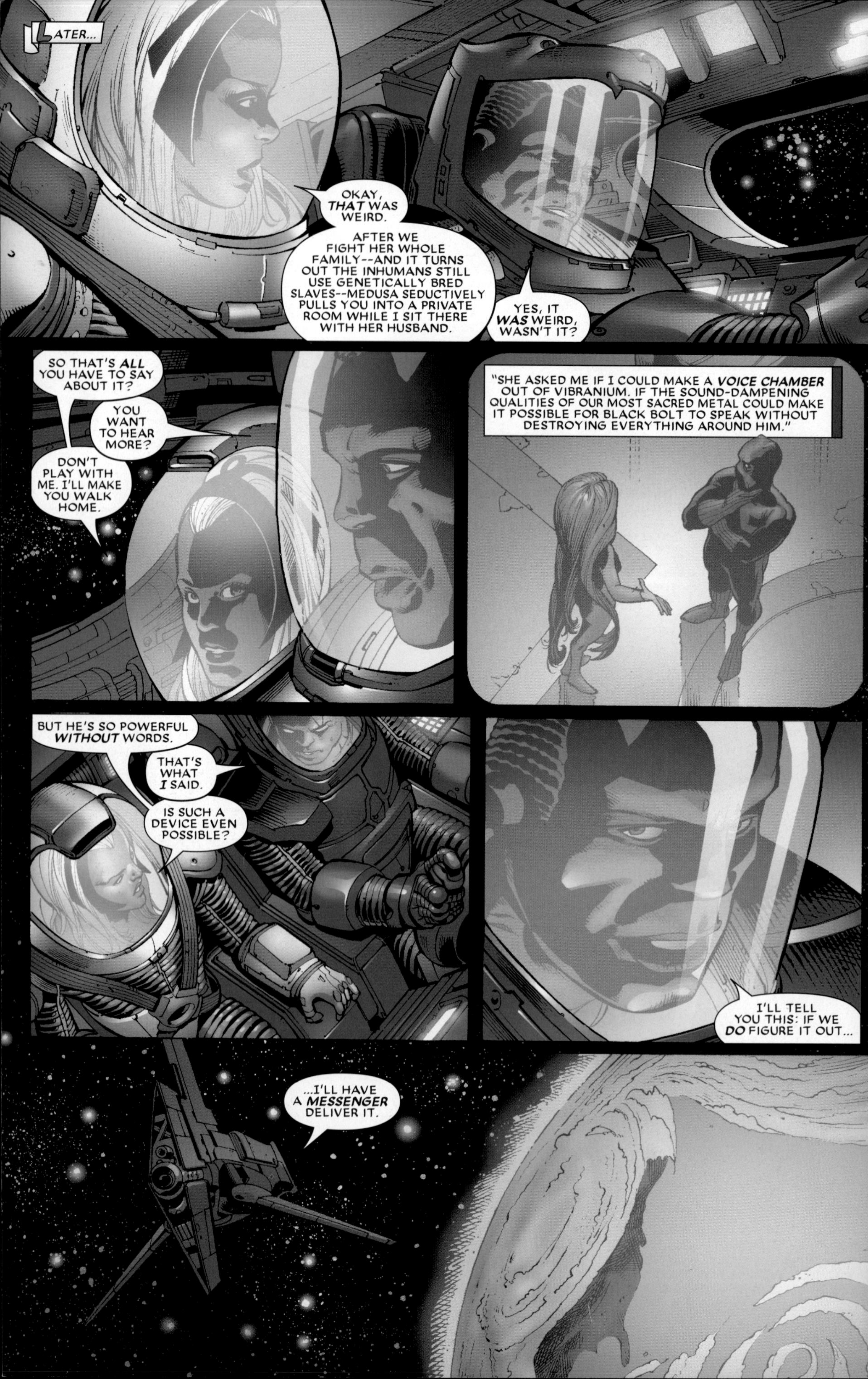
LATER...
OKAY, THAT WAS WEIRD.
AFTER WE FIGHT HER WHOLE FAMILY--AND IT TURNS OUT THE INHUMANS STILL USE GENETICALLY BRED SLAVES--MEDUSA SEDUCTIVELY PULLS YOU INTO A PRIVATE ROOM WHILE I SIT THERE WITH HER HUSBAND.
YES, IT WAS WEIRD, WASN'T IT?
SO THAT'S ALL YOU HAVE TO SAY ABOUT IT?
YOU WANT TO HEAR MORE?
DON'T PLAY WITH ME. I'LL MAKE YOU WALK HOME.
"SHE ASKED ME IF I COULD MAKE A VOICE CHAMBER OUT OF VIBRANIUM. IF THE SOUND-DAMPENING QUALITIES OF OUR MOST SACRED METAL COULD MAKE IT POSSIBLE FOR BLACK BOLT TO SPEAK WITHOUT DESTROYING EVERYTHING AROUND HIM."
BUT HE'S SO POWERFUL WITHOUT WORDS.
THAT'S WHAT I SAID.
IS SUCH A DEVICE EVEN POSSIBLE?
I'LL TELL YOU THIS: IF WE DO FIGURE IT OUT...
...I'LL HAVE A MESSENGER DELIVER IT.

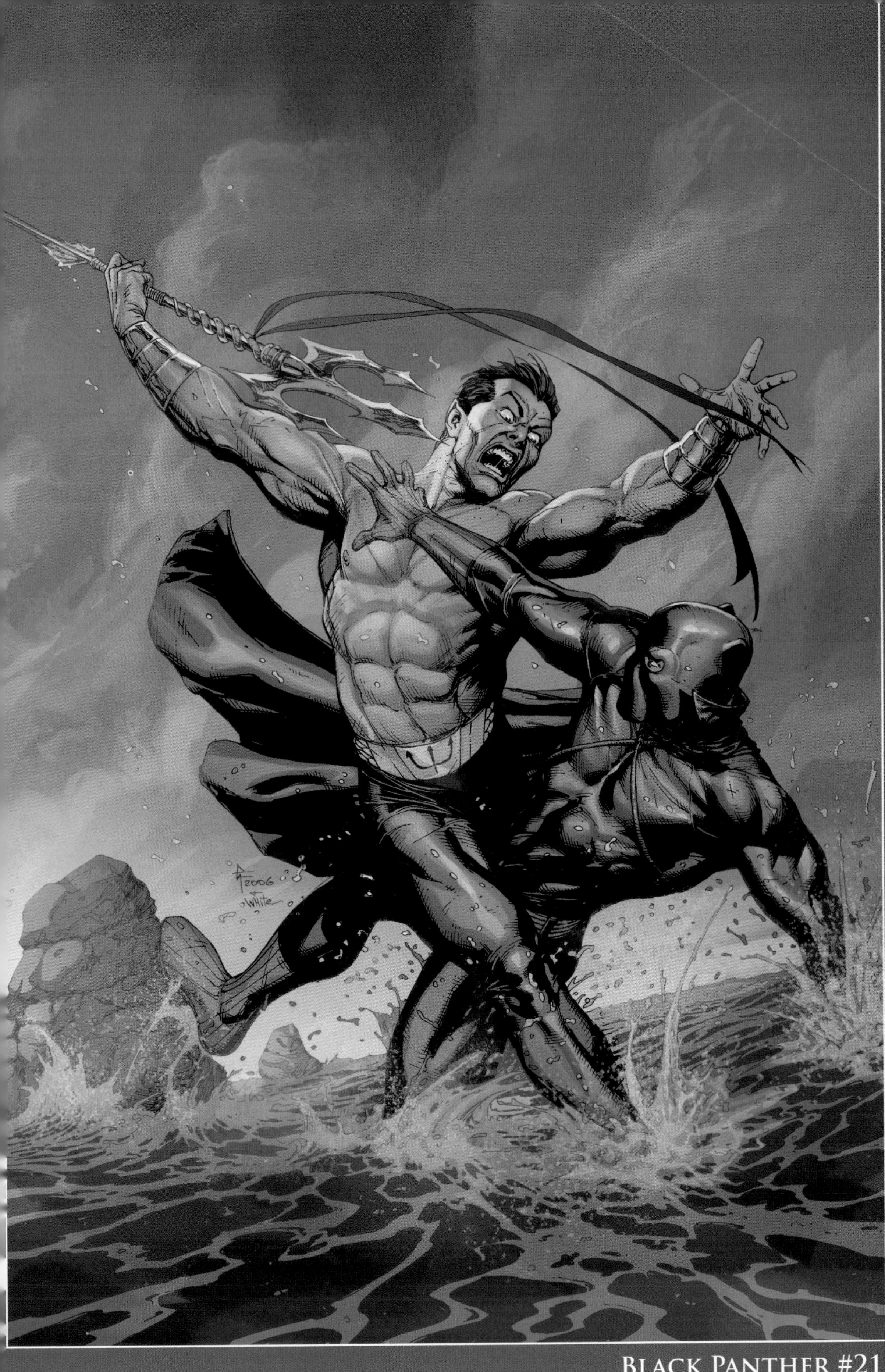
2006
White

Black Panther #21

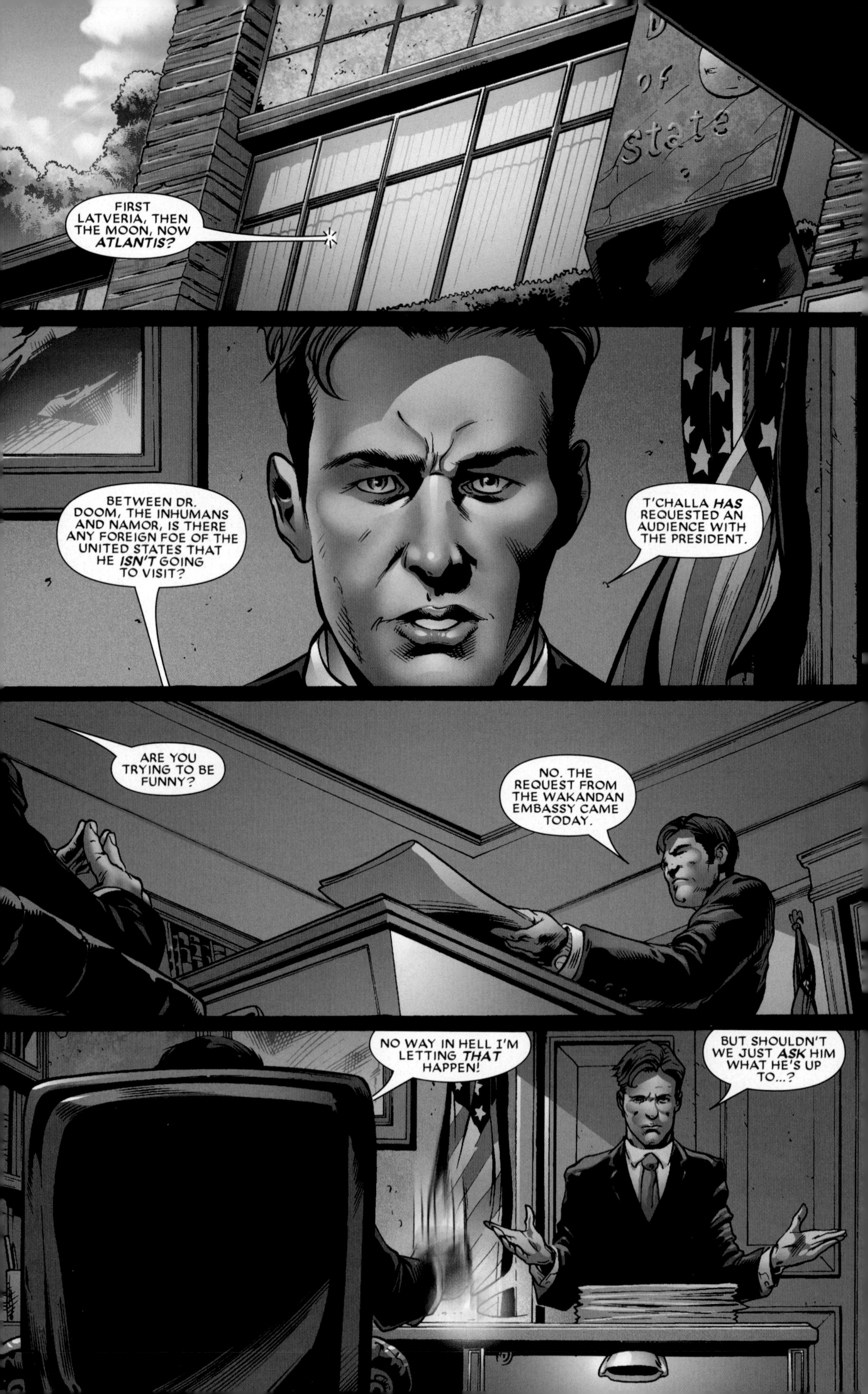
of
state
FIRST LATVERIA, THEN THE MOON, NOW *ATLANTIS?*
BETWEEN DR. DOOM, THE INHUMANS AND NAMOR, IS THERE ANY FOREIGN FOE OF THE UNITED STATES THAT HE *ISN'T* GOING TO VISIT?
T'CHALLA *HAS* REQUESTED AN AUDIENCE WITH THE PRESIDENT.
ARE YOU TRYING TO BE FUNNY?
NO. THE REQUEST FROM THE WAKANDAN EMBASSY CAME TODAY.
NO WAY IN HELL I'M LETTING *THAT* HAPPEN!
BUT SHOULDN'T WE JUST *ASK* HIM WHAT HE'S UP TO...?

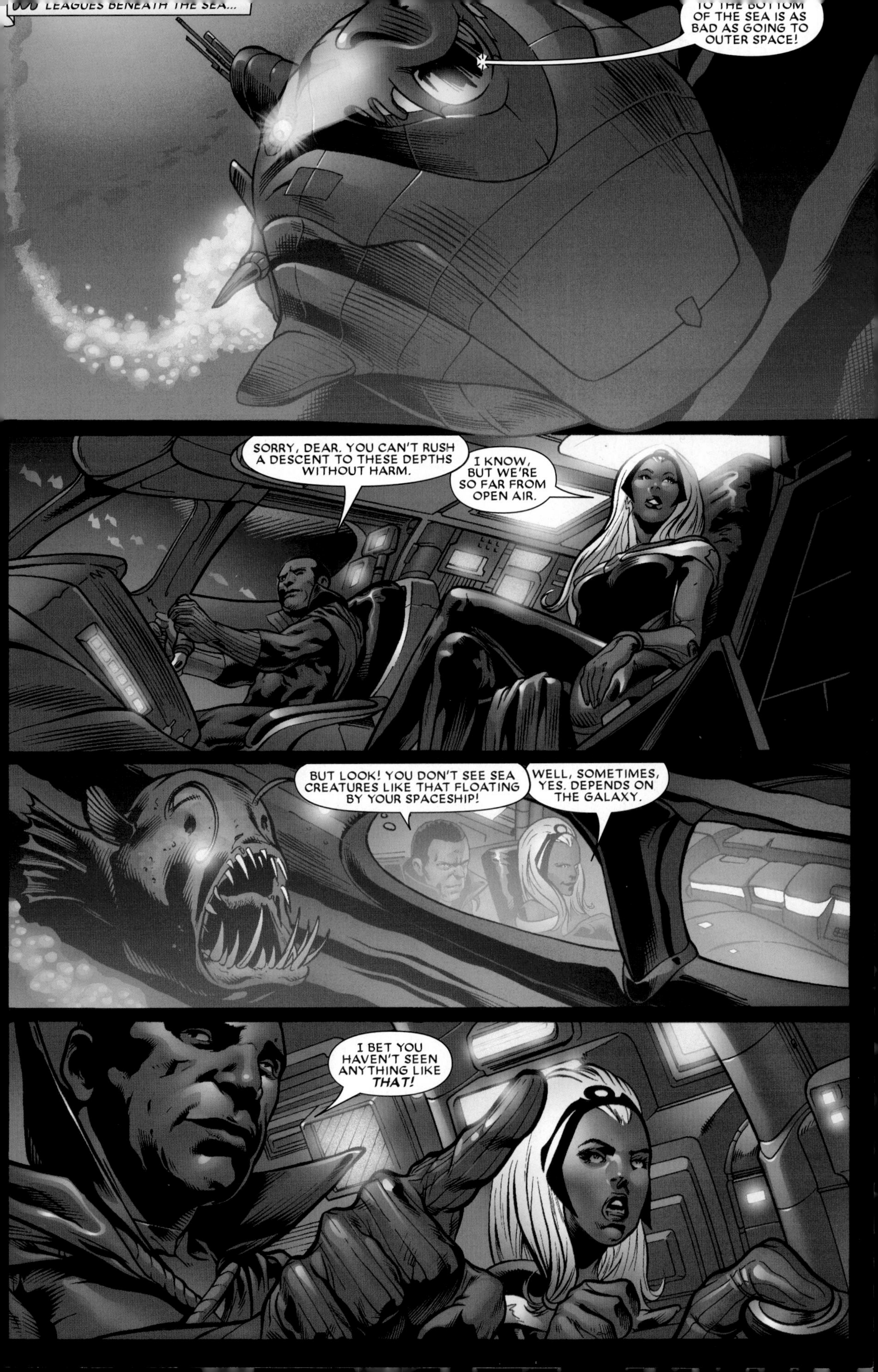

LEAGUES BENEATH THE SEA...
TO THE BOTTOM OF THE SEA IS AS BAD AS GOING TO OUTER SPACE!
SORRY, DEAR. YOU CAN'T RUSH A DESCENT TO THESE DEPTHS WITHOUT HARM.
I KNOW, BUT WE'RE SO FAR FROM OPEN AIR.
BUT LOOK! YOU DON'T SEE SEA CREATURES LIKE THAT FLOATING BY YOUR SPACESHIP!
WELL, SOMETIMES, YES. DEPENDS ON THE GALAXY.
I BET YOU HAVEN'T SEEN ANYTHING LIKE *THAT!*

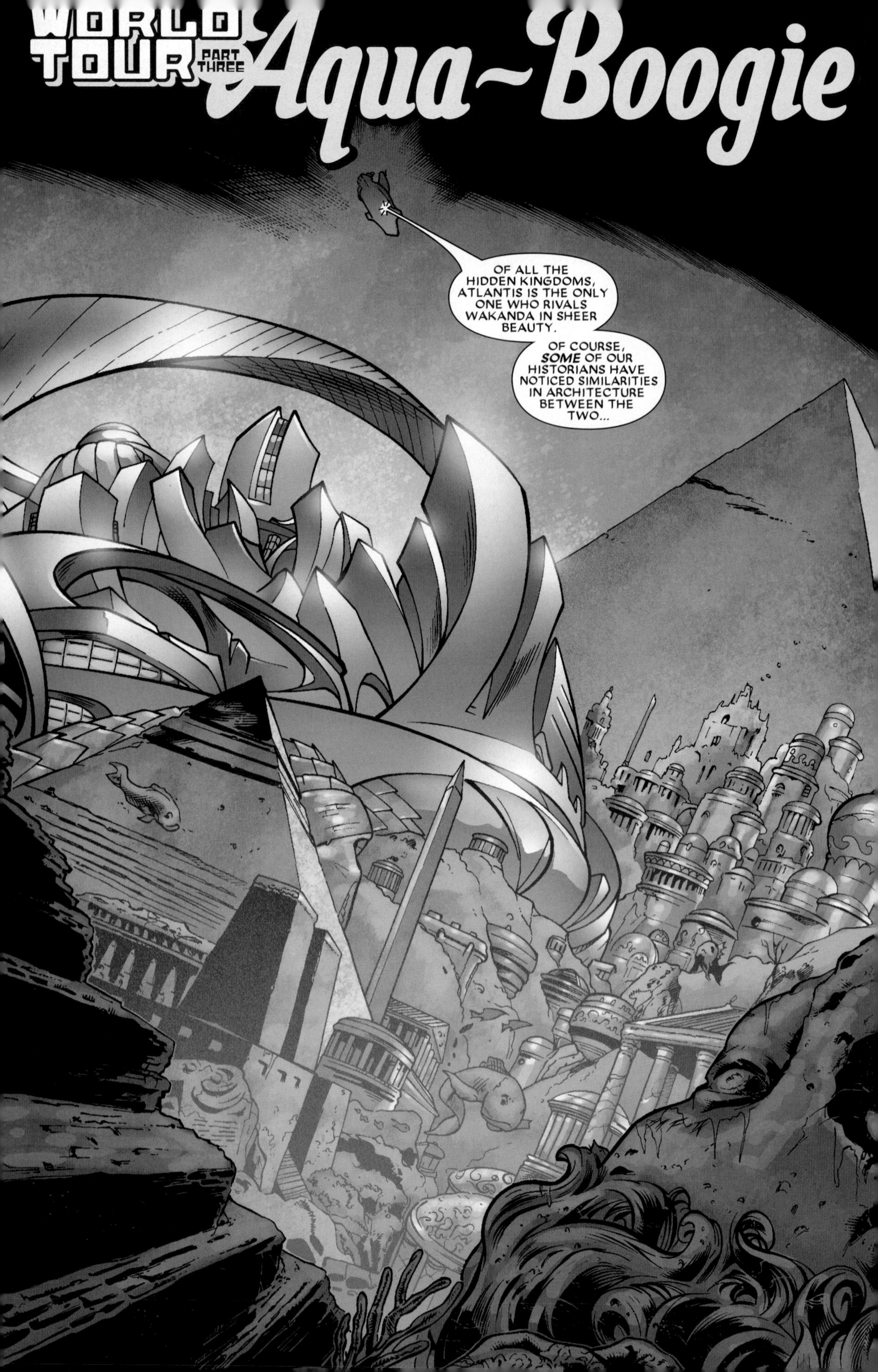
WORLD TOUR PART THREE
Aqua~Boogie
OF ALL THE HIDDEN KINGDOMS, ATLANTIS IS THE ONLY ONE WHO RIVALS WAKANDA IN SHEER BEAUTY.
OF COURSE, SOME OF OUR HISTORIANS HAVE NOTICED SIMILARITIES IN ARCHITECTURE BETWEEN THE TWO...

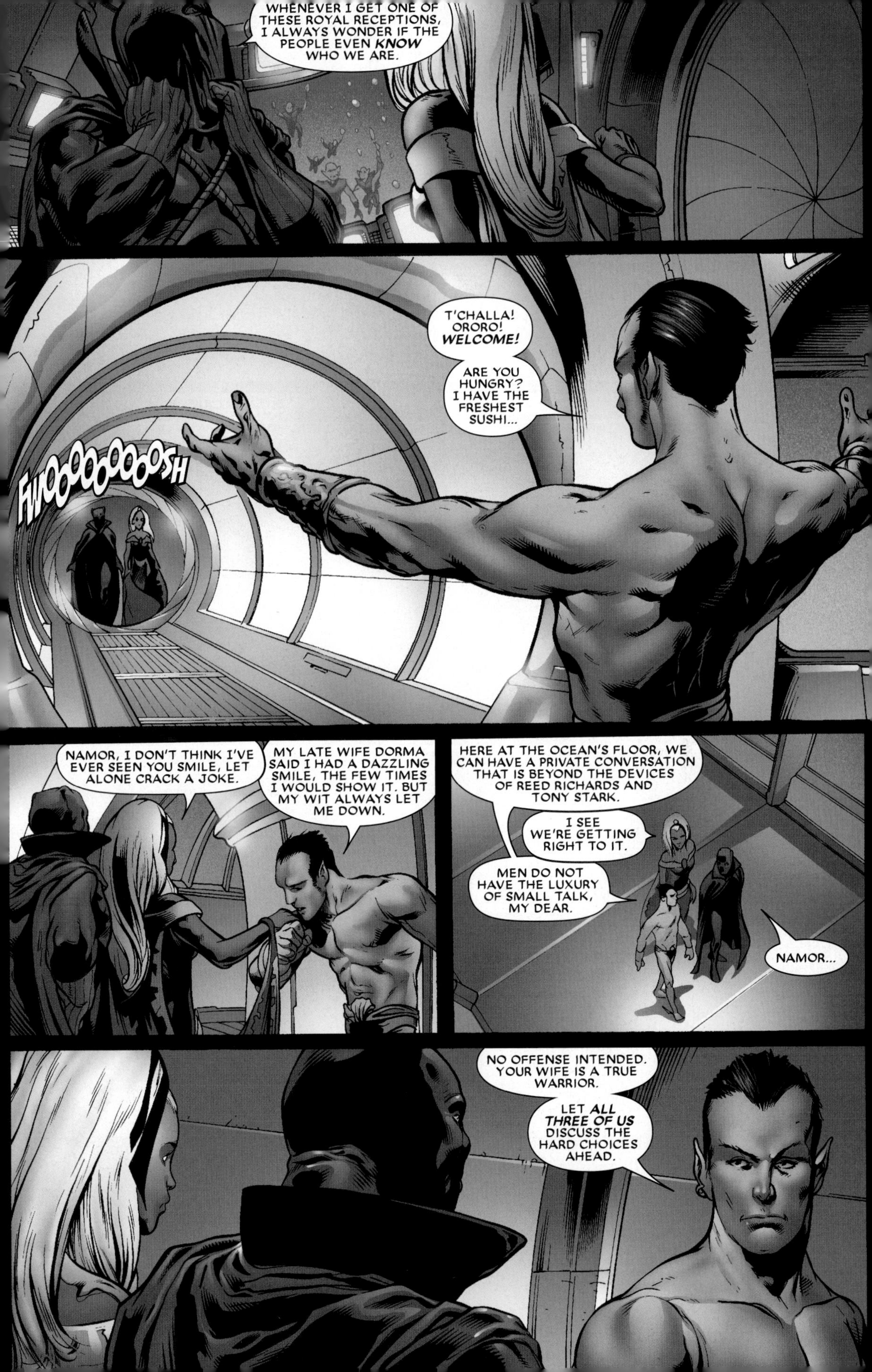
WHENEVER I GET ONE OF THESE ROYAL RECEPTIONS, I ALWAYS WONDER IF THE PEOPLE EVEN *KNOW* WHO WE ARE.
T'CHALLA! ORORO! ***WELCOME!***
ARE YOU HUNGRY? I HAVE THE FRESHEST SUSHI...
FWOOOOOOOOOSH
NAMOR, I DON'T THINK I'VE EVER SEEN YOU SMILE, LET ALONE CRACK A JOKE.
MY LATE WIFE DORMA SAID I HAD A DAZZLING SMILE, THE FEW TIMES I WOULD SHOW IT. BUT MY WIT ALWAYS LET ME DOWN.
HERE AT THE OCEAN'S FLOOR, WE CAN HAVE A PRIVATE CONVERSATION THAT IS BEYOND THE DEVICES OF REED RICHARDS AND TONY STARK.
I SEE WE'RE GETTING RIGHT TO IT.
MEN DO NOT HAVE THE LUXURY OF SMALL TALK, MY DEAR.
NAMOR...
NO OFFENSE INTENDED. YOUR WIFE IS A TRUE WARRIOR.
LET ***ALL THREE OF US*** DISCUSS THE HARD CHOICES AHEAD.

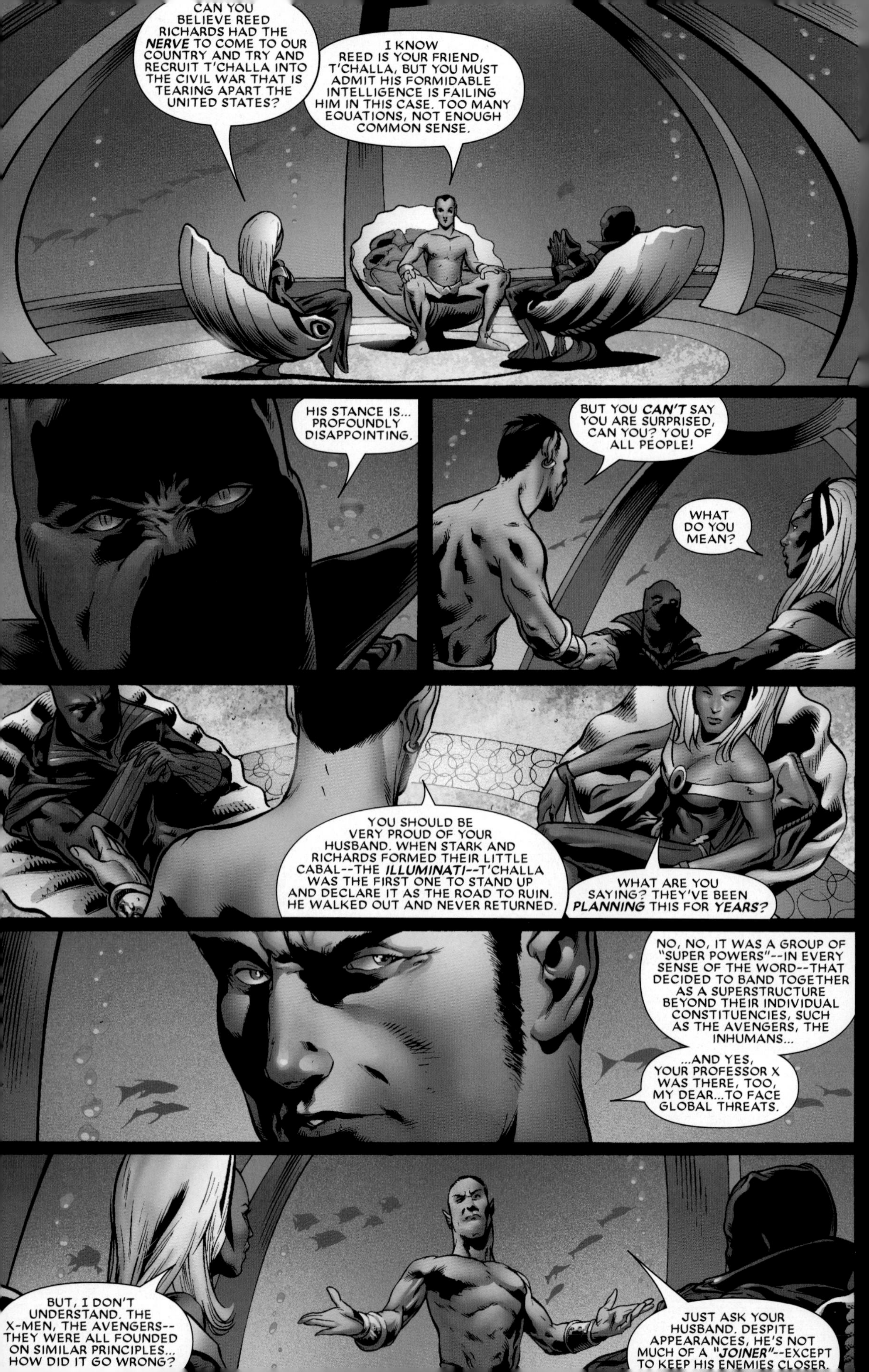
CAN YOU BELIEVE REED RICHARDS HAD THE NERVE TO COME TO OUR COUNTRY AND TRY AND RECRUIT T'CHALLA INTO THE CIVIL WAR THAT IS TEARING APART THE UNITED STATES?
I KNOW REED IS YOUR FRIEND, T'CHALLA, BUT YOU MUST ADMIT HIS FORMIDABLE INTELLIGENCE IS FAILING HIM IN THIS CASE. TOO MANY EQUATIONS, NOT ENOUGH COMMON SENSE.
HIS STANCE IS... PROFOUNDLY DISAPPOINTING.
BUT YOU CAN'T SAY YOU ARE SURPRISED, CAN YOU? YOU OF ALL PEOPLE!
WHAT DO YOU MEAN?
YOU SHOULD BE VERY PROUD OF YOUR HUSBAND. WHEN STARK AND RICHARDS FORMED THEIR LITTLE CABAL--THE ILLUMINATI--T'CHALLA WAS THE FIRST ONE TO STAND UP AND DECLARE IT AS THE ROAD TO RUIN. HE WALKED OUT AND NEVER RETURNED.
WHAT ARE YOU SAYING? THEY'VE BEEN PLANNING THIS FOR YEARS?
NO, NO, IT WAS A GROUP OF "SUPER POWERS"--IN EVERY SENSE OF THE WORD--THAT DECIDED TO BAND TOGETHER AS A SUPERSTRUCTURE BEYOND THEIR INDIVIDUAL CONSTITUENCIES, SUCH AS THE AVENGERS, THE INHUMANS...
...AND YES, YOUR PROFESSOR X WAS THERE, TOO, MY DEAR...TO FACE GLOBAL THREATS.
BUT, I DON'T UNDERSTAND. THE X-MEN, THE AVENGERS--THEY WERE ALL FOUNDED ON SIMILAR PRINCIPLES... HOW DID IT GO WRONG?
JUST ASK YOUR HUSBAND. DESPITE APPEARANCES, HE'S NOT MUCH OF A "JOINER"--EXCEPT TO KEEP HIS ENEMIES CLOSER.

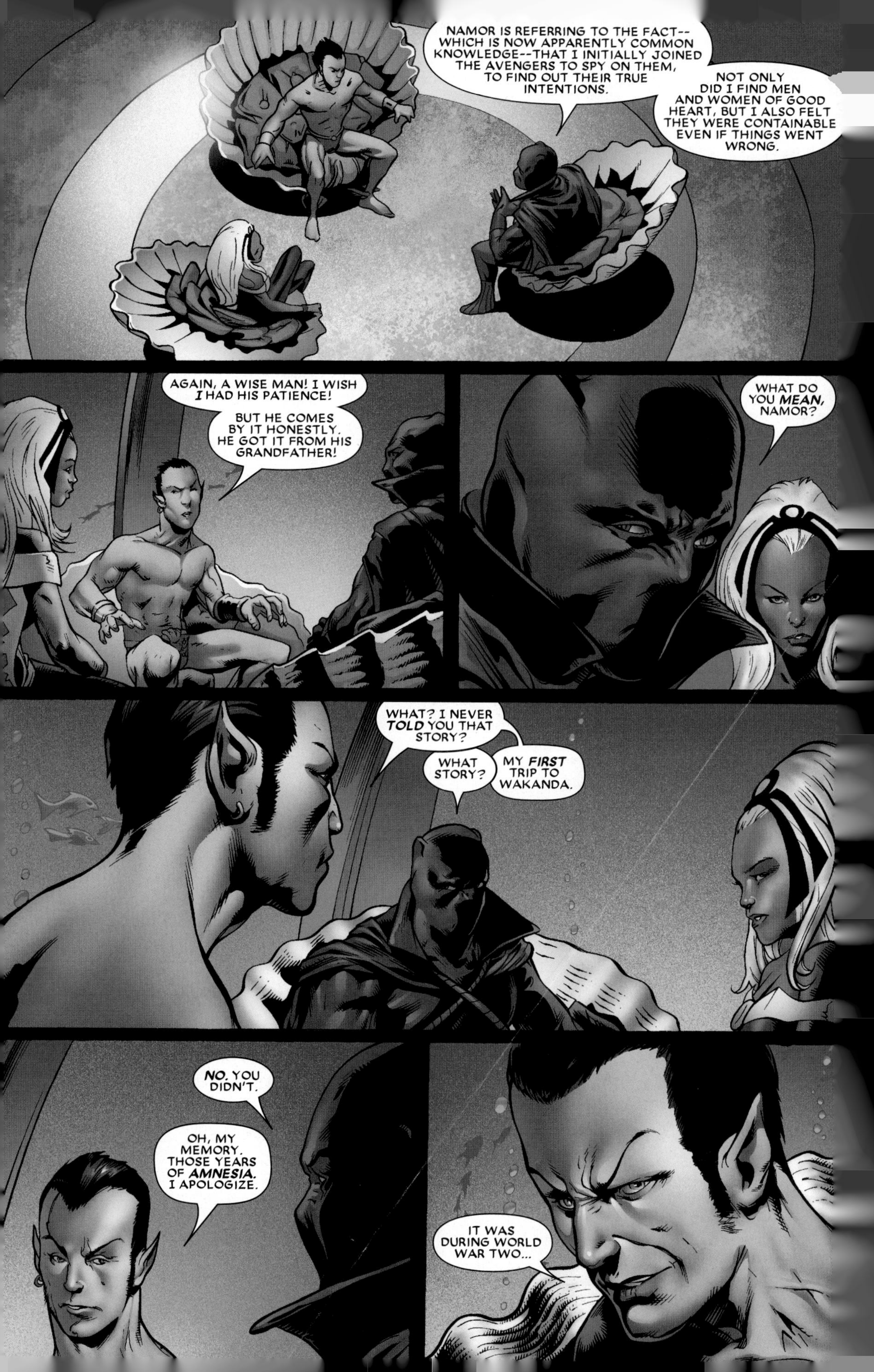
NAMOR IS REFERRING TO THE FACT--WHICH IS NOW APPARENTLY COMMON KNOWLEDGE--THAT I INITIALLY JOINED THE AVENGERS TO SPY ON THEM, TO FIND OUT THEIR TRUE INTENTIONS.
NOT ONLY DID I FIND MEN AND WOMEN OF GOOD HEART, BUT I ALSO FELT THEY WERE CONTAINABLE EVEN IF THINGS WENT WRONG.
AGAIN, A WISE MAN! I WISH *I* HAD HIS PATIENCE!
BUT HE COMES BY IT HONESTLY. HE GOT IT FROM HIS GRANDFATHER!
WHAT DO YOU *MEAN,* NAMOR?
WHAT? I NEVER *TOLD* YOU THAT STORY?
WHAT STORY?
MY *FIRST* TRIP TO WAKANDA.
NO. YOU DIDN'T.
OH, MY MEMORY. THOSE YEARS OF *AMNESIA.* I APOLOGIZE.
IT WAS DURING WORLD WAR TWO...

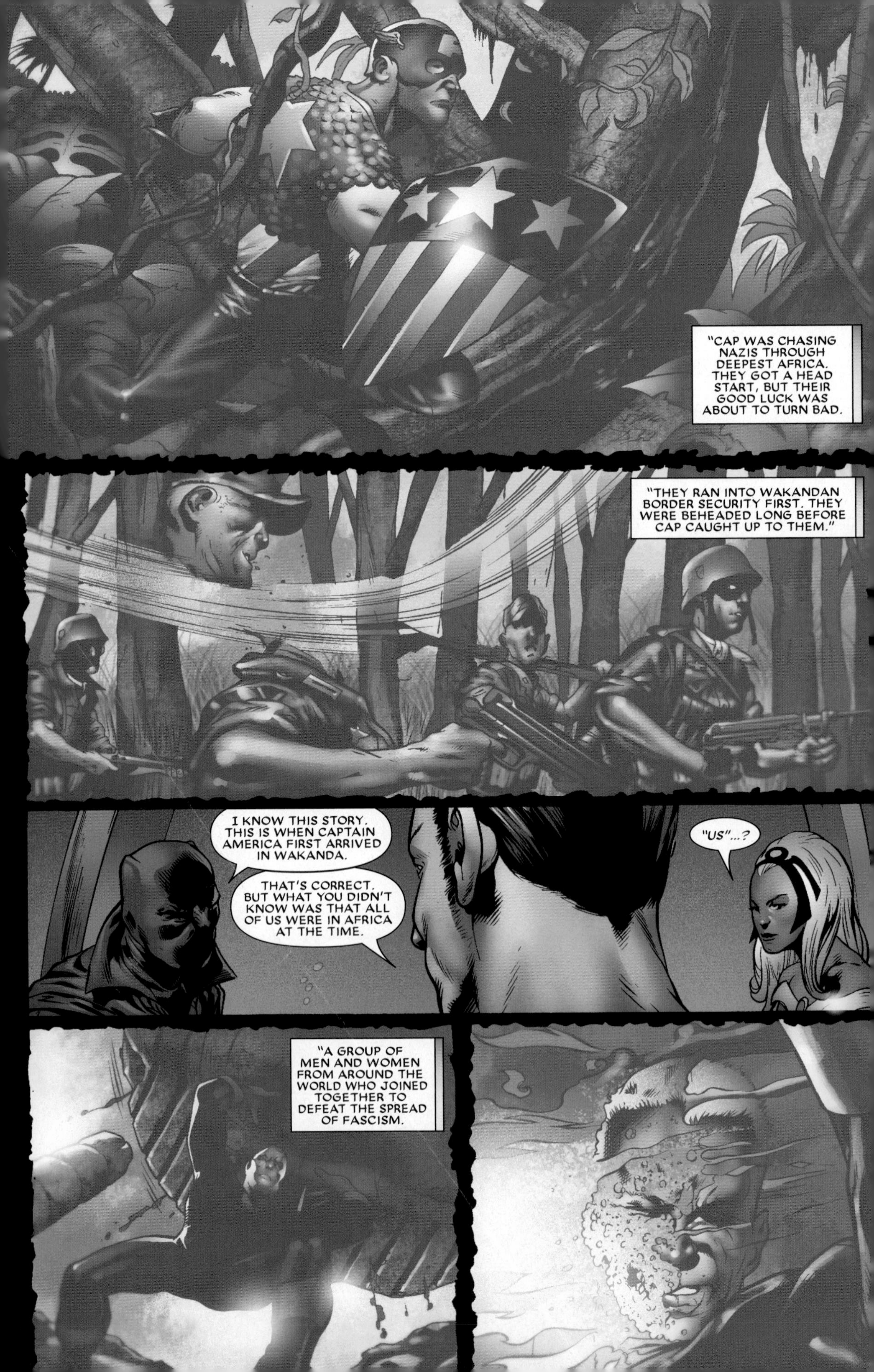
"CAP WAS CHASING NAZIS THROUGH DEEPEST AFRICA. THEY GOT A HEAD START, BUT THEIR GOOD LUCK WAS ABOUT TO TURN BAD.
"THEY RAN INTO WAKANDAN BORDER SECURITY FIRST. THEY WERE BEHEADED LONG BEFORE CAP CAUGHT UP TO THEM."
I KNOW THIS STORY. THIS IS WHEN CAPTAIN AMERICA FIRST ARRIVED IN WAKANDA.
THAT'S CORRECT. BUT WHAT YOU DIDN'T KNOW WAS THAT ALL OF US WERE IN AFRICA AT THE TIME.
"US"...?
"A GROUP OF MEN AND WOMEN FROM AROUND THE WORLD WHO JOINED TOGETHER TO DEFEAT THE SPREAD OF FASCISM.

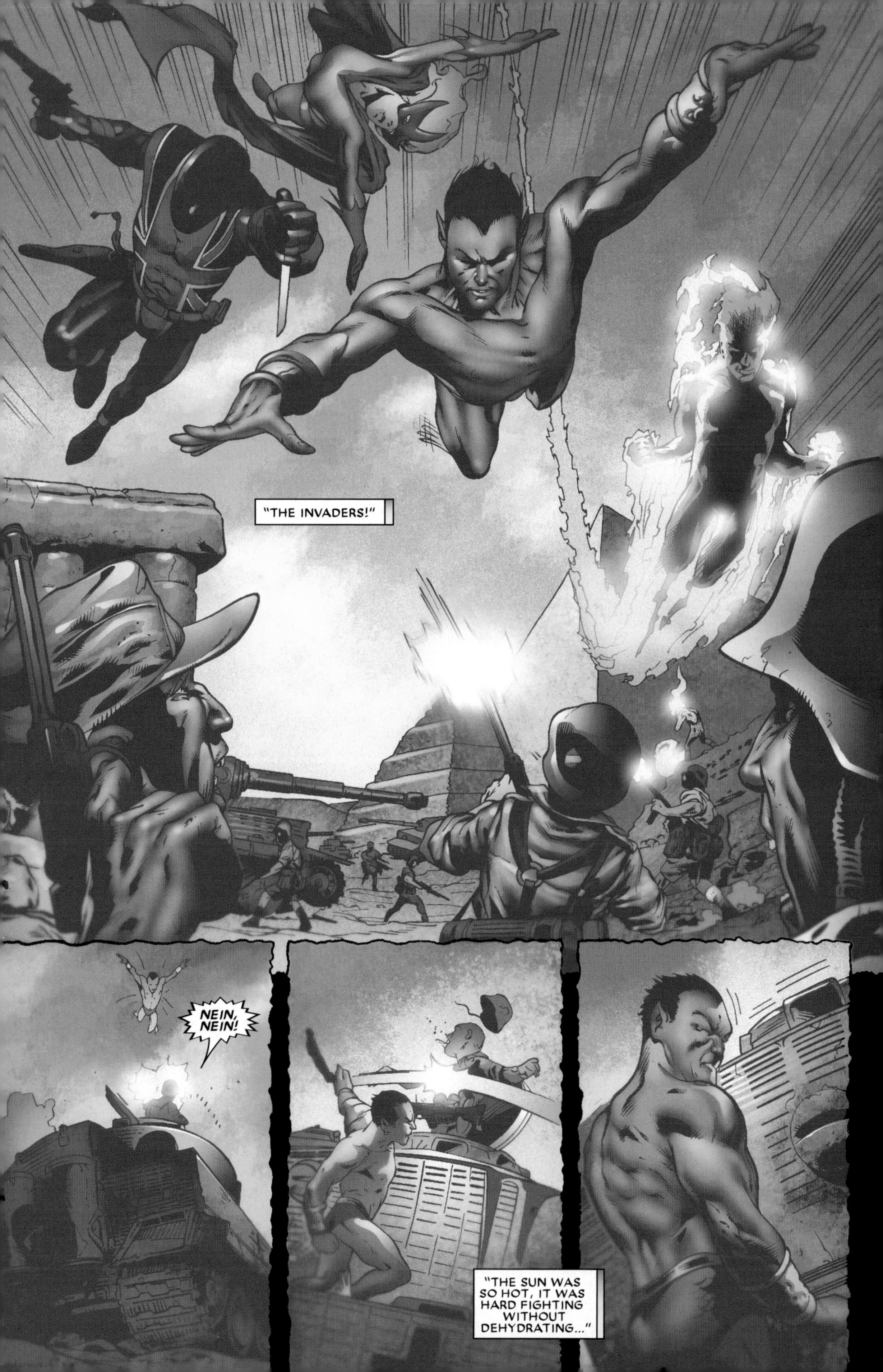
"THE INVADERS!"
NEIN, NEIN!
"THE SUN WAS SO HOT, IT WAS HARD FIGHTING WITHOUT DEHYDRATING..."

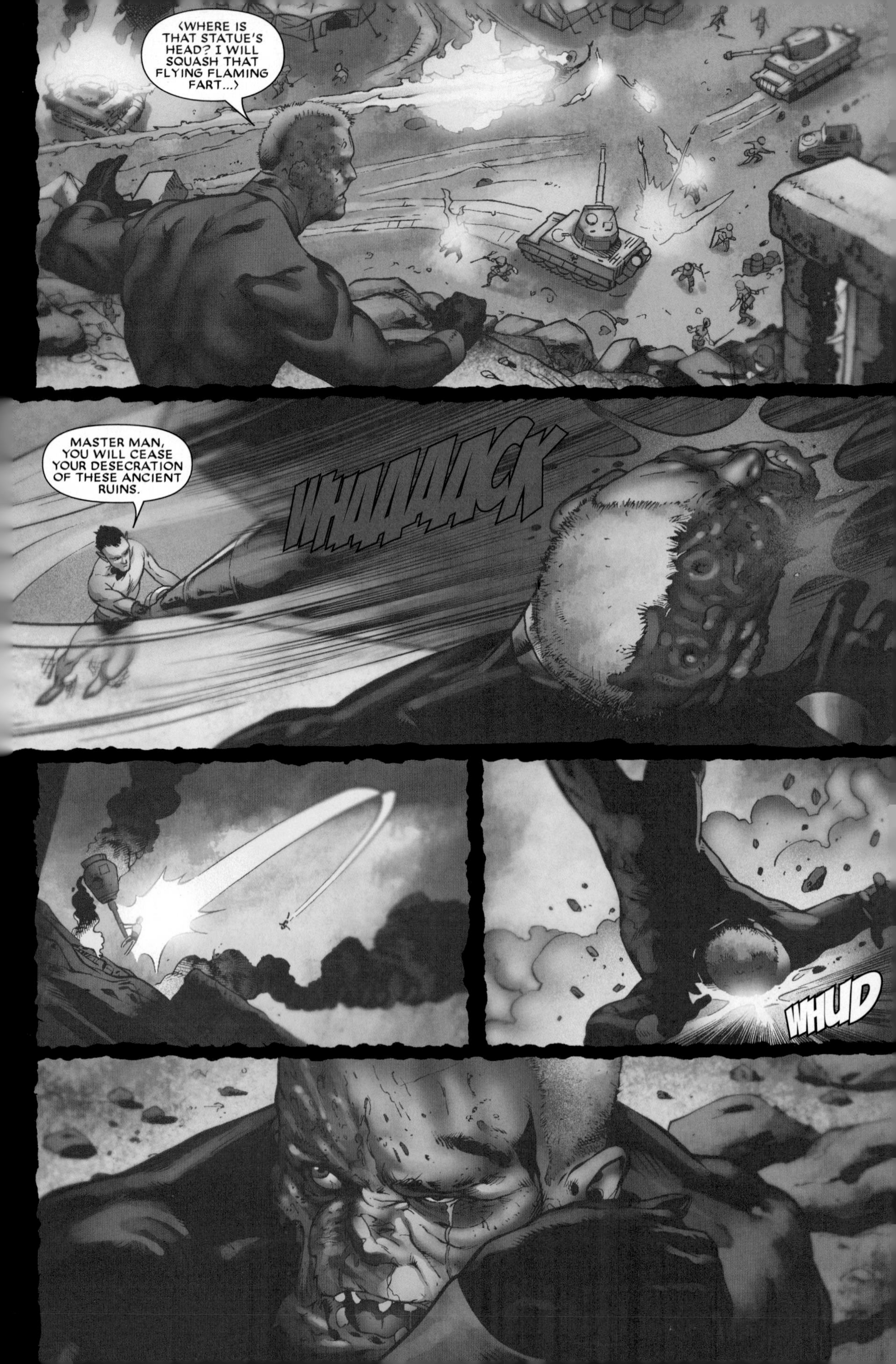

‹WHERE IS THAT STATUE'S HEAD? I WILL SQUASH THAT FLYING FLAMING FART...›
MASTER MAN, YOU WILL CEASE YOUR DESECRATION OF THESE ANCIENT RUINS.
WHAAAACK
WHUD

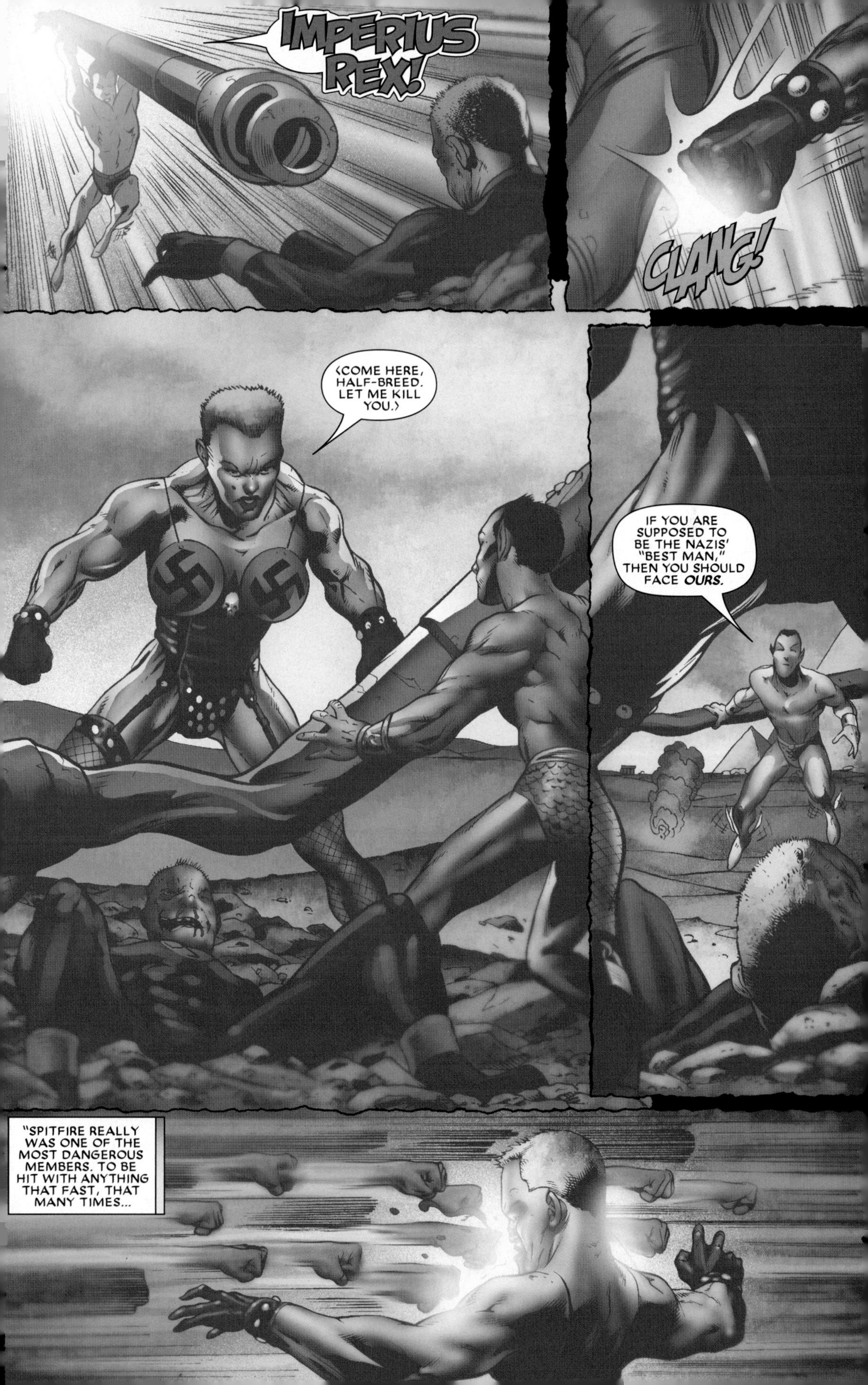
IMPERIUS REX!
CLANG!
‹COME HERE, HALF-BREED. LET ME KILL YOU.›
IF YOU ARE SUPPOSED TO BE THE NAZIS' "BEST MAN," THEN YOU SHOULD FACE *OURS*.
"SPITFIRE REALLY WAS ONE OF THE MOST DANGEROUS MEMBERS. TO BE HIT WITH ANYTHING THAT FAST, THAT MANY TIMES...

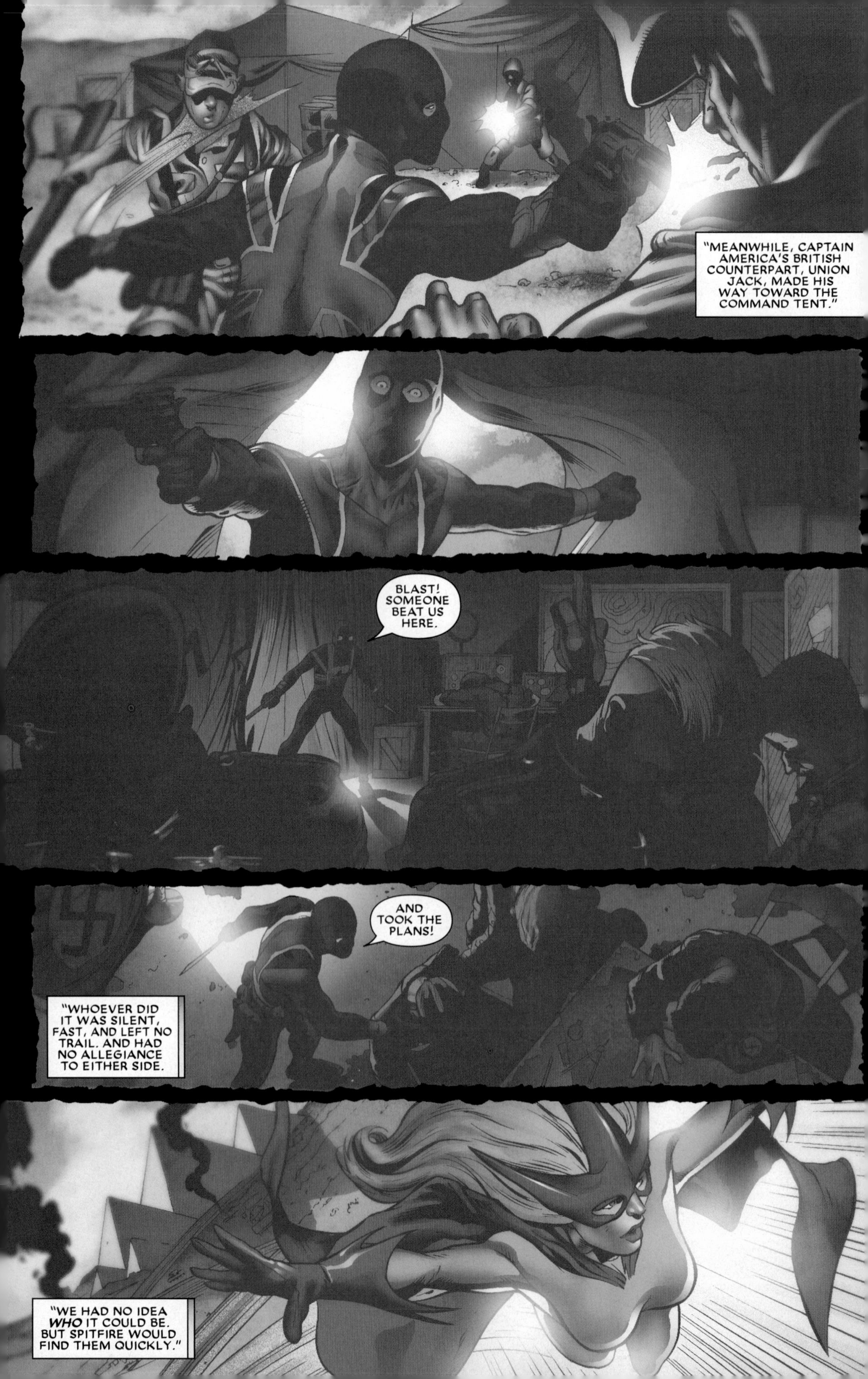
"MEANWHILE, CAPTAIN AMERICA'S BRITISH COUNTERPART, UNION JACK, MADE HIS WAY TOWARD THE COMMAND TENT."
BLAST! SOMEONE BEAT US HERE.
AND TOOK THE PLANS!
"WHOEVER DID IT WAS SILENT, FAST, AND LEFT NO TRAIL. AND HAD NO ALLEGIANCE TO EITHER SIDE.
"WE HAD NO IDEA *WHO* IT COULD BE. BUT SPITFIRE WOULD FIND THEM QUICKLY."

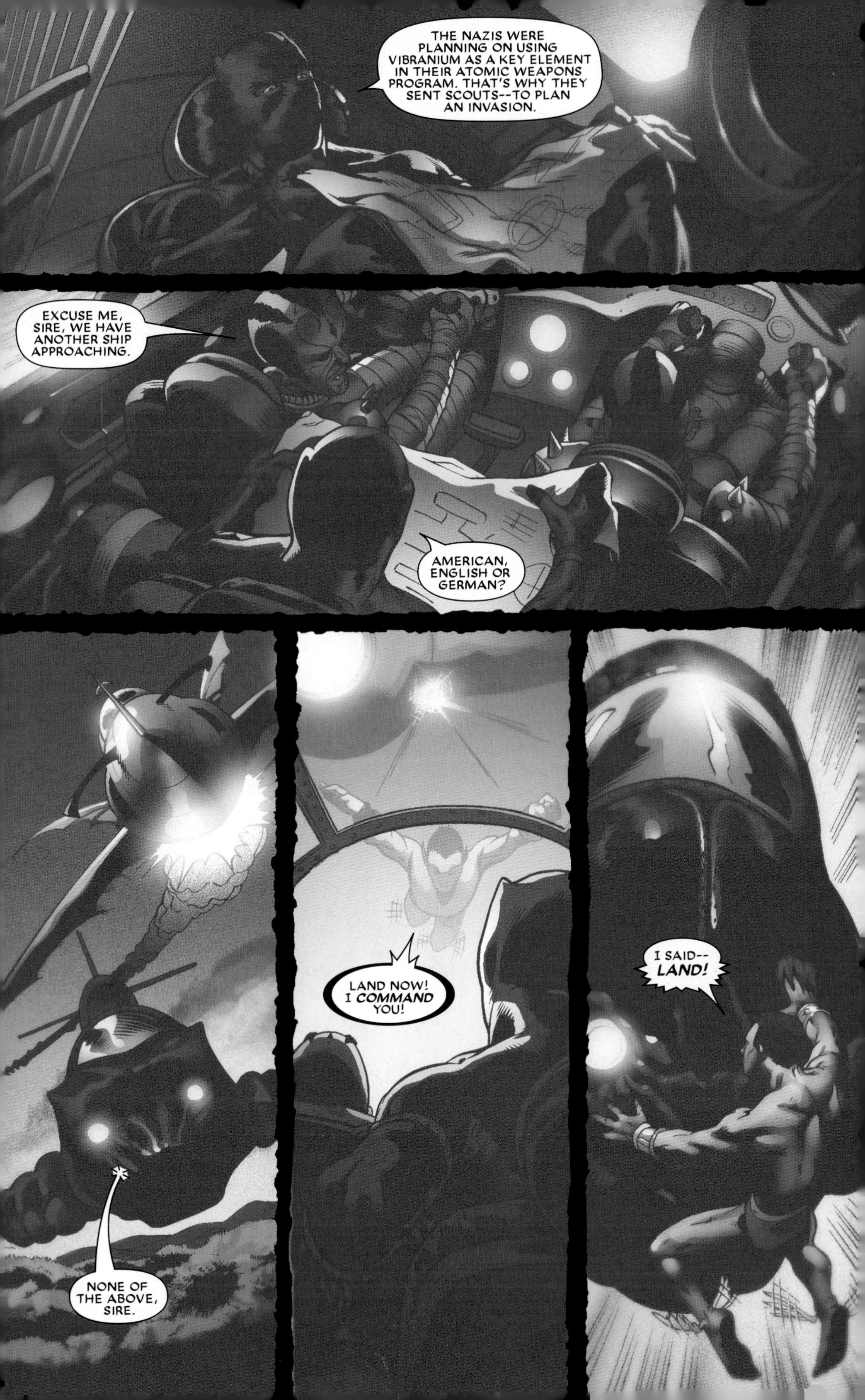
THE NAZIS WERE PLANNING ON USING VIBRANIUM AS A KEY ELEMENT IN THEIR ATOMIC WEAPONS PROGRAM. THAT'S WHY THEY SENT SCOUTS--TO PLAN AN INVASION.
EXCUSE ME, SIRE, WE HAVE ANOTHER SHIP APPROACHING.
AMERICAN, ENGLISH OR GERMAN?
NONE OF THE ABOVE, SIRE.
LAND NOW! I **COMMAND** YOU!
I SAID-- **LAND!**

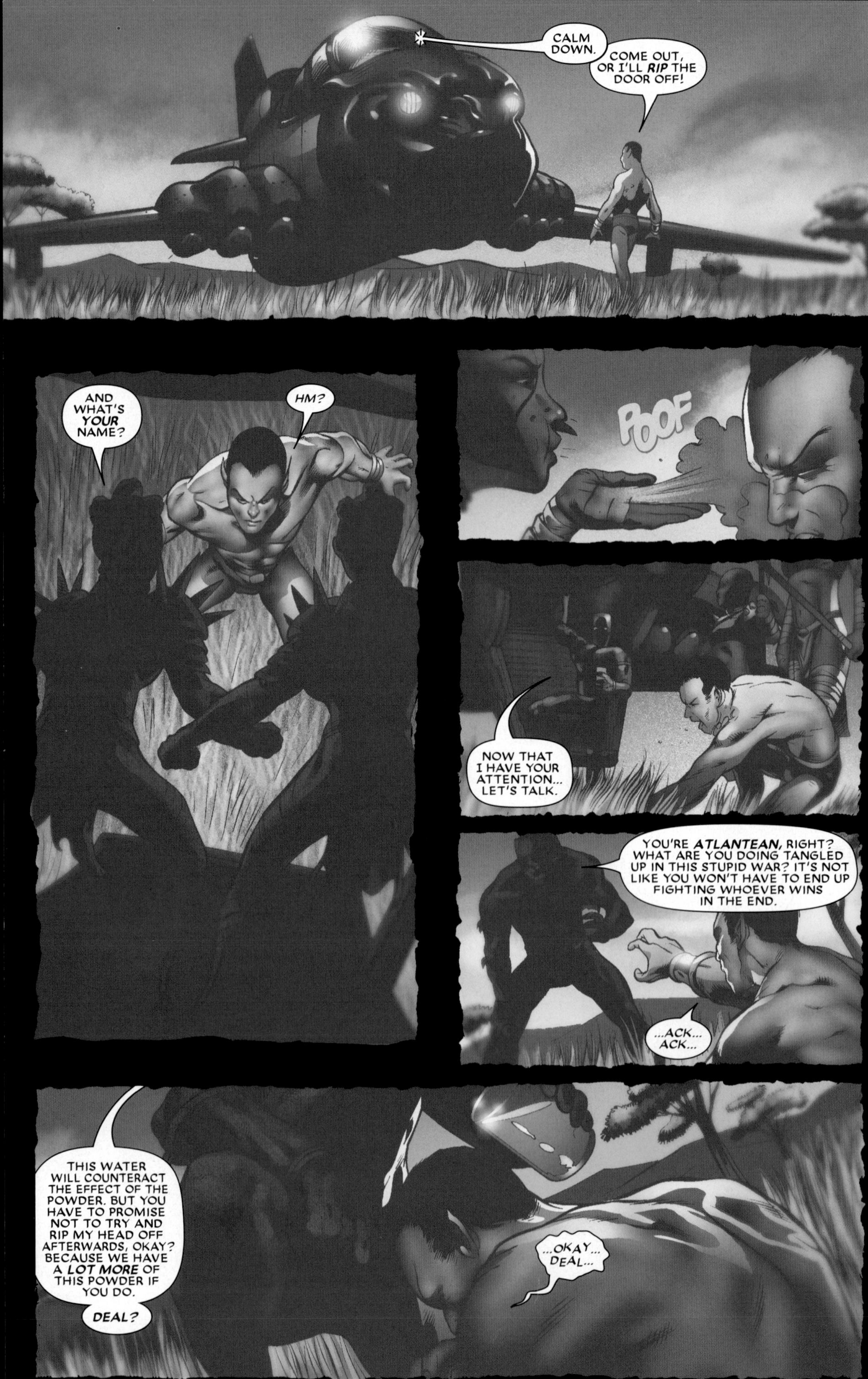

CALM DOWN.
COME OUT, OR I'LL RIP THE DOOR OFF!
AND WHAT'S YOUR NAME?
HM?
POOF
NOW THAT I HAVE YOUR ATTENTION... LET'S TALK.
YOU'RE ATLANTEAN, RIGHT? WHAT ARE YOU DOING TANGLED UP IN THIS STUPID WAR? IT'S NOT LIKE YOU WON'T HAVE TO END UP FIGHTING WHOEVER WINS IN THE END.
...ACK... ACK...
THIS WATER WILL COUNTERACT THE EFFECT OF THE POWDER. BUT YOU HAVE TO PROMISE NOT TO TRY AND RIP MY HEAD OFF AFTERWARDS, OKAY? BECAUSE WE HAVE A LOT MORE OF THIS POWDER IF YOU DO.
DEAL?
...OKAY... DEAL...

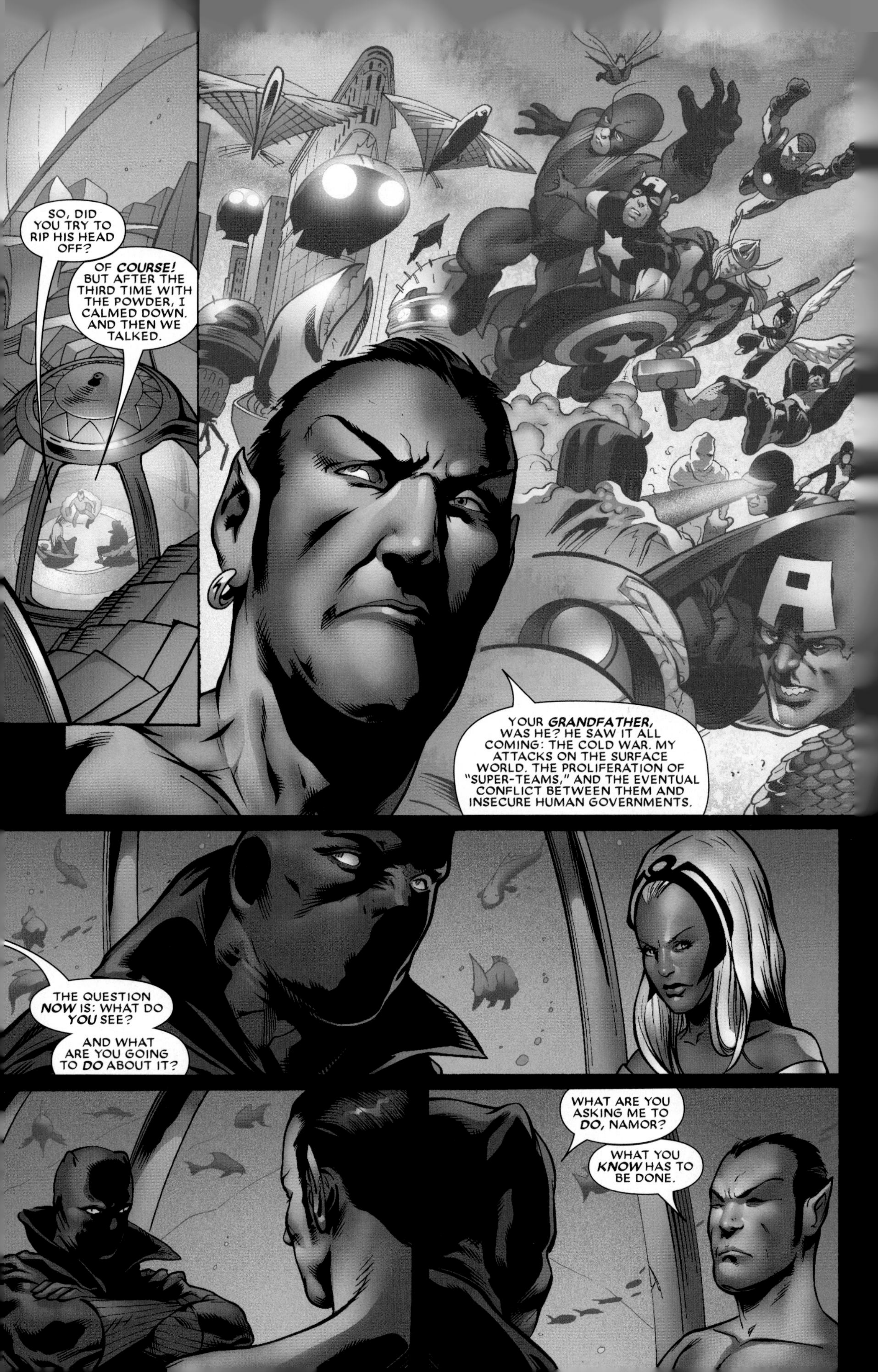
SO, DID YOU TRY TO RIP HIS HEAD OFF?
OF COURSE! BUT AFTER THE THIRD TIME WITH THE POWDER, I CALMED DOWN. AND THEN WE TALKED.
YOUR GRANDFATHER, WAS HE? HE SAW IT ALL COMING: THE COLD WAR. MY ATTACKS ON THE SURFACE WORLD. THE PROLIFERATION OF "SUPER-TEAMS," AND THE EVENTUAL CONFLICT BETWEEN THEM AND INSECURE HUMAN GOVERNMENTS.
THE QUESTION NOW IS: WHAT DO YOU SEE?
AND WHAT ARE YOU GOING TO DO ABOUT IT?
WHAT ARE YOU ASKING ME TO DO, NAMOR?
WHAT YOU KNOW HAS TO BE DONE.

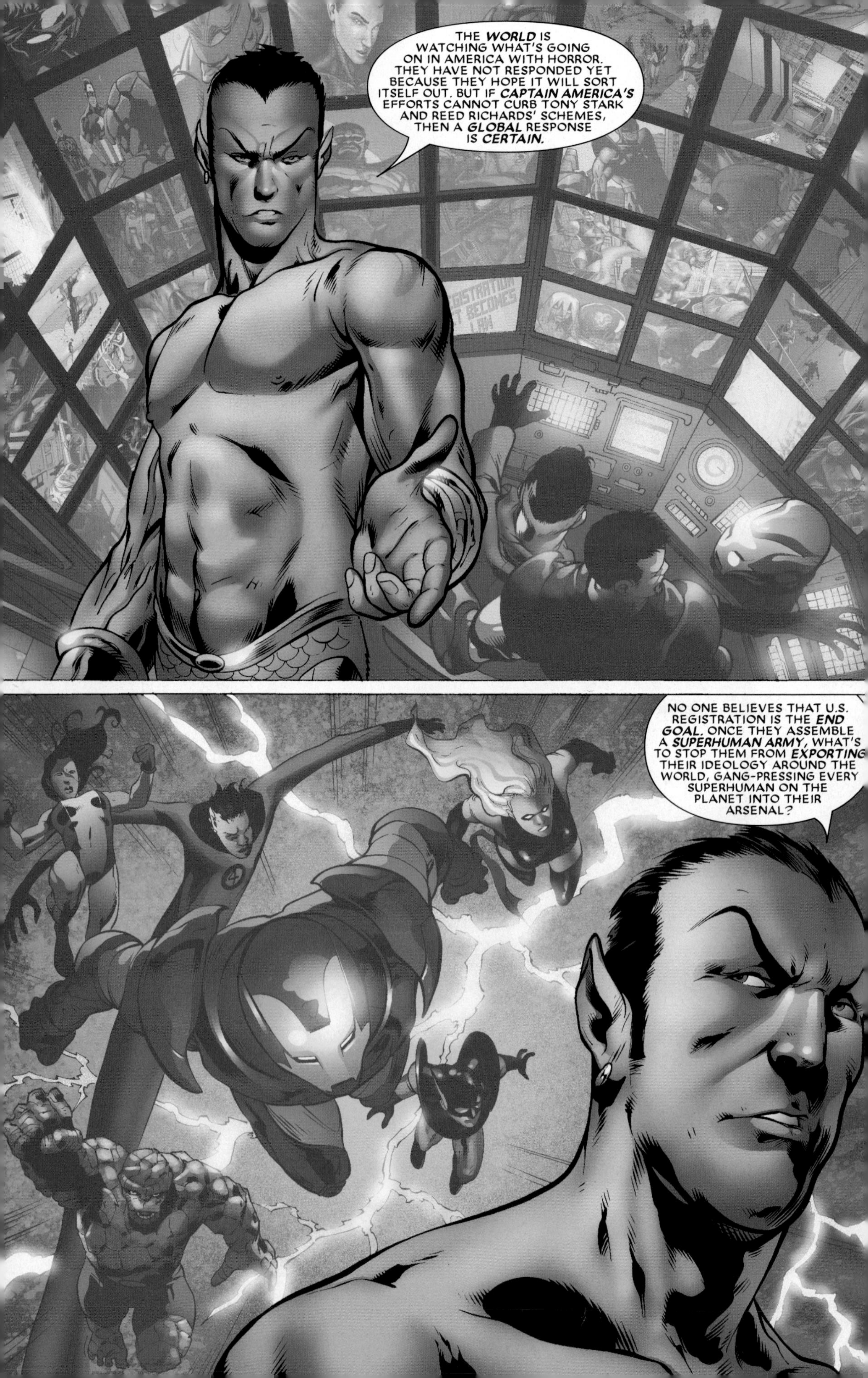
THE WORLD IS WATCHING WHAT'S GOING ON IN AMERICA WITH HORROR. THEY HAVE NOT RESPONDED YET BECAUSE THEY HOPE IT WILL SORT ITSELF OUT. BUT IF CAPTAIN AMERICA'S EFFORTS CANNOT CURB TONY STARK AND REED RICHARDS' SCHEMES, THEN A GLOBAL RESPONSE IS CERTAIN.
NO ONE BELIEVES THAT U.S. REGISTRATION IS THE END GOAL. ONCE THEY ASSEMBLE A SUPERHUMAN ARMY, WHAT'S TO STOP THEM FROM EXPORTING THEIR IDEOLOGY AROUND THE WORLD, GANG-PRESSING EVERY SUPERHUMAN ON THE PLANET INTO THEIR ARSENAL?

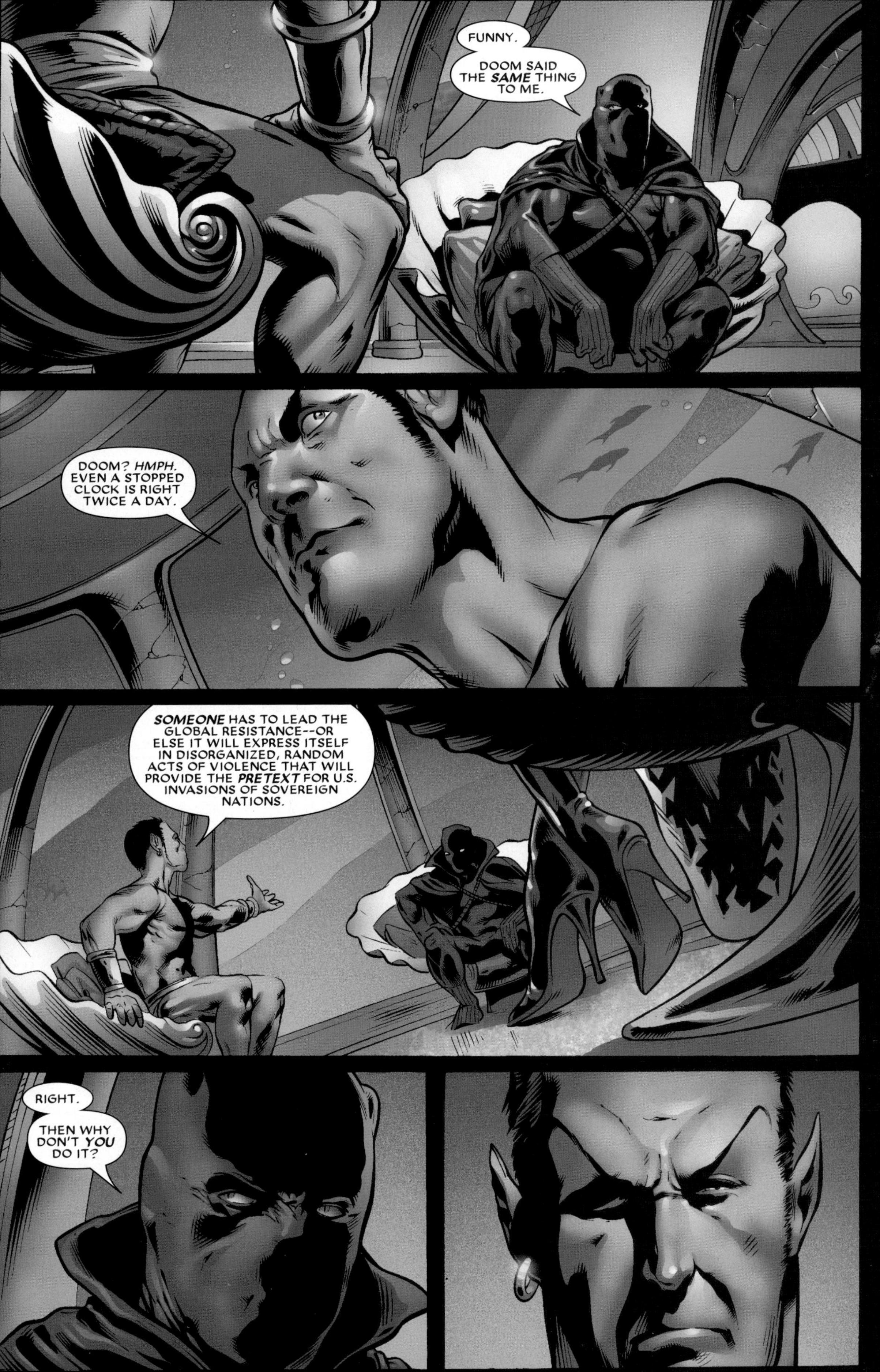
FUNNY.
DOOM SAID THE SAME THING TO ME.
DOOM? HMPH. EVEN A STOPPED CLOCK IS RIGHT TWICE A DAY.
SOMEONE HAS TO LEAD THE GLOBAL RESISTANCE--OR ELSE IT WILL EXPRESS ITSELF IN DISORGANIZED, RANDOM ACTS OF VIOLENCE THAT WILL PROVIDE THE PRETEXT FOR U.S. INVASIONS OF SOVEREIGN NATIONS.
RIGHT.
THEN WHY DON'T YOU DO IT?

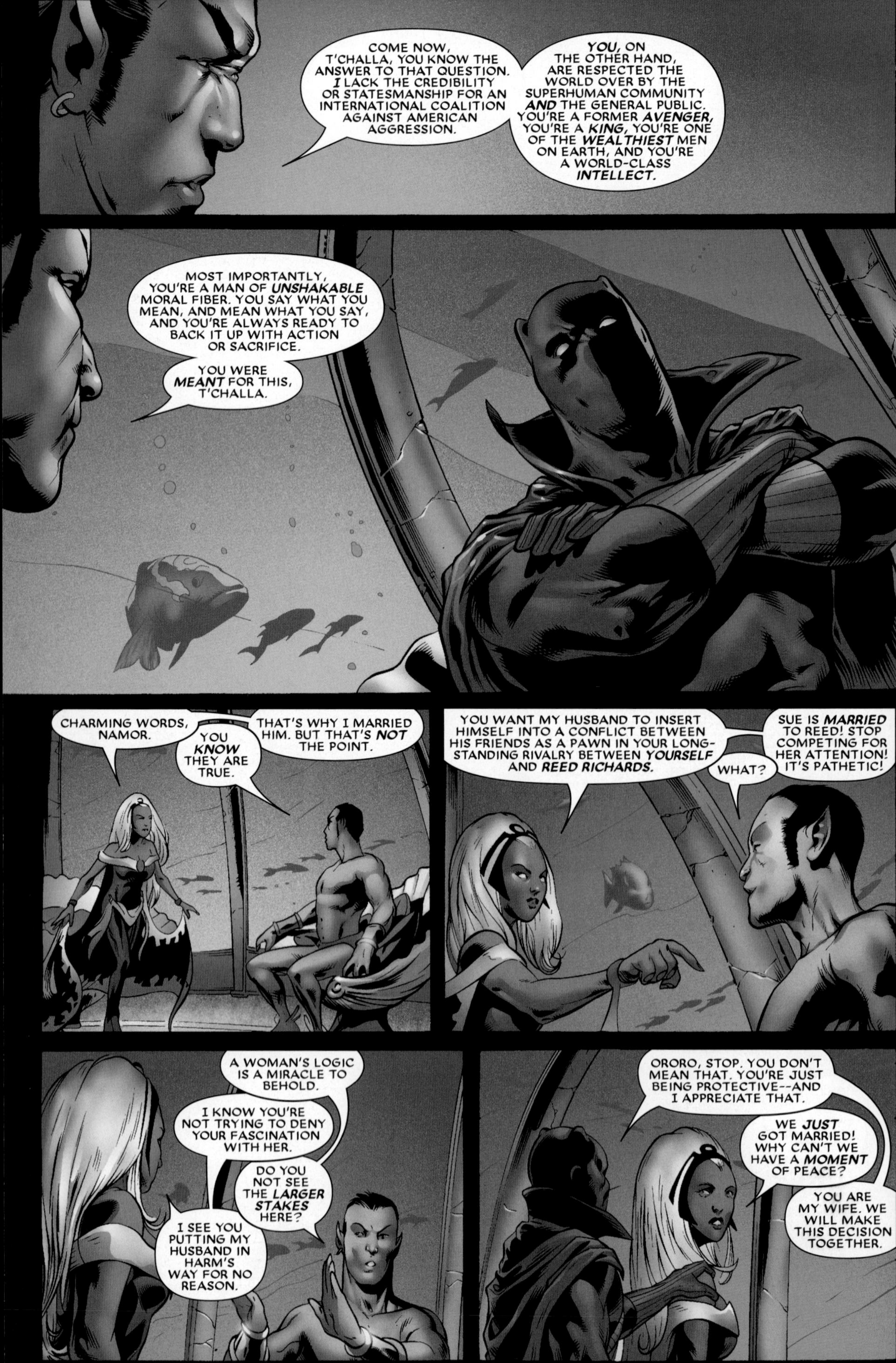
COME NOW, T'CHALLA, YOU KNOW THE ANSWER TO THAT QUESTION. *I* LACK THE CREDIBILITY OR STATESMANSHIP FOR AN INTERNATIONAL COALITION AGAINST AMERICAN AGGRESSION.
YOU, ON THE OTHER HAND, ARE RESPECTED THE WORLD OVER BY THE SUPERHUMAN COMMUNITY *AND* THE GENERAL PUBLIC. YOU'RE A FORMER *AVENGER,* YOU'RE A *KING,* YOU'RE ONE OF THE *WEALTHIEST* MEN ON EARTH, AND YOU'RE A WORLD-CLASS *INTELLECT.*
MOST IMPORTANTLY, YOU'RE A MAN OF *UNSHAKABLE* MORAL FIBER. YOU SAY WHAT YOU MEAN, AND MEAN WHAT YOU SAY, AND YOU'RE ALWAYS READY TO BACK IT UP WITH ACTION OR SACRIFICE.
YOU WERE *MEANT* FOR THIS, T'CHALLA.
CHARMING WORDS, NAMOR.
YOU *KNOW* THEY ARE TRUE.
THAT'S WHY I MARRIED HIM. BUT THAT'S *NOT* THE POINT.
YOU WANT MY HUSBAND TO INSERT HIMSELF INTO A CONFLICT BETWEEN HIS FRIENDS AS A PAWN IN YOUR LONG-STANDING RIVALRY BETWEEN *YOURSELF* AND *REED RICHARDS.*
WHAT?
SUE IS *MARRIED* TO REED! STOP COMPETING FOR HER ATTENTION! IT'S PATHETIC!
A WOMAN'S LOGIC IS A MIRACLE TO BEHOLD.
I KNOW YOU'RE NOT TRYING TO DENY YOUR FASCINATION WITH HER.
DO YOU NOT SEE THE *LARGER STAKES* HERE?
I SEE YOU PUTTING MY HUSBAND IN HARM'S WAY FOR NO REASON.
ORORO, STOP. YOU DON'T MEAN THAT. YOU'RE JUST BEING PROTECTIVE--AND I APPRECIATE THAT.
WE *JUST* GOT MARRIED! WHY CAN'T WE HAVE A *MOMENT* OF PEACE?
YOU ARE MY WIFE. WE WILL MAKE THIS DECISION TOGETHER.

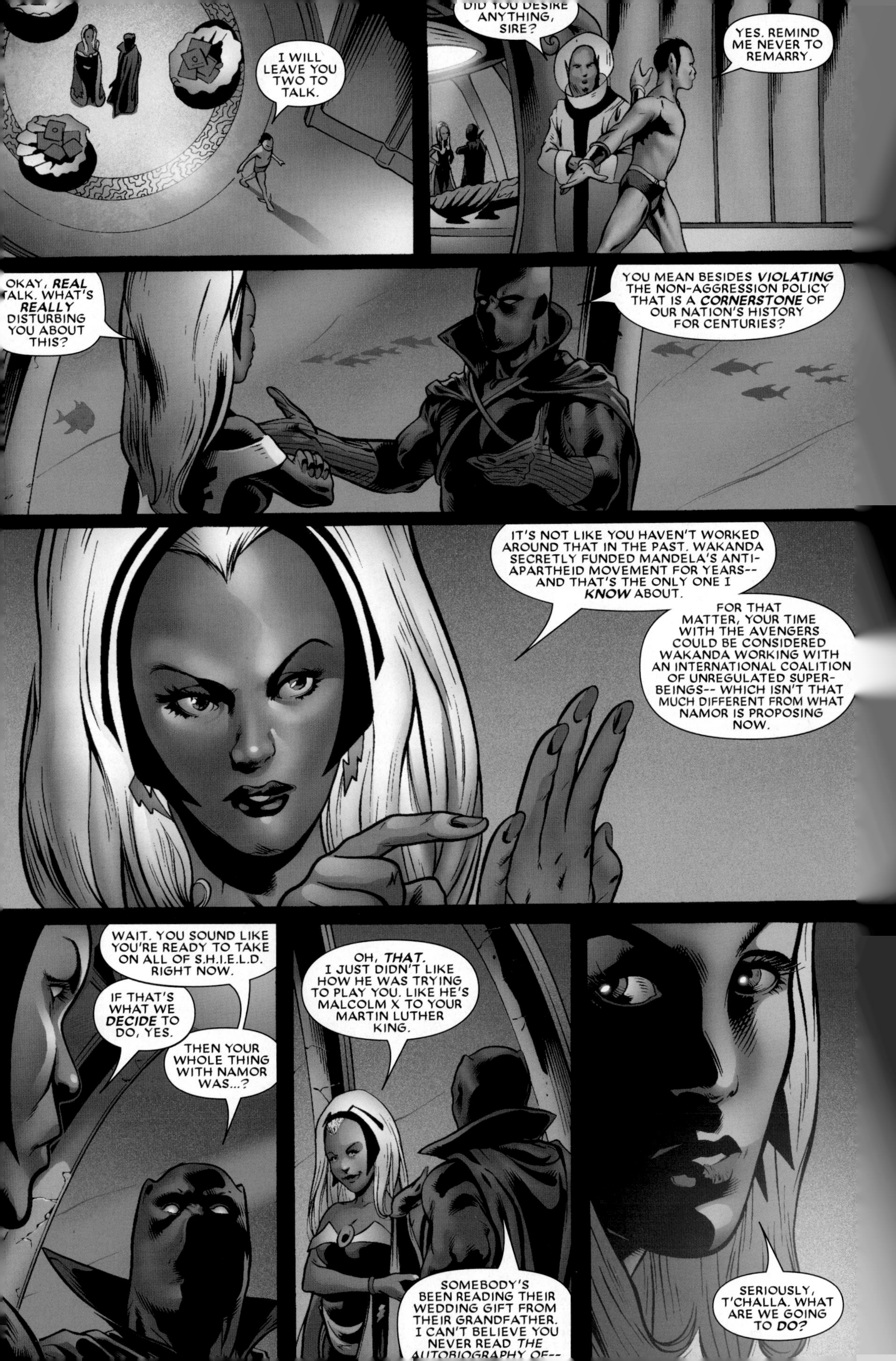
I WILL LEAVE YOU TWO TO TALK.
DID YOU DESIRE ANYTHING, SIRE?
YES. REMIND ME NEVER TO REMARRY.
OKAY, REAL TALK. WHAT'S REALLY DISTURBING YOU ABOUT THIS?
YOU MEAN BESIDES VIOLATING THE NON-AGGRESSION POLICY THAT IS A CORNERSTONE OF OUR NATION'S HISTORY FOR CENTURIES?
IT'S NOT LIKE YOU HAVEN'T WORKED AROUND THAT IN THE PAST. WAKANDA SECRETLY FUNDED MANDELA'S ANTI-APARTHEID MOVEMENT FOR YEARS-- AND THAT'S THE ONLY ONE I KNOW ABOUT.
FOR THAT MATTER, YOUR TIME WITH THE AVENGERS COULD BE CONSIDERED WAKANDA WORKING WITH AN INTERNATIONAL COALITION OF UNREGULATED SUPER-BEINGS-- WHICH ISN'T THAT MUCH DIFFERENT FROM WHAT NAMOR IS PROPOSING NOW.
WAIT. YOU SOUND LIKE YOU'RE READY TO TAKE ON ALL OF S.H.I.E.L.D. RIGHT NOW.
IF THAT'S WHAT WE DECIDE TO DO, YES.
THEN YOUR WHOLE THING WITH NAMOR WAS...?
OH, THAT. I JUST DIDN'T LIKE HOW HE WAS TRYING TO PLAY YOU. LIKE HE'S MALCOLM X TO YOUR MARTIN LUTHER KING.
SOMEBODY'S BEEN READING THEIR WEDDING GIFT FROM THEIR GRANDFATHER. I CAN'T BELIEVE YOU NEVER READ THE AUTOBIOGRAPHY OF--
SERIOUSLY, T'CHALLA. WHAT ARE WE GOING TO DO?

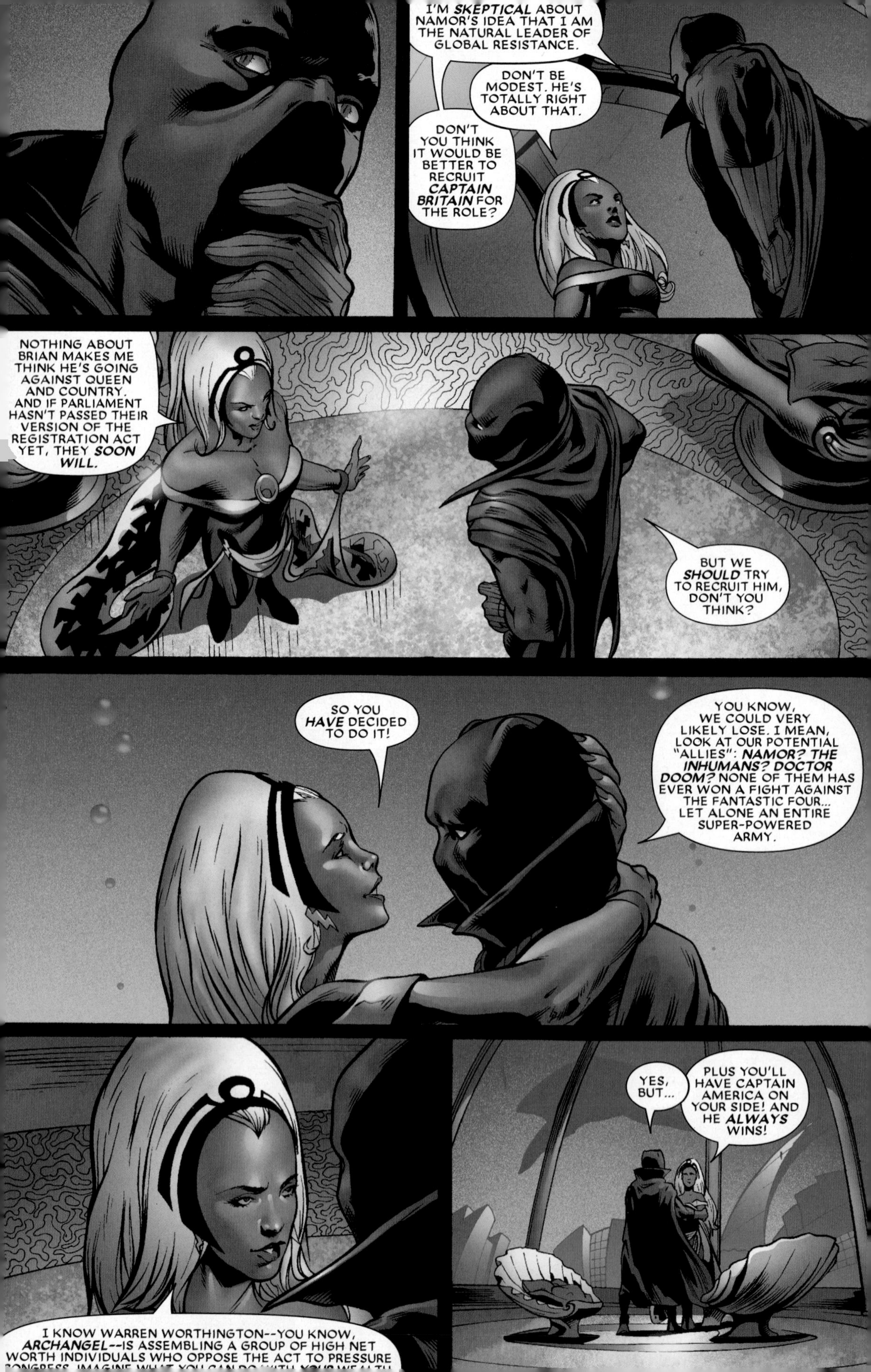
I'M SKEPTICAL ABOUT NAMOR'S IDEA THAT I AM THE NATURAL LEADER OF GLOBAL RESISTANCE.
DON'T BE MODEST. HE'S TOTALLY RIGHT ABOUT THAT.
DON'T YOU THINK IT WOULD BE BETTER TO RECRUIT CAPTAIN BRITAIN FOR THE ROLE?
NOTHING ABOUT BRIAN MAKES ME THINK HE'S GOING AGAINST QUEEN AND COUNTRY. AND IF PARLIAMENT HASN'T PASSED THEIR VERSION OF THE REGISTRATION ACT YET, THEY SOON WILL.
BUT WE SHOULD TRY TO RECRUIT HIM, DON'T YOU THINK?
SO YOU HAVE DECIDED TO DO IT!
YOU KNOW, WE COULD VERY LIKELY LOSE. I MEAN, LOOK AT OUR POTENTIAL "ALLIES": NAMOR? THE INHUMANS? DOCTOR DOOM? NONE OF THEM HAS EVER WON A FIGHT AGAINST THE FANTASTIC FOUR... LET ALONE AN ENTIRE SUPER-POWERED ARMY.
I KNOW WARREN WORTHINGTON--YOU KNOW, ARCHANGEL--IS ASSEMBLING A GROUP OF HIGH NET WORTH INDIVIDUALS WHO OPPOSE THE ACT TO PRESSURE
YES, BUT...
PLUS YOU'LL HAVE CAPTAIN AMERICA ON YOUR SIDE! AND HE ALWAYS WINS!

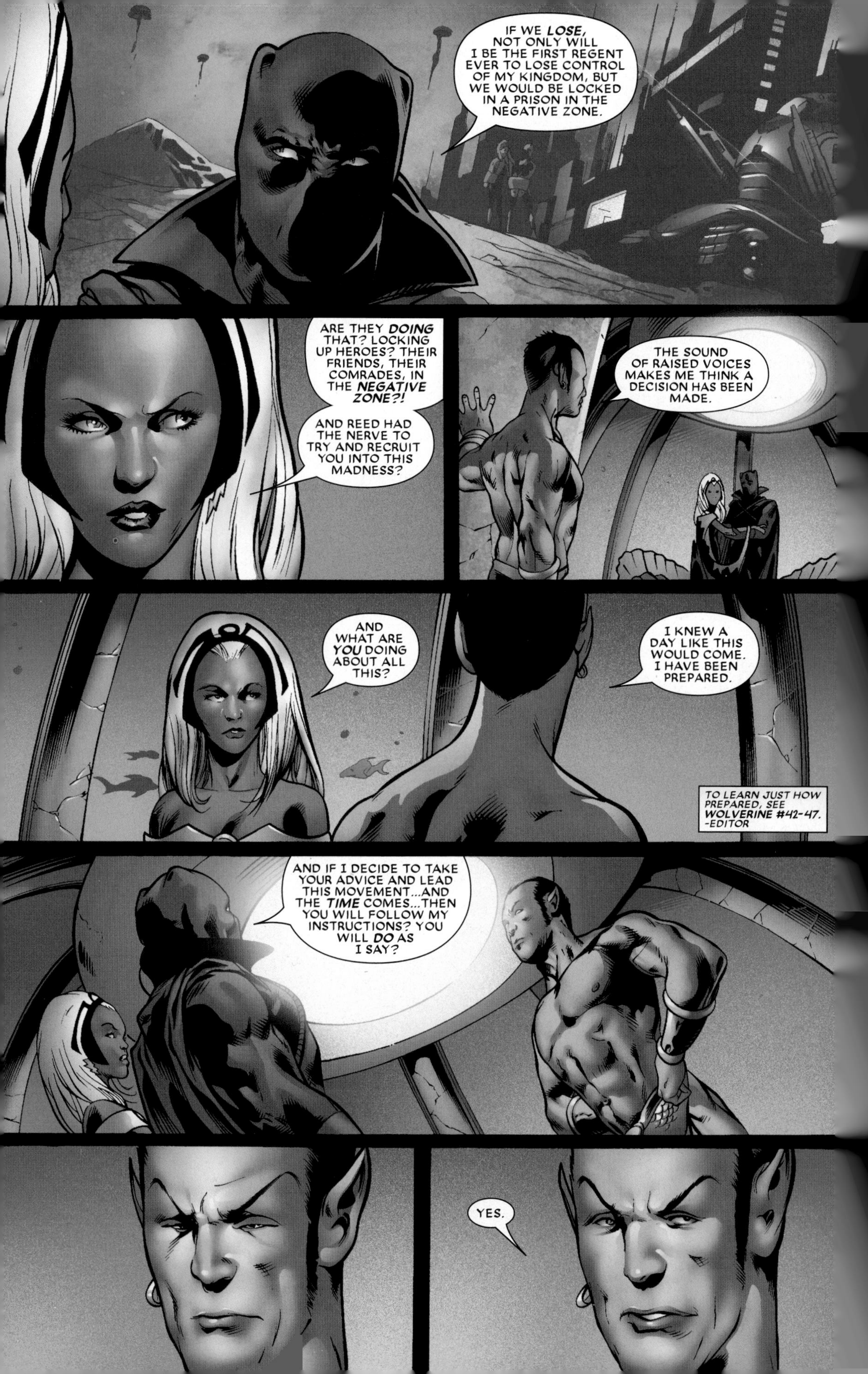
IF WE LOSE, NOT ONLY WILL I BE THE FIRST REGENT EVER TO LOSE CONTROL OF MY KINGDOM, BUT WE WOULD BE LOCKED IN A PRISON IN THE NEGATIVE ZONE.
ARE THEY DOING THAT? LOCKING UP HEROES? THEIR FRIENDS, THEIR COMRADES, IN THE NEGATIVE ZONE?!
AND REED HAD THE NERVE TO TRY AND RECRUIT YOU INTO THIS MADNESS?
THE SOUND OF RAISED VOICES MAKES ME THINK A DECISION HAS BEEN MADE.
AND WHAT ARE YOU DOING ABOUT ALL THIS?
I KNEW A DAY LIKE THIS WOULD COME. I HAVE BEEN PREPARED.
TO LEARN JUST HOW PREPARED, SEE WOLVERINE #42-47. -EDITOR
AND IF I DECIDE TO TAKE YOUR ADVICE AND LEAD THIS MOVEMENT...AND THE TIME COMES...THEN YOU WILL FOLLOW MY INSTRUCTIONS? YOU WILL DO AS I SAY?
YES.

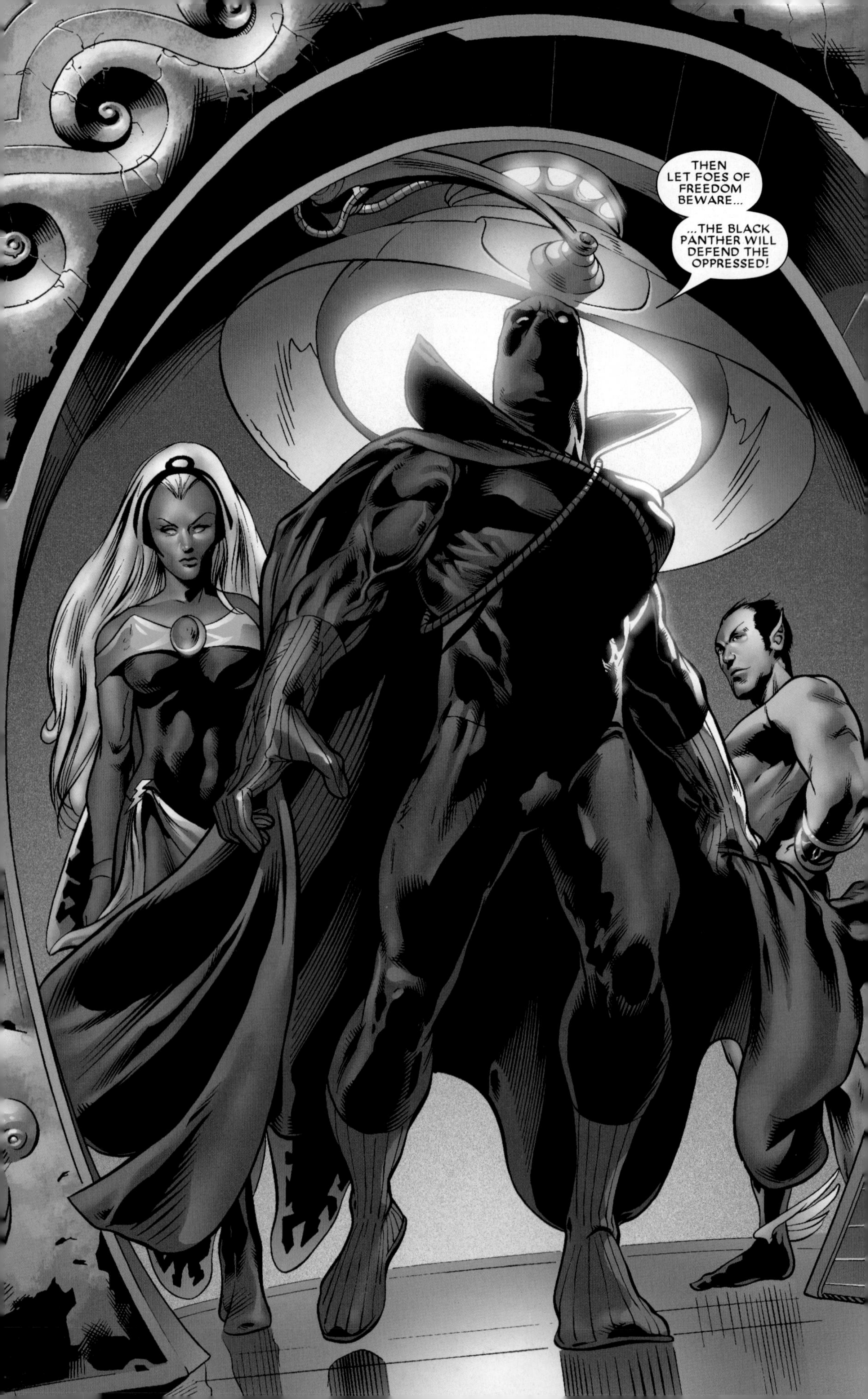
THEN LET FOES OF FREEDOM BEWARE...
...THE BLACK PANTHER WILL DEFEND THE OPPRESSED!

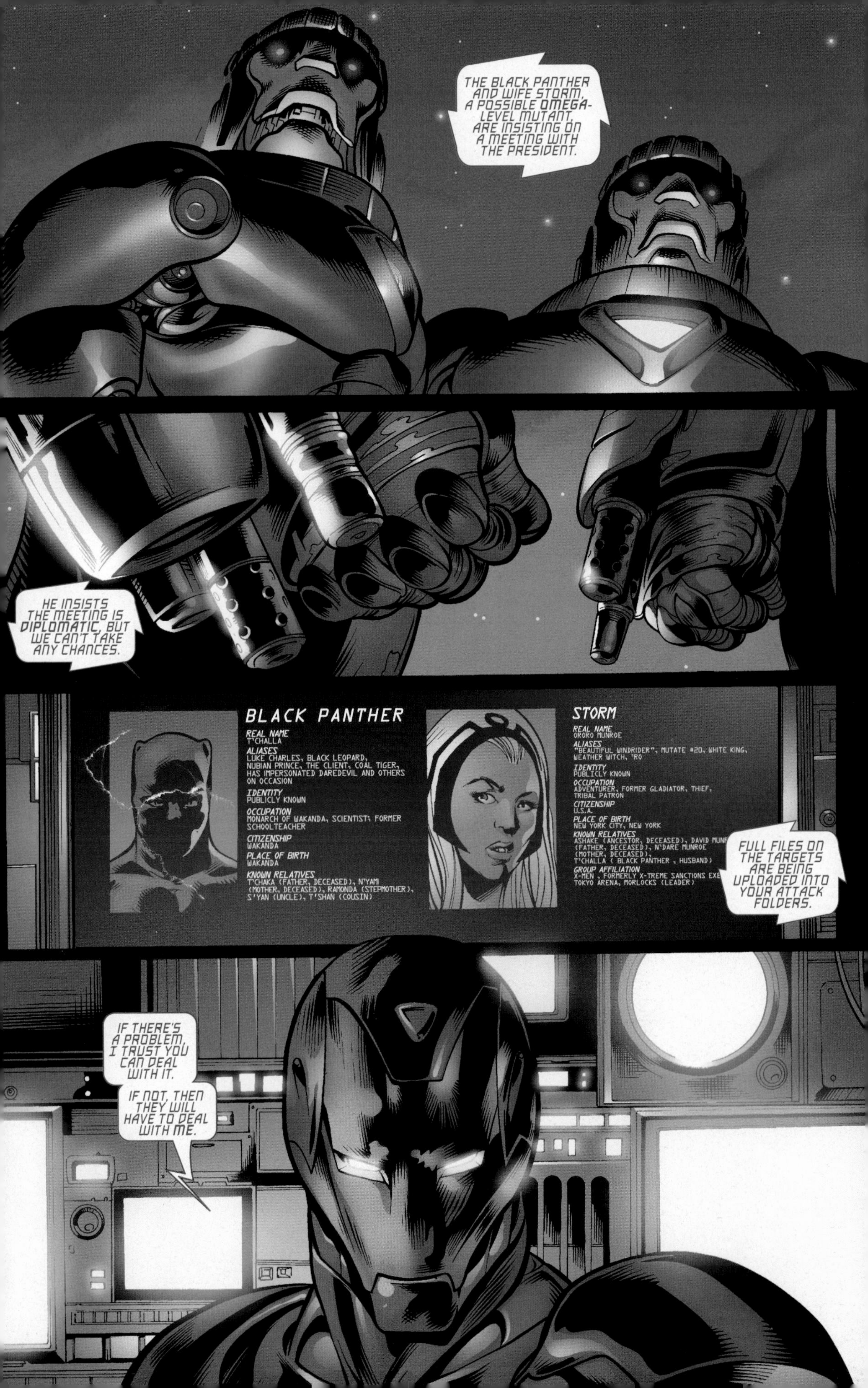

THE BLACK PANTHER AND WIFE STORM, A POSSIBLE OMEGA-LEVEL MUTANT, ARE INSISTING ON A MEETING WITH THE PRESIDENT.
HE INSISTS THE MEETING IS DIPLOMATIC, BUT WE CAN'T TAKE ANY CHANCES.
BLACK PANTHER
REAL NAME
T'CHALLA
ALIASES
LUKE CHARLES, BLACK LEOPARD, NUBIAN PRINCE, THE CLIENT, COAL TIGER, HAS IMPERSONATED DAREDEVIL AND OTHERS ON OCCASION
IDENTITY
PUBLICLY KNOWN
OCCUPATION
MONARCH OF WAKANDA, SCIENTIST; FORMER SCHOOLTEACHER
CITIZENSHIP
WAKANDA
PLACE OF BIRTH
WAKANDA
KNOWN RELATIVES
T'CHAKA (FATHER, DECEASED), N'YAMI (MOTHER, DECEASED), RAMONDA (STEPMOTHER), S'YAN (UNCLE), T'SHAN (COUSIN)
STORM
REAL NAME
ORORO MUNROE
ALIASES
"BEAUTIFUL WINDRIDER", MUTATE #20, WHITE KING, WEATHER WITCH, 'RO
IDENTITY
PUBLICLY KNOWN
OCCUPATION
ADVENTURER, FORMER GLADIATOR, THIEF, TRIBAL PATRON
CITIZENSHIP
U.S.A.
PLACE OF BIRTH
NEW YORK CITY, NEW YORK
KNOWN RELATIVES
ASHAKE (ANCESTOR, DECEASED), DAVID MUNR (FATHER, DECEASED), N'DARE MUNROE (MOTHER, DECEASED), T'CHALLA (BLACK PANTHER , HUSBAND)
GROUP AFFILIATION
X-MEN , FORMERLY X-TREME SANCTIONS EXE TOKYO ARENA, MORLOCKS (LEADER)
FULL FILES ON THE TARGETS ARE BEING UPLOADED INTO YOUR ATTACK FOLDERS.
IF THERE'S A PROBLEM, I TRUST YOU CAN DEAL WITH IT.
IF NOT, THEN THEY WILL HAVE TO DEAL WITH ME.

BLACK PANTHER

A MARVEL COMICS EVENT

CIVIL WAR

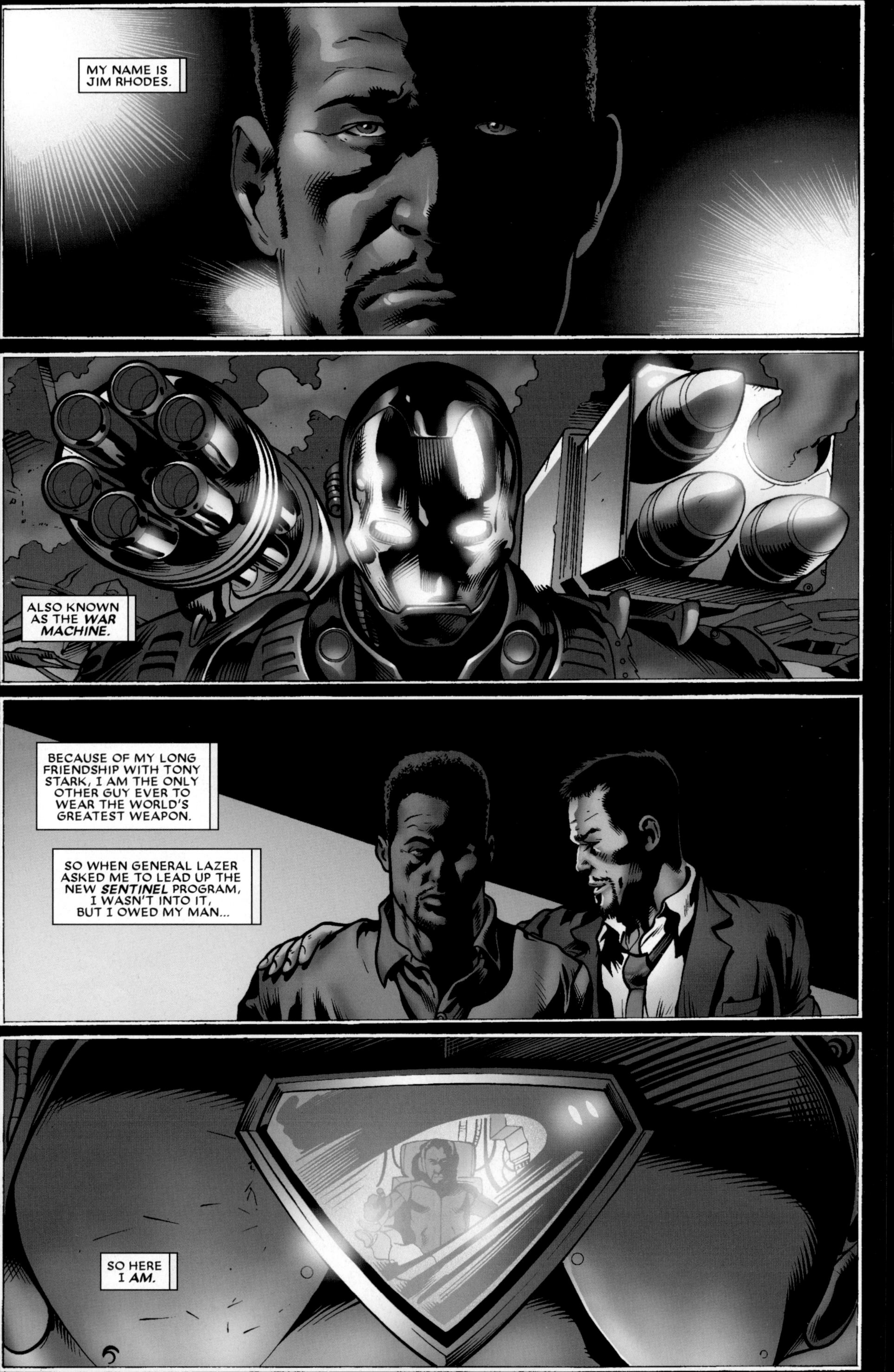
MY NAME IS JIM RHODES.
ALSO KNOWN AS THE *WAR MACHINE.*
BECAUSE OF MY LONG FRIENDSHIP WITH TONY STARK, I AM THE ONLY OTHER GUY EVER TO WEAR THE WORLD'S GREATEST WEAPON.
SO WHEN GENERAL LAZER ASKED ME TO LEAD UP THE NEW *SENTINEL* PROGRAM, I WASN'T INTO IT, BUT I OWED MY MAN...
SO HERE I *AM.*

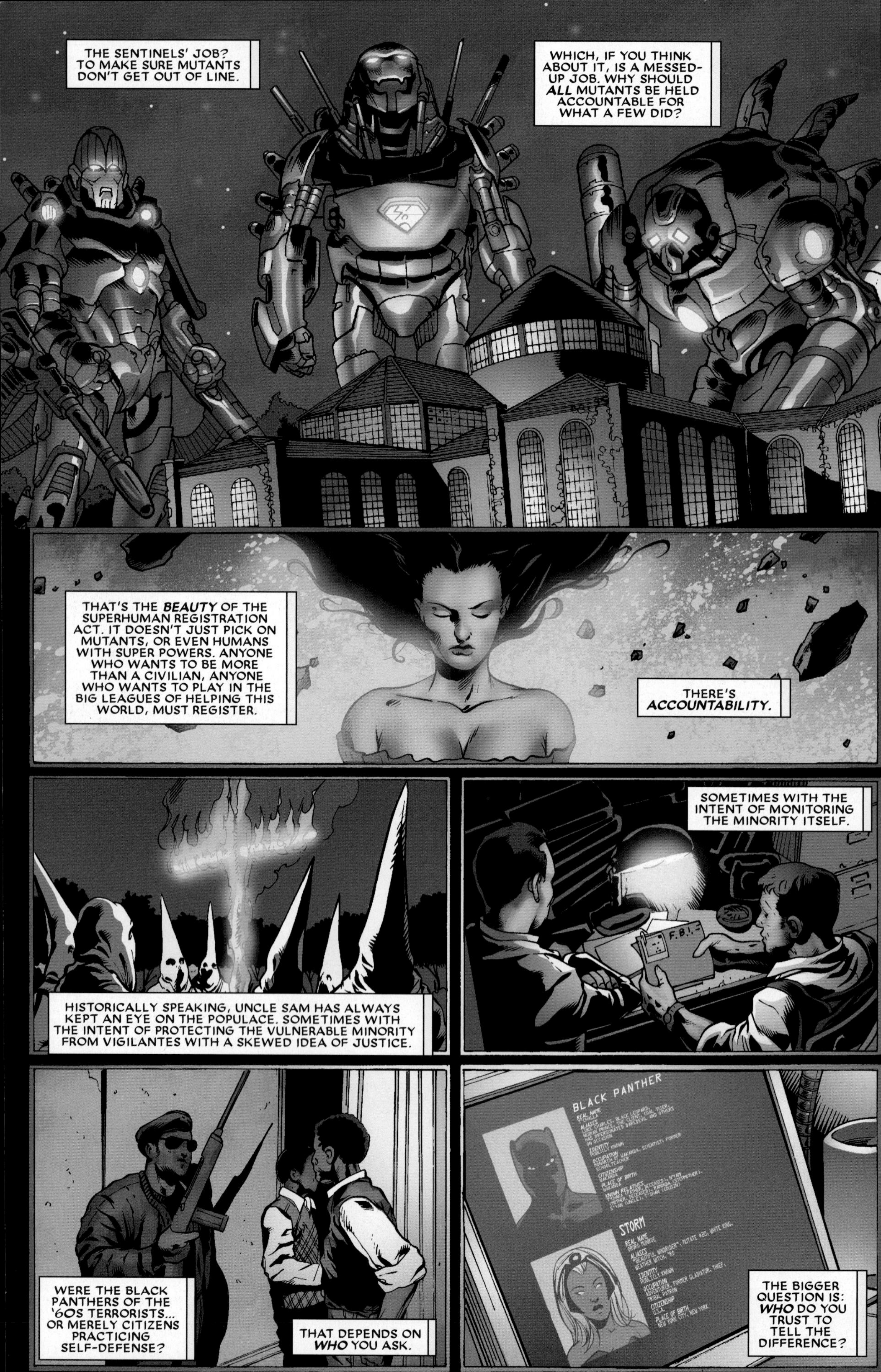
THE SENTINELS' JOB? TO MAKE SURE MUTANTS DON'T GET OUT OF LINE.
WHICH, IF YOU THINK ABOUT IT, IS A MESSED-UP JOB. WHY SHOULD *ALL* MUTANTS BE HELD ACCOUNTABLE FOR WHAT A FEW DID?
THAT'S THE *BEAUTY* OF THE SUPERHUMAN REGISTRATION ACT. IT DOESN'T JUST PICK ON MUTANTS, OR EVEN HUMANS WITH SUPER POWERS. ANYONE WHO WANTS TO BE MORE THAN A CIVILIAN, ANYONE WHO WANTS TO PLAY IN THE BIG LEAGUES OF HELPING THIS WORLD, MUST REGISTER.
THERE'S *ACCOUNTABILITY.*
HISTORICALLY SPEAKING, UNCLE SAM HAS ALWAYS KEPT AN EYE ON THE POPULACE. SOMETIMES WITH THE INTENT OF PROTECTING THE VULNERABLE MINORITY FROM VIGILANTES WITH A SKEWED IDEA OF JUSTICE.
SOMETIMES WITH THE INTENT OF MONITORING THE MINORITY ITSELF.
F.B.I.
WERE THE BLACK PANTHERS OF THE '60S TERRORISTS... OR MERELY CITIZENS PRACTICING SELF-DEFENSE?
THAT DEPENDS ON *WHO* YOU ASK.
BLACK PANTHER
STORM
THE BIGGER QUESTION IS: *WHO* DO YOU TRUST TO TELL THE DIFFERENCE?

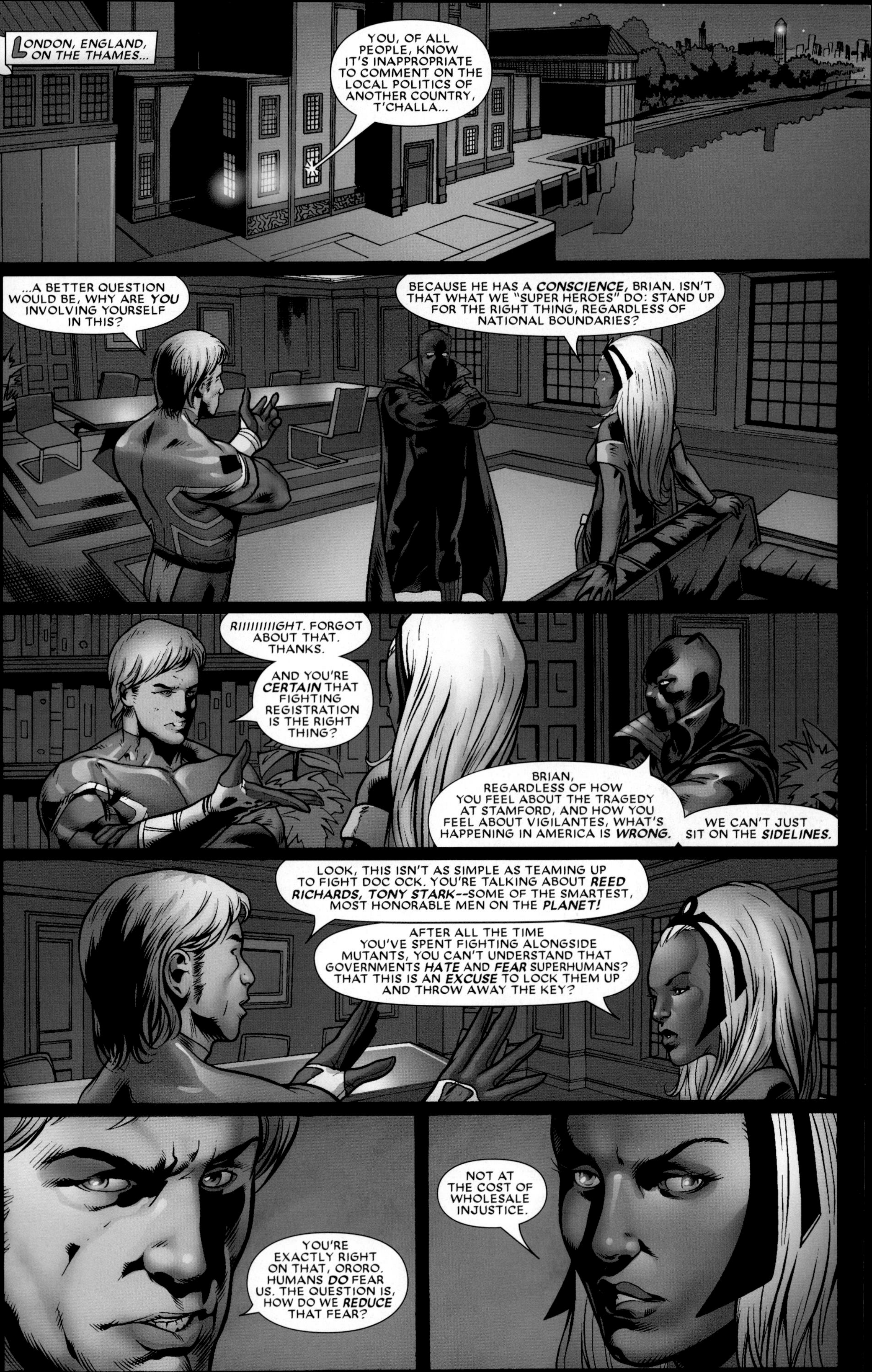
LONDON, ENGLAND, ON THE THAMES...
YOU, OF ALL PEOPLE, KNOW IT'S INAPPROPRIATE TO COMMENT ON THE LOCAL POLITICS OF ANOTHER COUNTRY, T'CHALLA...
...A BETTER QUESTION WOULD BE, WHY ARE YOU INVOLVING YOURSELF IN THIS?
BECAUSE HE HAS A CONSCIENCE, BRIAN. ISN'T THAT WHAT WE "SUPER HEROES" DO: STAND UP FOR THE RIGHT THING, REGARDLESS OF NATIONAL BOUNDARIES?
RIIIIIIIIGHT. FORGOT ABOUT THAT. THANKS.
AND YOU'RE CERTAIN THAT FIGHTING REGISTRATION IS THE RIGHT THING?
BRIAN, REGARDLESS OF HOW YOU FEEL ABOUT THE TRAGEDY AT STAMFORD, AND HOW YOU FEEL ABOUT VIGILANTES, WHAT'S HAPPENING IN AMERICA IS WRONG.
WE CAN'T JUST SIT ON THE SIDELINES.
LOOK, THIS ISN'T AS SIMPLE AS TEAMING UP TO FIGHT DOC OCK. YOU'RE TALKING ABOUT REED RICHARDS, TONY STARK--SOME OF THE SMARTEST, MOST HONORABLE MEN ON THE PLANET!
AFTER ALL THE TIME YOU'VE SPENT FIGHTING ALONGSIDE MUTANTS, YOU CAN'T UNDERSTAND THAT GOVERNMENTS HATE AND FEAR SUPERHUMANS? THAT THIS IS AN EXCUSE TO LOCK THEM UP AND THROW AWAY THE KEY?
NOT AT THE COST OF WHOLESALE INJUSTICE.
YOU'RE EXACTLY RIGHT ON THAT, ORORO. HUMANS DO FEAR US. THE QUESTION IS, HOW DO WE REDUCE THAT FEAR?

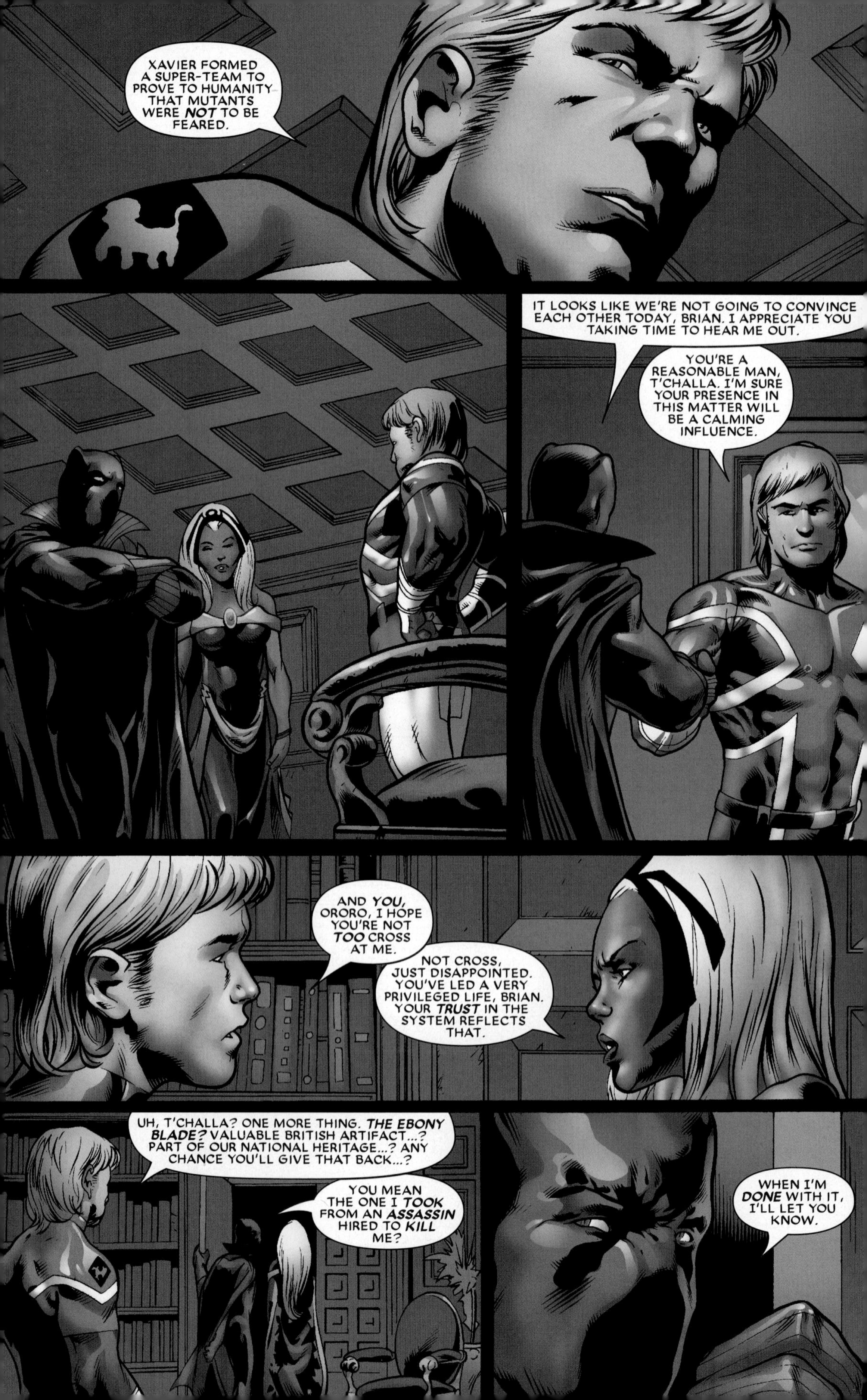
XAVIER FORMED A SUPER-TEAM TO PROVE TO HUMANITY THAT MUTANTS WERE NOT TO BE FEARED.
IT LOOKS LIKE WE'RE NOT GOING TO CONVINCE EACH OTHER TODAY, BRIAN. I APPRECIATE YOU TAKING TIME TO HEAR ME OUT.
YOU'RE A REASONABLE MAN, T'CHALLA. I'M SURE YOUR PRESENCE IN THIS MATTER WILL BE A CALMING INFLUENCE.
AND YOU, ORORO, I HOPE YOU'RE NOT TOO CROSS AT ME.
NOT CROSS, JUST DISAPPOINTED. YOU'VE LED A VERY PRIVILEGED LIFE, BRIAN. YOUR TRUST IN THE SYSTEM REFLECTS THAT.
UH, T'CHALLA? ONE MORE THING. THE EBONY BLADE? VALUABLE BRITISH ARTIFACT...? PART OF OUR NATIONAL HERITAGE...? ANY CHANCE YOU'LL GIVE THAT BACK...?
YOU MEAN THE ONE I TOOK FROM AN ASSASSIN HIRED TO KILL ME?
WHEN I'M DONE WITH IT, I'LL LET YOU KNOW.

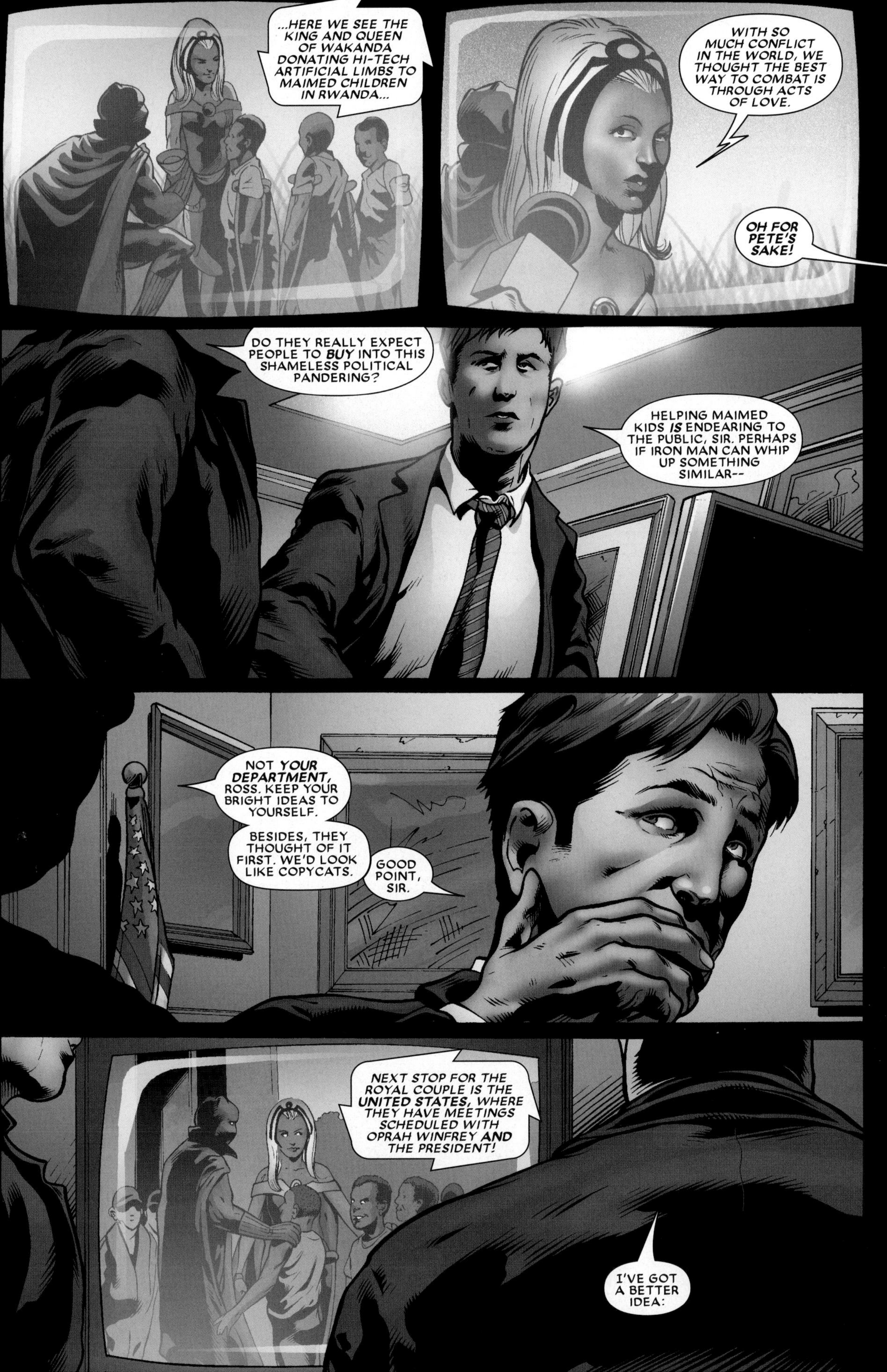
...HERE WE SEE THE KING AND QUEEN OF WAKANDA DONATING HI-TECH ARTIFICIAL LIMBS TO MAIMED CHILDREN IN RWANDA...
WITH SO MUCH CONFLICT IN THE WORLD, WE THOUGHT THE BEST WAY TO COMBAT IS THROUGH ACTS OF LOVE.
OH FOR PETE'S SAKE!
DO THEY REALLY EXPECT PEOPLE TO BUY INTO THIS SHAMELESS POLITICAL PANDERING?
HELPING MAIMED KIDS IS ENDEARING TO THE PUBLIC, SIR. PERHAPS IF IRON MAN CAN WHIP UP SOMETHING SIMILAR--
NOT YOUR DEPARTMENT, ROSS. KEEP YOUR BRIGHT IDEAS TO YOURSELF.
BESIDES, THEY THOUGHT OF IT FIRST. WE'D LOOK LIKE COPYCATS.
GOOD POINT, SIR.
NEXT STOP FOR THE ROYAL COUPLE IS THE UNITED STATES, WHERE THEY HAVE MEETINGS SCHEDULED WITH OPRAH WINFREY AND THE PRESIDENT!
I'VE GOT A BETTER IDEA:

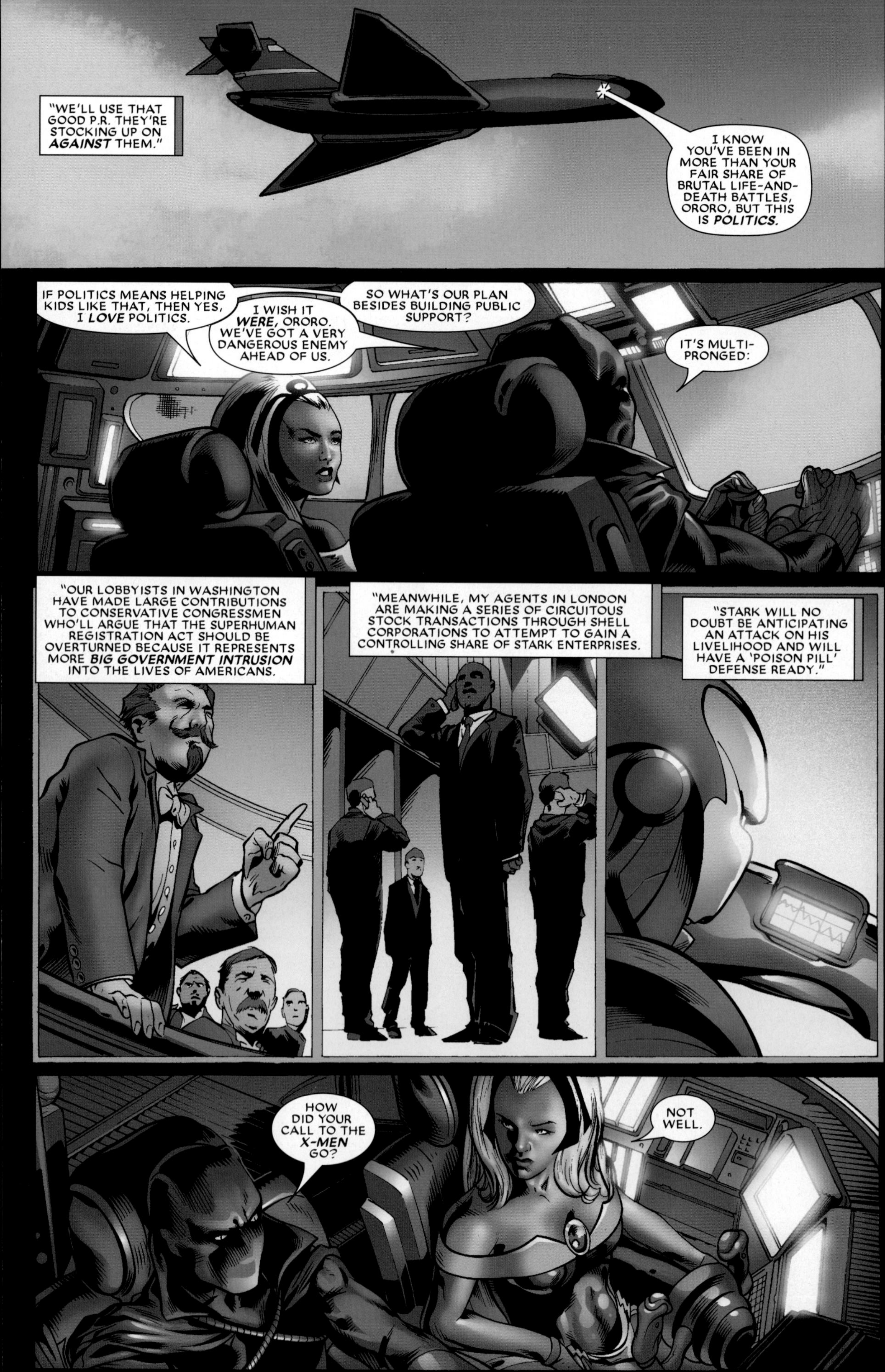
"WE'LL USE THAT GOOD P.R. THEY'RE STOCKING UP ON AGAINST THEM."
I KNOW YOU'VE BEEN IN MORE THAN YOUR FAIR SHARE OF BRUTAL LIFE-AND-DEATH BATTLES, ORORO, BUT THIS IS POLITICS.
IF POLITICS MEANS HELPING KIDS LIKE THAT, THEN YES, I LOVE POLITICS.
I WISH IT WERE, ORORO. WE'VE GOT A VERY DANGEROUS ENEMY AHEAD OF US.
SO WHAT'S OUR PLAN BESIDES BUILDING PUBLIC SUPPORT?
IT'S MULTI-PRONGED:
"OUR LOBBYISTS IN WASHINGTON HAVE MADE LARGE CONTRIBUTIONS TO CONSERVATIVE CONGRESSMEN WHO'LL ARGUE THAT THE SUPERHUMAN REGISTRATION ACT SHOULD BE OVERTURNED BECAUSE IT REPRESENTS MORE BIG GOVERNMENT INTRUSION INTO THE LIVES OF AMERICANS.
"MEANWHILE, MY AGENTS IN LONDON ARE MAKING A SERIES OF CIRCUITOUS STOCK TRANSACTIONS THROUGH SHELL CORPORATIONS TO ATTEMPT TO GAIN A CONTROLLING SHARE OF STARK ENTERPRISES.
"STARK WILL NO DOUBT BE ANTICIPATING AN ATTACK ON HIS LIVELIHOOD AND WILL HAVE A 'POISON PILL' DEFENSE READY."
HOW DID YOUR CALL TO THE X-MEN GO?
NOT WELL.

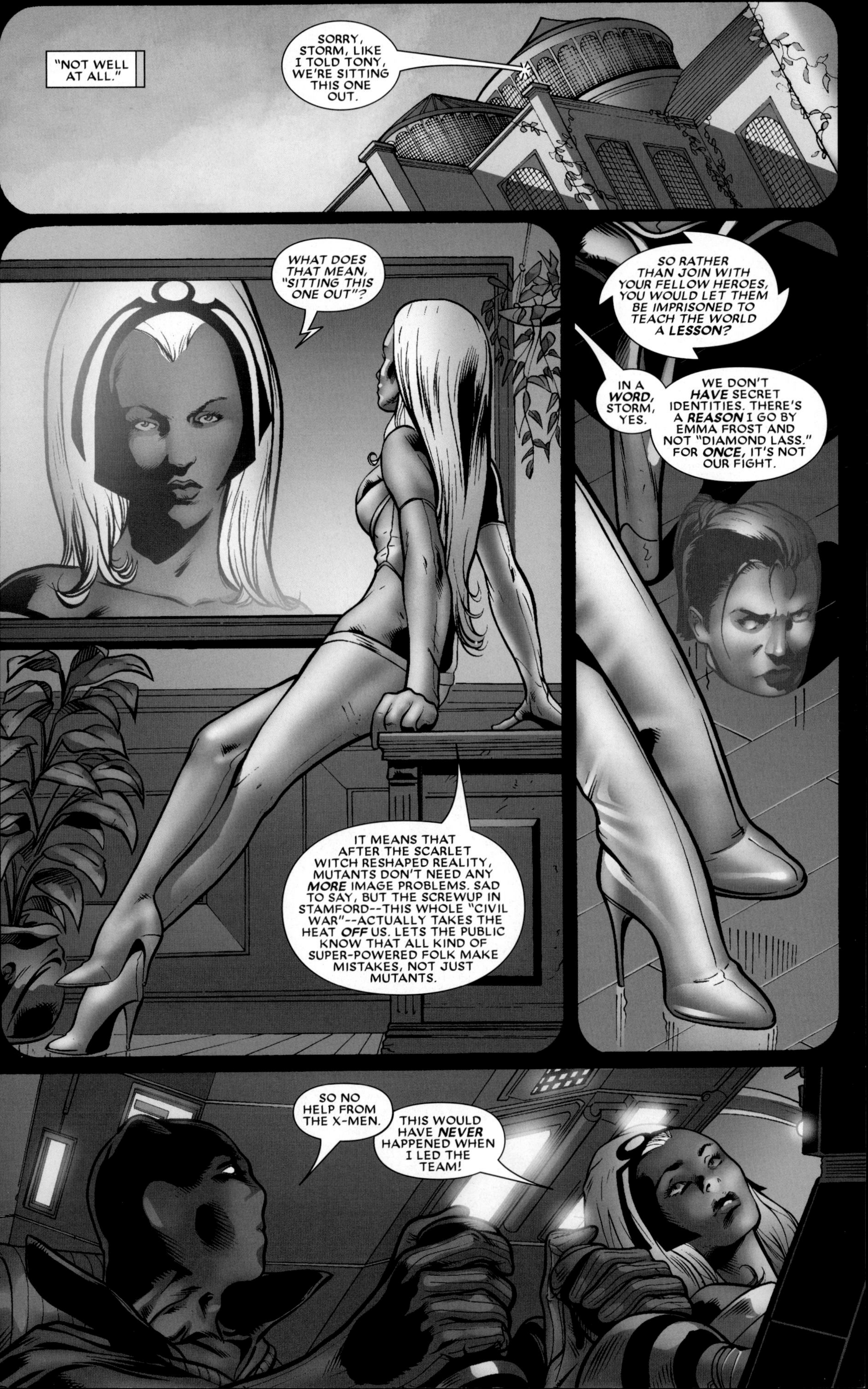

"NOT WELL AT ALL."
SORRY, STORM, LIKE I TOLD TONY, WE'RE SITTING THIS ONE OUT.
WHAT DOES THAT MEAN, "SITTING THIS ONE OUT"?
IT MEANS THAT AFTER THE SCARLET WITCH RESHAPED REALITY, MUTANTS DON'T NEED ANY MORE IMAGE PROBLEMS. SAD TO SAY, BUT THE SCREWUP IN STAMFORD--THIS WHOLE "CIVIL WAR"--ACTUALLY TAKES THE HEAT OFF US. LETS THE PUBLIC KNOW THAT ALL KIND OF SUPER-POWERED FOLK MAKE MISTAKES, NOT JUST MUTANTS.
SO RATHER THAN JOIN WITH YOUR FELLOW HEROES, YOU WOULD LET THEM BE IMPRISONED TO TEACH THE WORLD A LESSON?
IN A WORD, STORM, YES.
WE DON'T HAVE SECRET IDENTITIES. THERE'S A REASON I GO BY EMMA FROST AND NOT "DIAMOND LASS." FOR ONCE, IT'S NOT OUR FIGHT.
SO NO HELP FROM THE X-MEN.
THIS WOULD HAVE NEVER HAPPENED WHEN I LED THE TEAM!

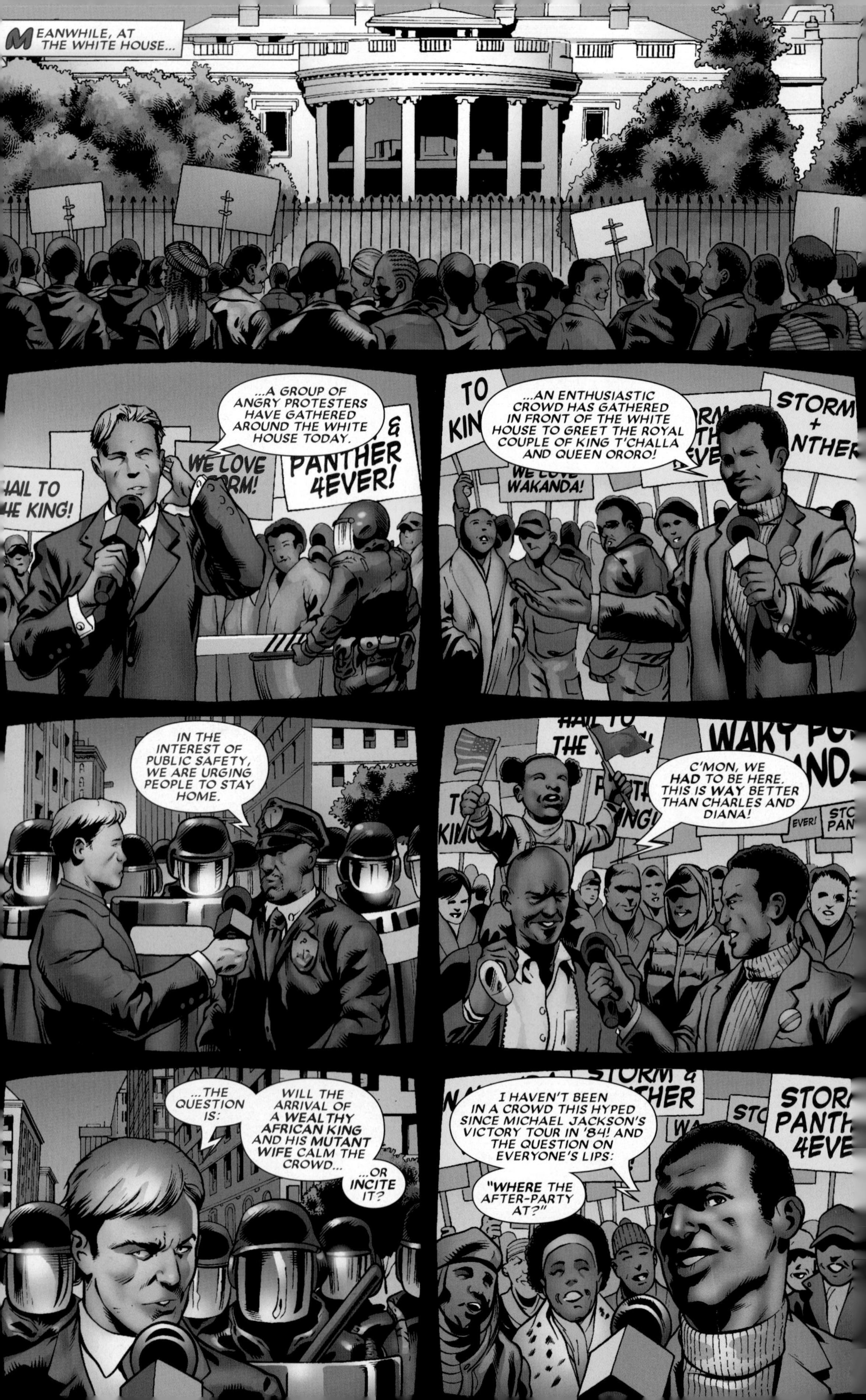
MEANWHILE, AT THE WHITE HOUSE...
...A GROUP OF ANGRY PROTESTERS HAVE GATHERED AROUND THE WHITE HOUSE TODAY.
WE LOVE STORM!
HAIL TO THE KING!
PANTHER 4EVER!
...AN ENTHUSIASTIC CROWD HAS GATHERED IN FRONT OF THE WHITE HOUSE TO GREET THE ROYAL COUPLE OF KING T'CHALLA AND QUEEN ORORO!
WE LOVE WAKANDA!
STORM + PANTHER
IN THE INTEREST OF PUBLIC SAFETY, WE ARE URGING PEOPLE TO STAY HOME.
C'MON, WE HAD TO BE HERE. THIS IS WAY BETTER THAN CHARLES AND DIANA!
...THE QUESTION IS:
WILL THE ARRIVAL OF A WEALTHY AFRICAN KING AND HIS MUTANT WIFE CALM THE CROWD...
...OR INCITE IT?
I HAVEN'T BEEN IN A CROWD THIS HYPED SINCE MICHAEL JACKSON'S VICTORY TOUR IN '84! AND THE QUESTION ON EVERYONE'S LIPS:
"WHERE THE AFTER-PARTY AT?"

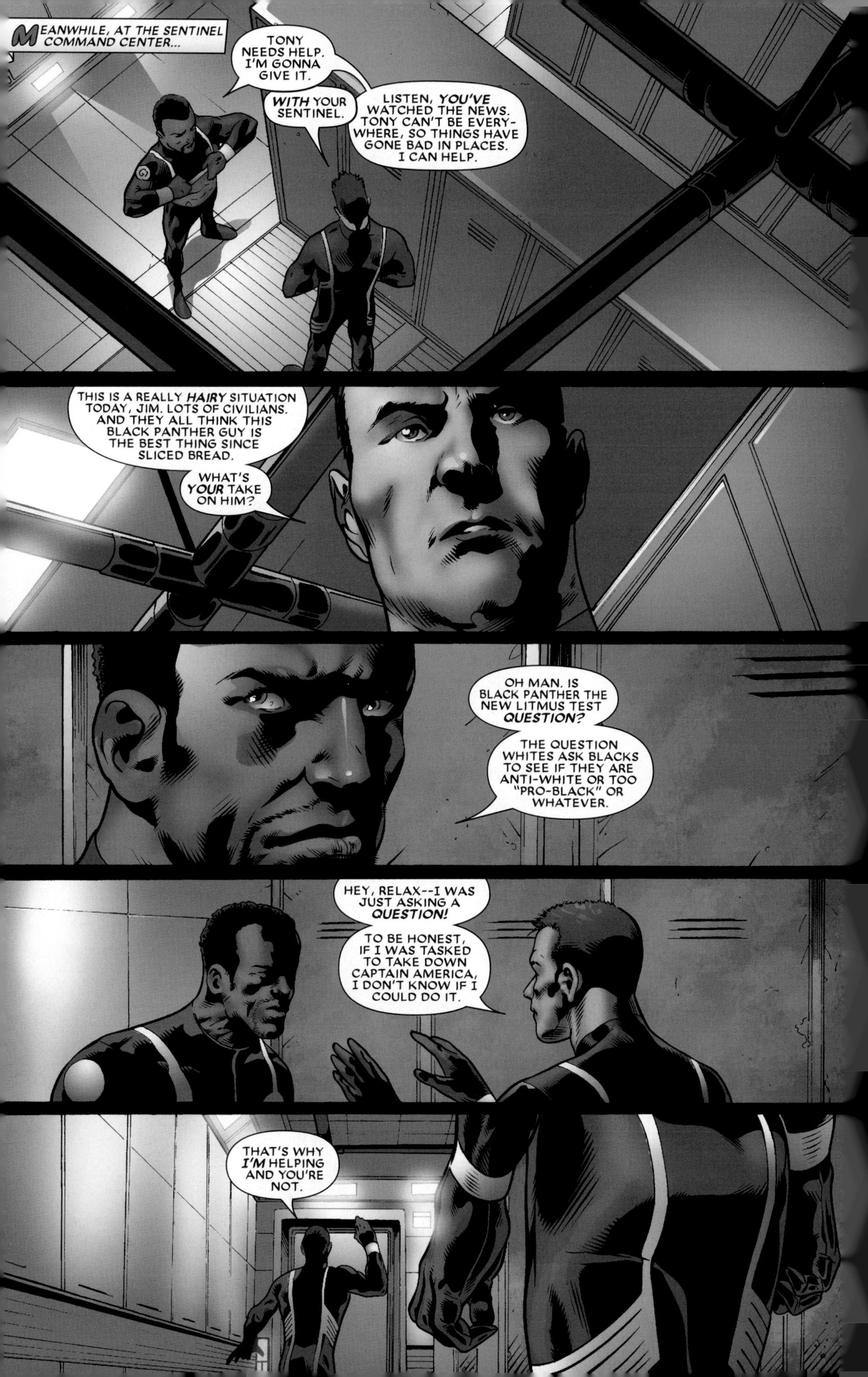
MEANWHILE, AT THE SENTINEL COMMAND CENTER...
TONY NEEDS HELP. I'M GONNA GIVE IT.
WITH YOUR SENTINEL.
LISTEN, YOU'VE WATCHED THE NEWS. TONY CAN'T BE EVERY-WHERE, SO THINGS HAVE GONE BAD IN PLACES. I CAN HELP.
THIS IS A REALLY HAIRY SITUATION TODAY, JIM. LOTS OF CIVILIANS. AND THEY ALL THINK THIS BLACK PANTHER GUY IS THE BEST THING SINCE SLICED BREAD.
WHAT'S YOUR TAKE ON HIM?
OH MAN. IS BLACK PANTHER THE NEW LITMUS TEST QUESTION?
THE QUESTION WHITES ASK BLACKS TO SEE IF THEY ARE ANTI-WHITE OR TOO "PRO-BLACK" OR WHATEVER.
HEY, RELAX--I WAS JUST ASKING A QUESTION!
TO BE HONEST, IF I WAS TASKED TO TAKE DOWN CAPTAIN AMERICA, I DON'T KNOW IF I COULD DO IT.
THAT'S WHY I'M HELPING AND YOU'RE NOT.

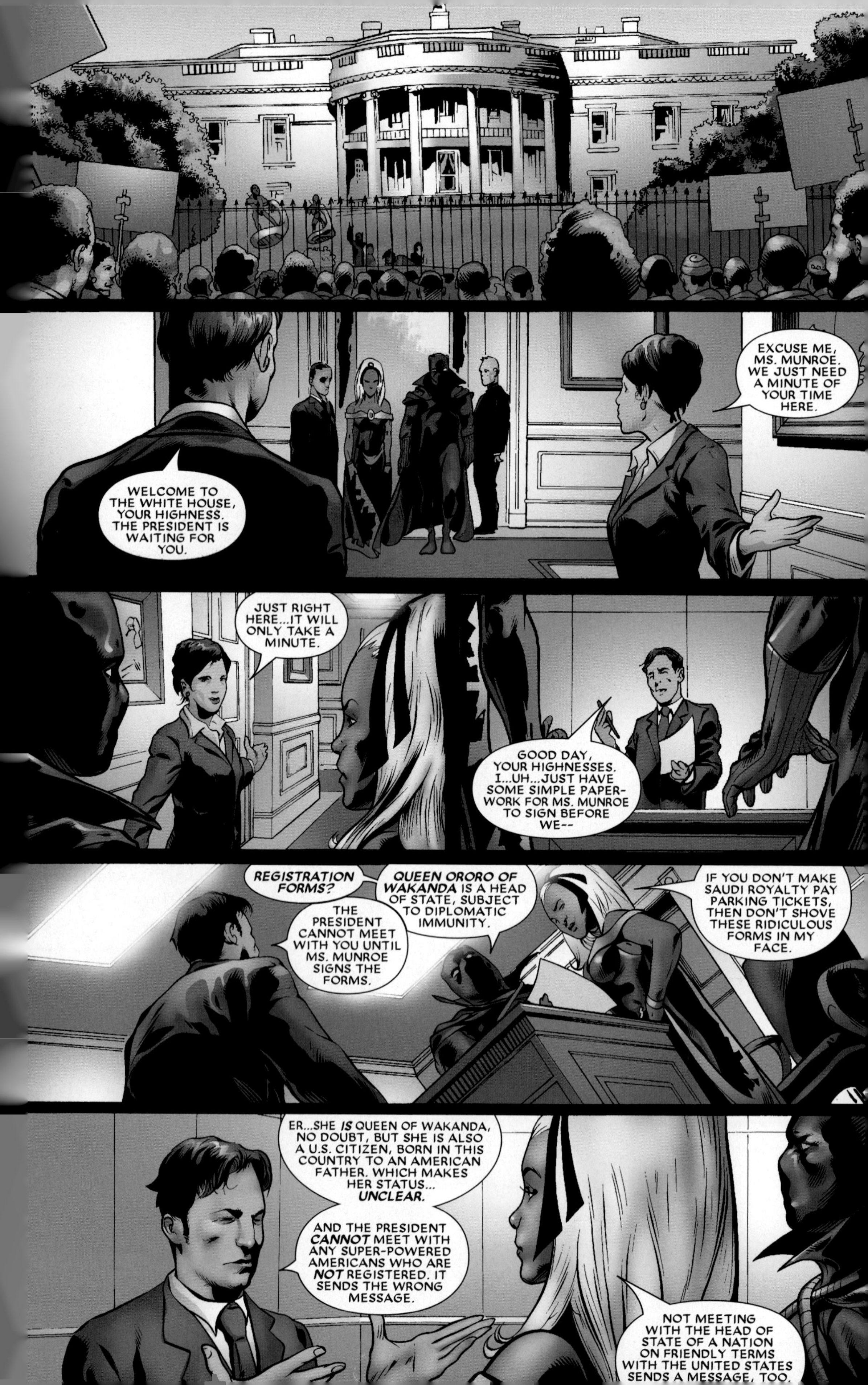

EXCUSE ME, MS. MUNROE. WE JUST NEED A MINUTE OF YOUR TIME HERE.
WELCOME TO THE WHITE HOUSE, YOUR HIGHNESS. THE PRESIDENT IS WAITING FOR YOU.
JUST RIGHT HERE...IT WILL ONLY TAKE A MINUTE.
GOOD DAY, YOUR HIGHNESSES. I...UH...JUST HAVE SOME SIMPLE PAPER-WORK FOR MS. MUNROE TO SIGN BEFORE WE--
REGISTRATION FORMS?
THE PRESIDENT CANNOT MEET WITH YOU UNTIL MS. MUNROE SIGNS THE FORMS.
QUEEN ORORO OF WAKANDA IS A HEAD OF STATE, SUBJECT TO DIPLOMATIC IMMUNITY.
IF YOU DON'T MAKE SAUDI ROYALTY PAY PARKING TICKETS, THEN DON'T SHOVE THESE RIDICULOUS FORMS IN MY FACE.
ER...SHE IS QUEEN OF WAKANDA, NO DOUBT, BUT SHE IS ALSO A U.S. CITIZEN, BORN IN THIS COUNTRY TO AN AMERICAN FATHER. WHICH MAKES HER STATUS... UNCLEAR.
AND THE PRESIDENT CANNOT MEET WITH ANY SUPER-POWERED AMERICANS WHO ARE NOT REGISTERED. IT SENDS THE WRONG MESSAGE.
NOT MEETING WITH THE HEAD OF STATE OF A NATION ON FRIENDLY TERMS WITH THE UNITED STATES SENDS A MESSAGE, TOO.

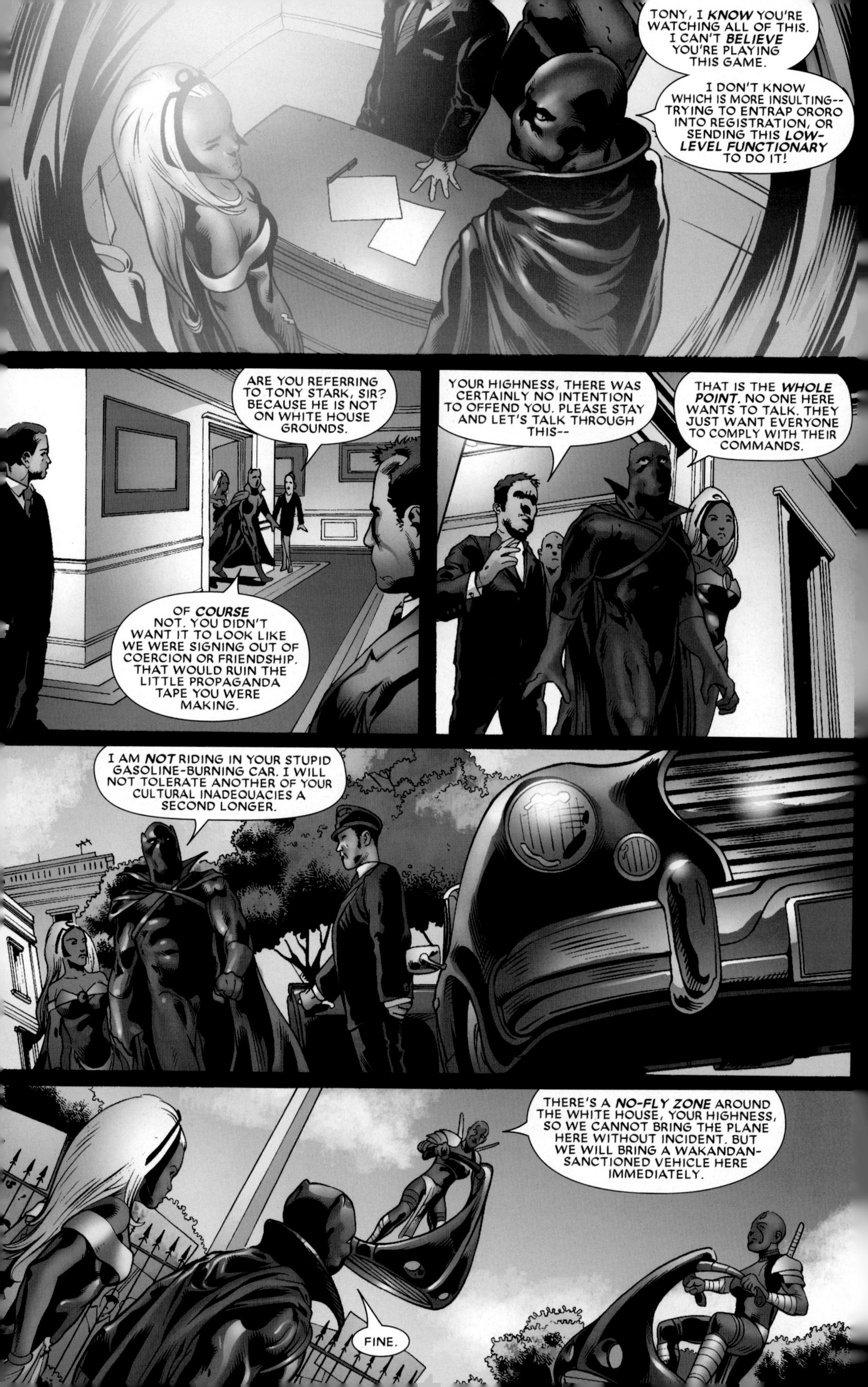

TONY, I KNOW YOU'RE WATCHING ALL OF THIS. I CAN'T BELIEVE YOU'RE PLAYING THIS GAME.
I DON'T KNOW WHICH IS MORE INSULTING-- TRYING TO ENTRAP ORORO INTO REGISTRATION, OR SENDING THIS LOW-LEVEL FUNCTIONARY TO DO IT!
ARE YOU REFERRING TO TONY STARK, SIR? BECAUSE HE IS NOT ON WHITE HOUSE GROUNDS.
OF COURSE NOT. YOU DIDN'T WANT IT TO LOOK LIKE WE WERE SIGNING OUT OF COERCION OR FRIENDSHIP. THAT WOULD RUIN THE LITTLE PROPAGANDA TAPE YOU WERE MAKING.
YOUR HIGHNESS, THERE WAS CERTAINLY NO INTENTION TO OFFEND YOU. PLEASE STAY AND LET'S TALK THROUGH THIS--
THAT IS THE WHOLE POINT. NO ONE HERE WANTS TO TALK. THEY JUST WANT EVERYONE TO COMPLY WITH THEIR COMMANDS.
I AM NOT RIDING IN YOUR STUPID GASOLINE-BURNING CAR. I WILL NOT TOLERATE ANOTHER OF YOUR CULTURAL INADEQUACIES A SECOND LONGER.
THERE'S A NO-FLY ZONE AROUND THE WHITE HOUSE, YOUR HIGHNESS, SO WE CANNOT BRING THE PLANE HERE WITHOUT INCIDENT. BUT WE WILL BRING A WAKANDAN-SANCTIONED VEHICLE HERE IMMEDIATELY.
FINE.

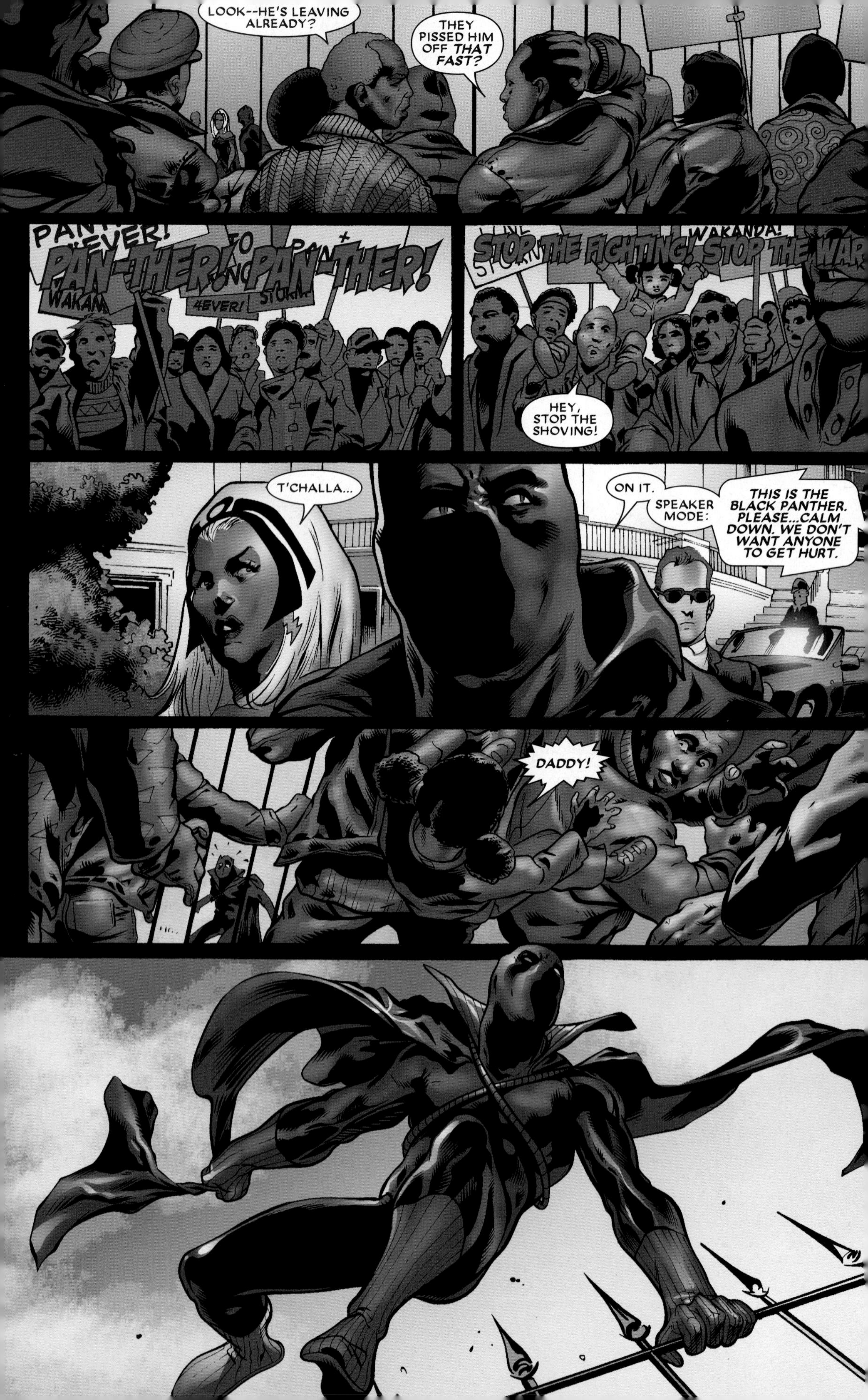
LOOK--HE'S LEAVING ALREADY?
THEY PISSED HIM OFF THAT FAST?
PAN-THER! PAN-THER!
4EVER!
STOP THE FIGHTING! STOP THE WAR
WAKANDA!
HEY, STOP THE SHOVING!
T'CHALLA...
ON IT.
SPEAKER MODE:
THIS IS THE BLACK PANTHER. PLEASE...CALM DOWN. WE DON'T WANT ANYONE TO GET HURT.
DADDY!

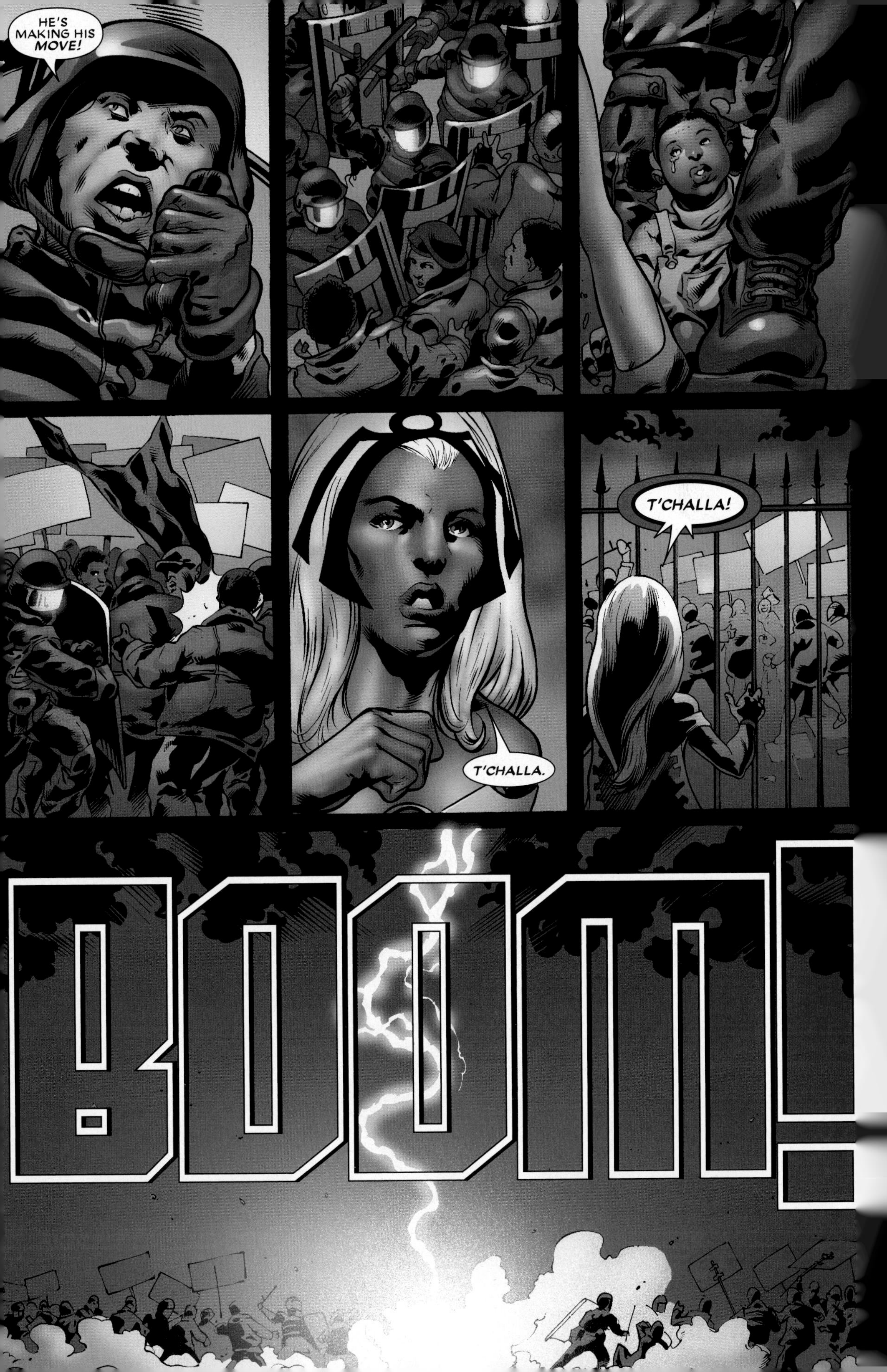
HE'S MAKING HIS MOVE!
T'CHALLA.
T'CHALLA!
BOOM!

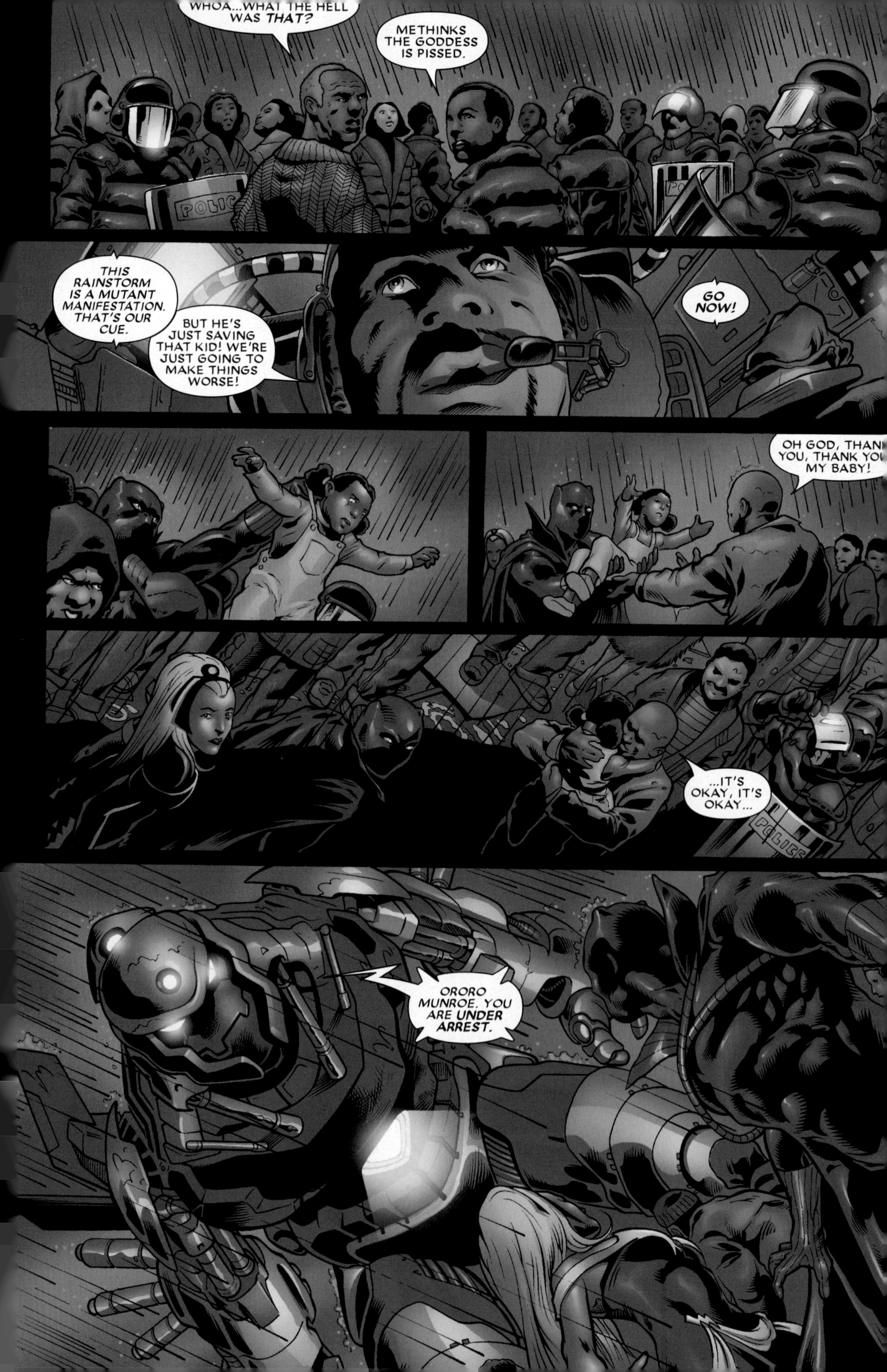
WHOA...WHAT THE HELL WAS THAT?
METHINKS THE GODDESS IS PISSED.
THIS RAINSTORM IS A MUTANT MANIFESTATION. THAT'S OUR CUE.
BUT HE'S JUST SAVING THAT KID! WE'RE JUST GOING TO MAKE THINGS WORSE!
GO NOW!
OH GOD, THAN YOU, THANK YO MY BABY!
...IT'S OKAY, IT'S OKAY...
ORORO MUNROE. YOU ARE UNDER ARREST.

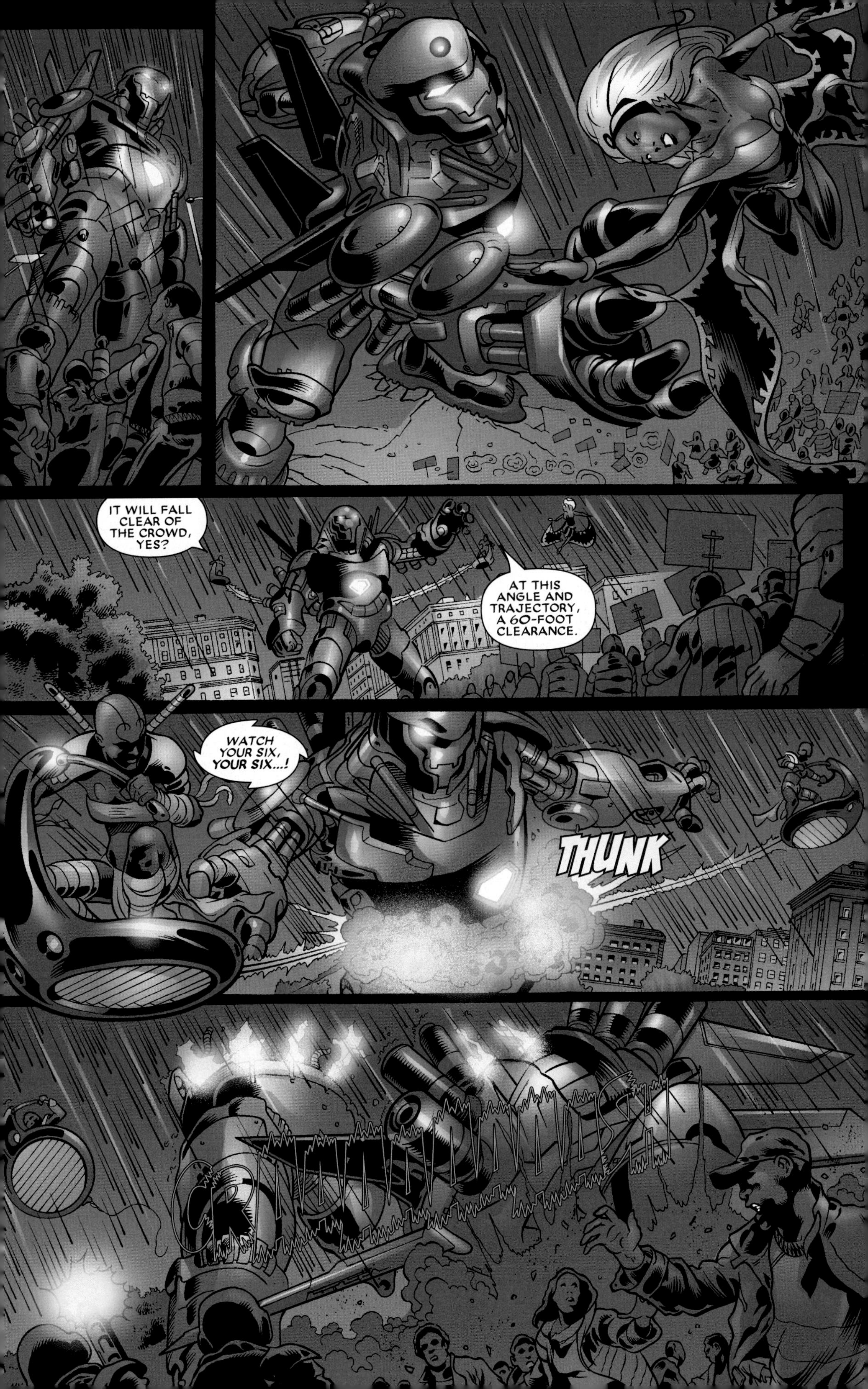
IT WILL FALL CLEAR OF THE CROWD, YES?
AT THIS ANGLE AND TRAJECTORY, A 60-FOOT CLEARANCE.
WATCH YOUR SIX, YOUR SIX...!
THUNK

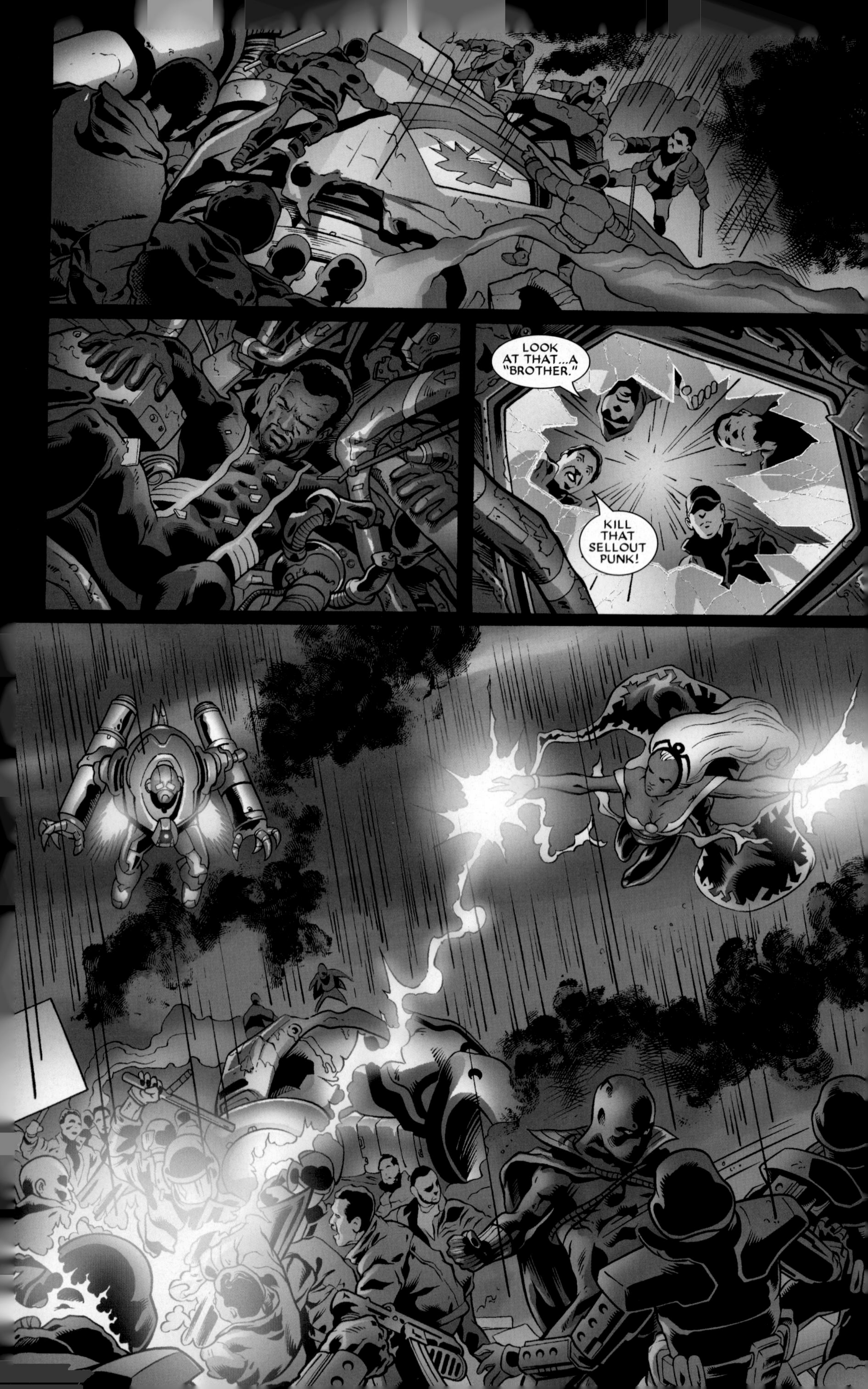
LOOK AT THAT...A "BROTHER."
KILL THAT SELLOUT PUNK!

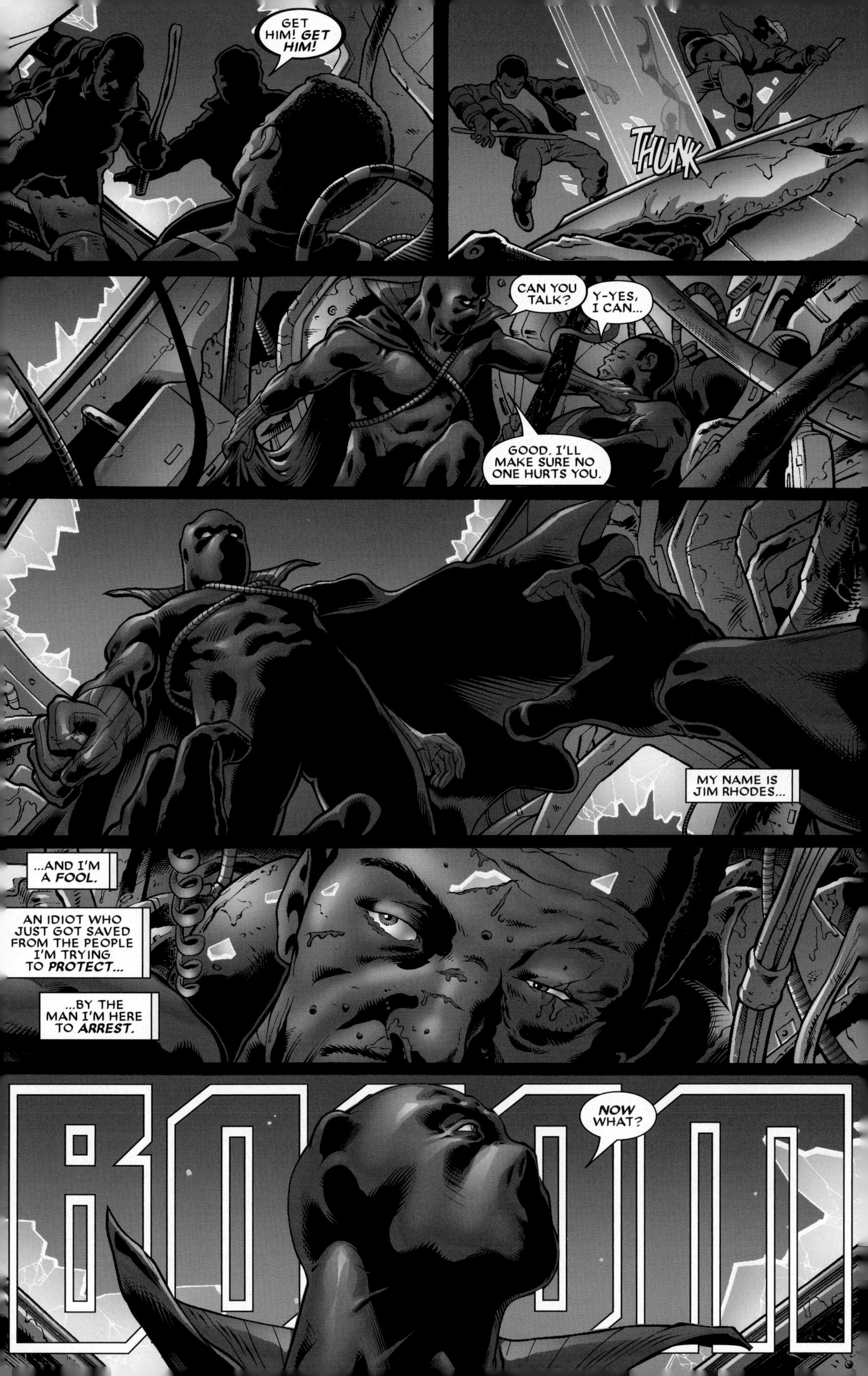

GET HIM! GET HIM!
THUNK
CAN YOU TALK?
Y-YES, I CAN...
GOOD. I'LL MAKE SURE NO ONE HURTS YOU.
MY NAME IS JIM RHODES...
...AND I'M A FOOL.
AN IDIOT WHO JUST GOT SAVED FROM THE PEOPLE I'M TRYING TO PROTECT...
...BY THE MAN I'M HERE TO ARREST.
NOW WHAT?

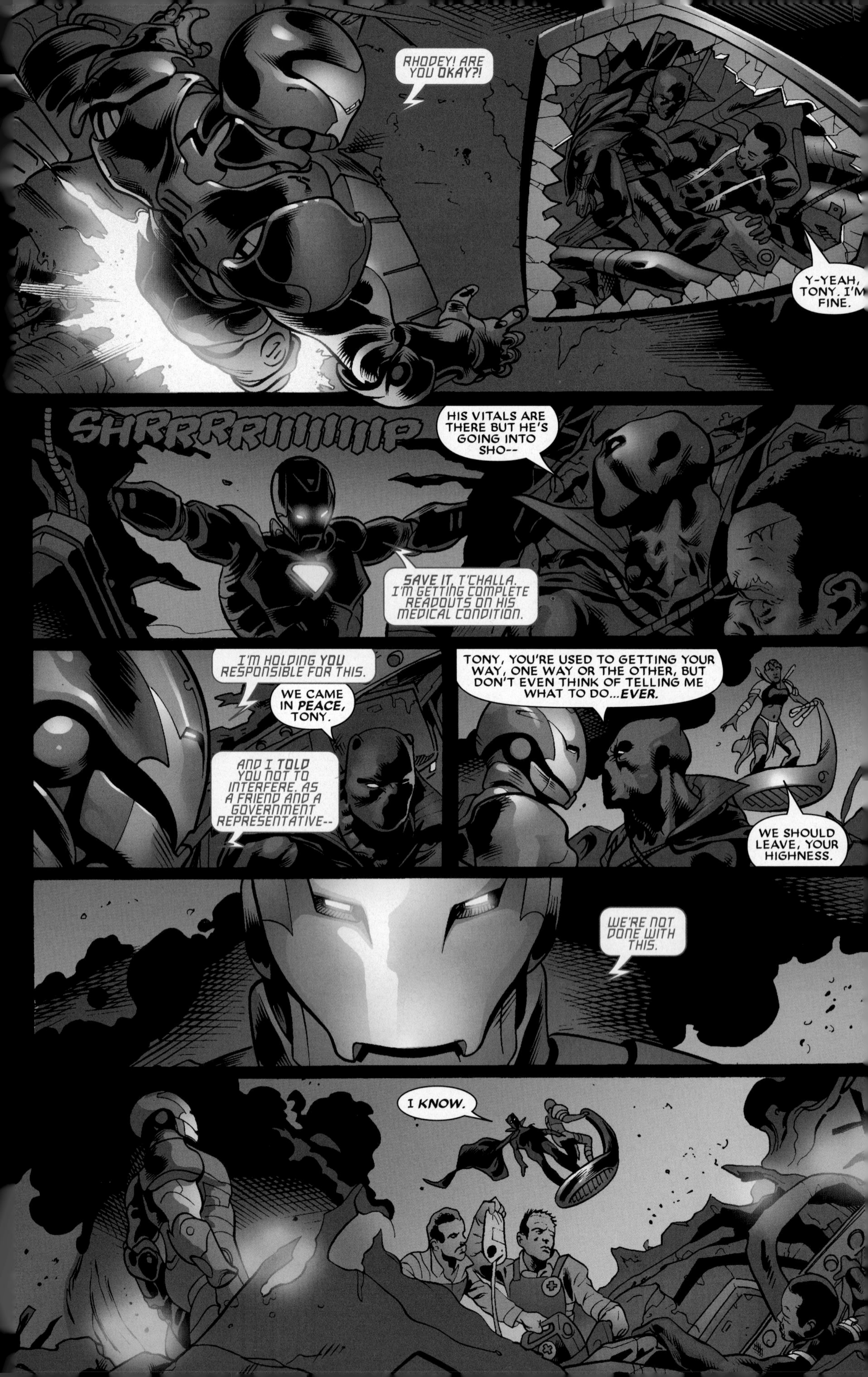
RHODEY! ARE YOU OKAY?!
Y-YEAH, TONY. I'M FINE.
SHRRRRIIIIIIIP
HIS VITALS ARE THERE BUT HE'S GOING INTO SHO--
SAVE IT, T'CHALLA. I'M GETTING COMPLETE READOUTS ON HIS MEDICAL CONDITION.
I'M HOLDING YOU RESPONSIBLE FOR THIS.
WE CAME IN PEACE, TONY.
AND I TOLD YOU NOT TO INTERFERE. AS A FRIEND AND A GOVERNMENT REPRESENTATIVE--
TONY, YOU'RE USED TO GETTING YOUR WAY, ONE WAY OR THE OTHER, BUT DON'T EVEN THINK OF TELLING ME WHAT TO DO...EVER.
WE SHOULD LEAVE, YOUR HIGHNESS.
WE'RE NOT DONE WITH THIS.
I KNOW.

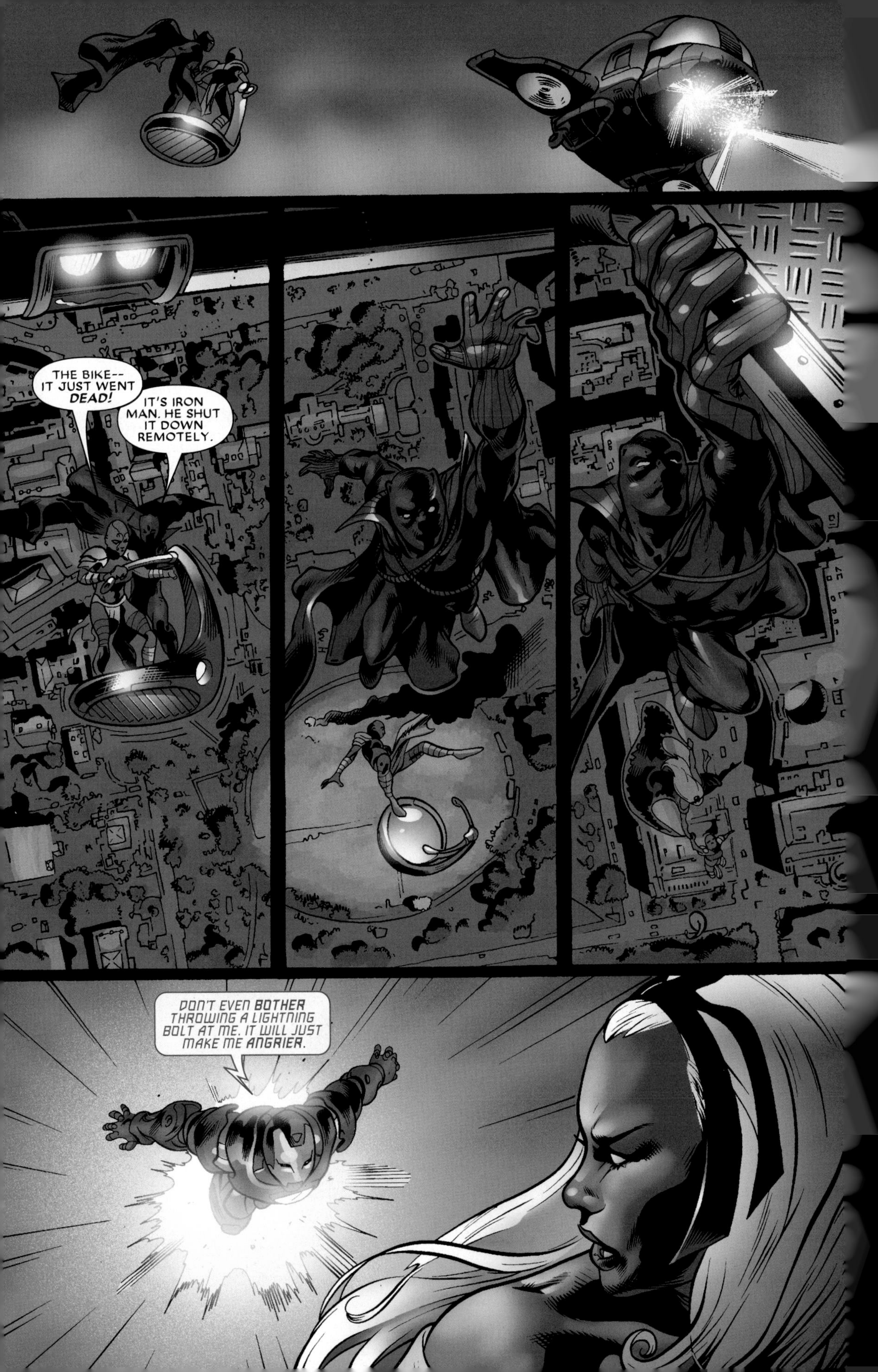
THE BIKE-- IT JUST WENT DEAD!
IT'S IRON MAN. HE SHUT IT DOWN REMOTELY.
DON'T EVEN BOTHER THROWING A LIGHTNING BOLT AT ME. IT WILL JUST MAKE ME ANGRIER.

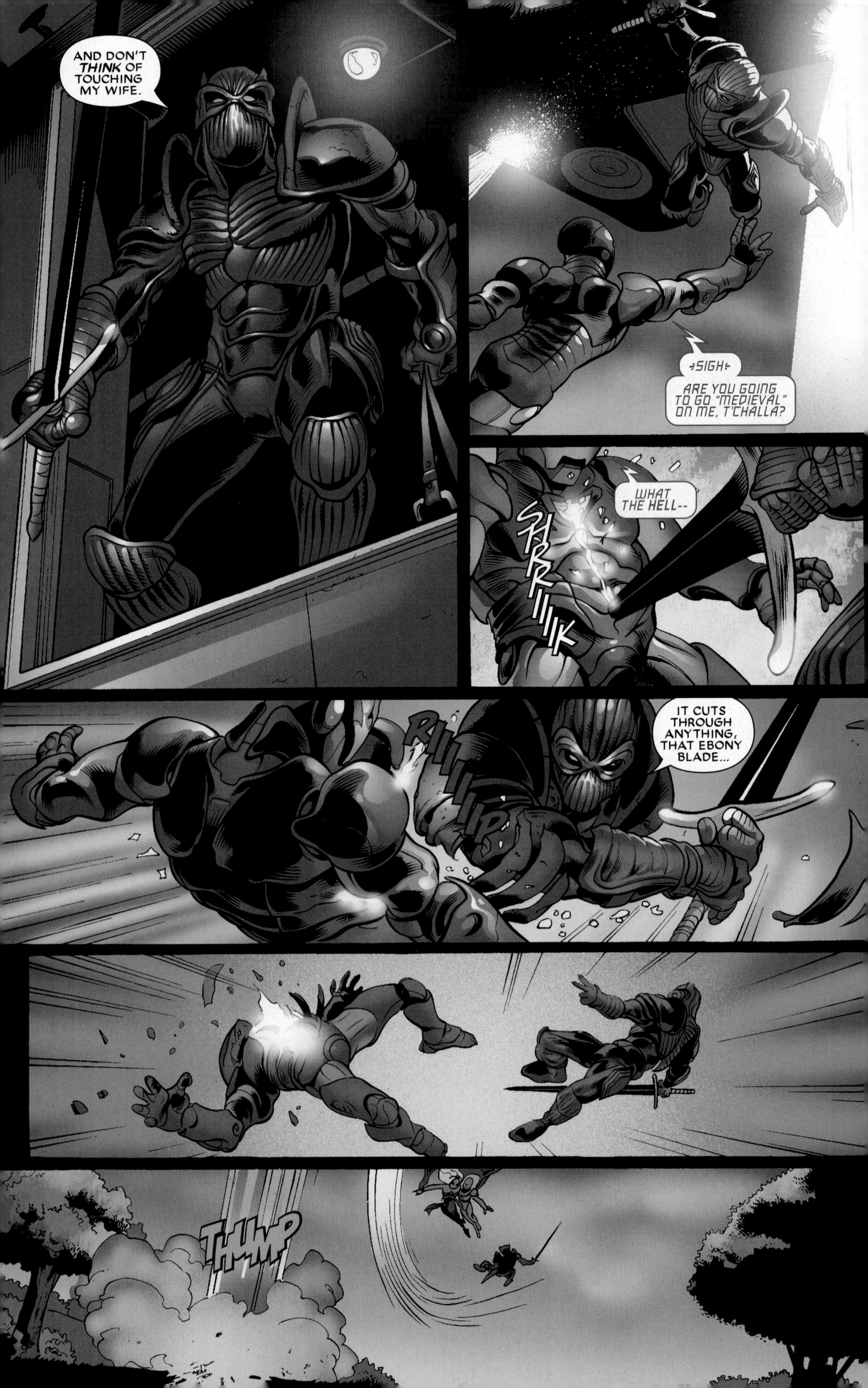
AND DON'T THINK OF TOUCHING MY WIFE.
⊰SIGH⊱
ARE YOU GOING TO GO "MEDIEVAL" ON ME, T'CHALLA?
WHAT THE HELL--
SHRRIIIIIK
IT CUTS THROUGH ANYTHING, THAT EBONY BLADE...
RIIIIIIP
THUMP

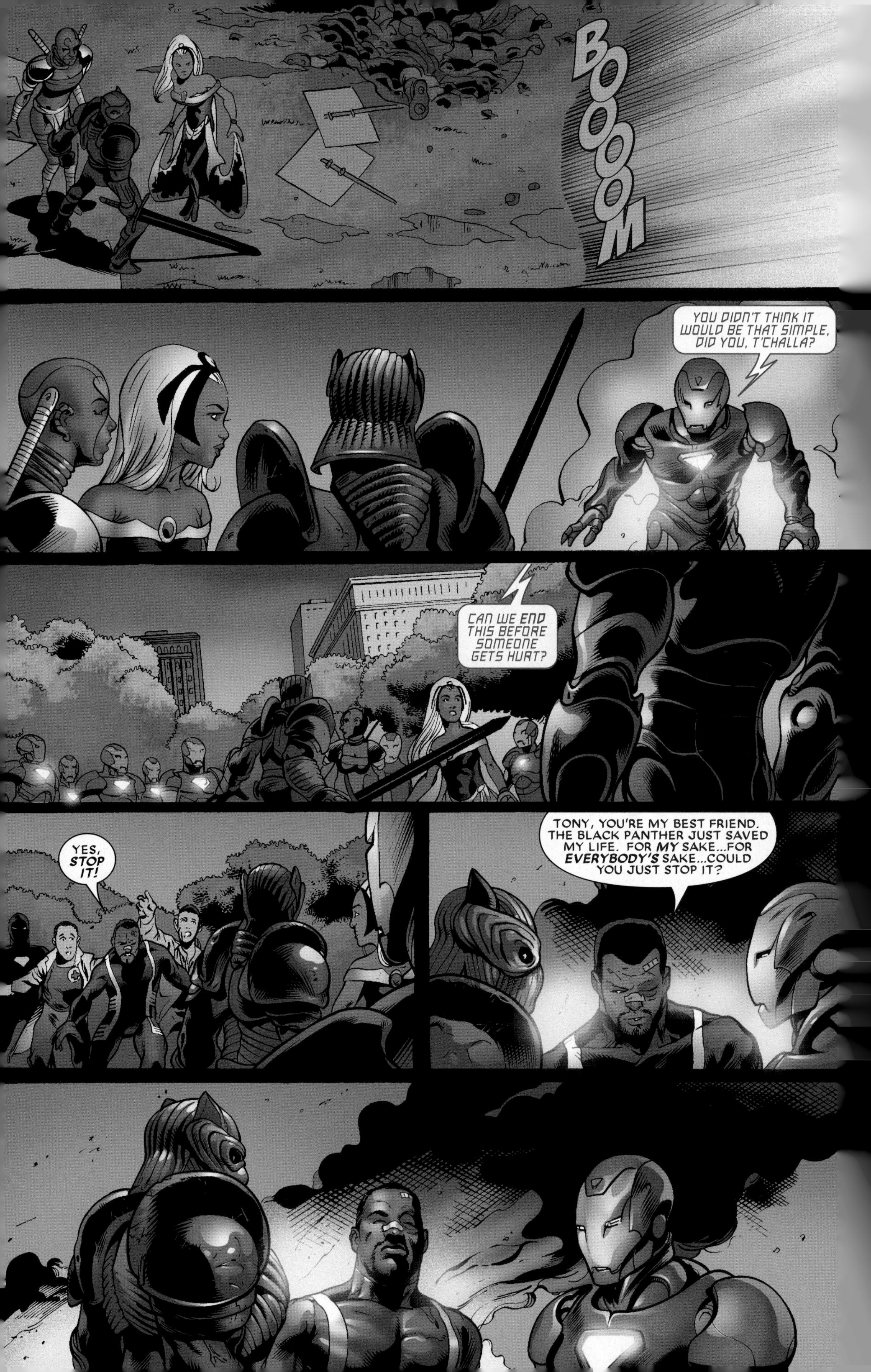
BOOOOM
YOU DIDN'T THINK IT WOULD BE THAT SIMPLE, DID YOU, T'CHALLA?
CAN WE END THIS BEFORE SOMEONE GETS HURT?
YES, STOP IT!
TONY, YOU'RE MY BEST FRIEND. THE BLACK PANTHER JUST SAVED MY LIFE. FOR MY SAKE...FOR EVERYBODY'S SAKE...COULD YOU JUST STOP IT?

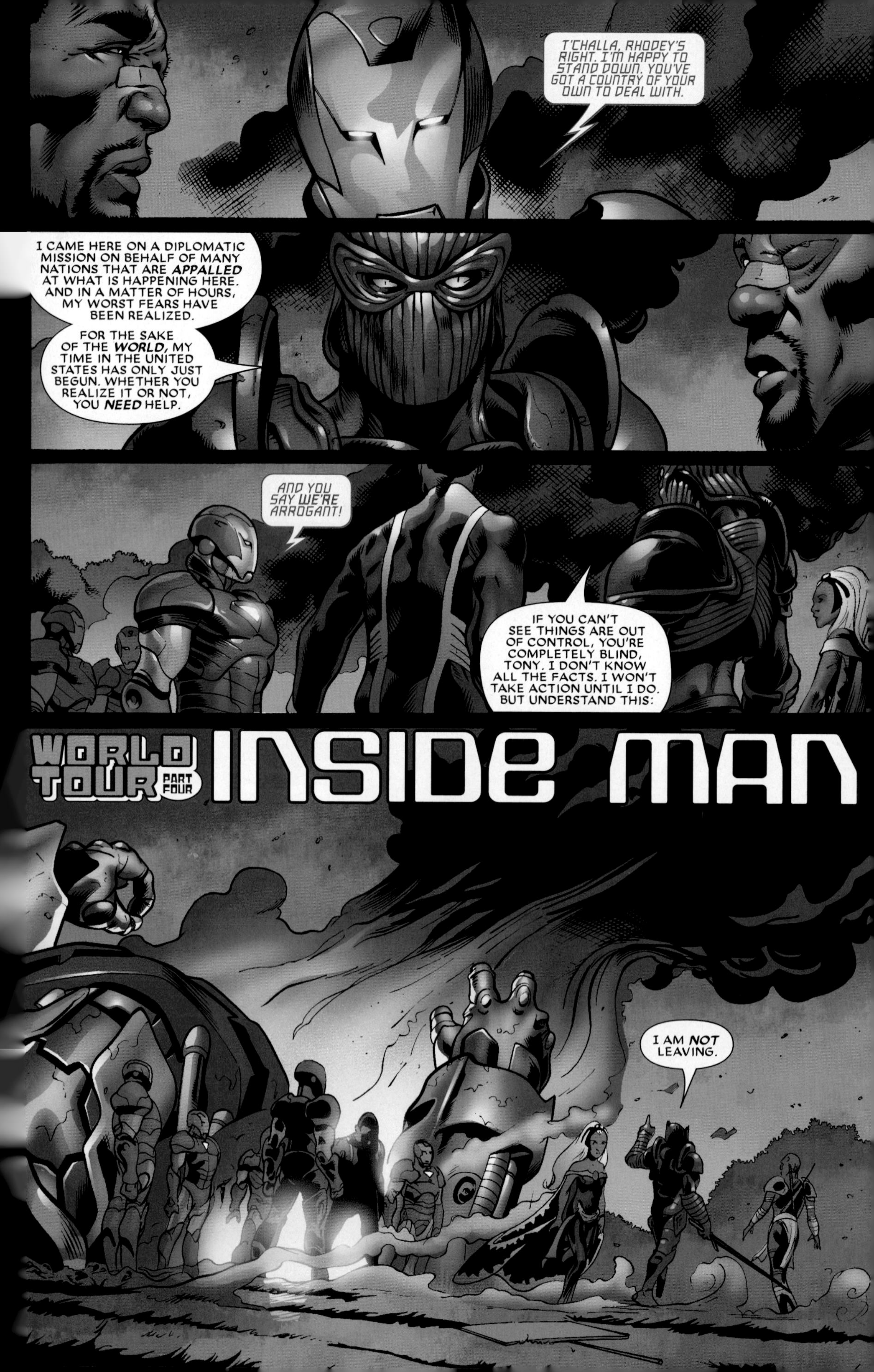
T'CHALLA, RHODEY'S RIGHT. I'M HAPPY TO STAND DOWN. YOU'VE GOT A COUNTRY OF YOUR OWN TO DEAL WITH.
I CAME HERE ON A DIPLOMATIC MISSION ON BEHALF OF MANY NATIONS THAT ARE APPALLED AT WHAT IS HAPPENING HERE. AND IN A MATTER OF HOURS, MY WORST FEARS HAVE BEEN REALIZED.
FOR THE SAKE OF THE WORLD, MY TIME IN THE UNITED STATES HAS ONLY JUST BEGUN. WHETHER YOU REALIZE IT OR NOT, YOU NEED HELP.
AND YOU SAY WE'RE ARROGANT!
IF YOU CAN'T SEE THINGS ARE OUT OF CONTROL, YOU'RE COMPLETELY BLIND, TONY. I DON'T KNOW ALL THE FACTS. I WON'T TAKE ACTION UNTIL I DO. BUT UNDERSTAND THIS:
WORLD TOUR PART FOUR
INSIDE MAN
I AM NOT LEAVING.

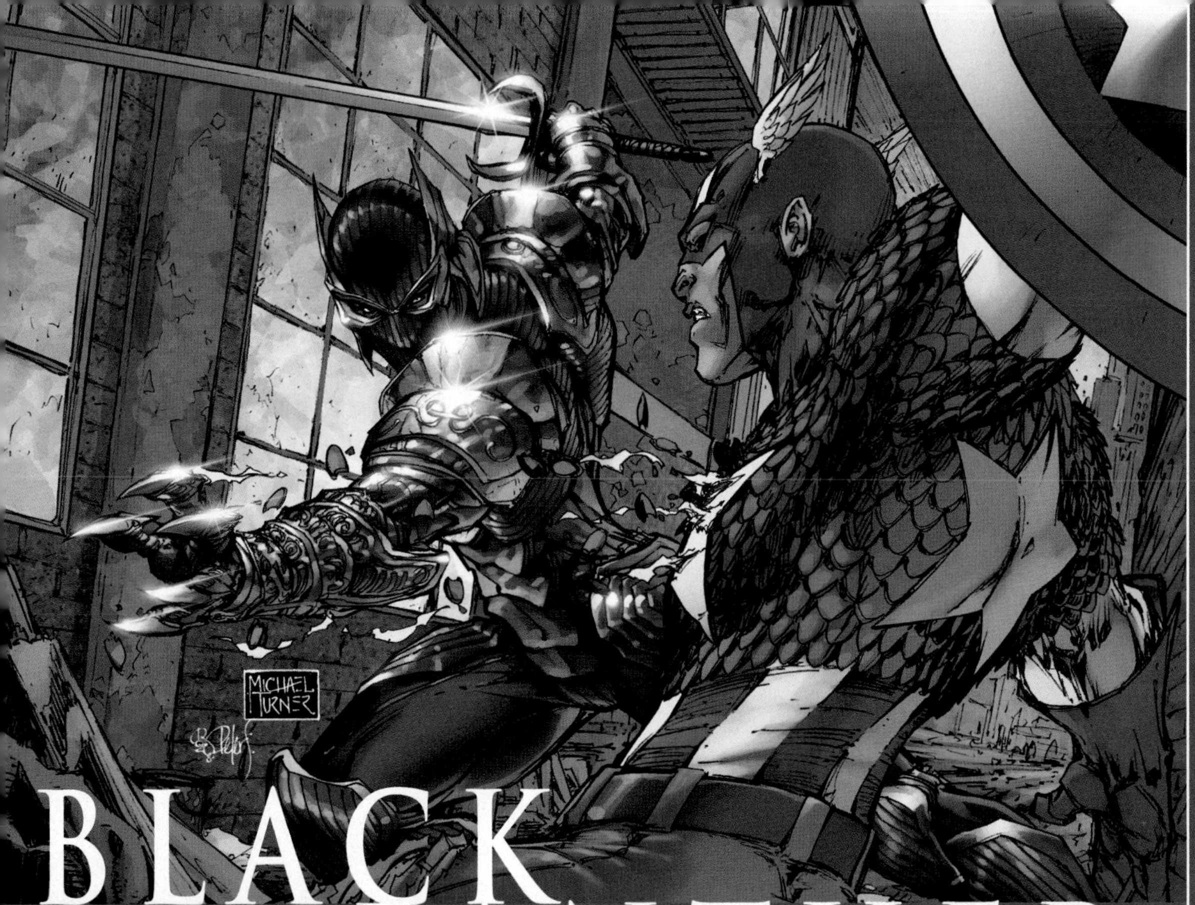
MICHAEL TURNER

BLACK PANTHER

A MARVEL COMICS EVENT

CIVIL WAR

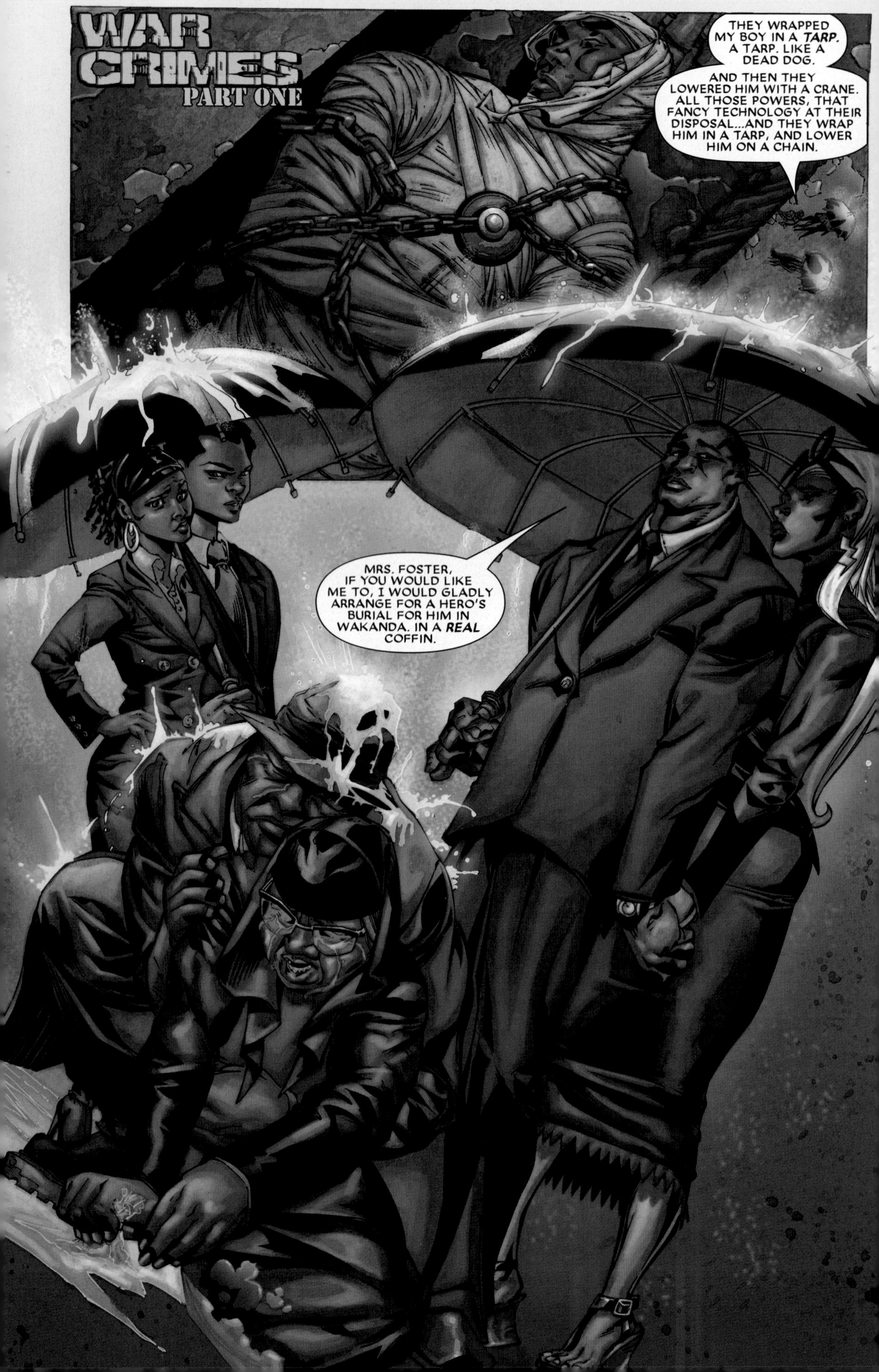
WAR CRIMES
PART ONE
THEY WRAPPED MY BOY IN A *TARP.* A TARP. LIKE A DEAD DOG.
AND THEN THEY LOWERED HIM WITH A CRANE. ALL THOSE POWERS, THAT FANCY TECHNOLOGY AT THEIR DISPOSAL...AND THEY WRAP HIM IN A TARP, AND LOWER HIM ON A CHAIN.
MRS. FOSTER, IF YOU WOULD LIKE ME TO, I WOULD GLADLY ARRANGE FOR A HERO'S BURIAL FOR HIM IN WAKANDA. IN A *REAL* COFFIN.

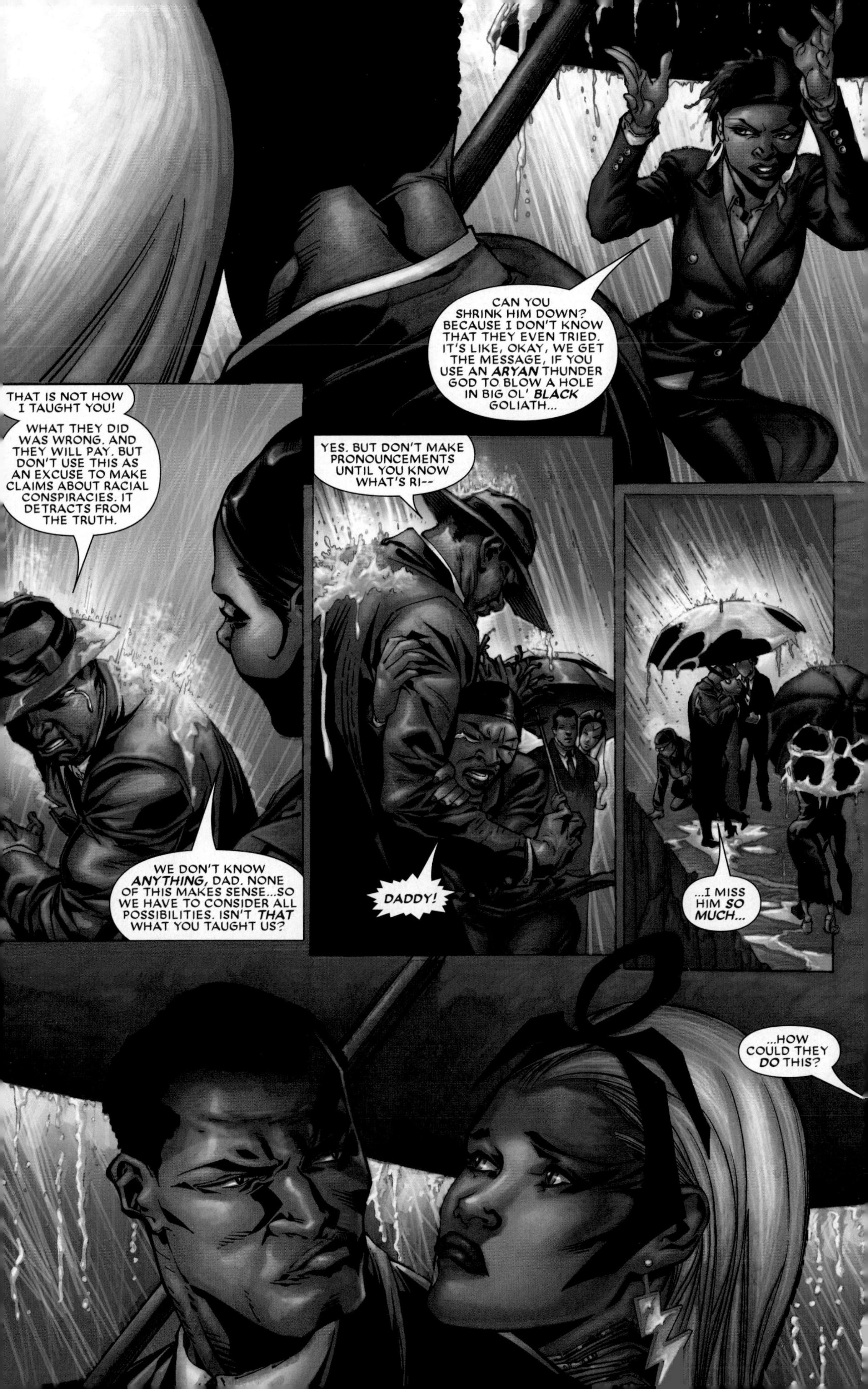
CAN YOU SHRINK HIM DOWN? BECAUSE I DON'T KNOW THAT THEY EVEN TRIED. IT'S LIKE, OKAY, WE GET THE MESSAGE, IF YOU USE AN ARYAN THUNDER GOD TO BLOW A HOLE IN BIG OL' BLACK GOLIATH...
THAT IS NOT HOW I TAUGHT YOU!
WHAT THEY DID WAS WRONG. AND THEY WILL PAY. BUT DON'T USE THIS AS AN EXCUSE TO MAKE CLAIMS ABOUT RACIAL CONSPIRACIES. IT DETRACTS FROM THE TRUTH.
WE DON'T KNOW ANYTHING, DAD. NONE OF THIS MAKES SENSE...SO WE HAVE TO CONSIDER ALL POSSIBILITIES. ISN'T THAT WHAT YOU TAUGHT US?
YES. BUT DON'T MAKE PRONOUNCEMENTS UNTIL YOU KNOW WHAT'S RI--
DADDY!
...I MISS HIM SO MUCH...
...HOW COULD THEY DO THIS?

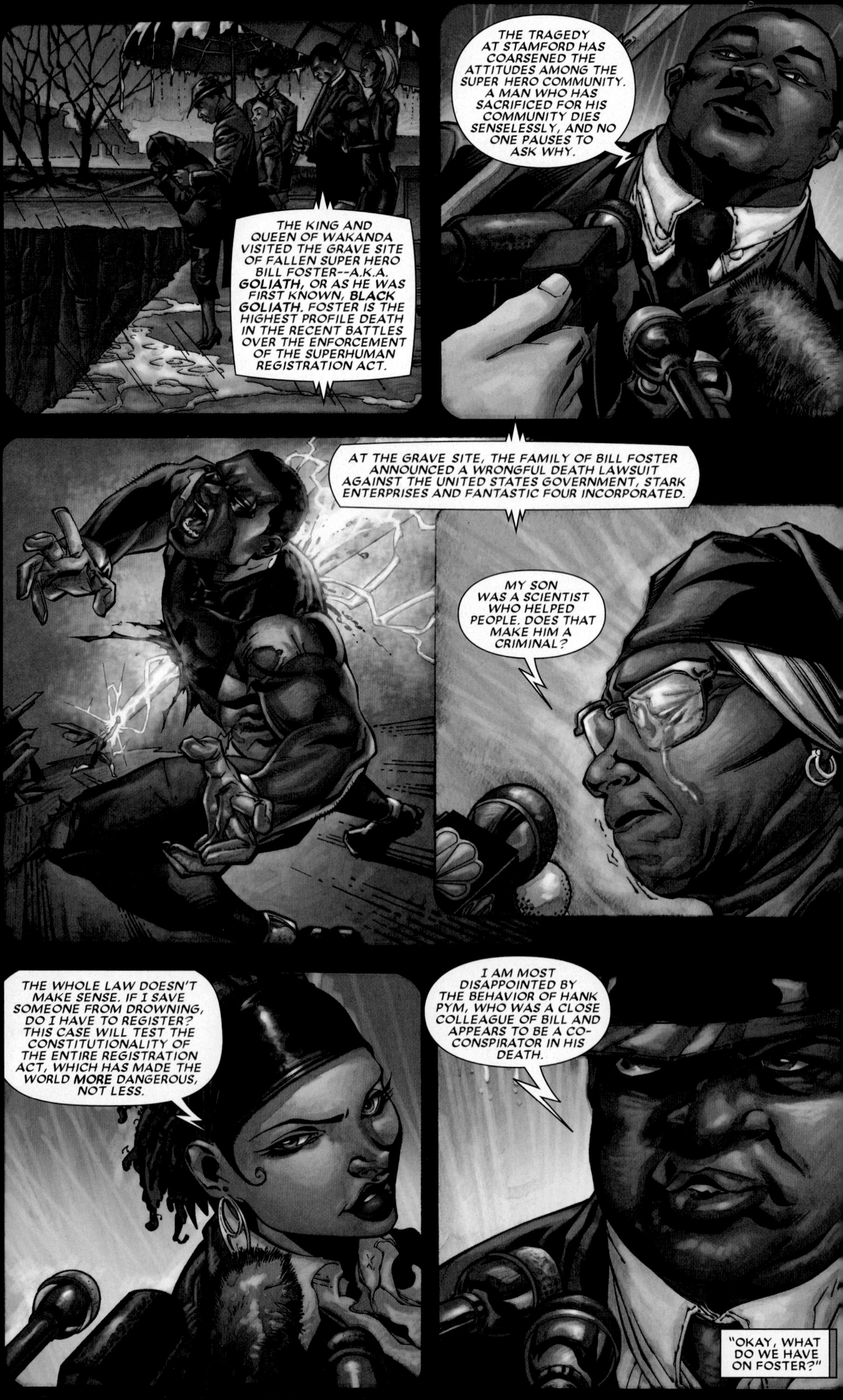
THE KING AND QUEEN OF WAKANDA VISITED THE GRAVE SITE OF FALLEN SUPER HERO BILL FOSTER--A.K.A. GOLIATH, OR AS HE WAS FIRST KNOWN, BLACK GOLIATH. FOSTER IS THE HIGHEST PROFILE DEATH IN THE RECENT BATTLES OVER THE ENFORCEMENT OF THE SUPERHUMAN REGISTRATION ACT.
THE TRAGEDY AT STAMFORD HAS COARSENED THE ATTITUDES AMONG THE SUPER HERO COMMUNITY. A MAN WHO HAS SACRIFICED FOR HIS COMMUNITY DIES SENSELESSLY, AND NO ONE PAUSES TO ASK WHY.
AT THE GRAVE SITE, THE FAMILY OF BILL FOSTER ANNOUNCED A WRONGFUL DEATH LAWSUIT AGAINST THE UNITED STATES GOVERNMENT, STARK ENTERPRISES AND FANTASTIC FOUR INCORPORATED.
MY SON WAS A SCIENTIST WHO HELPED PEOPLE. DOES THAT MAKE HIM A CRIMINAL?
THE WHOLE LAW DOESN'T MAKE SENSE. IF I SAVE SOMEONE FROM DROWNING, DO I HAVE TO REGISTER? THIS CASE WILL TEST THE CONSTITUTIONALITY OF THE ENTIRE REGISTRATION ACT, WHICH HAS MADE THE WORLD MORE DANGEROUS, NOT LESS.
I AM MOST DISAPPOINTED BY THE BEHAVIOR OF HANK PYM, WHO WAS A CLOSE COLLEAGUE OF BILL AND APPEARS TO BE A CO-CONSPIRATOR IN HIS DEATH.
"OKAY, WHAT DO WE HAVE ON FOSTER?"

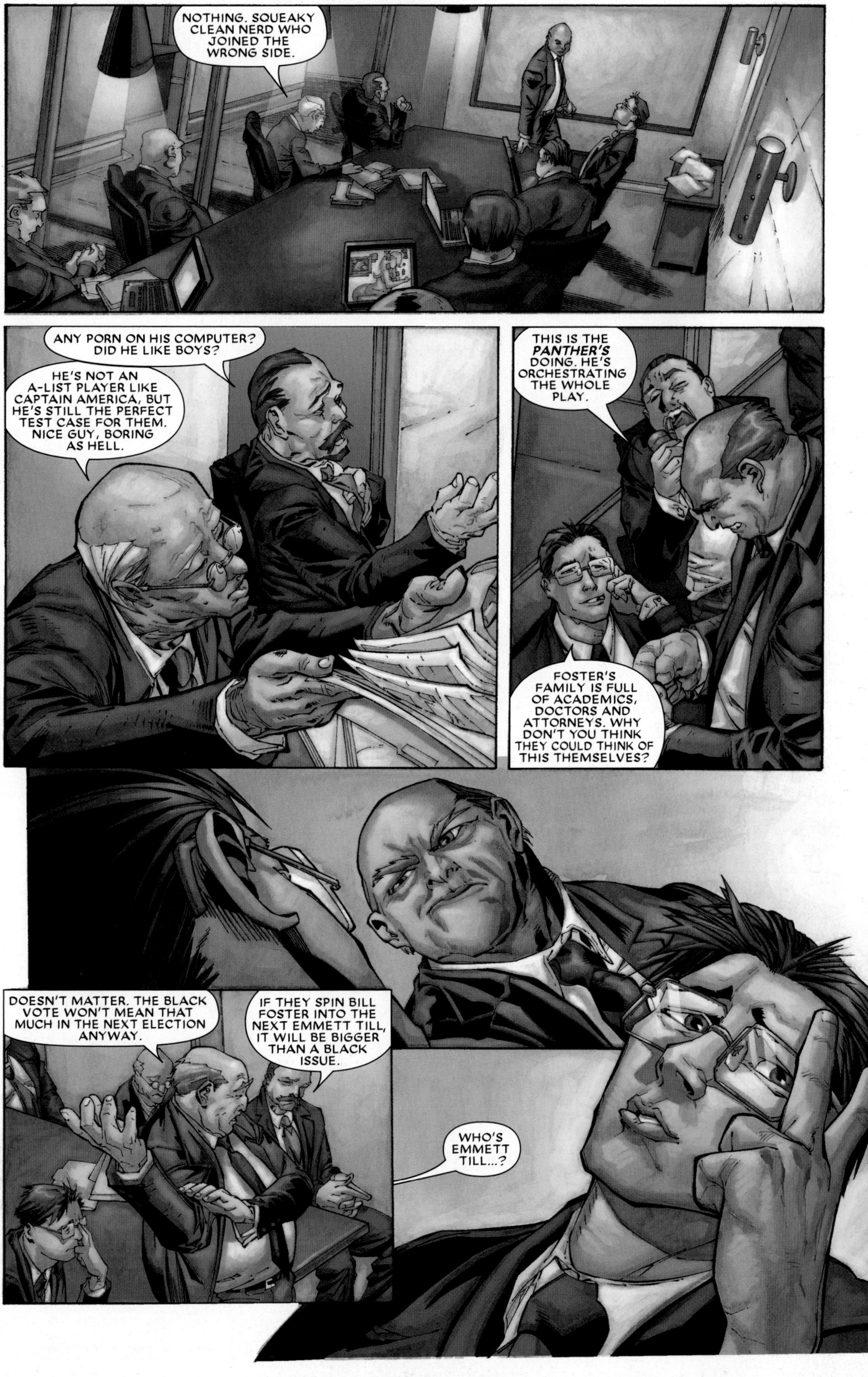
NOTHING. SQUEAKY CLEAN NERD WHO JOINED THE WRONG SIDE.
ANY PORN ON HIS COMPUTER? DID HE LIKE BOYS?
HE'S NOT AN A-LIST PLAYER LIKE CAPTAIN AMERICA, BUT HE'S STILL THE PERFECT TEST CASE FOR THEM. NICE GUY, BORING AS HELL.
THIS IS THE PANTHER'S DOING. HE'S ORCHESTRATING THE WHOLE PLAY.
FOSTER'S FAMILY IS FULL OF ACADEMICS, DOCTORS AND ATTORNEYS. WHY DON'T YOU THINK THEY COULD THINK OF THIS THEMSELVES?
DOESN'T MATTER. THE BLACK VOTE WON'T MEAN THAT MUCH IN THE NEXT ELECTION ANYWAY.
IF THEY SPIN BILL FOSTER INTO THE NEXT EMMETT TILL, IT WILL BE BIGGER THAN A BLACK ISSUE.
WHO'S EMMETT TILL...?

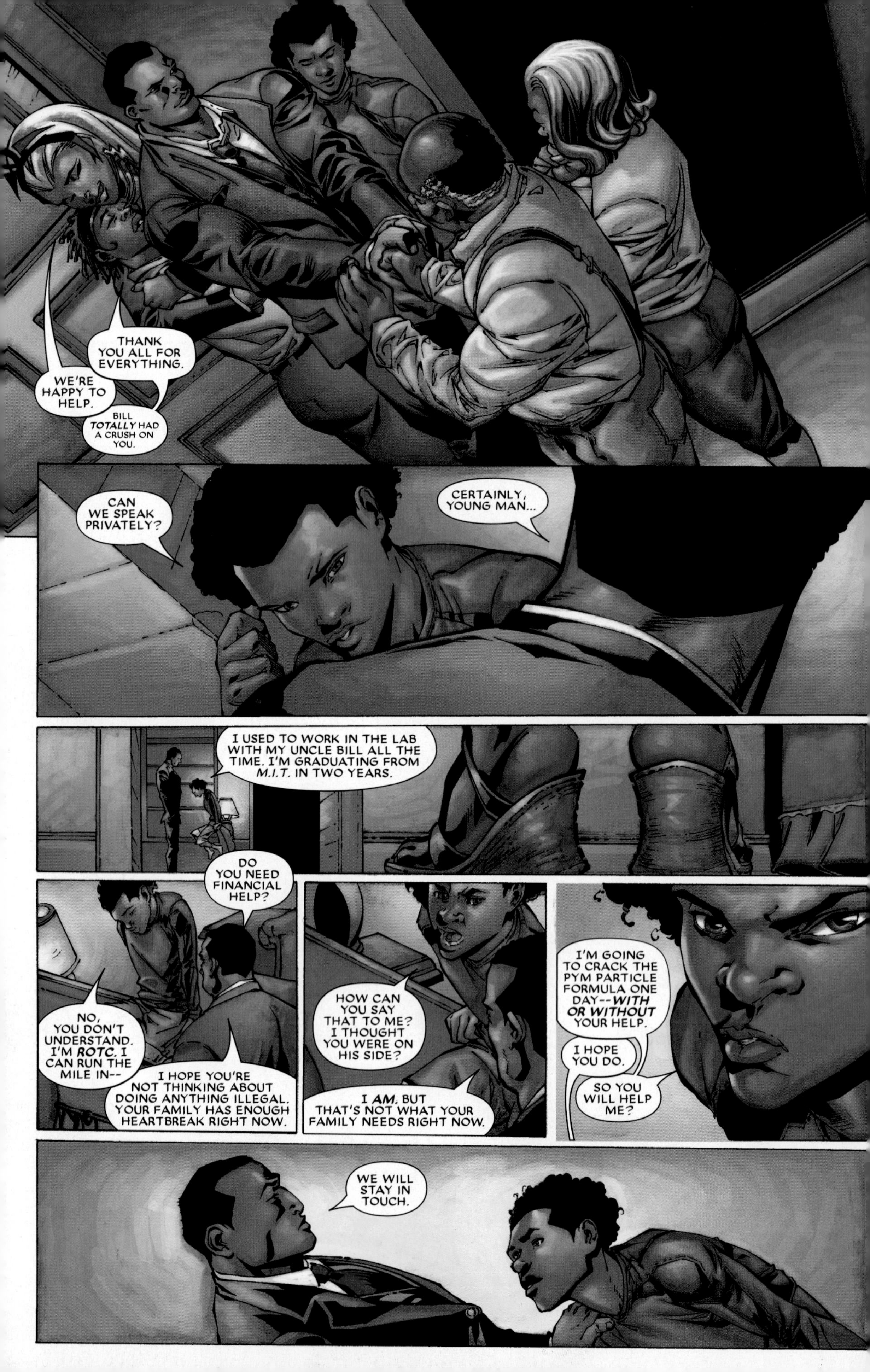
THANK YOU ALL FOR EVERYTHING.
WE'RE HAPPY TO HELP.
BILL *TOTALLY* HAD A CRUSH ON YOU.
CAN WE SPEAK PRIVATELY?
CERTAINLY, YOUNG MAN...
I USED TO WORK IN THE LAB WITH MY UNCLE BILL ALL THE TIME. I'M GRADUATING FROM *M.I.T.* IN TWO YEARS.
DO YOU NEED FINANCIAL HELP?
NO, YOU DON'T UNDERSTAND. I'M *ROTC.* I CAN RUN THE MILE IN--
I HOPE YOU'RE NOT THINKING ABOUT DOING ANYTHING ILLEGAL. YOUR FAMILY HAS ENOUGH HEARTBREAK RIGHT NOW.
HOW CAN YOU SAY THAT TO ME? I THOUGHT YOU WERE ON HIS SIDE?
I *AM.* BUT THAT'S NOT WHAT YOUR FAMILY NEEDS RIGHT NOW.
I'M GOING TO CRACK THE PYM PARTICLE FORMULA ONE DAY--*WITH OR WITHOUT* YOUR HELP.
I HOPE YOU DO.
SO YOU WILL HELP ME?
WE WILL STAY IN TOUCH.

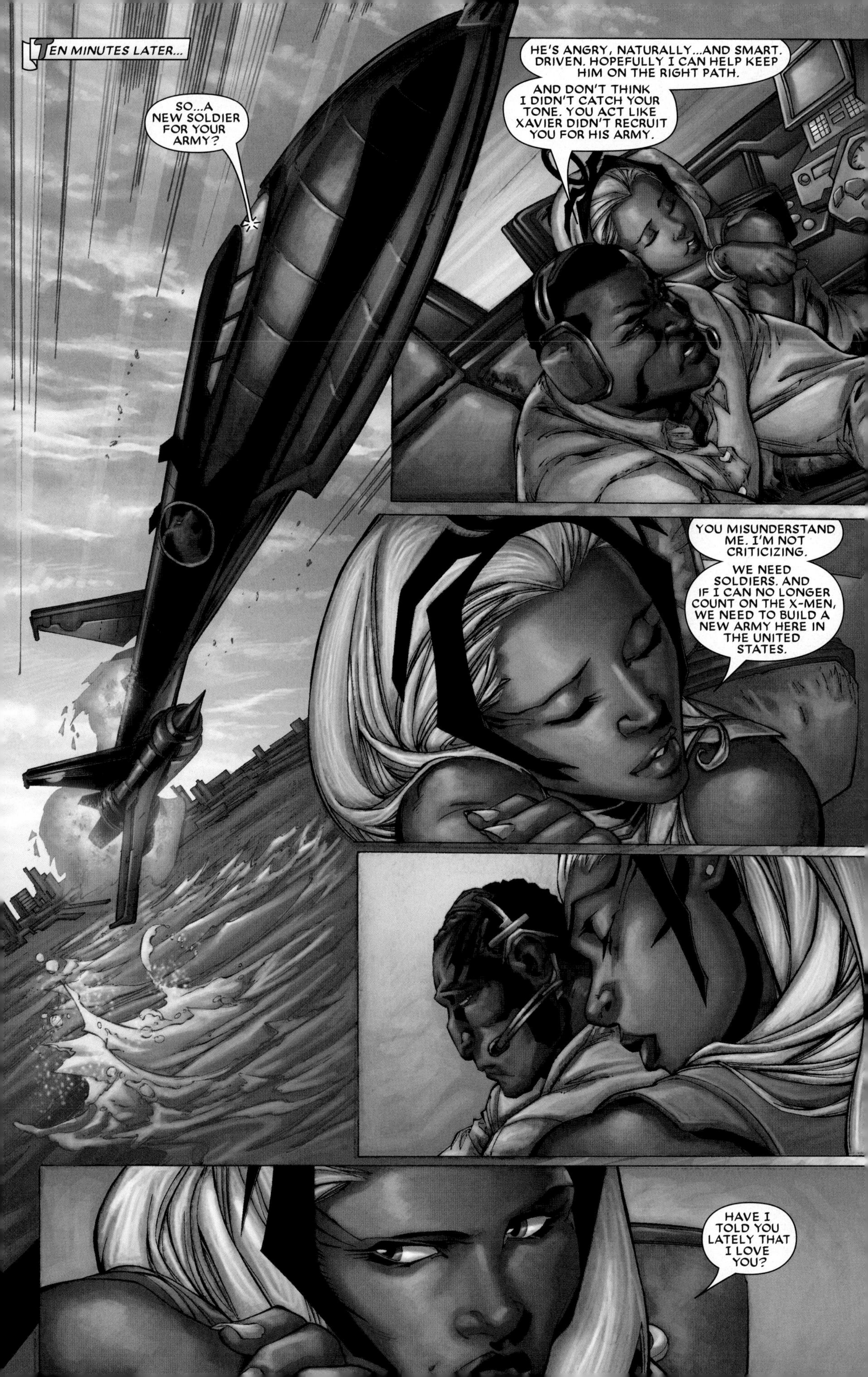
TEN MINUTES LATER...
SO...A NEW SOLDIER FOR YOUR ARMY?
HE'S ANGRY, NATURALLY...AND SMART. DRIVEN. HOPEFULLY I CAN HELP KEEP HIM ON THE RIGHT PATH.
AND DON'T THINK I DIDN'T CATCH YOUR TONE. YOU ACT LIKE XAVIER DIDN'T RECRUIT YOU FOR HIS ARMY.
YOU MISUNDERSTAND ME. I'M NOT CRITICIZING.
WE NEED SOLDIERS. AND IF I CAN NO LONGER COUNT ON THE X-MEN, WE NEED TO BUILD A NEW ARMY HERE IN THE UNITED STATES.
HAVE I TOLD YOU LATELY THAT I LOVE YOU?

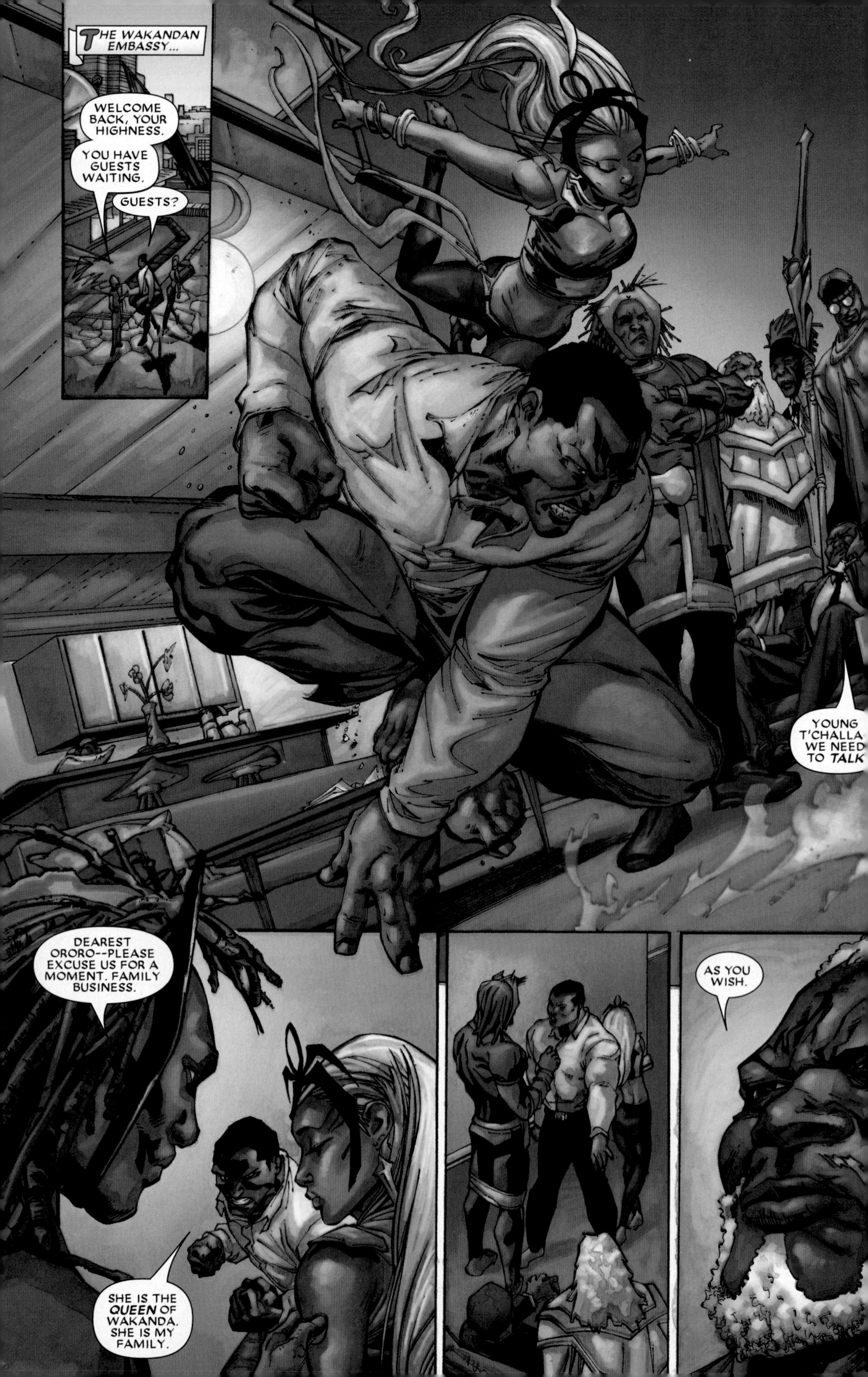
THE WAKANDAN EMBASSY...
WELCOME BACK, YOUR HIGHNESS.
YOU HAVE GUESTS WAITING.
GUESTS?
YOUNG T'CHALLA WE NEED TO TALK
DEAREST ORORO--PLEASE EXCUSE US FOR A MOMENT. FAMILY BUSINESS.
SHE IS THE QUEEN OF WAKANDA. SHE IS MY FAMILY.
AS YOU WISH.

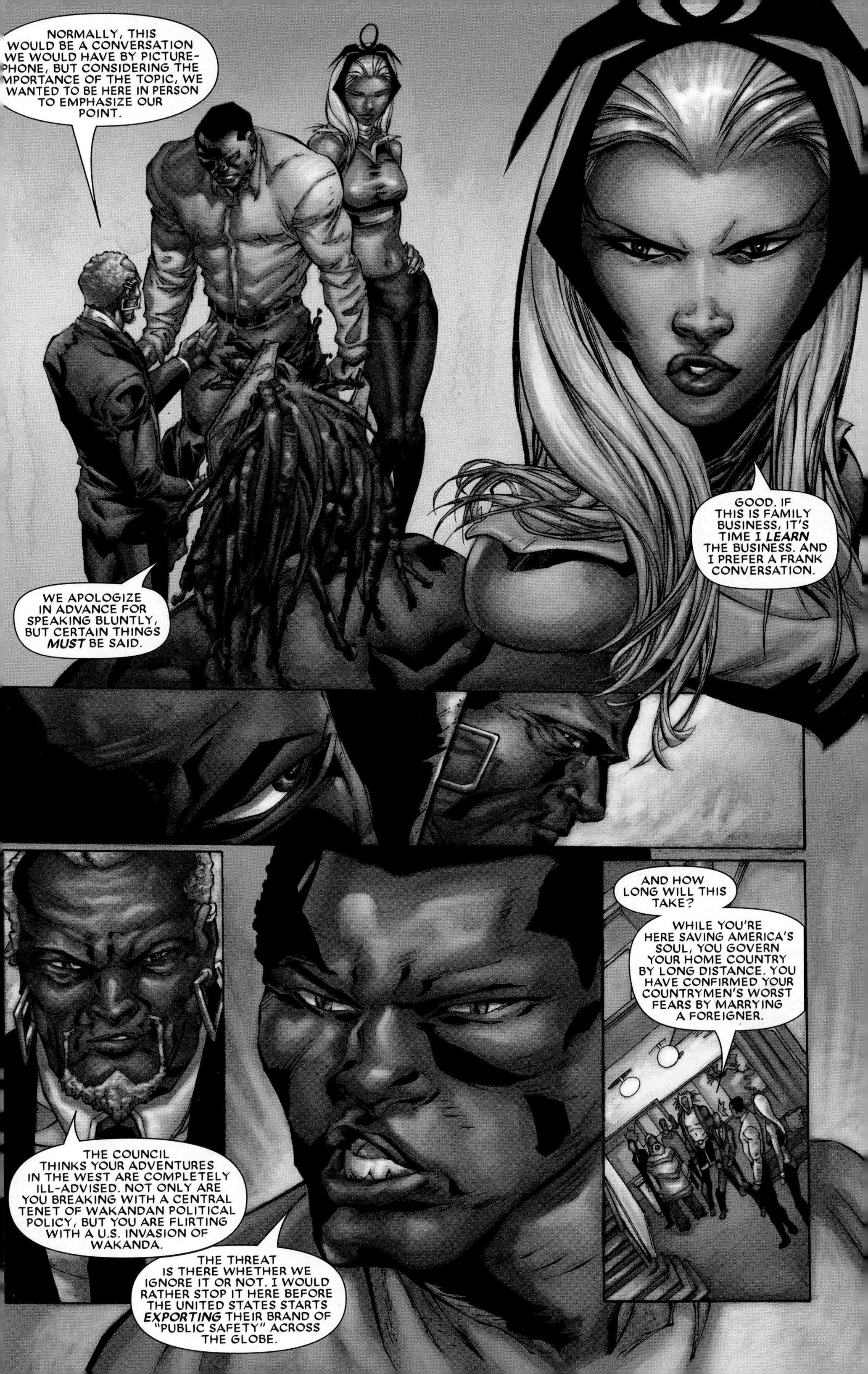
NORMALLY, THIS WOULD BE A CONVERSATION WE WOULD HAVE BY PICTURE-PHONE, BUT CONSIDERING THE IMPORTANCE OF THE TOPIC, WE WANTED TO BE HERE IN PERSON TO EMPHASIZE OUR POINT.
WE APOLOGIZE IN ADVANCE FOR SPEAKING BLUNTLY, BUT CERTAIN THINGS *MUST* BE SAID.
GOOD. IF THIS IS FAMILY BUSINESS, IT'S TIME I *LEARN* THE BUSINESS. AND I PREFER A FRANK CONVERSATION.
THE COUNCIL THINKS YOUR ADVENTURES IN THE WEST ARE COMPLETELY ILL-ADVISED. NOT ONLY ARE YOU BREAKING WITH A CENTRAL TENET OF WAKANDAN POLITICAL POLICY, BUT YOU ARE FLIRTING WITH A U.S. INVASION OF WAKANDA.
THE THREAT IS THERE WHETHER WE IGNORE IT OR NOT. I WOULD RATHER STOP IT HERE BEFORE THE UNITED STATES STARTS *EXPORTING* THEIR BRAND OF "PUBLIC SAFETY" ACROSS THE GLOBE.
AND HOW LONG WILL THIS TAKE?
WHILE YOU'RE HERE SAVING AMERICA'S SOUL, YOU GOVERN YOUR HOME COUNTRY BY LONG DISTANCE. YOU HAVE CONFIRMED YOUR COUNTRYMEN'S WORST FEARS BY MARRYING A FOREIGNER.

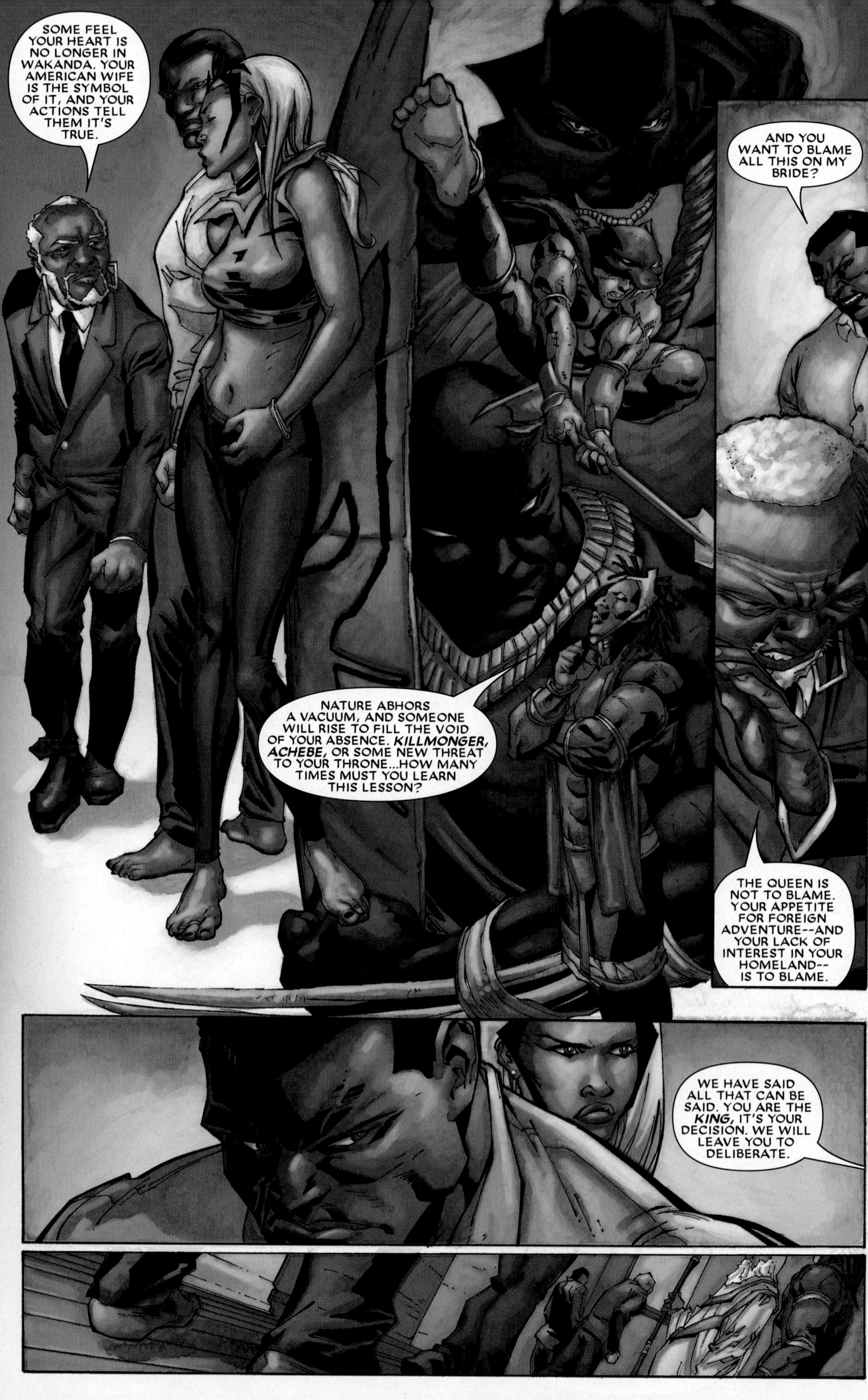
SOME FEEL YOUR HEART IS NO LONGER IN WAKANDA. YOUR AMERICAN WIFE IS THE SYMBOL OF IT, AND YOUR ACTIONS TELL THEM IT'S TRUE.
AND YOU WANT TO BLAME ALL THIS ON MY BRIDE?
NATURE ABHORS A VACUUM, AND SOMEONE WILL RISE TO FILL THE VOID OF YOUR ABSENCE. *KILLMONGER, ACHEBE,* OR SOME NEW THREAT TO YOUR THRONE...HOW MANY TIMES MUST YOU LEARN THIS LESSON?
THE QUEEN IS NOT TO BLAME. YOUR APPETITE FOR FOREIGN ADVENTURE--AND YOUR LACK OF INTEREST IN YOUR HOMELAND--IS TO BLAME.
WE HAVE SAID ALL THAT CAN BE SAID. YOU ARE THE *KING,* IT'S YOUR DECISION. WE WILL LEAVE YOU TO DELIBERATE.

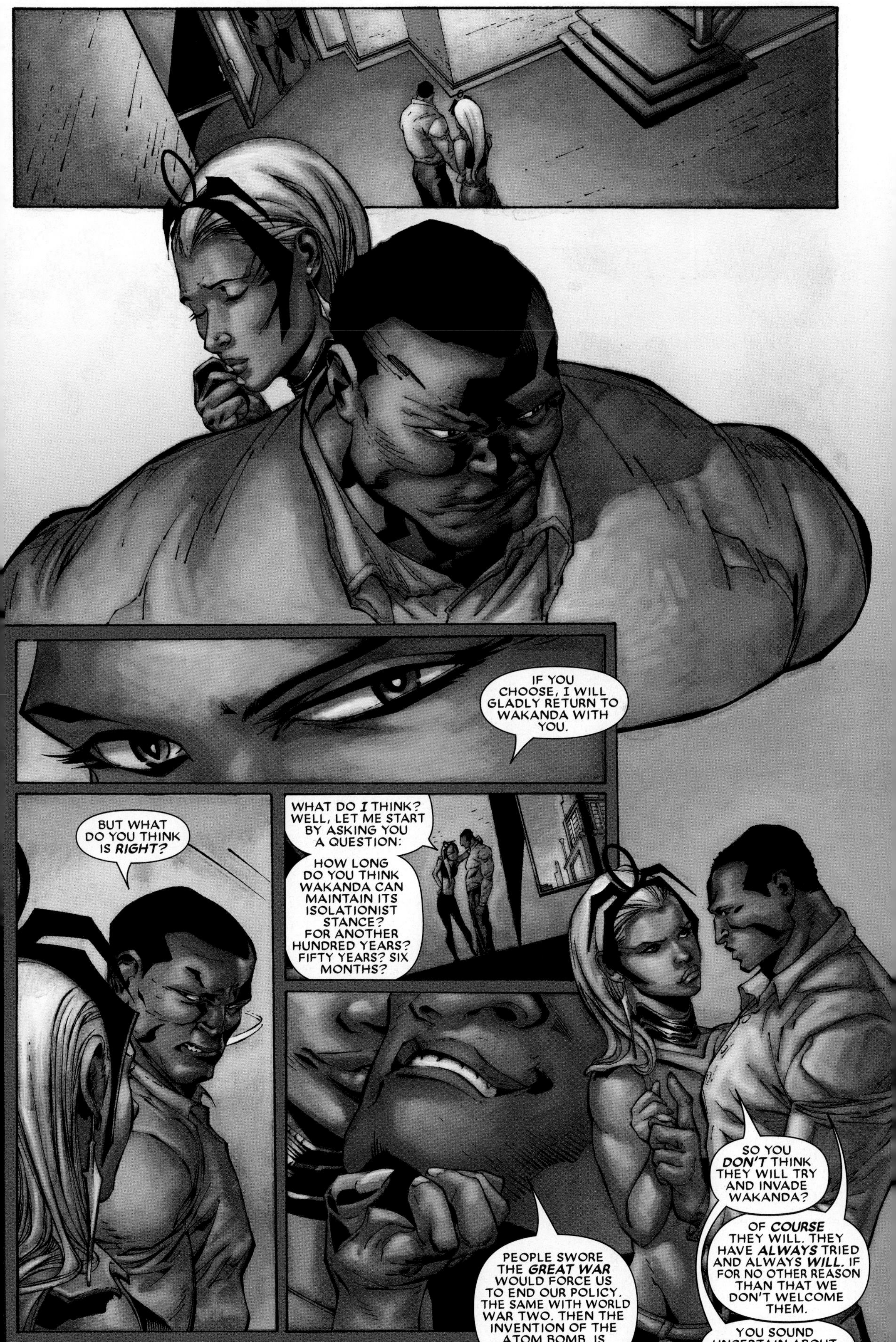

IF YOU CHOOSE, I WILL GLADLY RETURN TO WAKANDA WITH YOU.
BUT WHAT DO YOU THINK IS RIGHT?
WHAT DO I THINK? WELL, LET ME START BY ASKING YOU A QUESTION:
HOW LONG DO YOU THINK WAKANDA CAN MAINTAIN ITS ISOLATIONIST STANCE? FOR ANOTHER HUNDRED YEARS? FIFTY YEARS? SIX MONTHS?
PEOPLE SWORE THE GREAT WAR WOULD FORCE US TO END OUR POLICY. THE SAME WITH WORLD WAR TWO. THEN THE INVENTION OF THE ATOM BOMB. IS THIS REALLY ANY DIFFERENT?
SO YOU DON'T THINK THEY WILL TRY AND INVADE WAKANDA?
OF COURSE THEY WILL. THEY HAVE ALWAYS TRIED AND ALWAYS WILL. IF FOR NO OTHER REASON THAN THAT WE DON'T WELCOME THEM.
YOU SOUND UNCERTAIN ABOUT WHICH DIRECTION TO GO, T'CHALLA.

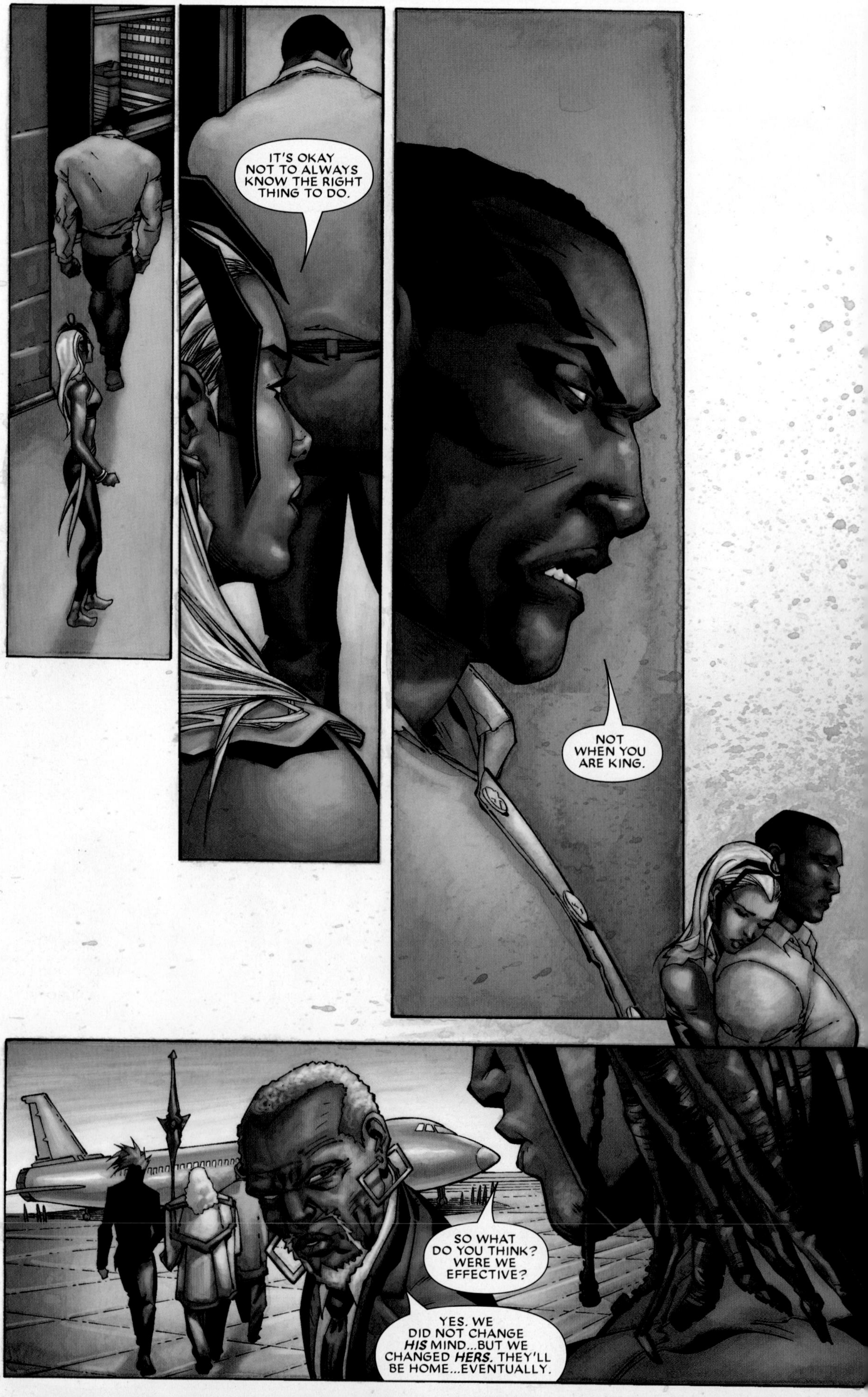
IT'S OKAY NOT TO ALWAYS KNOW THE RIGHT THING TO DO.
NOT WHEN YOU ARE KING.
SO WHAT DO YOU THINK? WERE WE EFFECTIVE?
YES. WE DID NOT CHANGE *HIS* MIND...BUT WE CHANGED *HERS*. THEY'LL BE HOME...EVENTUALLY.

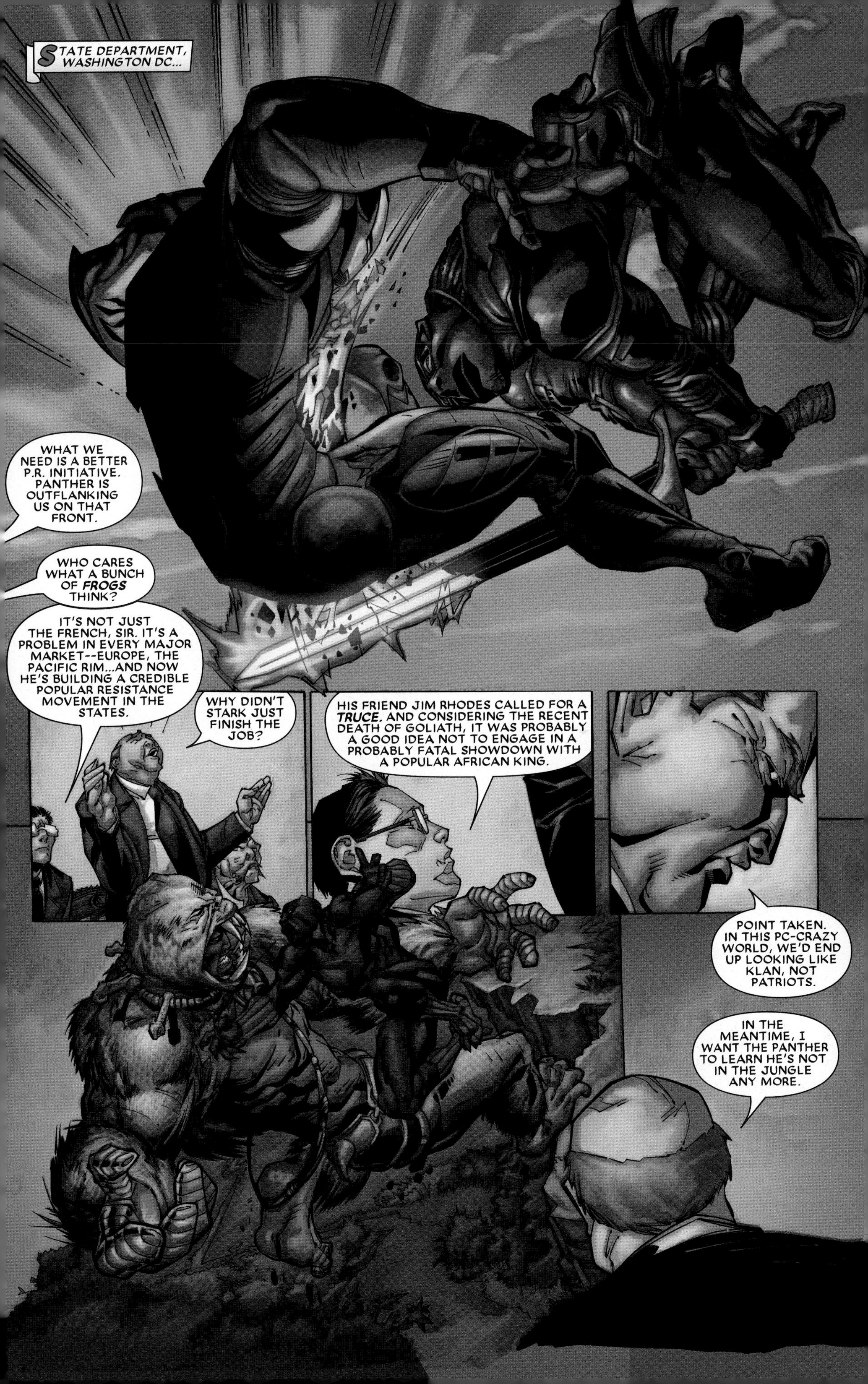
STATE DEPARTMENT, WASHINGTON DC...
WHAT WE NEED IS A BETTER P.R. INITIATIVE. PANTHER IS OUTFLANKING US ON THAT FRONT.
WHO CARES WHAT A BUNCH OF FROGS THINK?
IT'S NOT JUST THE FRENCH, SIR. IT'S A PROBLEM IN EVERY MAJOR MARKET--EUROPE, THE PACIFIC RIM...AND NOW HE'S BUILDING A CREDIBLE POPULAR RESISTANCE MOVEMENT IN THE STATES.
WHY DIDN'T STARK JUST FINISH THE JOB?
HIS FRIEND JIM RHODES CALLED FOR A TRUCE. AND CONSIDERING THE RECENT DEATH OF GOLIATH, IT WAS PROBABLY A GOOD IDEA NOT TO ENGAGE IN A PROBABLY FATAL SHOWDOWN WITH A POPULAR AFRICAN KING.
POINT TAKEN. IN THIS PC-CRAZY WORLD, WE'D END UP LOOKING LIKE KLAN, NOT PATRIOTS.
IN THE MEANTIME, I WANT THE PANTHER TO LEARN HE'S NOT IN THE JUNGLE ANY MORE.

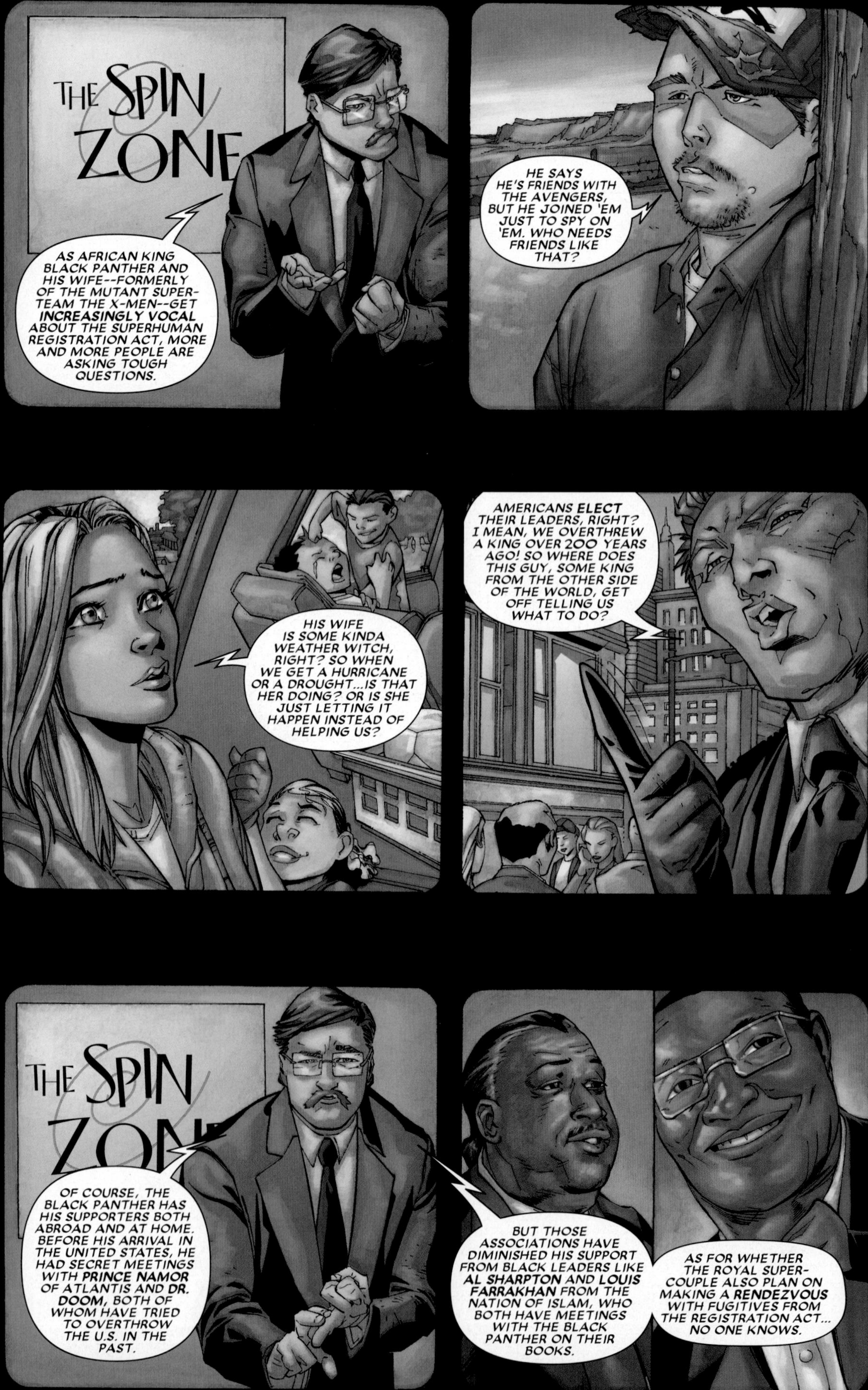
THE SPIN ZONE
AS AFRICAN KING BLACK PANTHER AND HIS WIFE--FORMERLY OF THE MUTANT SUPER-TEAM THE X-MEN--GET INCREASINGLY VOCAL ABOUT THE SUPERHUMAN REGISTRATION ACT, MORE AND MORE PEOPLE ARE ASKING TOUGH QUESTIONS.
HE SAYS HE'S FRIENDS WITH THE AVENGERS, BUT HE JOINED 'EM JUST TO SPY ON 'EM. WHO NEEDS FRIENDS LIKE THAT?
HIS WIFE IS SOME KINDA WEATHER WITCH, RIGHT? SO WHEN WE GET A HURRICANE OR A DROUGHT...IS THAT HER DOING? OR IS SHE JUST LETTING IT HAPPEN INSTEAD OF HELPING US?
AMERICANS ELECT THEIR LEADERS, RIGHT? I MEAN, WE OVERTHREW A KING OVER 200 YEARS AGO! SO WHERE DOES THIS GUY, SOME KING FROM THE OTHER SIDE OF THE WORLD, GET OFF TELLING US WHAT TO DO?
THE SPIN ZONE
OF COURSE, THE BLACK PANTHER HAS HIS SUPPORTERS BOTH ABROAD AND AT HOME. BEFORE HIS ARRIVAL IN THE UNITED STATES, HE HAD SECRET MEETINGS WITH PRINCE NAMOR OF ATLANTIS AND DR. DOOM, BOTH OF WHOM HAVE TRIED TO OVERTHROW THE U.S. IN THE PAST.
BUT THOSE ASSOCIATIONS HAVE DIMINISHED HIS SUPPORT FROM BLACK LEADERS LIKE AL SHARPTON AND LOUIS FARRAKHAN FROM THE NATION OF ISLAM, WHO BOTH HAVE MEETINGS WITH THE BLACK PANTHER ON THEIR BOOKS.
AS FOR WHETHER THE ROYAL SUPER-COUPLE ALSO PLAN ON MAKING A RENDEZVOUS WITH FUGITIVES FROM THE REGISTRATION ACT... NO ONE KNOWS.

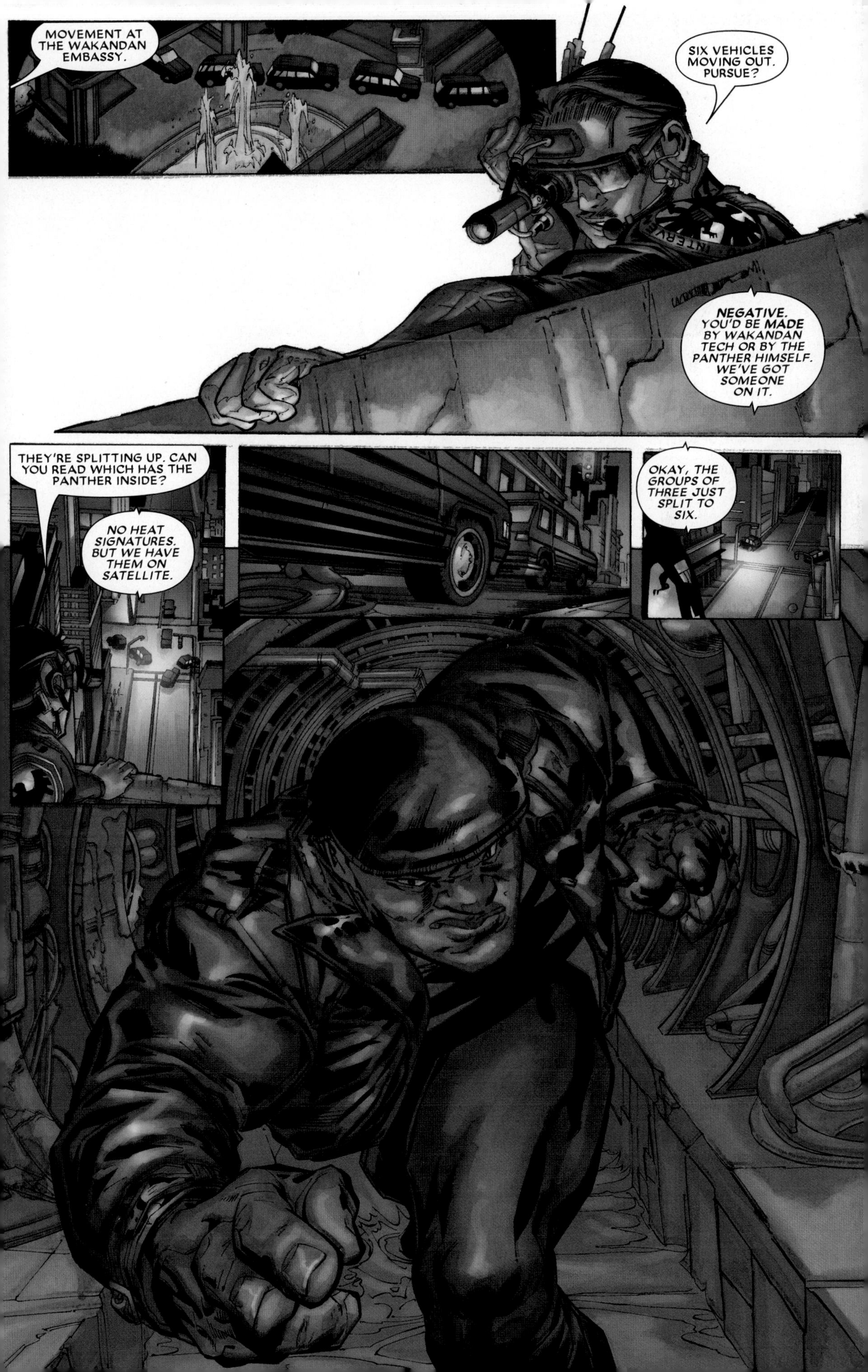
MOVEMENT AT THE WAKANDAN EMBASSY.
SIX VEHICLES MOVING OUT. PURSUE?
NEGATIVE. YOU'D BE MADE BY WAKANDAN TECH OR BY THE PANTHER HIMSELF. WE'VE GOT SOMEONE ON IT.
THEY'RE SPLITTING UP. CAN YOU READ WHICH HAS THE PANTHER INSIDE?
NO HEAT SIGNATURES. BUT WE HAVE THEM ON SATELLITE.
OKAY, THE GROUPS OF THREE JUST SPLIT TO SIX.

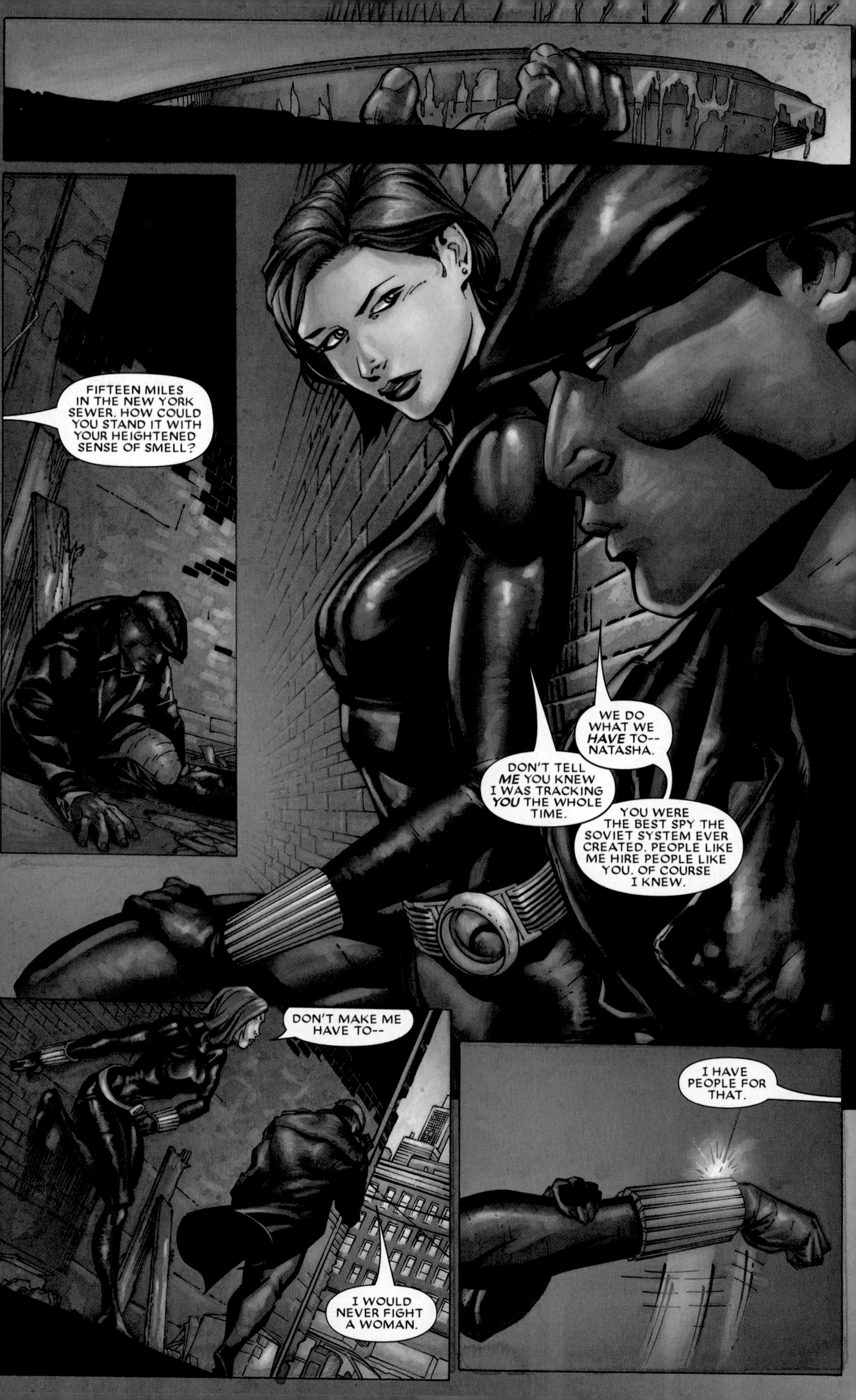

FIFTEEN MILES IN THE NEW YORK SEWER. HOW COULD YOU STAND IT WITH YOUR HEIGHTENED SENSE OF SMELL?
DON'T TELL *ME* YOU KNEW I WAS TRACKING *YOU* THE WHOLE TIME.
WE DO WHAT WE *HAVE* TO-- NATASHA.
YOU WERE THE BEST SPY THE SOVIET SYSTEM EVER CREATED. PEOPLE LIKE ME HIRE PEOPLE LIKE YOU. OF COURSE I KNEW.
DON'T MAKE ME HAVE TO--
I WOULD NEVER FIGHT A WOMAN.
I HAVE PEOPLE FOR THAT.

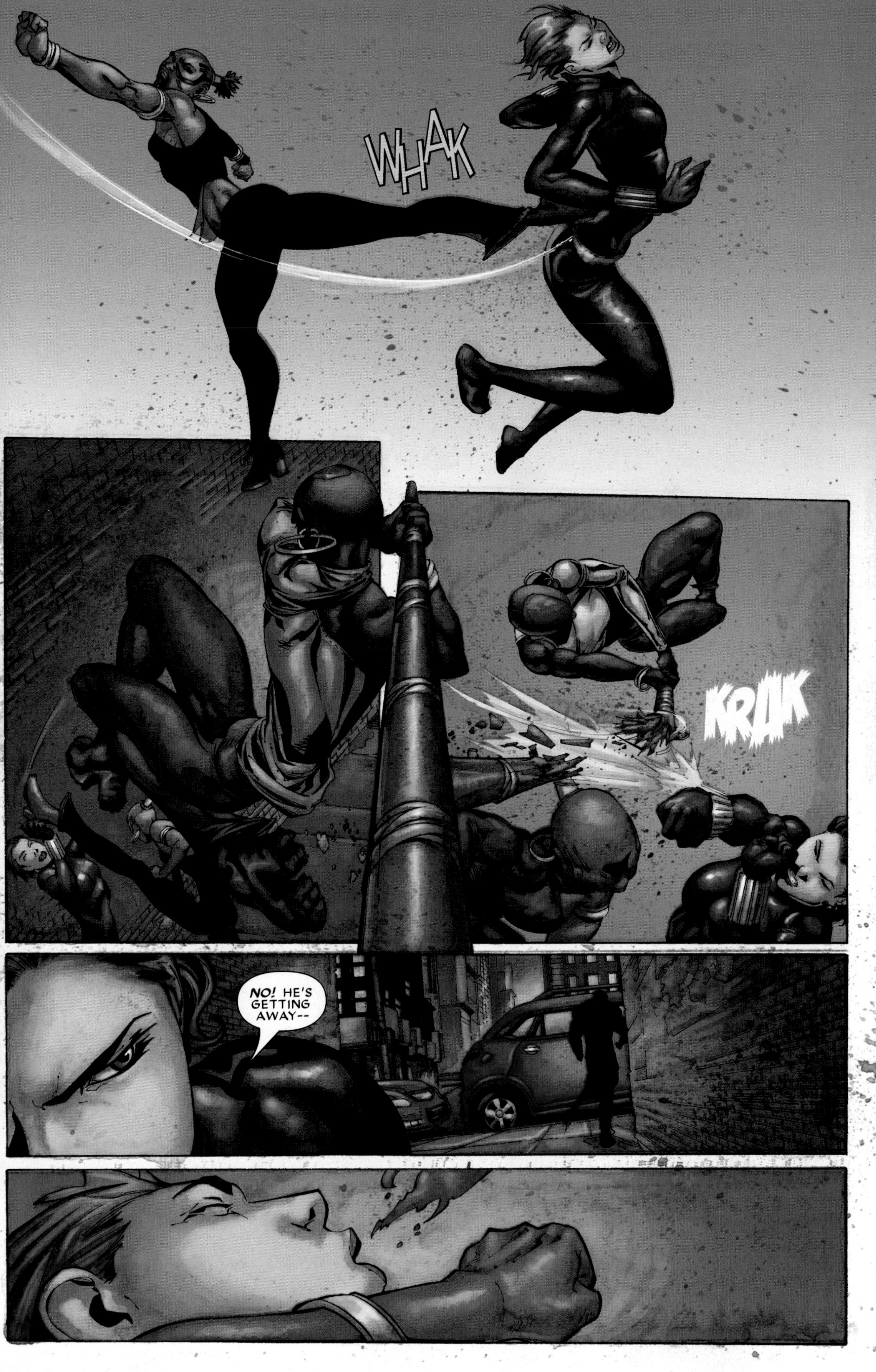
WHAK
KRAK
NO! HE'S GETTING AWAY--

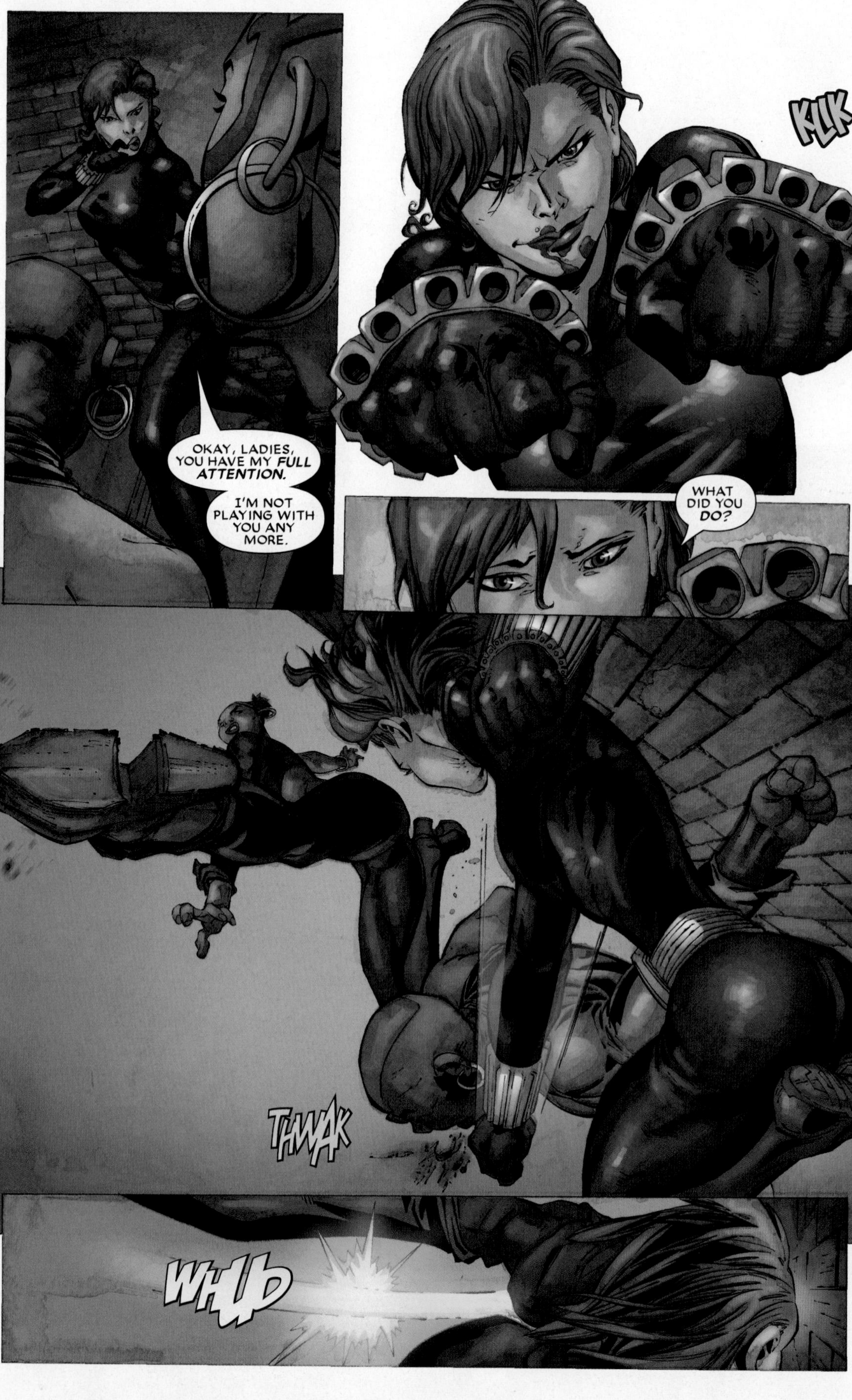
KLIK
OKAY, LADIES, YOU HAVE MY *FULL ATTENTION.*
I'M NOT PLAYING WITH YOU ANY MORE.
WHAT DID YOU *DO?*
THWAK
WHUD

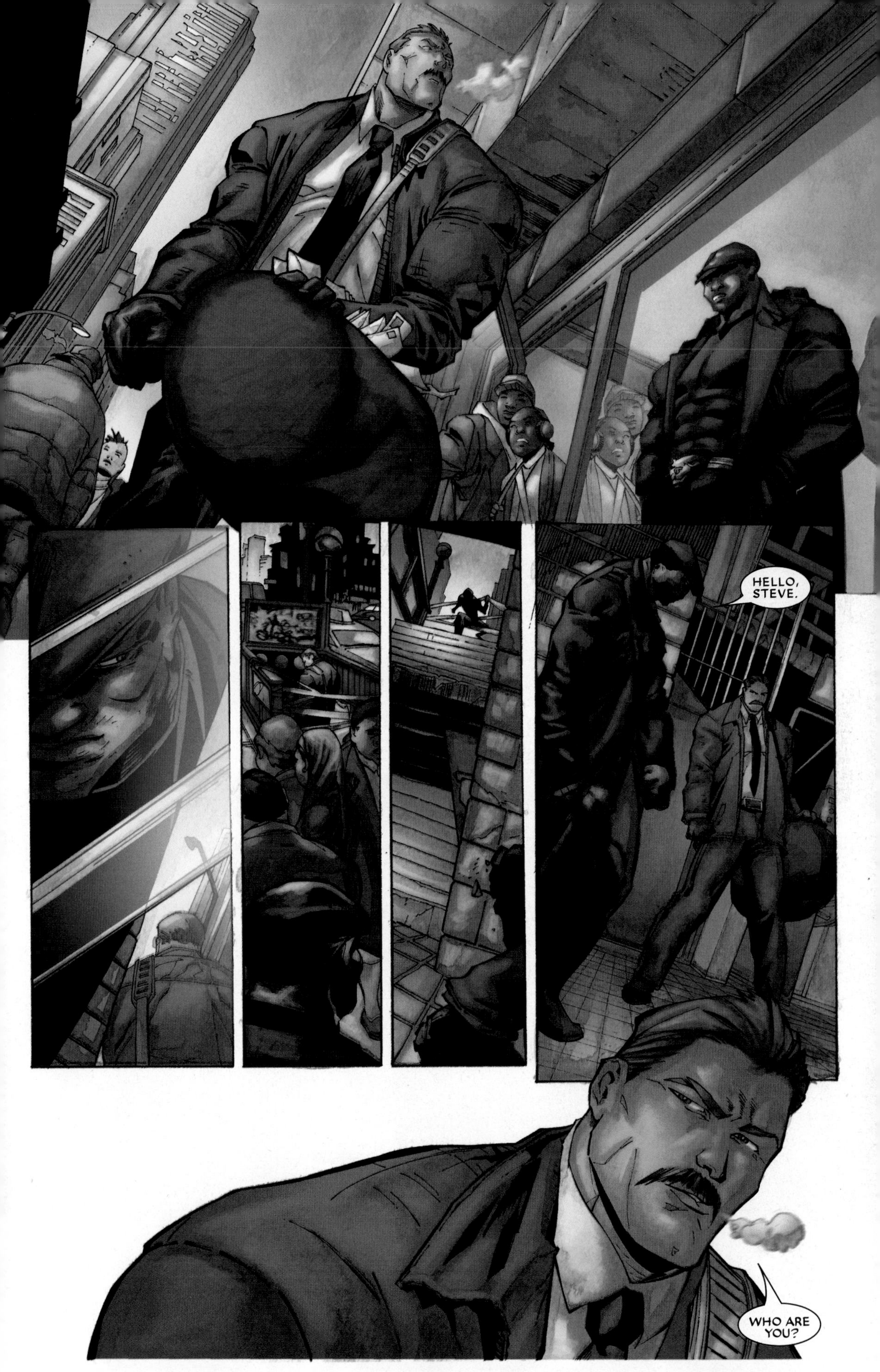
HELLO, STEVE.
WHO ARE YOU?

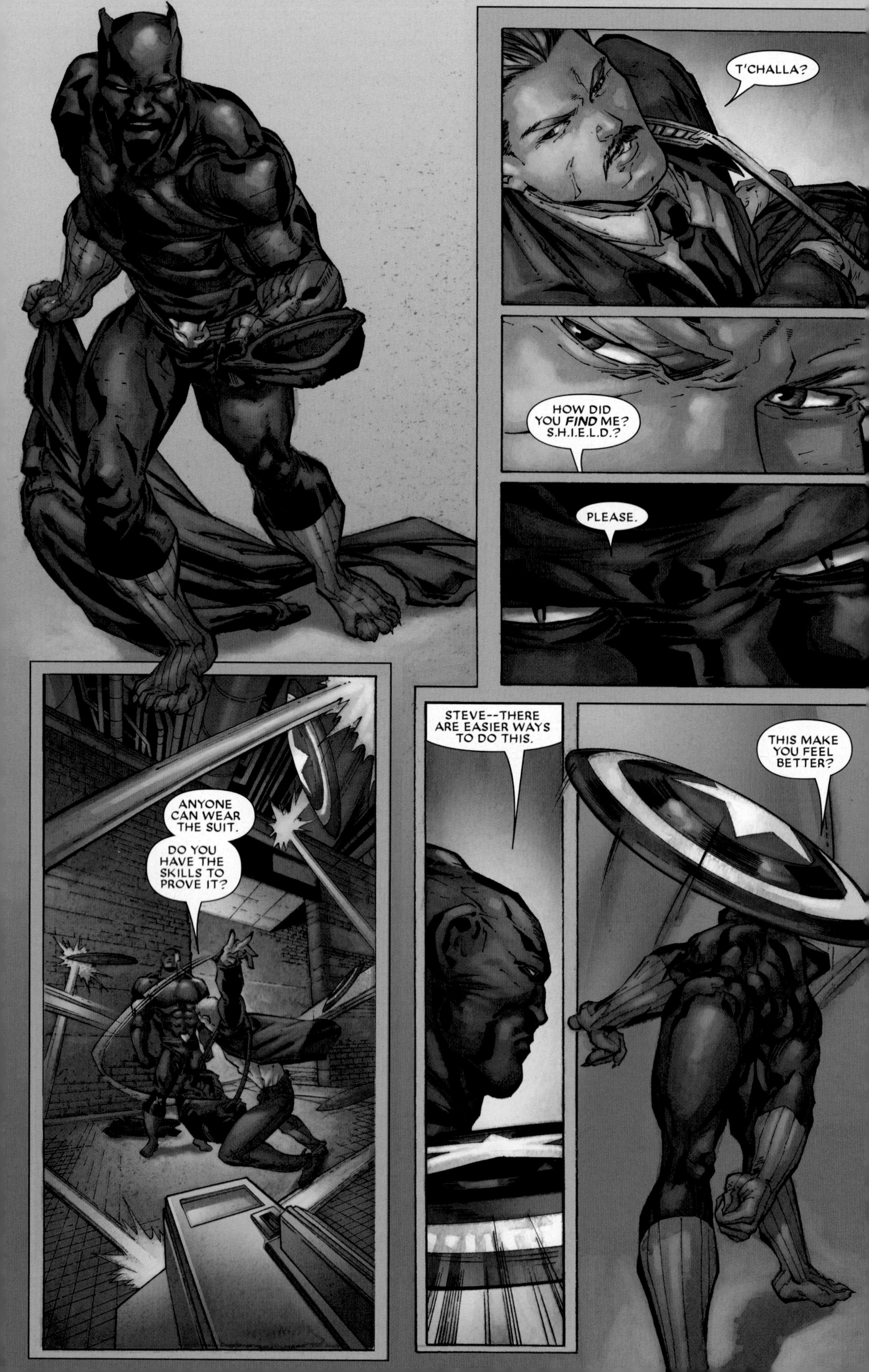
T'CHALLA?
HOW DID YOU *FIND* ME? S.H.I.E.L.D.?
PLEASE.
ANYONE CAN WEAR THE SUIT.
DO YOU HAVE THE SKILLS TO PROVE IT?
STEVE--THERE ARE EASIER WAYS TO DO THIS.
THIS MAKE YOU FEEL BETTER?

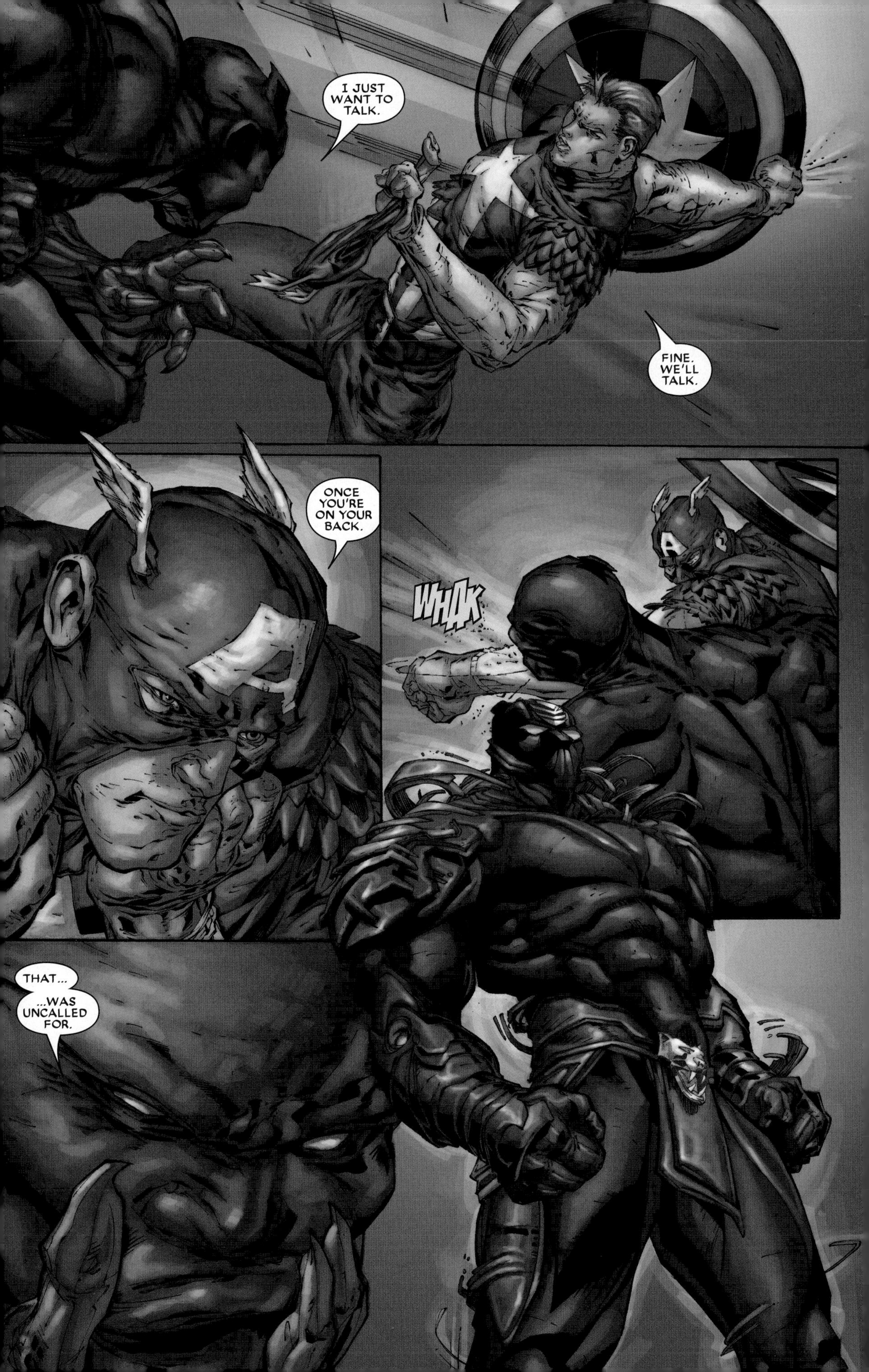

I JUST WANT TO TALK.
FINE. WE'LL TALK.
ONCE YOU'RE ON YOUR BACK.
WHAK
THAT...
...WAS UNCALLED FOR.

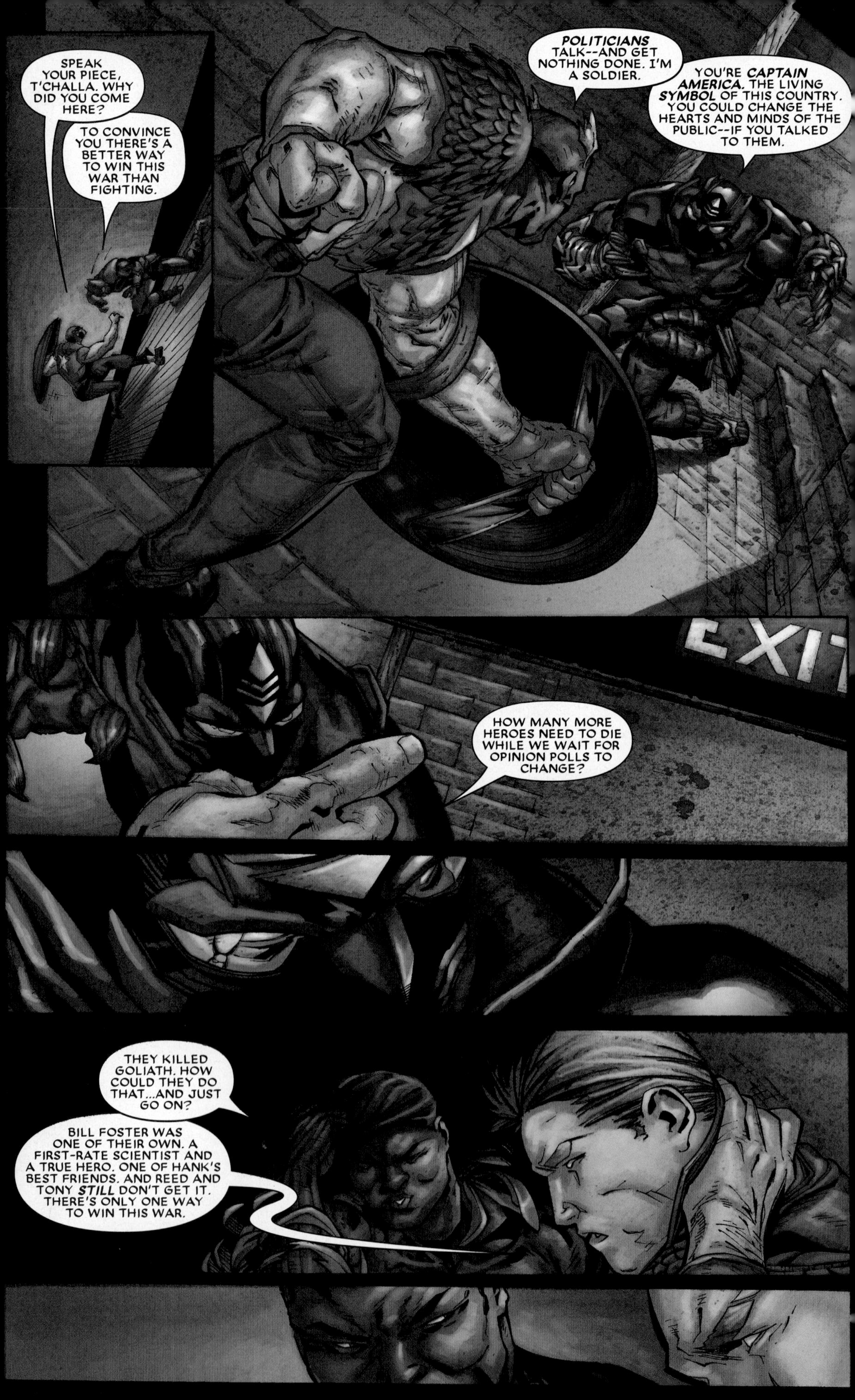
SPEAK YOUR PIECE, T'CHALLA. WHY DID YOU COME HERE?
TO CONVINCE YOU THERE'S A BETTER WAY TO WIN THIS WAR THAN FIGHTING.
POLITICIANS TALK--AND GET NOTHING DONE. I'M A SOLDIER.
YOU'RE CAPTAIN AMERICA. THE LIVING SYMBOL OF THIS COUNTRY. YOU COULD CHANGE THE HEARTS AND MINDS OF THE PUBLIC--IF YOU TALKED TO THEM.
EXIT
HOW MANY MORE HEROES NEED TO DIE WHILE WE WAIT FOR OPINION POLLS TO CHANGE?
THEY KILLED GOLIATH. HOW COULD THEY DO THAT...AND JUST GO ON?
BILL FOSTER WAS ONE OF THEIR OWN. A FIRST-RATE SCIENTIST AND A TRUE HERO. ONE OF HANK'S BEST FRIENDS. AND REED AND TONY STILL DON'T GET IT. THERE'S ONLY ONE WAY TO WIN THIS WAR.

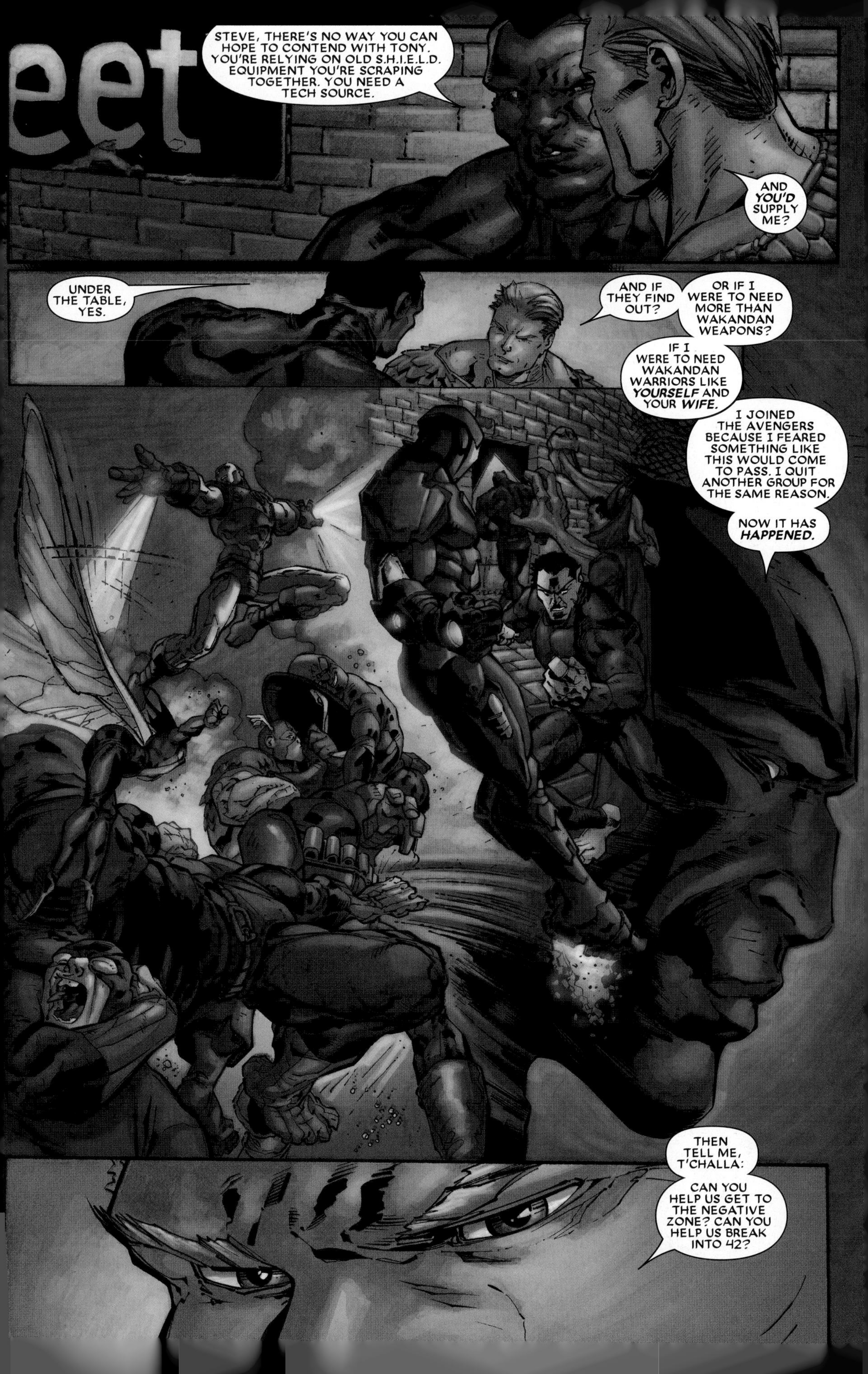
eet
STEVE, THERE'S NO WAY YOU CAN HOPE TO CONTEND WITH TONY. YOU'RE RELYING ON OLD S.H.I.E.L.D. EQUIPMENT YOU'RE SCRAPING TOGETHER. YOU NEED A TECH SOURCE.
AND YOU'D SUPPLY ME?
UNDER THE TABLE, YES.
AND IF THEY FIND OUT?
OR IF I WERE TO NEED MORE THAN WAKANDAN WEAPONS?
IF I WERE TO NEED WAKANDAN WARRIORS LIKE YOURSELF AND YOUR WIFE.
I JOINED THE AVENGERS BECAUSE I FEARED SOMETHING LIKE THIS WOULD COME TO PASS. I QUIT ANOTHER GROUP FOR THE SAME REASON.
NOW IT HAS HAPPENED.
THEN TELL ME, T'CHALLA:
CAN YOU HELP US GET TO THE NEGATIVE ZONE? CAN YOU HELP US BREAK INTO 42?

...IT WAS *TWO* OF THEM, SO LAY OFF.

I CAN'T TALK. A GUY WITH NO POWERS CUT MY CHEST PLATE OFF IN MID-AIR.

OF COURSE, IF RHODEY HADN'T JUMPED IN, I WOULD HAVE SOLVED THE WHOLE PROBLEM RIGHT *THEN*...

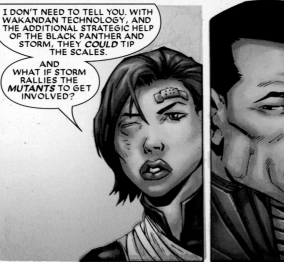

I DON'T NEED TO TELL YOU. WITH WAKANDAN TECHNOLOGY, AND THE ADDITIONAL STRATEGIC HELP OF THE BLACK PANTHER AND STORM, THEY *COULD* TIP THE SCALES.

AND WHAT IF STORM RALLIES THE *MUTANTS* TO GET INVOLVED?

TIME FOR THE *BIG GUNS*.

BLACK PANTHER
A MARVEL COMICS EVENT

CIVIL WAR

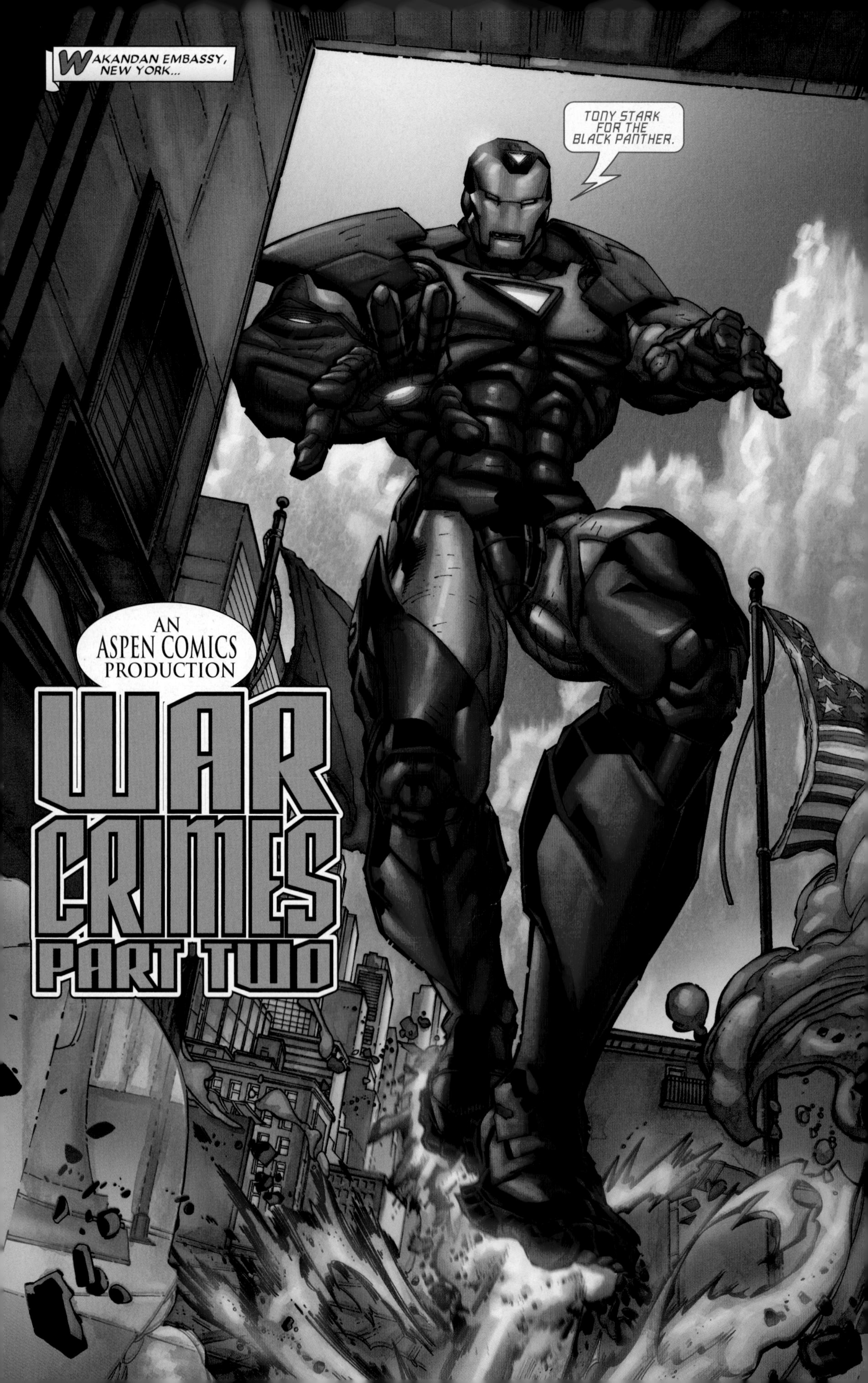
WAKANDAN EMBASSY, NEW YORK...
TONY STARK FOR THE BLACK PANTHER.
AN ASPEN COMICS PRODUCTION
WAR CRIMES PART TWO

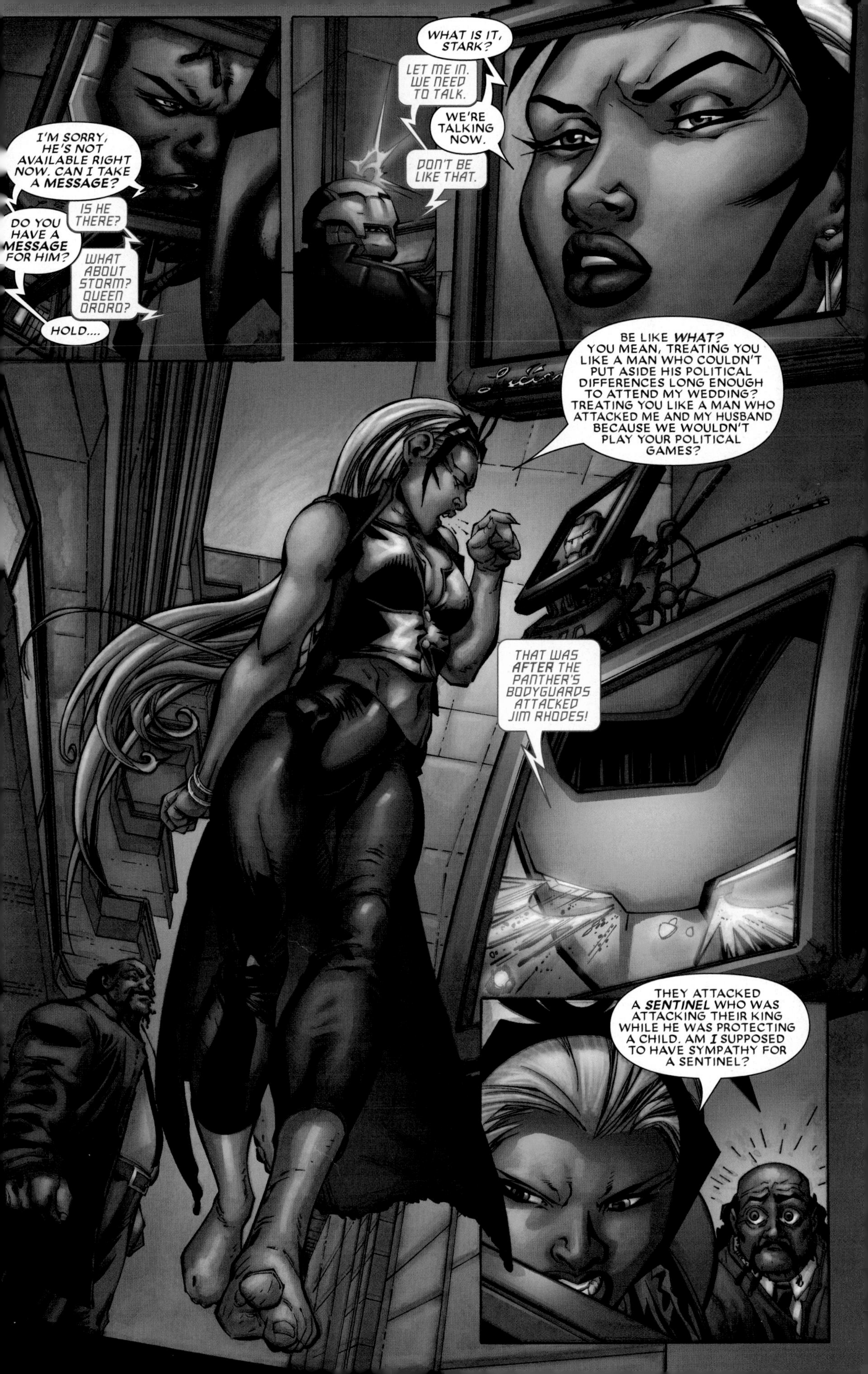
I'M SORRY, HE'S NOT AVAILABLE RIGHT NOW. CAN I TAKE A MESSAGE?
IS HE THERE?
DO YOU HAVE A MESSAGE FOR HIM?
WHAT ABOUT STORM? QUEEN ORORO?
HOLD....
WHAT IS IT, STARK?
LET ME IN. WE NEED TO TALK.
WE'RE TALKING NOW.
DON'T BE LIKE THAT.
BE LIKE WHAT? YOU MEAN, TREATING YOU LIKE A MAN WHO COULDN'T PUT ASIDE HIS POLITICAL DIFFERENCES LONG ENOUGH TO ATTEND MY WEDDING? TREATING YOU LIKE A MAN WHO ATTACKED ME AND MY HUSBAND BECAUSE WE WOULDN'T PLAY YOUR POLITICAL GAMES?
THAT WAS AFTER THE PANTHER'S BODYGUARDS ATTACKED JIM RHODES!
THEY ATTACKED A SENTINEL WHO WAS ATTACKING THEIR KING WHILE HE WAS PROTECTING A CHILD. AM I SUPPOSED TO HAVE SYMPATHY FOR A SENTINEL?

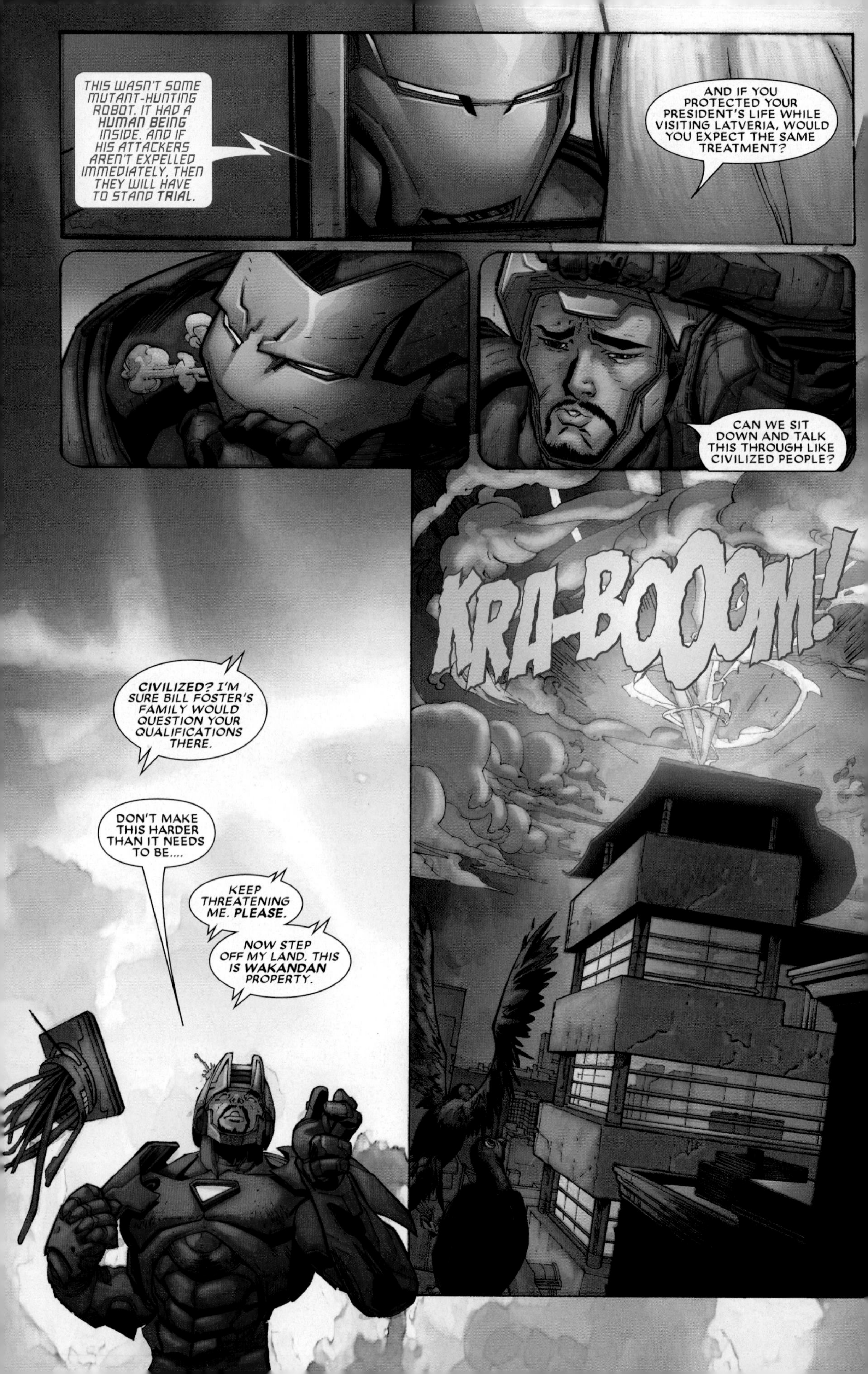
THIS WASN'T SOME MUTANT-HUNTING ROBOT. IT HAD A HUMAN BEING INSIDE. AND IF HIS ATTACKERS AREN'T EXPELLED IMMEDIATELY, THEN THEY WILL HAVE TO STAND TRIAL.
AND IF YOU PROTECTED YOUR PRESIDENT'S LIFE WHILE VISITING LATVERIA, WOULD YOU EXPECT THE SAME TREATMENT?
CAN WE SIT DOWN AND TALK THIS THROUGH LIKE CIVILIZED PEOPLE?
KRA-BOOOM!
CIVILIZED? I'M SURE BILL FOSTER'S FAMILY WOULD QUESTION YOUR QUALIFICATIONS THERE.
DON'T MAKE THIS HARDER THAN IT NEEDS TO BE....
KEEP THREATENING ME. PLEASE.
NOW STEP OFF MY LAND. THIS IS WAKANDAN PROPERTY.

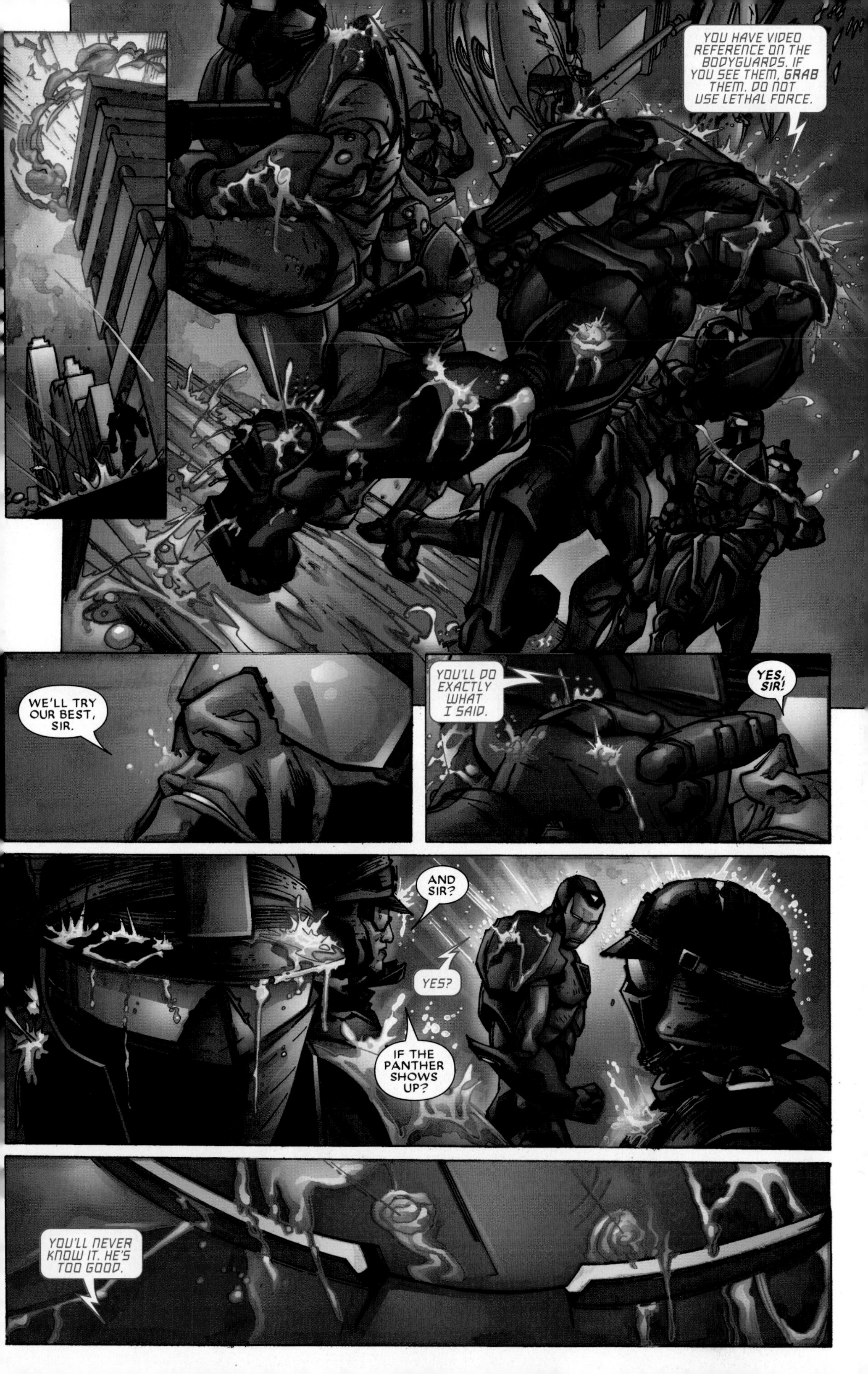
YOU HAVE VIDEO REFERENCE ON THE BODYGUARDS. IF YOU SEE THEM, GRAB THEM. DO NOT USE LETHAL FORCE.
WE'LL TRY OUR BEST, SIR.
YOU'LL DO EXACTLY WHAT I SAID.
YES, SIR!
AND SIR?
YES?
IF THE PANTHER SHOWS UP?
YOU'LL NEVER KNOW IT. HE'S TOO GOOD.

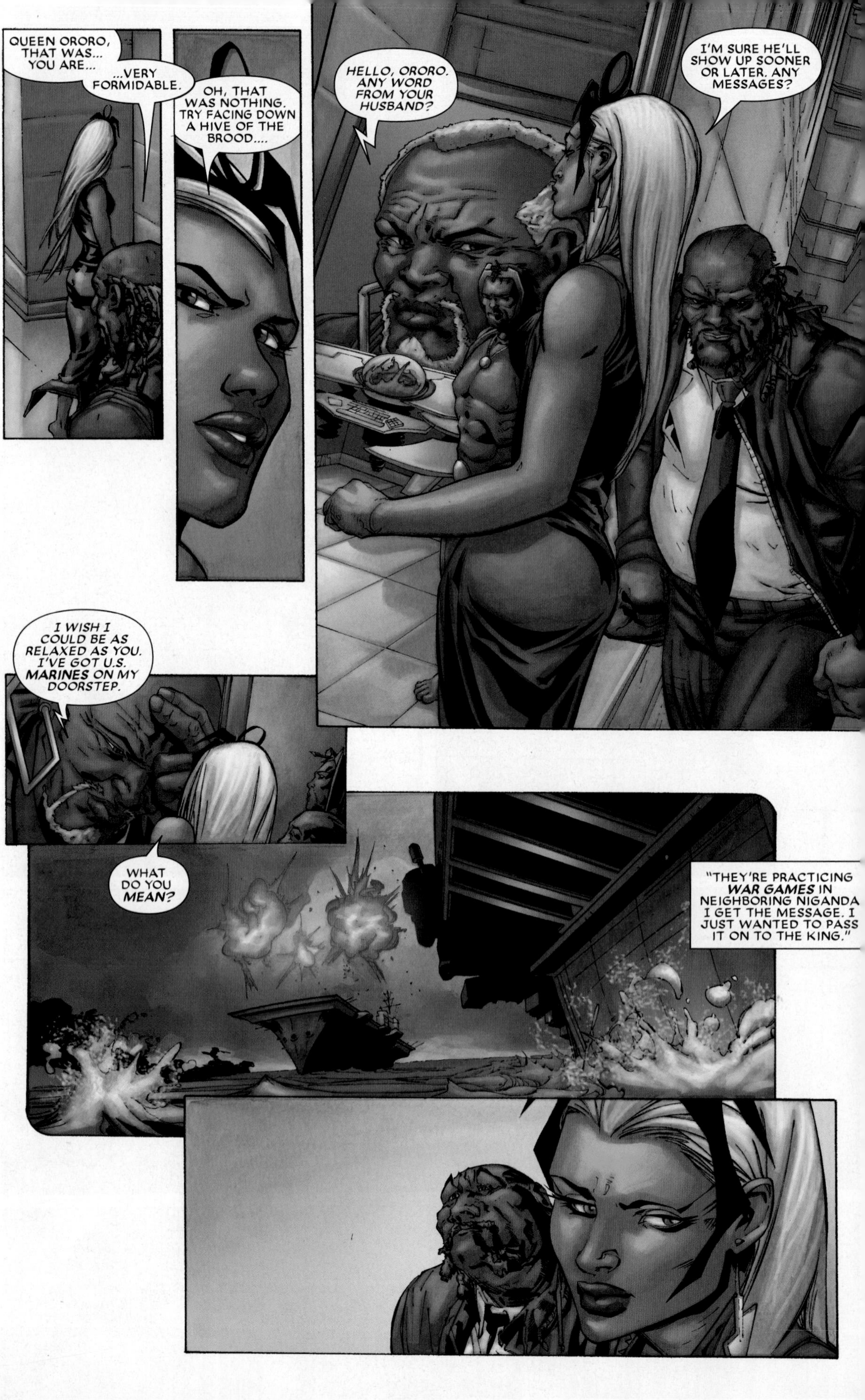
QUEEN ORORO, THAT WAS... YOU ARE...
...VERY FORMIDABLE.
OH, THAT WAS NOTHING. TRY FACING DOWN A HIVE OF THE BROOD....
HELLO, ORORO. ANY WORD FROM YOUR HUSBAND?
I'M SURE HE'LL SHOW UP SOONER OR LATER. ANY MESSAGES?
I WISH I COULD BE AS RELAXED AS YOU. I'VE GOT U.S. MARINES ON MY DOORSTEP.
WHAT DO YOU MEAN?
"THEY'RE PRACTICING WAR GAMES IN NEIGHBORING NIGANDA I GET THE MESSAGE. I JUST WANTED TO PASS IT ON TO THE KING."

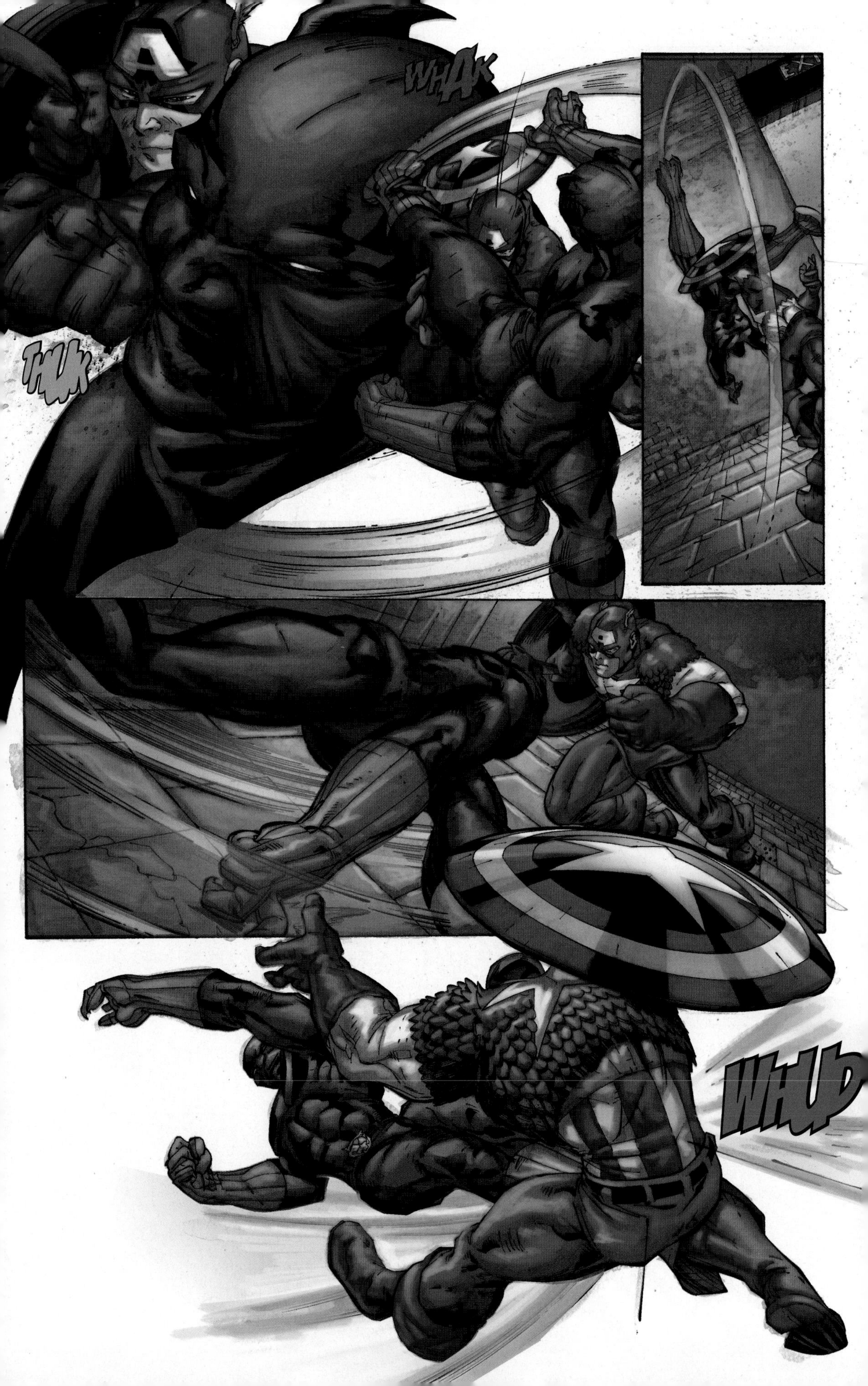
WHAK
THUK
WHUD

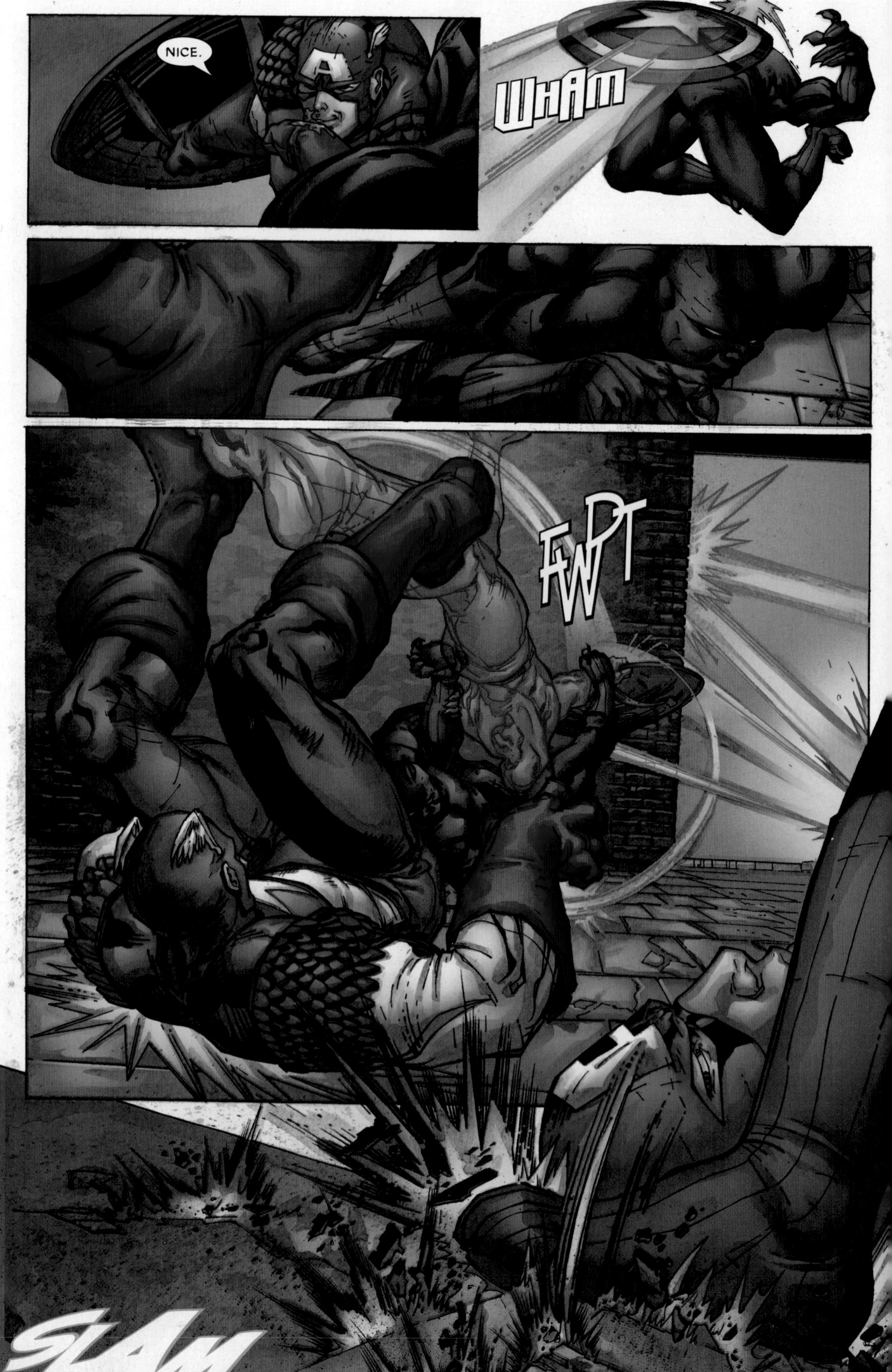
NICE.
WHAM
FWPT
SLAM

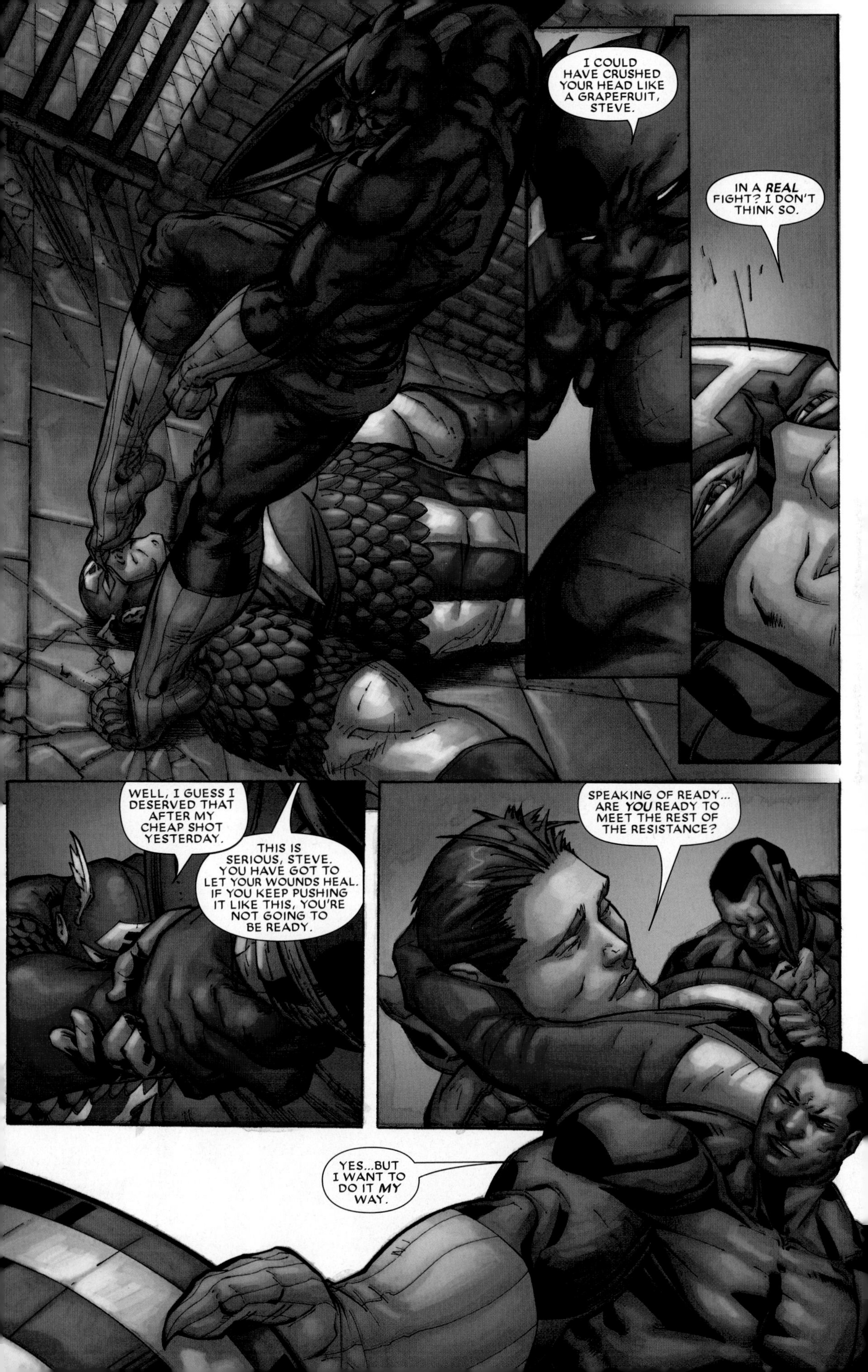
I COULD HAVE CRUSHED YOUR HEAD LIKE A GRAPEFRUIT, STEVE.
IN A *REAL* FIGHT? I DON'T THINK SO.
WELL, I GUESS I DESERVED THAT AFTER MY CHEAP SHOT YESTERDAY.
THIS IS SERIOUS, STEVE. YOU HAVE GOT TO LET YOUR WOUNDS HEAL. IF YOU KEEP PUSHING IT LIKE THIS, YOU'RE NOT GOING TO BE READY.
SPEAKING OF READY... ARE *YOU* READY TO MEET THE REST OF THE RESISTANCE?
YES...BUT I WANT TO DO IT *MY* WAY.

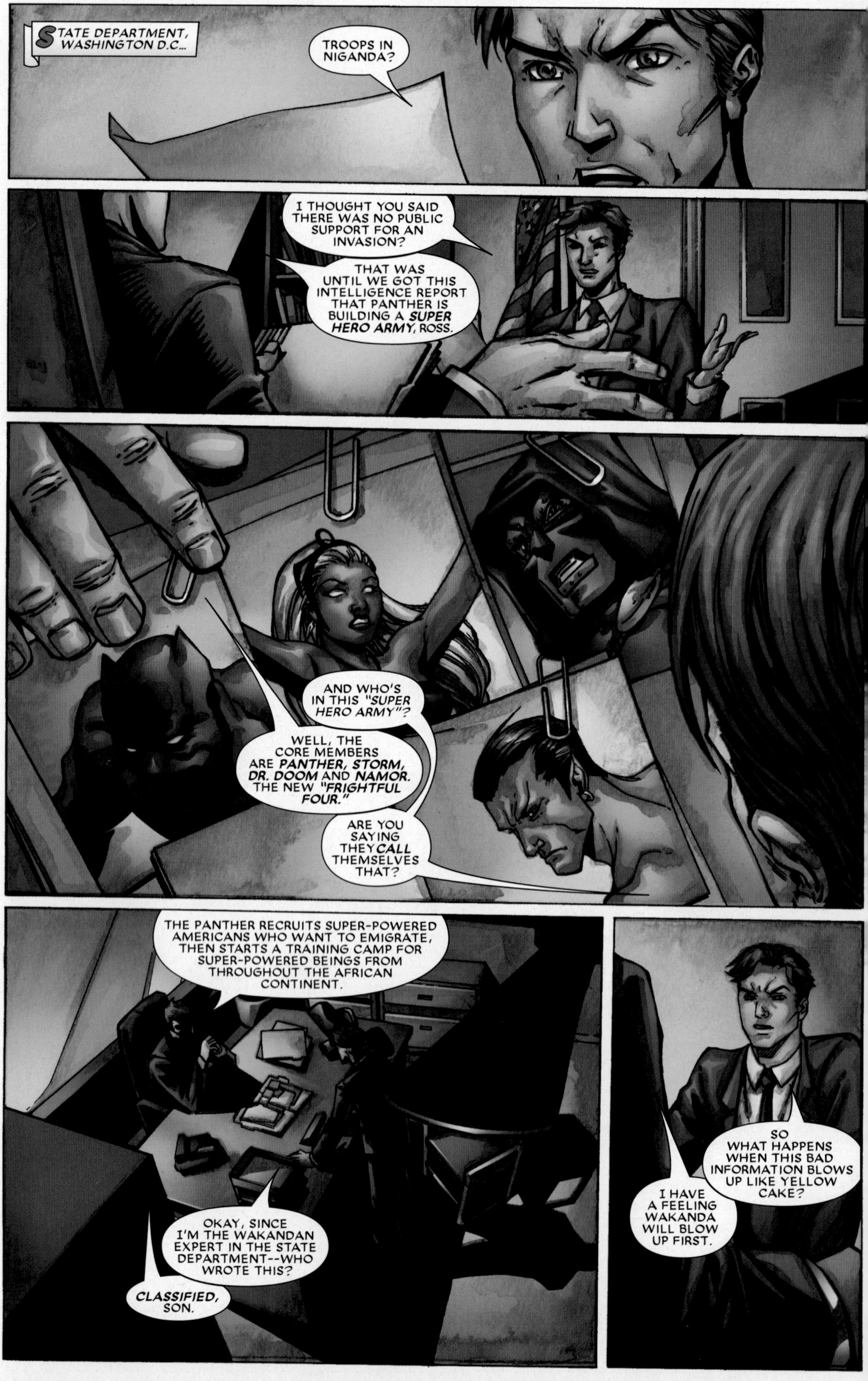
STATE DEPARTMENT, WASHINGTON D.C...
TROOPS IN NIGANDA?
I THOUGHT YOU SAID THERE WAS NO PUBLIC SUPPORT FOR AN INVASION?
THAT WAS UNTIL WE GOT THIS INTELLIGENCE REPORT THAT PANTHER IS BUILDING A SUPER HERO ARMY, ROSS.
AND WHO'S IN THIS "SUPER HERO ARMY"?
WELL, THE CORE MEMBERS ARE PANTHER, STORM, DR. DOOM AND NAMOR. THE NEW "FRIGHTFUL FOUR."
ARE YOU SAYING THEY CALL THEMSELVES THAT?
THE PANTHER RECRUITS SUPER-POWERED AMERICANS WHO WANT TO EMIGRATE, THEN STARTS A TRAINING CAMP FOR SUPER-POWERED BEINGS FROM THROUGHOUT THE AFRICAN CONTINENT.
OKAY, SINCE I'M THE WAKANDAN EXPERT IN THE STATE DEPARTMENT--WHO WROTE THIS?
CLASSIFIED, SON.
SO WHAT HAPPENS WHEN THIS BAD INFORMATION BLOWS UP LIKE YELLOW CAKE?
I HAVE A FEELING WAKANDA WILL BLOW UP FIRST.

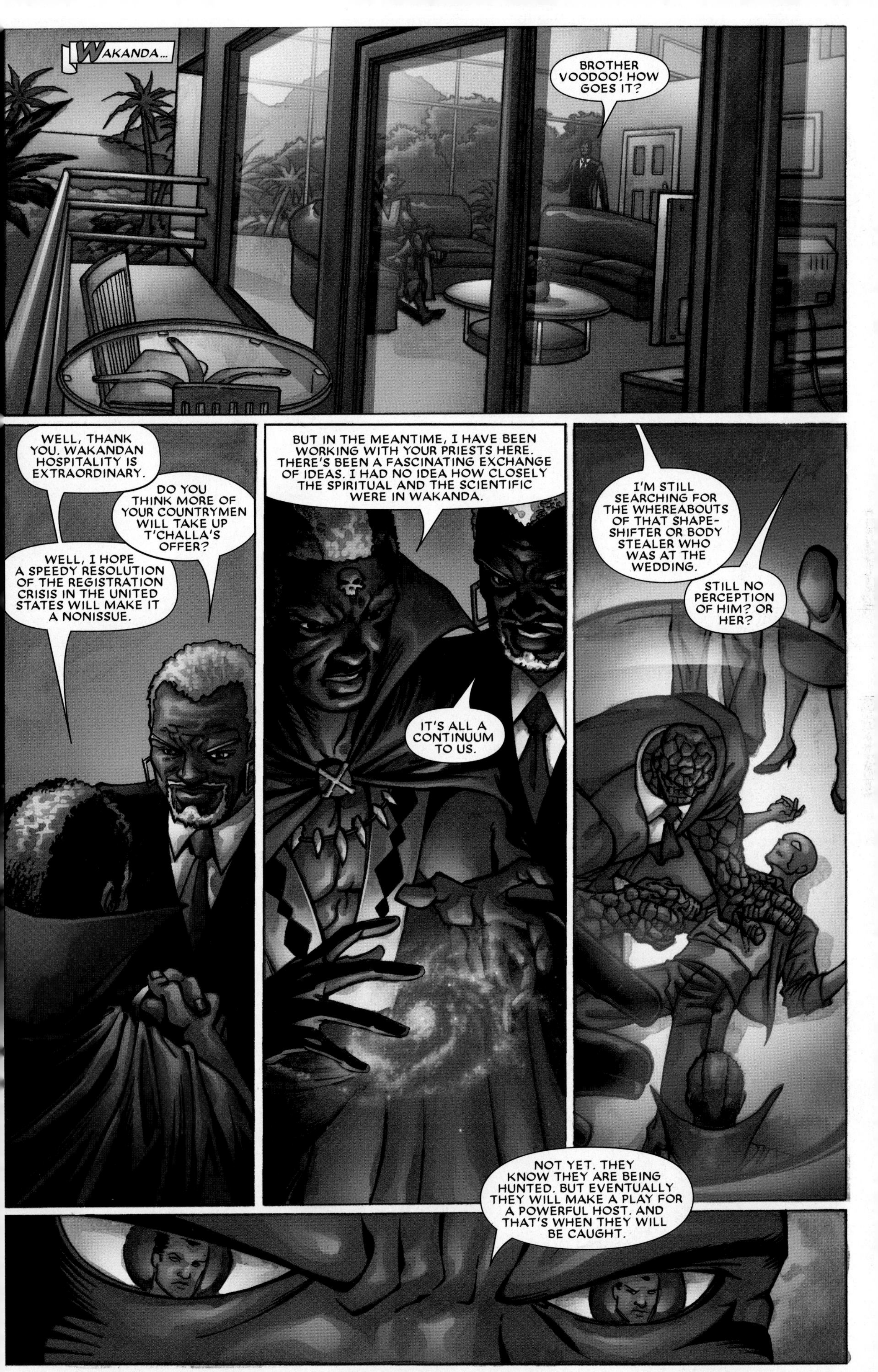
WAKANDA...
BROTHER VOODOO! HOW GOES IT?
WELL, THANK YOU. WAKANDAN HOSPITALITY IS EXTRAORDINARY.
DO YOU THINK MORE OF YOUR COUNTRYMEN WILL TAKE UP T'CHALLA'S OFFER?
WELL, I HOPE A SPEEDY RESOLUTION OF THE REGISTRATION CRISIS IN THE UNITED STATES WILL MAKE IT A NONISSUE.
BUT IN THE MEANTIME, I HAVE BEEN WORKING WITH YOUR PRIESTS HERE. THERE'S BEEN A FASCINATING EXCHANGE OF IDEAS. I HAD NO IDEA HOW CLOSELY THE SPIRITUAL AND THE SCIENTIFIC WERE IN WAKANDA.
IT'S ALL A CONTINUUM TO US.
I'M STILL SEARCHING FOR THE WHEREABOUTS OF THAT SHAPE-SHIFTER OR BODY STEALER WHO WAS AT THE WEDDING.
STILL NO PERCEPTION OF HIM? OR HER?
NOT YET. THEY KNOW THEY ARE BEING HUNTED. BUT EVENTUALLY THEY WILL MAKE A PLAY FOR A POWERFUL HOST. AND THAT'S WHEN THEY WILL BE CAUGHT.

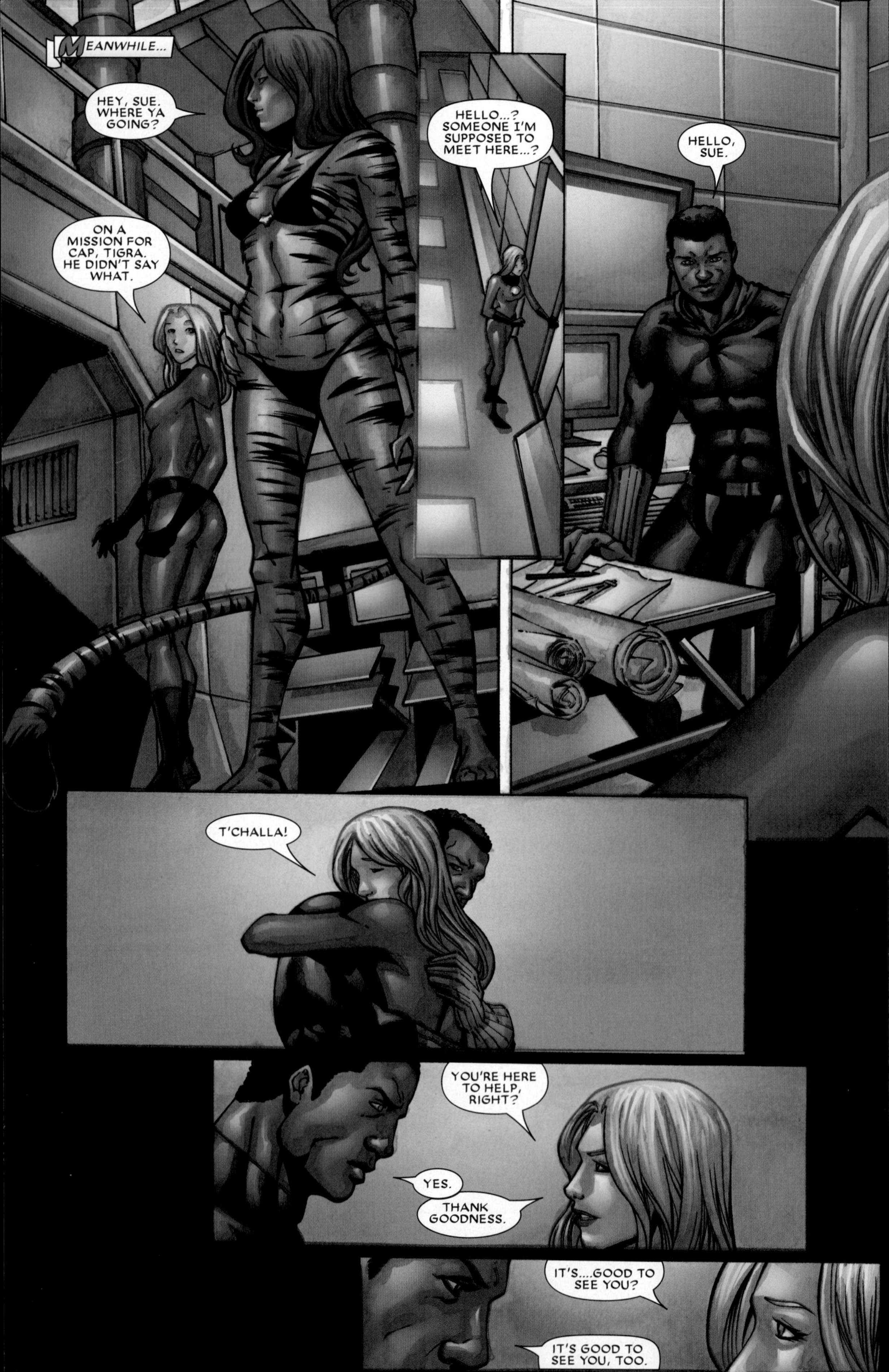
MEANWHILE...
HEY, SUE. WHERE YA GOING?
ON A MISSION FOR CAP, TIGRA. HE DIDN'T SAY WHAT.
HELLO...? SOMEONE I'M SUPPOSED TO MEET HERE...?
HELLO, SUE.
T'CHALLA!
YOU'RE HERE TO HELP, RIGHT?
YES.
THANK GOODNESS.
IT'S....GOOD TO SEE YOU?
IT'S GOOD TO SEE YOU, TOO.

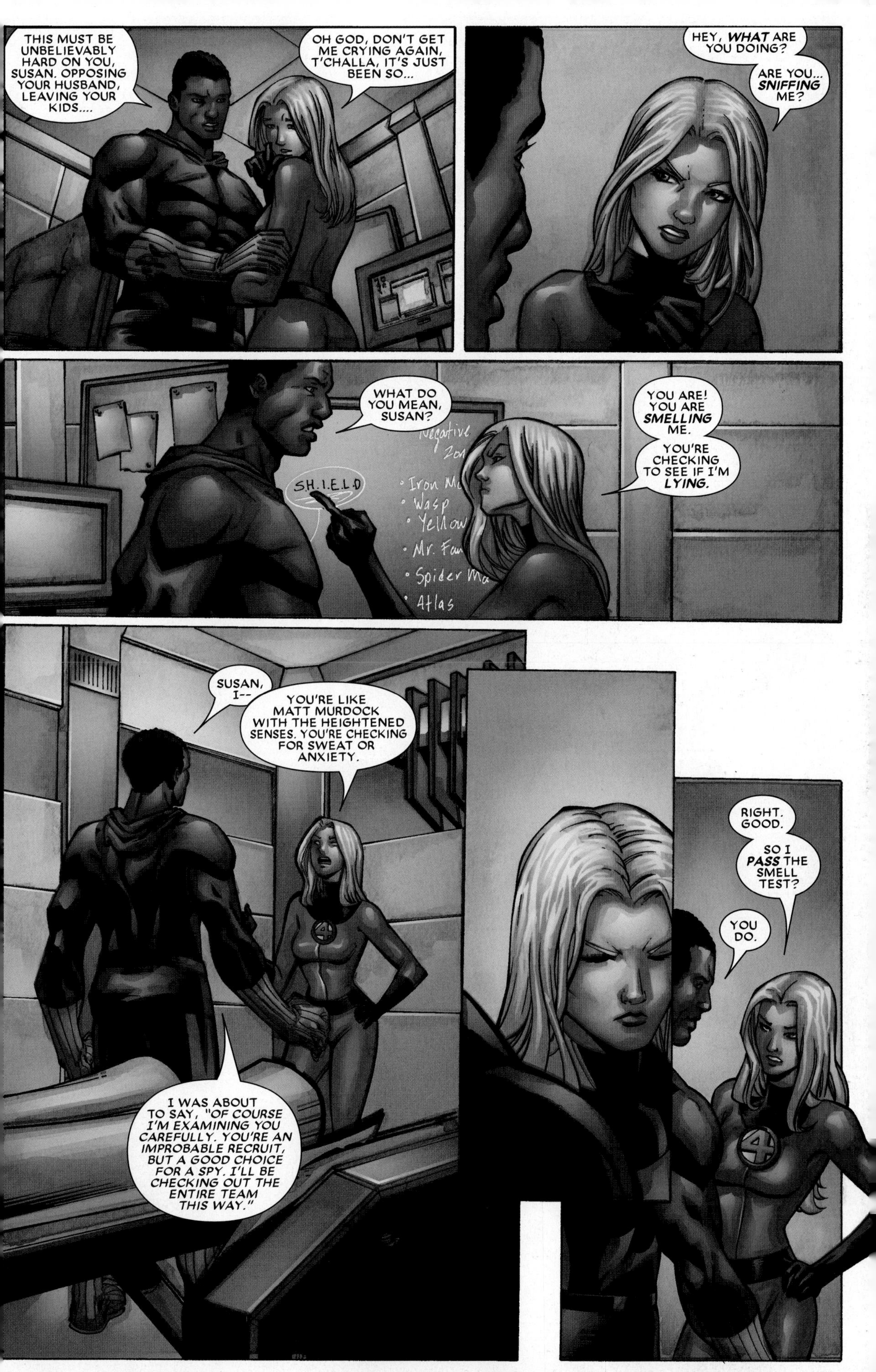
THIS MUST BE UNBELIEVABLY HARD ON YOU, SUSAN. OPPOSING YOUR HUSBAND, LEAVING YOUR KIDS....
OH GOD, DON'T GET ME CRYING AGAIN, T'CHALLA, IT'S JUST BEEN SO...
HEY, WHAT ARE YOU DOING?
ARE YOU... SNIFFING ME?
WHAT DO YOU MEAN, SUSAN?
S.H.I.E.L.D
Negative Zo
• Iron M
• Wasp
• Yellow
• Mr. Fan
• Spider Ma
• Atlas
YOU ARE! YOU ARE SMELLING ME.
YOU'RE CHECKING TO SEE IF I'M LYING.
SUSAN, I--
YOU'RE LIKE MATT MURDOCK WITH THE HEIGHTENED SENSES. YOU'RE CHECKING FOR SWEAT OR ANXIETY.
I WAS ABOUT TO SAY, "OF COURSE I'M EXAMINING YOU CAREFULLY. YOU'RE AN IMPROBABLE RECRUIT, BUT A GOOD CHOICE FOR A SPY. I'LL BE CHECKING OUT THE ENTIRE TEAM THIS WAY."
RIGHT. GOOD.
SO I PASS THE SMELL TEST?
YOU DO.

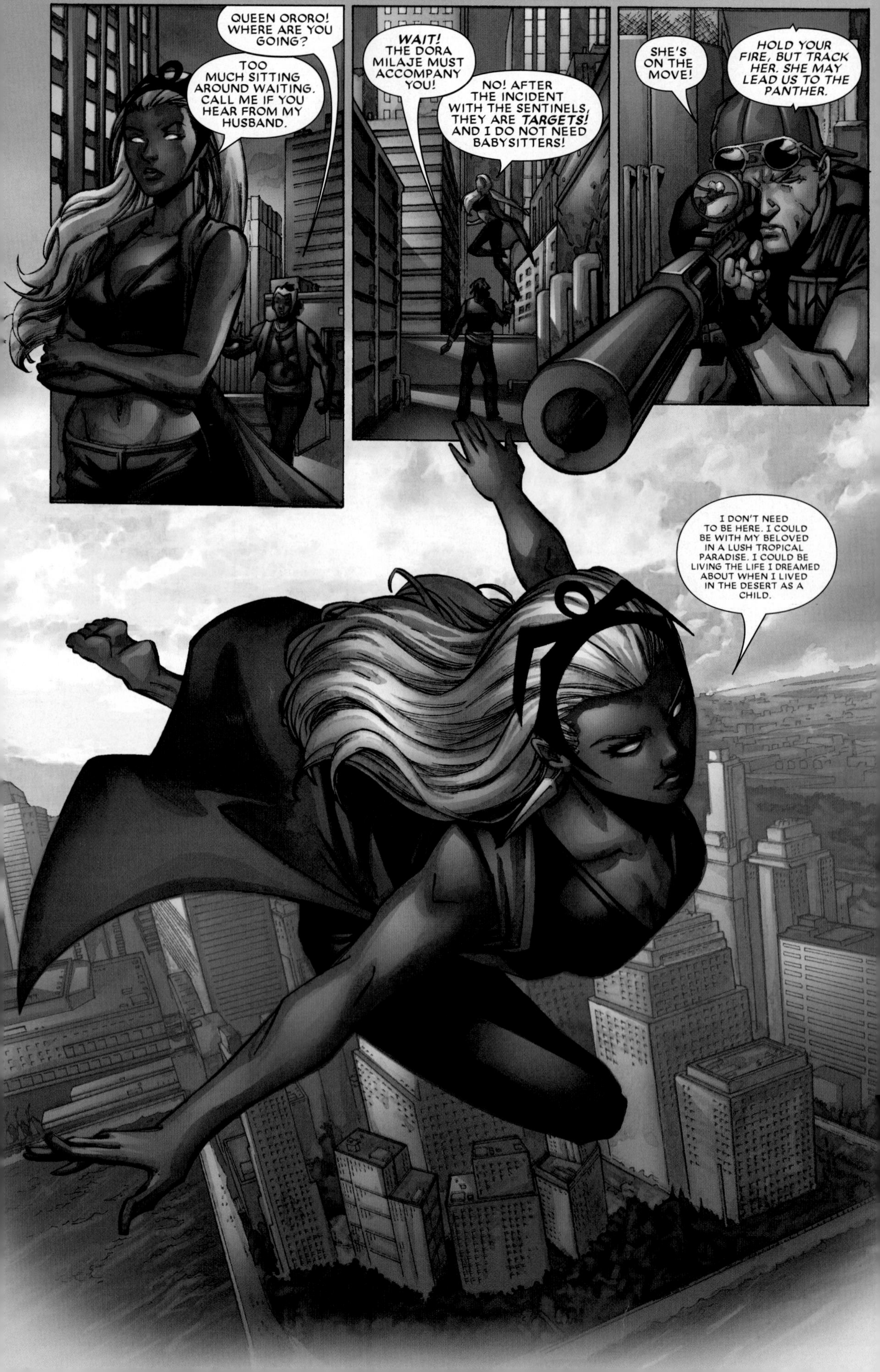
QUEEN ORORO! WHERE ARE YOU GOING?
TOO MUCH SITTING AROUND WAITING. CALL ME IF YOU HEAR FROM MY HUSBAND.
WAIT! THE DORA MILAJE MUST ACCOMPANY YOU!
NO! AFTER THE INCIDENT WITH THE SENTINELS, THEY ARE TARGETS! AND I DO NOT NEED BABYSITTERS!
SHE'S ON THE MOVE!
HOLD YOUR FIRE, BUT TRACK HER. SHE MAY LEAD US TO THE PANTHER.
I DON'T NEED TO BE HERE. I COULD BE WITH MY BELOVED IN A LUSH TROPICAL PARADISE. I COULD BE LIVING THE LIFE I DREAMED ABOUT WHEN I LIVED IN THE DESERT AS A CHILD.

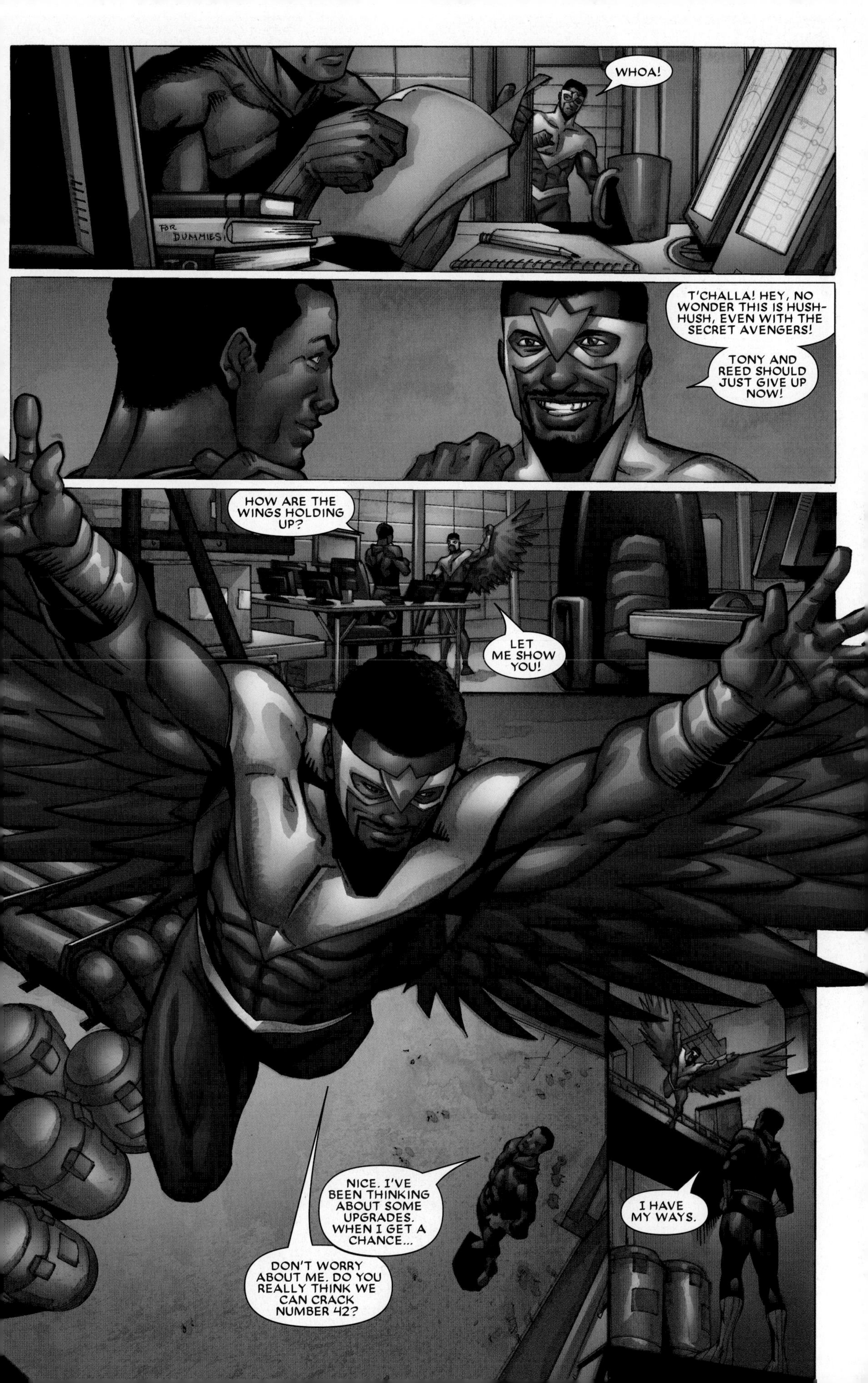
WHOA!
FOR DUMMIES
T'CHALLA! HEY, NO WONDER THIS IS HUSH-HUSH, EVEN WITH THE SECRET AVENGERS!
TONY AND REED SHOULD JUST GIVE UP NOW!
HOW ARE THE WINGS HOLDING UP?
LET ME SHOW YOU!
NICE. I'VE BEEN THINKING ABOUT SOME UPGRADES. WHEN I GET A CHANCE...
DON'T WORRY ABOUT ME. DO YOU REALLY THINK WE CAN CRACK NUMBER 42?
I HAVE MY WAYS.

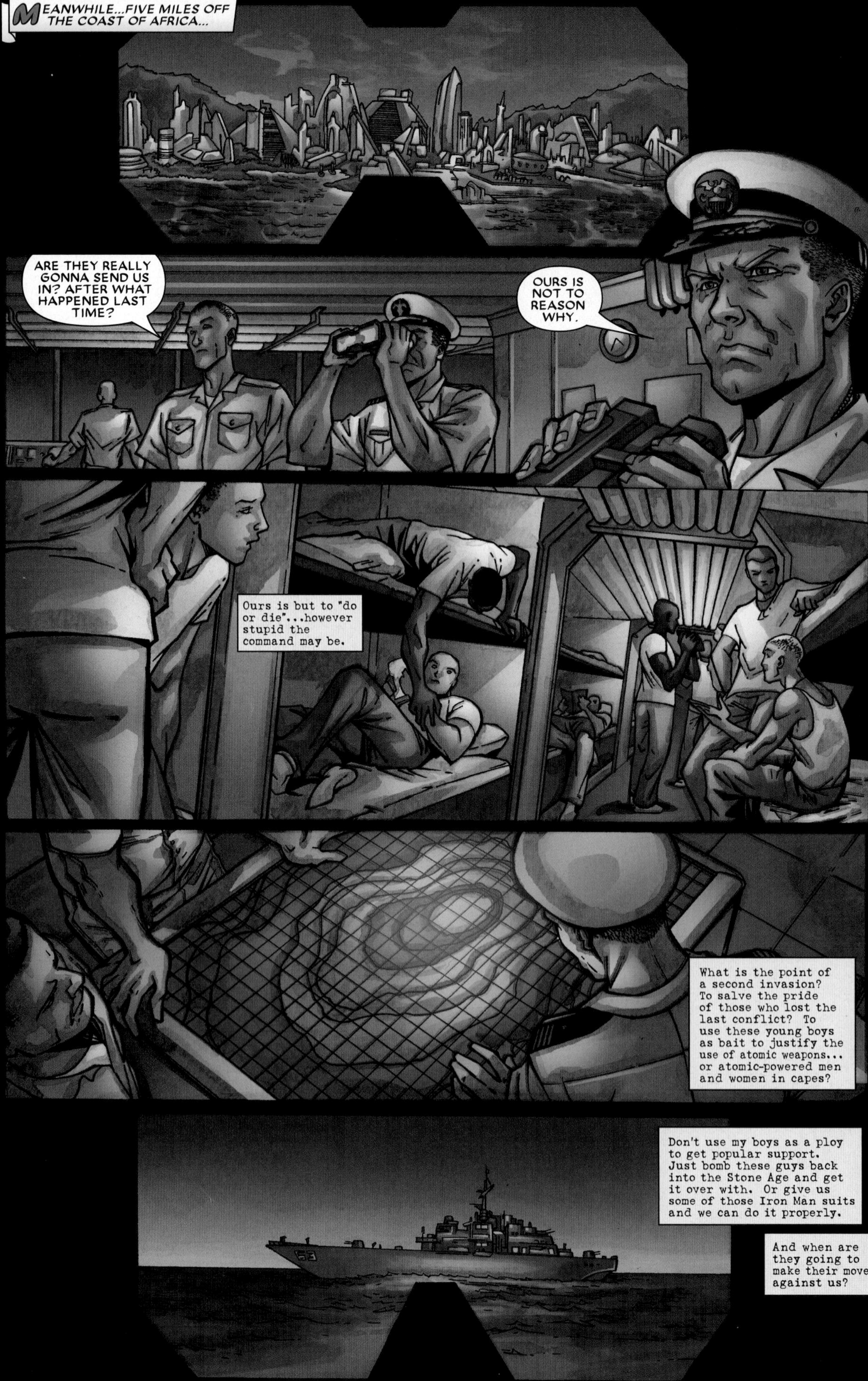
MEANWHILE...FIVE MILES OFF THE COAST OF AFRICA...
ARE THEY REALLY GONNA SEND US IN? AFTER WHAT HAPPENED LAST TIME?
OURS IS NOT TO REASON WHY.
Ours is but to "do or die"...however stupid the command may be.
What is the point of a second invasion? To salve the pride of those who lost the last conflict? To use these young boys as bait to justify the use of atomic weapons... or atomic-powered men and women in capes?
Don't use my boys as a ploy to get popular support. Just bomb these guys back into the Stone Age and get it over with. Or give us some of those Iron Man suits and we can do it properly.
And when are they going to make their move against us?

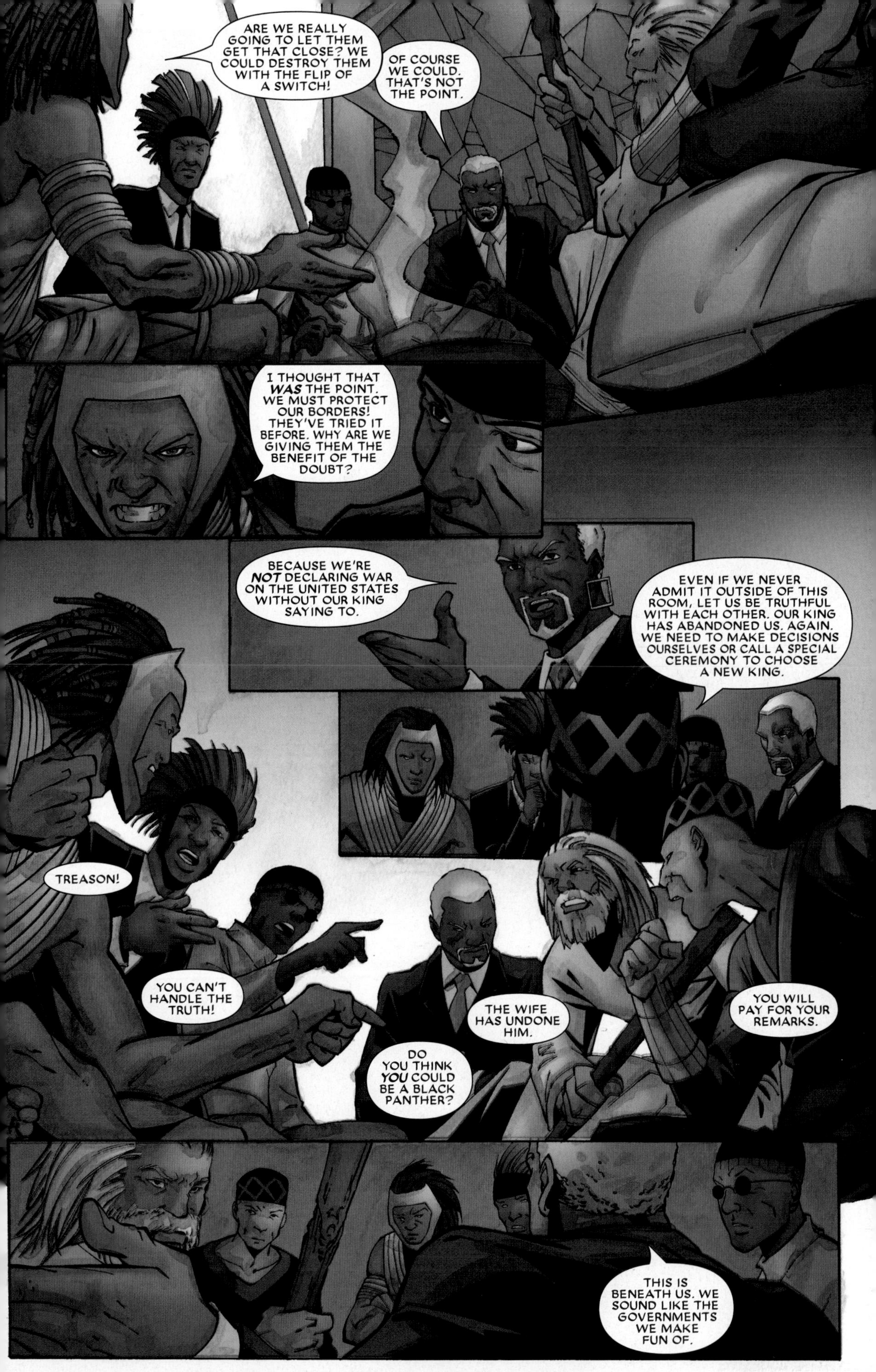
ARE WE REALLY GOING TO LET THEM GET THAT CLOSE? WE COULD DESTROY THEM WITH THE FLIP OF A SWITCH!
OF COURSE WE COULD. THAT'S NOT THE POINT.
I THOUGHT THAT WAS THE POINT. WE MUST PROTECT OUR BORDERS! THEY'VE TRIED IT BEFORE. WHY ARE WE GIVING THEM THE BENEFIT OF THE DOUBT?
BECAUSE WE'RE NOT DECLARING WAR ON THE UNITED STATES WITHOUT OUR KING SAYING TO.
EVEN IF WE NEVER ADMIT IT OUTSIDE OF THIS ROOM, LET US BE TRUTHFUL WITH EACH OTHER. OUR KING HAS ABANDONED US. AGAIN. WE NEED TO MAKE DECISIONS OURSELVES OR CALL A SPECIAL CEREMONY TO CHOOSE A NEW KING.
TREASON!
YOU CAN'T HANDLE THE TRUTH!
DO YOU THINK YOU COULD BE A BLACK PANTHER?
THE WIFE HAS UNDONE HIM.
YOU WILL PAY FOR YOUR REMARKS.
THIS IS BENEATH US. WE SOUND LIKE THE GOVERNMENTS WE MAKE FUN OF.

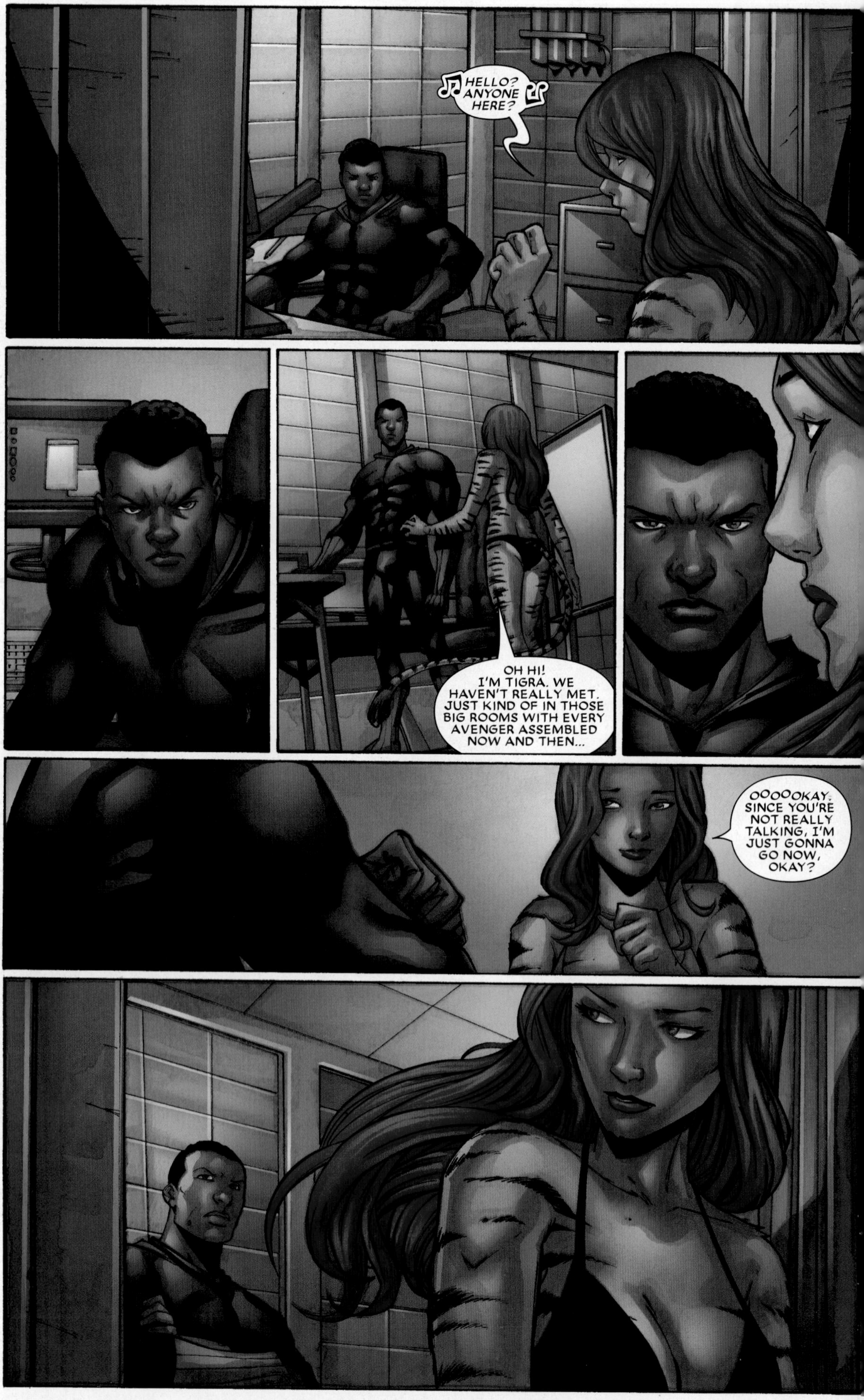
HELLO? ANYONE HERE?
OH HI! I'M TIGRA. WE HAVEN'T REALLY MET. JUST KIND OF IN THOSE BIG ROOMS WITH EVERY AVENGER ASSEMBLED NOW AND THEN...
OOOOOKAY. SINCE YOU'RE NOT REALLY TALKING, I'M JUST GONNA GO NOW, OKAY?

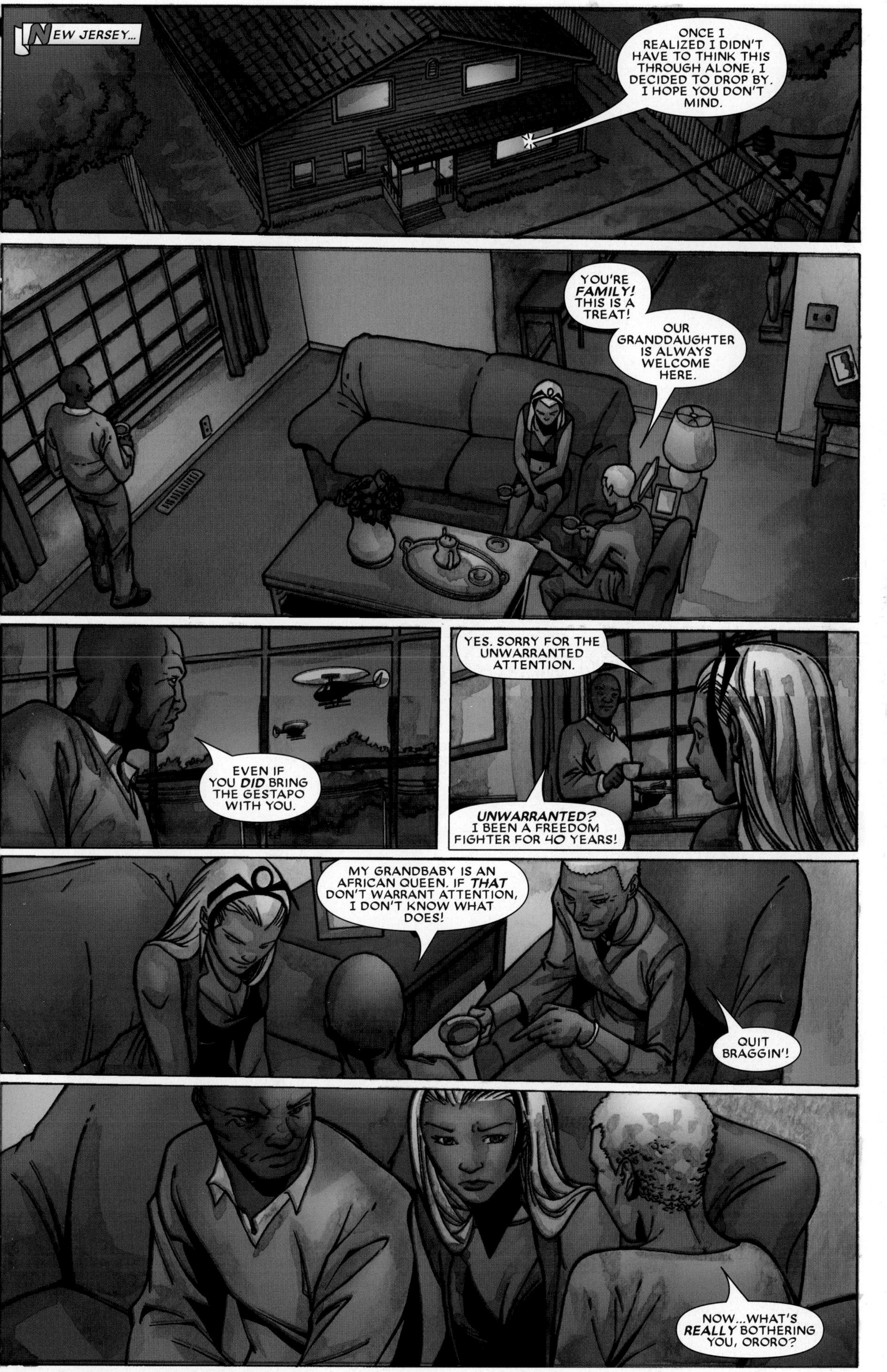
NEW JERSEY...
ONCE I REALIZED I DIDN'T HAVE TO THINK THIS THROUGH ALONE, I DECIDED TO DROP BY. I HOPE YOU DON'T MIND.
YOU'RE FAMILY! THIS IS A TREAT!
OUR GRANDDAUGHTER IS ALWAYS WELCOME HERE.
EVEN IF YOU DID BRING THE GESTAPO WITH YOU.
YES. SORRY FOR THE UNWARRANTED ATTENTION.
UNWARRANTED? I BEEN A FREEDOM FIGHTER FOR 40 YEARS!
MY GRANDBABY IS AN AFRICAN QUEEN. IF THAT DON'T WARRANT ATTENTION, I DON'T KNOW WHAT DOES!
QUIT BRAGGIN'!
NOW...WHAT'S REALLY BOTHERING YOU, ORORO?

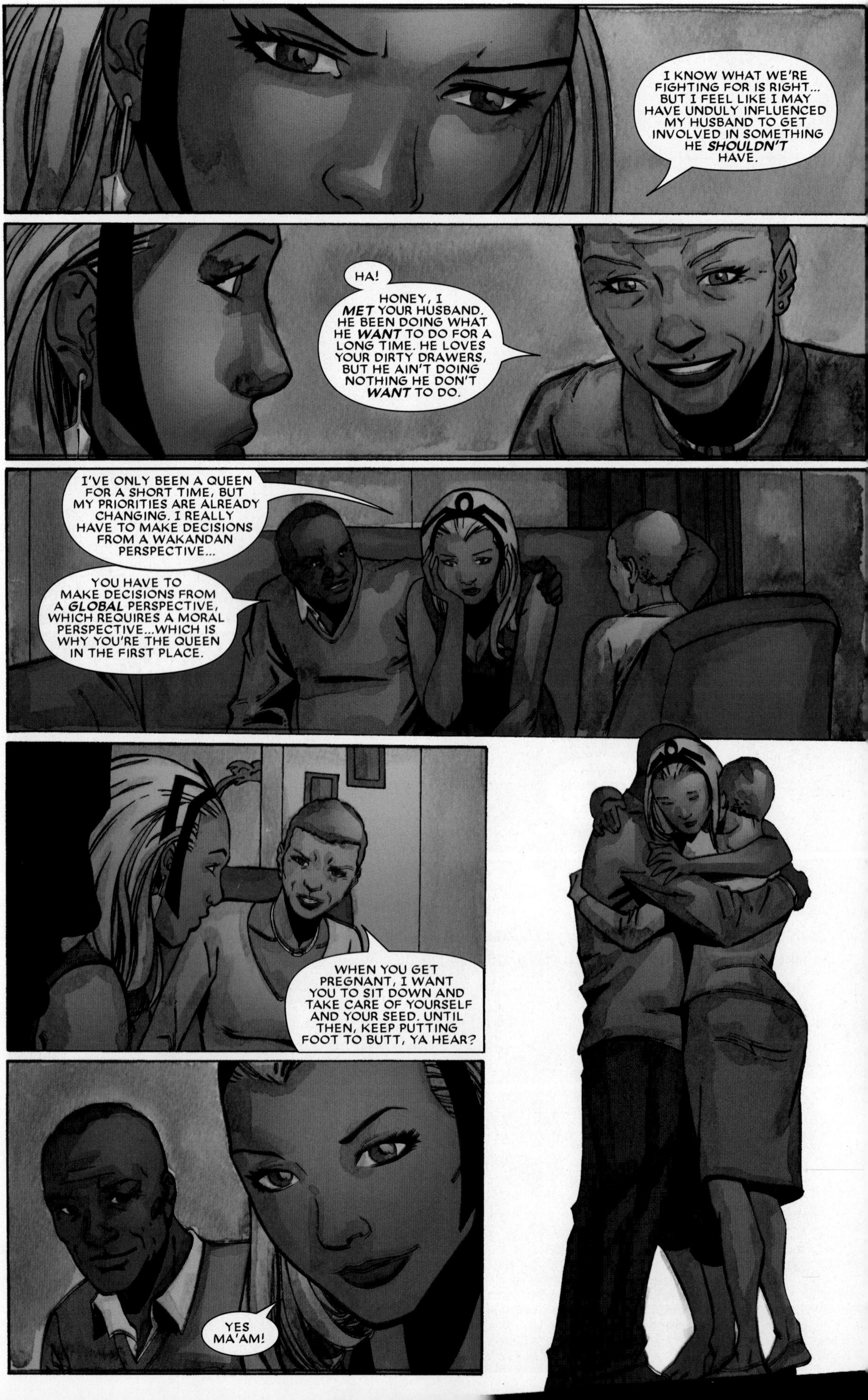
I KNOW WHAT WE'RE FIGHTING FOR IS RIGHT... BUT I FEEL LIKE I MAY HAVE UNDULY INFLUENCED MY HUSBAND TO GET INVOLVED IN SOMETHING HE SHOULDN'T HAVE.
HA!
HONEY, I MET YOUR HUSBAND. HE BEEN DOING WHAT HE WANT TO DO FOR A LONG TIME. HE LOVES YOUR DIRTY DRAWERS, BUT HE AIN'T DOING NOTHING HE DON'T WANT TO DO.
I'VE ONLY BEEN A QUEEN FOR A SHORT TIME, BUT MY PRIORITIES ARE ALREADY CHANGING. I REALLY HAVE TO MAKE DECISIONS FROM A WAKANDAN PERSPECTIVE...
YOU HAVE TO MAKE DECISIONS FROM A GLOBAL PERSPECTIVE, WHICH REQUIRES A MORAL PERSPECTIVE...WHICH IS WHY YOU'RE THE QUEEN IN THE FIRST PLACE.
WHEN YOU GET PREGNANT, I WANT YOU TO SIT DOWN AND TAKE CARE OF YOURSELF AND YOUR SEED. UNTIL THEN, KEEP PUTTING FOOT TO BUTT, YA HEAR?
YES MA'AM!

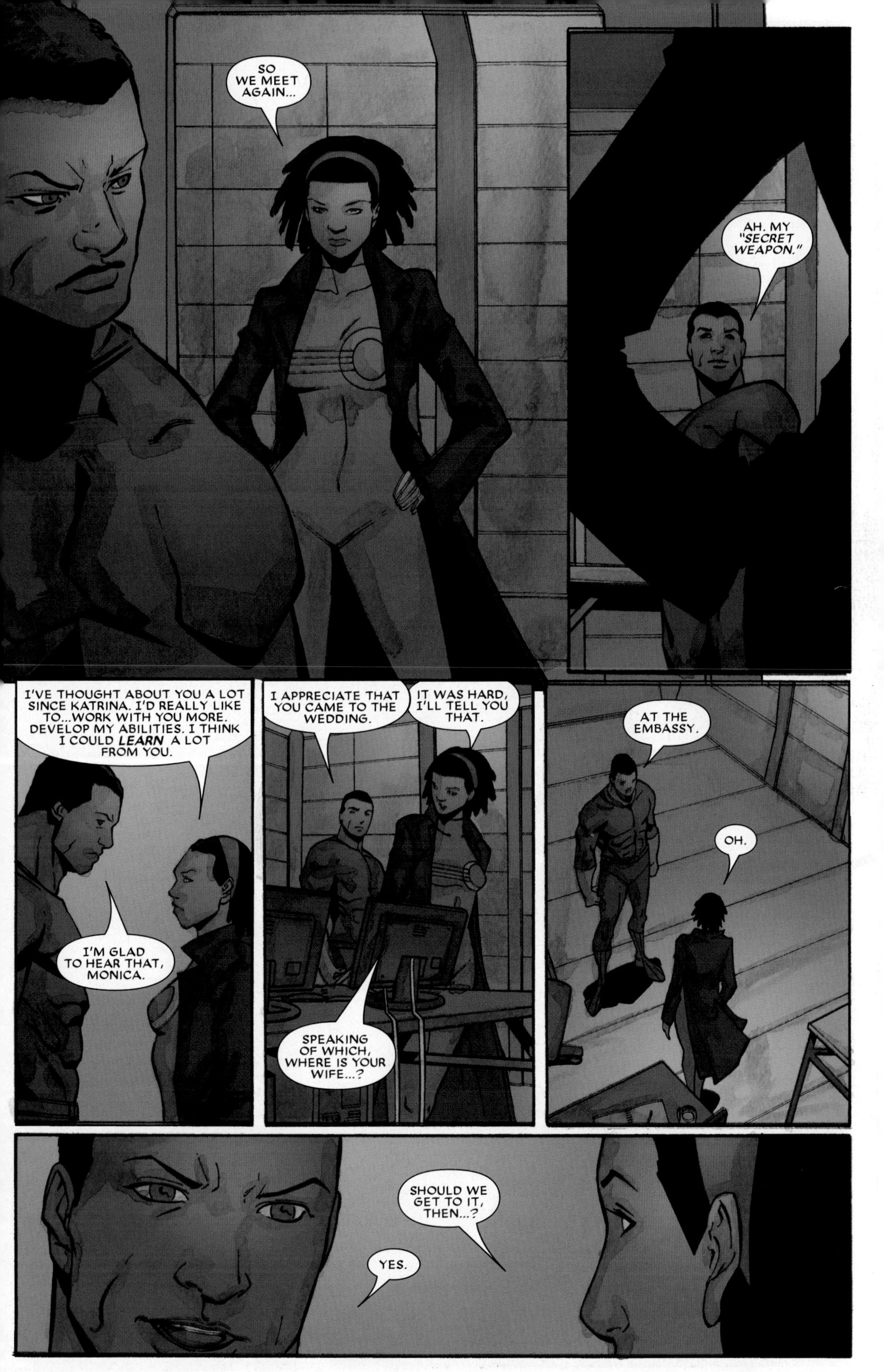
SO WE MEET AGAIN...
AH. MY "SECRET WEAPON."
I'VE THOUGHT ABOUT YOU A LOT SINCE KATRINA. I'D REALLY LIKE TO...WORK WITH YOU MORE. DEVELOP MY ABILITIES. I THINK I COULD LEARN A LOT FROM YOU.
I'M GLAD TO HEAR THAT, MONICA.
I APPRECIATE THAT YOU CAME TO THE WEDDING.
IT WAS HARD, I'LL TELL YOU THAT.
SPEAKING OF WHICH, WHERE IS YOUR WIFE...?
AT THE EMBASSY.
OH.
SHOULD WE GET TO IT, THEN...?
YES.

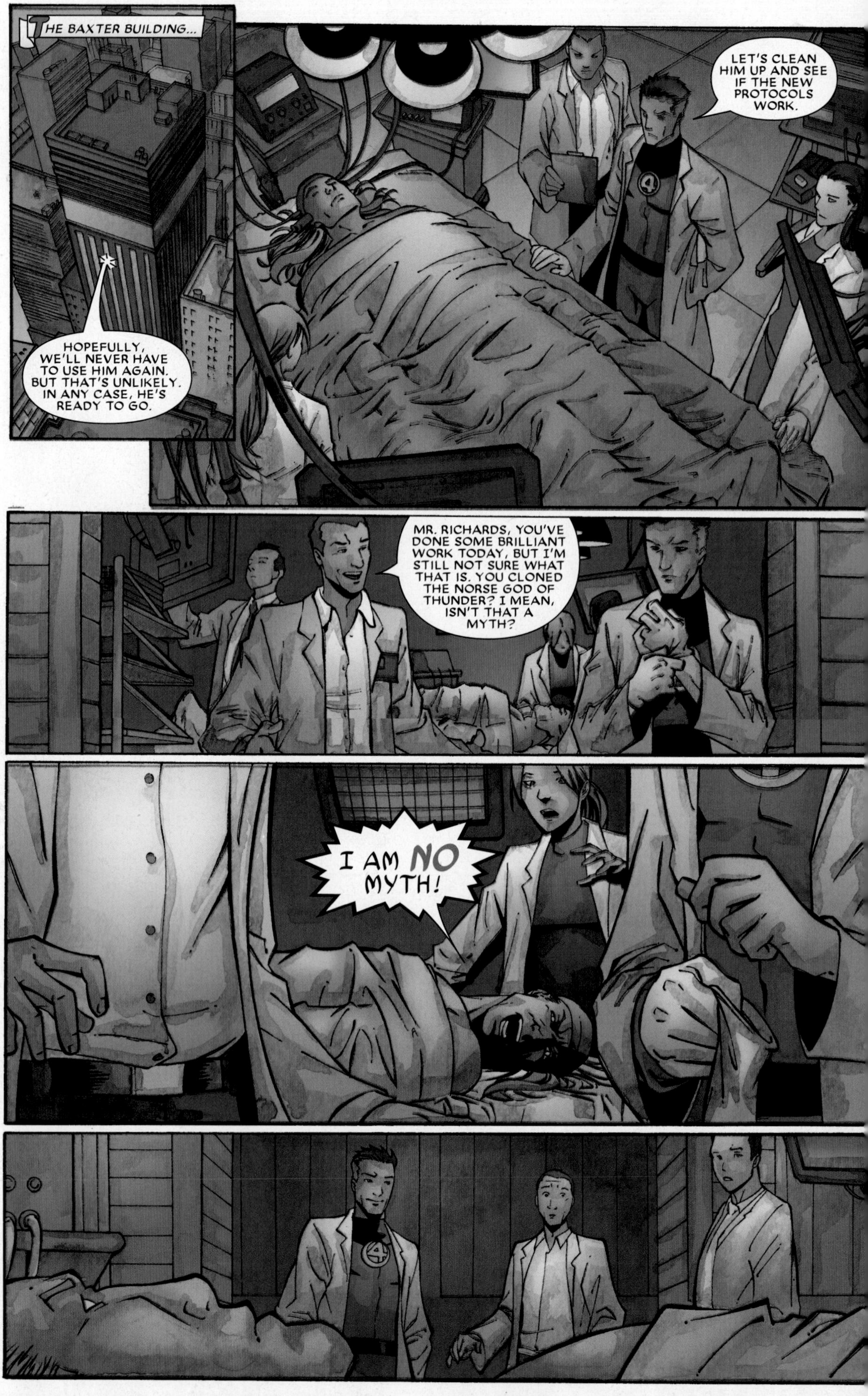
THE BAXTER BUILDING...
HOPEFULLY, WE'LL NEVER HAVE TO USE HIM AGAIN. BUT THAT'S UNLIKELY. IN ANY CASE, HE'S READY TO GO.
LET'S CLEAN HIM UP AND SEE IF THE NEW PROTOCOLS WORK.
MR. RICHARDS, YOU'VE DONE SOME BRILLIANT WORK TODAY, BUT I'M STILL NOT SURE WHAT THAT IS. YOU CLONED THE NORSE GOD OF THUNDER? I MEAN, ISN'T THAT A MYTH?
I AM NO MYTH!

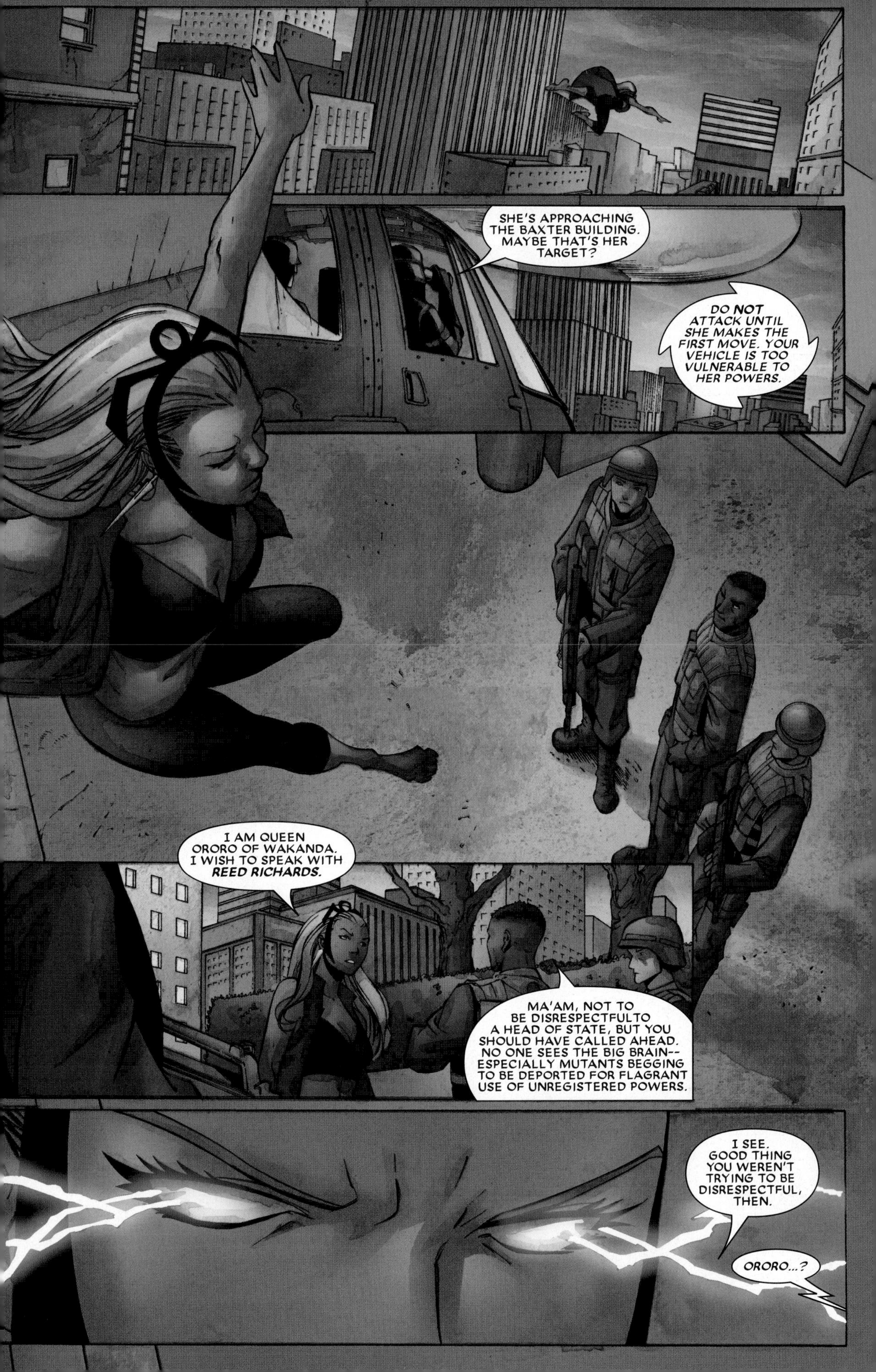

SHE'S APPROACHING THE BAXTER BUILDING. MAYBE THAT'S HER TARGET?
DO NOT ATTACK UNTIL SHE MAKES THE FIRST MOVE. YOUR VEHICLE IS TOO VULNERABLE TO HER POWERS.
I AM QUEEN ORORO OF WAKANDA. I WISH TO SPEAK WITH REED RICHARDS.
MA'AM, NOT TO BE DISRESPECTFULTO A HEAD OF STATE, BUT YOU SHOULD HAVE CALLED AHEAD. NO ONE SEES THE BIG BRAIN-- ESPECIALLY MUTANTS BEGGING TO BE DEPORTED FOR FLAGRANT USE OF UNREGISTERED POWERS.
I SEE. GOOD THING YOU WEREN'T TRYING TO BE DISRESPECTFUL, THEN.
ORORO...?

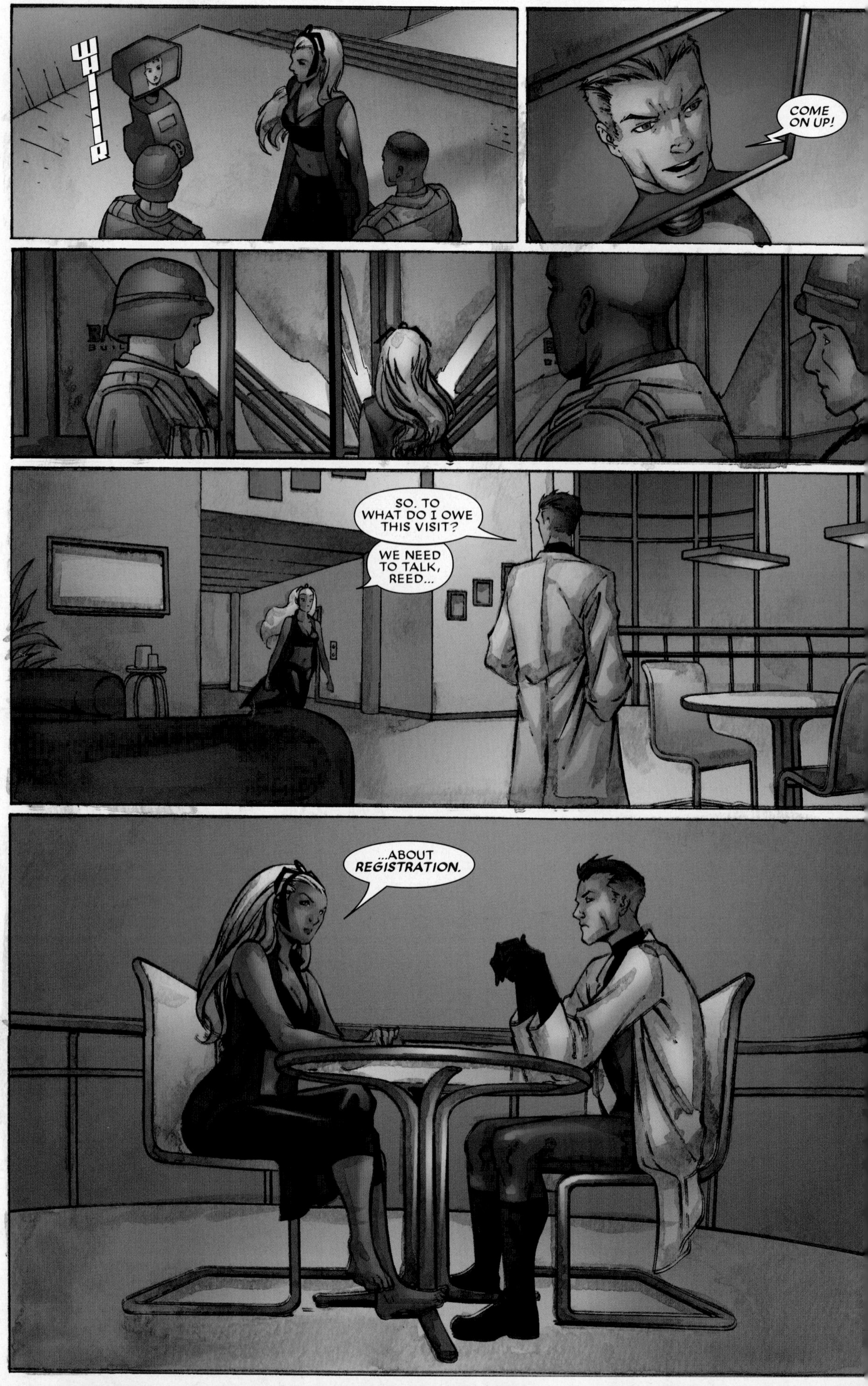
WHIIIR
COME ON UP!
SO. TO WHAT DO I OWE THIS VISIT?
WE NEED TO TALK, REED...
...ABOUT *REGISTRATION.*

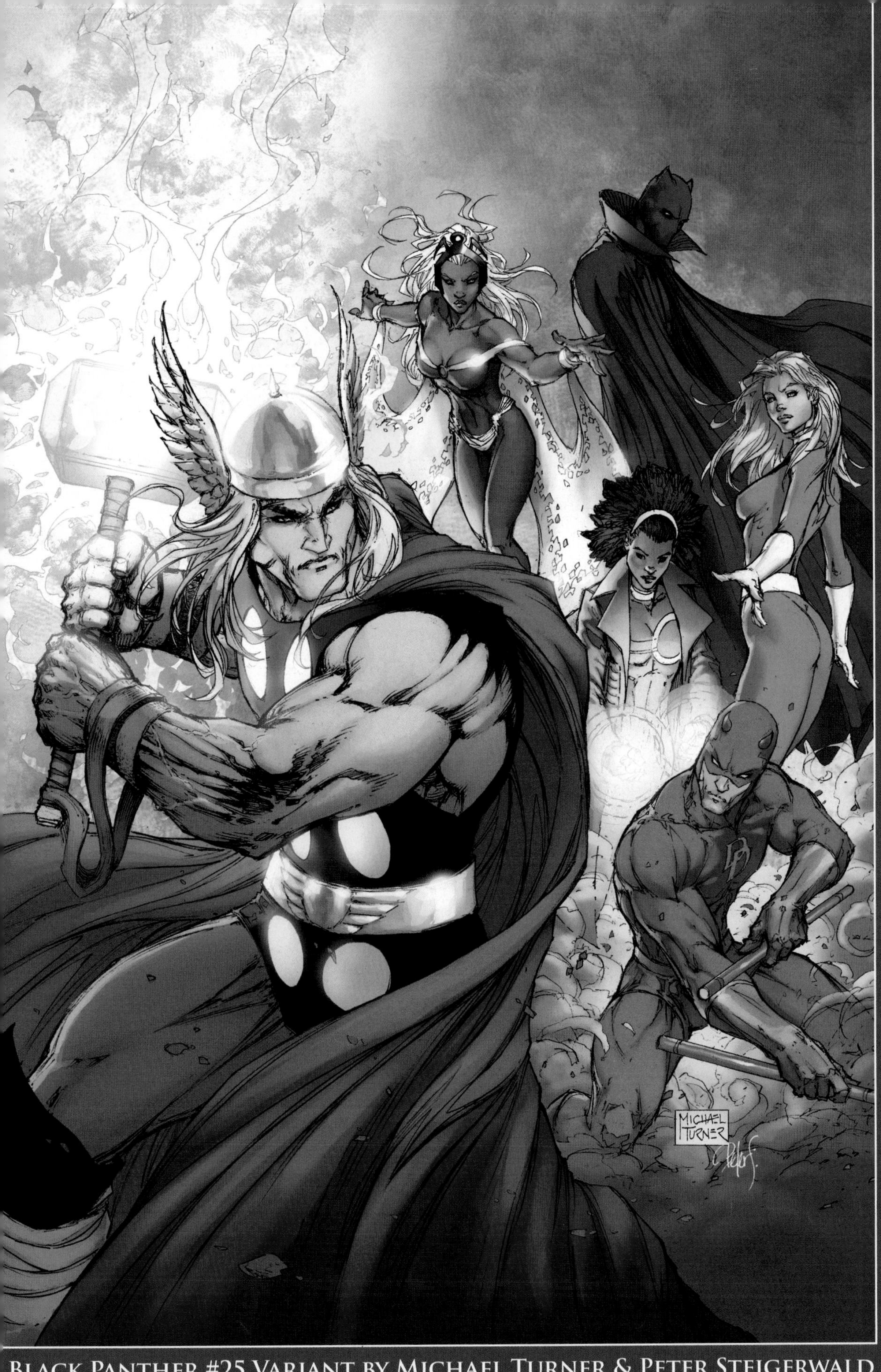
MICHAEL TURNER

BLACK PANTHER #25 VARIANT BY MICHAEL TURNER & PETER STEIGERWALD

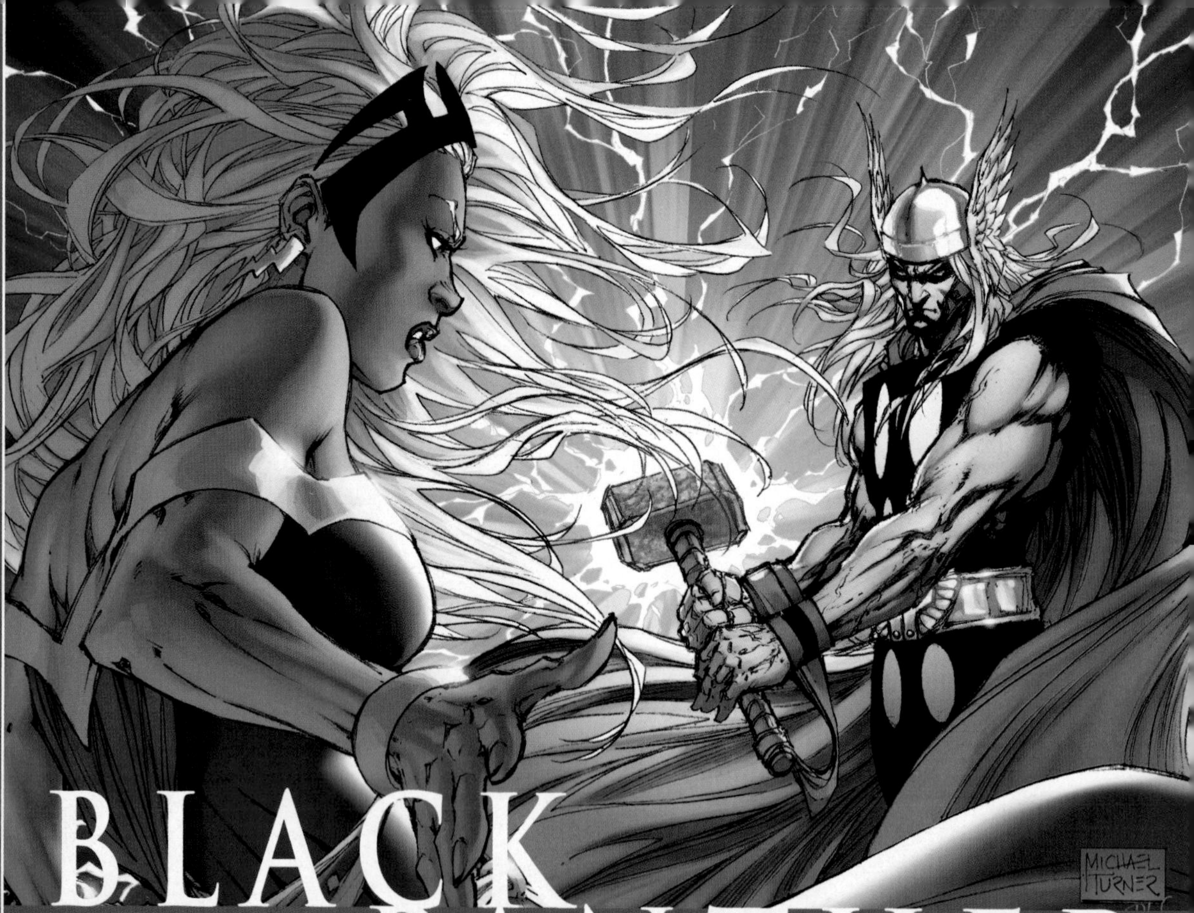
MICHAEL TURNER

BLACK PANTHER

A MARVEL COMICS EVENT

CIVIL WAR

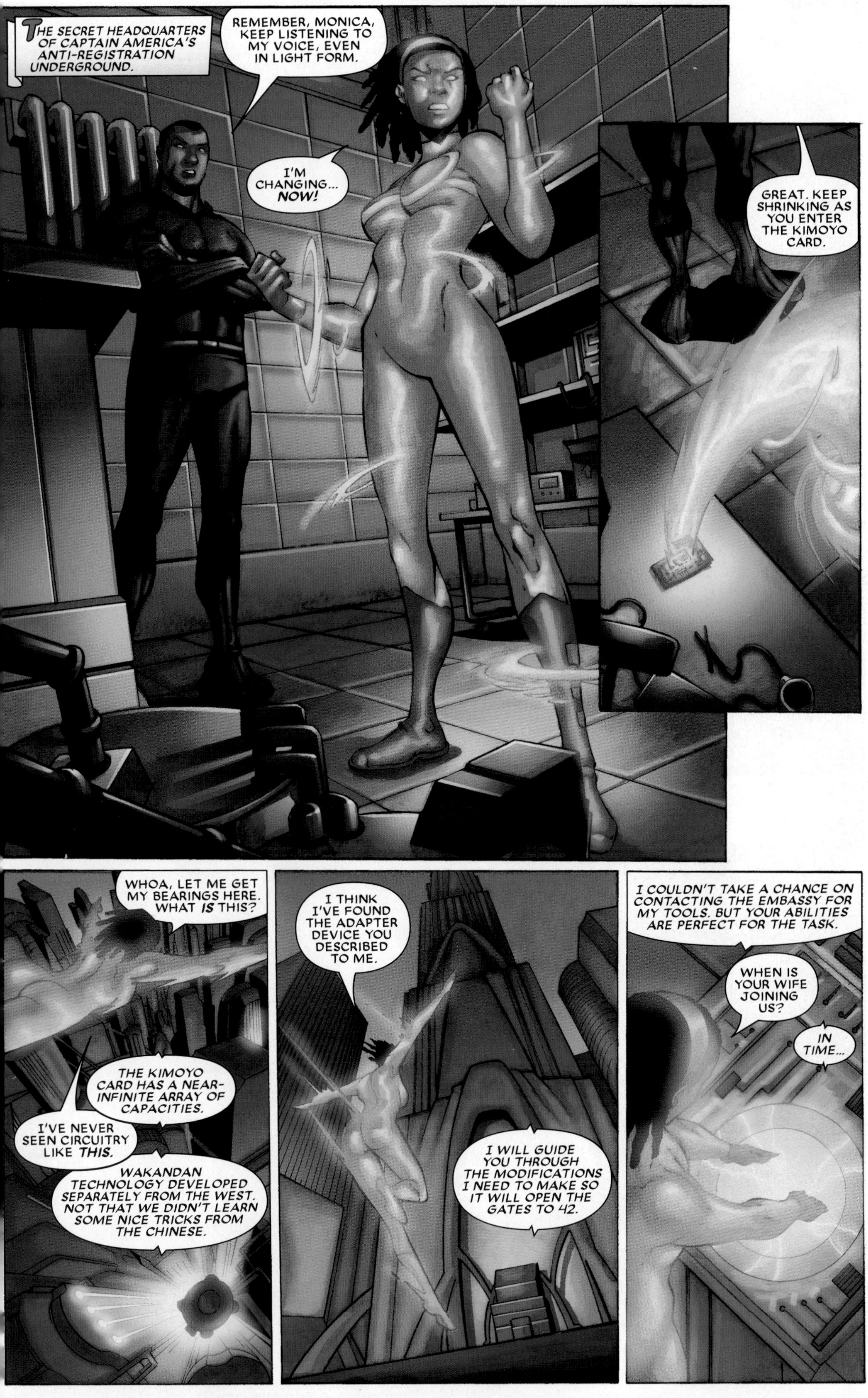
THE SECRET HEADQUARTERS OF CAPTAIN AMERICA'S ANTI-REGISTRATION UNDERGROUND.
REMEMBER, MONICA, KEEP LISTENING TO MY VOICE, EVEN IN LIGHT FORM.
I'M CHANGING... NOW!
GREAT. KEEP SHRINKING AS YOU ENTER THE KIMOYO CARD.
WHOA, LET ME GET MY BEARINGS HERE. WHAT IS THIS?
THE KIMOYO CARD HAS A NEAR-INFINITE ARRAY OF CAPACITIES.
I'VE NEVER SEEN CIRCUITRY LIKE THIS.
WAKANDAN TECHNOLOGY DEVELOPED SEPARATELY FROM THE WEST. NOT THAT WE DIDN'T LEARN SOME NICE TRICKS FROM THE CHINESE.
I THINK I'VE FOUND THE ADAPTER DEVICE YOU DESCRIBED TO ME.
I WILL GUIDE YOU THROUGH THE MODIFICATIONS I NEED TO MAKE SO IT WILL OPEN THE GATES TO 42.
I COULDN'T TAKE A CHANCE ON CONTACTING THE EMBASSY FOR MY TOOLS. BUT YOUR ABILITIES ARE PERFECT FOR THE TASK.
WHEN IS YOUR WIFE JOINING US?
IN TIME...

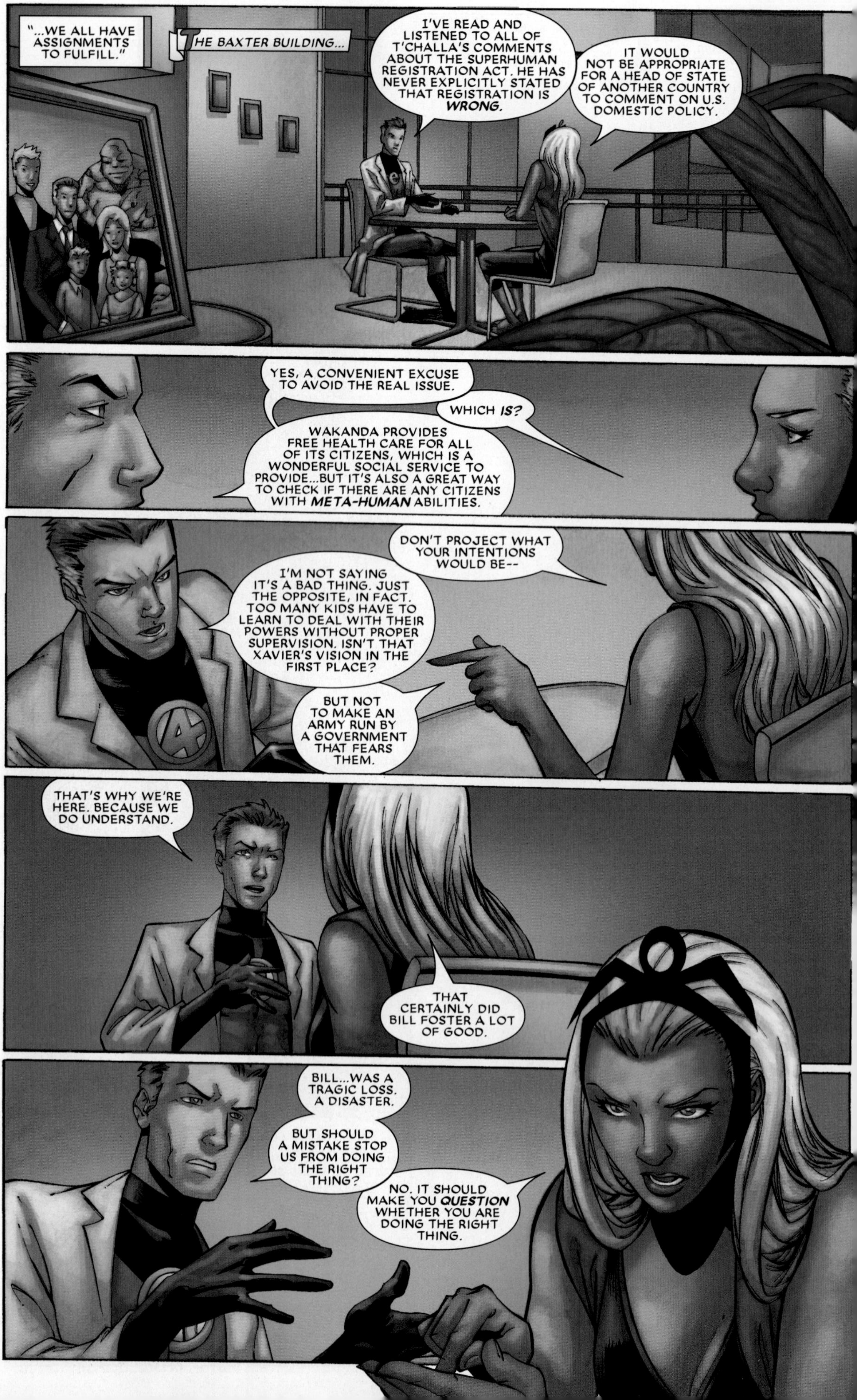
"...WE ALL HAVE ASSIGNMENTS TO FULFILL."
THE BAXTER BUILDING...
I'VE READ AND LISTENED TO ALL OF T'CHALLA'S COMMENTS ABOUT THE SUPERHUMAN REGISTRATION ACT. HE HAS NEVER EXPLICITLY STATED THAT REGISTRATION IS WRONG.
IT WOULD NOT BE APPROPRIATE FOR A HEAD OF STATE OF ANOTHER COUNTRY TO COMMENT ON U.S. DOMESTIC POLICY.
YES, A CONVENIENT EXCUSE TO AVOID THE REAL ISSUE.
WHICH IS?
WAKANDA PROVIDES FREE HEALTH CARE FOR ALL OF ITS CITIZENS, WHICH IS A WONDERFUL SOCIAL SERVICE TO PROVIDE...BUT IT'S ALSO A GREAT WAY TO CHECK IF THERE ARE ANY CITIZENS WITH META-HUMAN ABILITIES.
DON'T PROJECT WHAT YOUR INTENTIONS WOULD BE--
I'M NOT SAYING IT'S A BAD THING. JUST THE OPPOSITE, IN FACT. TOO MANY KIDS HAVE TO LEARN TO DEAL WITH THEIR POWERS WITHOUT PROPER SUPERVISION. ISN'T THAT XAVIER'S VISION IN THE FIRST PLACE?
BUT NOT TO MAKE AN ARMY RUN BY A GOVERNMENT THAT FEARS THEM.
THAT'S WHY WE'RE HERE. BECAUSE WE DO UNDERSTAND.
THAT CERTAINLY DID BILL FOSTER A LOT OF GOOD.
BILL...WAS A TRAGIC LOSS. A DISASTER.
BUT SHOULD A MISTAKE STOP US FROM DOING THE RIGHT THING?
NO. IT SHOULD MAKE YOU QUESTION WHETHER YOU ARE DOING THE RIGHT THING.

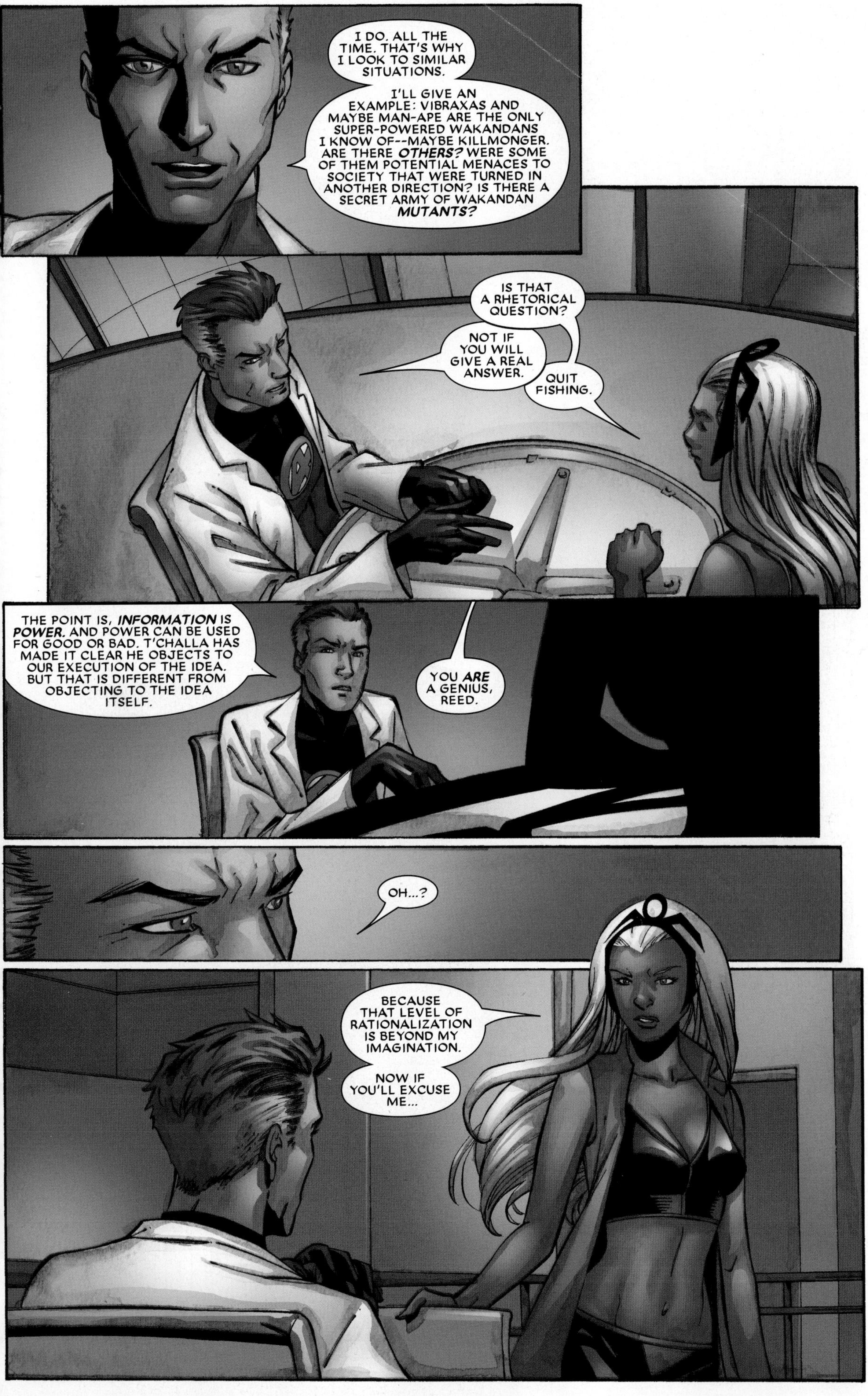
I DO. ALL THE TIME. THAT'S WHY I LOOK TO SIMILAR SITUATIONS.
I'LL GIVE AN EXAMPLE: VIBRAXAS AND MAYBE MAN-APE ARE THE ONLY SUPER-POWERED WAKANDANS I KNOW OF--MAYBE KILLMONGER. ARE THERE *OTHERS?* WERE SOME OF THEM POTENTIAL MENACES TO SOCIETY THAT WERE TURNED IN ANOTHER DIRECTION? IS THERE A SECRET ARMY OF WAKANDAN *MUTANTS?*
IS THAT A RHETORICAL QUESTION?
NOT IF YOU WILL GIVE A REAL ANSWER.
QUIT FISHING.
THE POINT IS, *INFORMATION* IS *POWER*. AND POWER CAN BE USED FOR GOOD OR BAD. T'CHALLA HAS MADE IT CLEAR HE OBJECTS TO OUR EXECUTION OF THE IDEA. BUT THAT IS DIFFERENT FROM OBJECTING TO THE IDEA ITSELF.
YOU *ARE* A GENIUS, REED.
OH...?
BECAUSE THAT LEVEL OF RATIONALIZATION IS BEYOND MY IMAGINATION.
NOW IF YOU'LL EXCUSE ME...

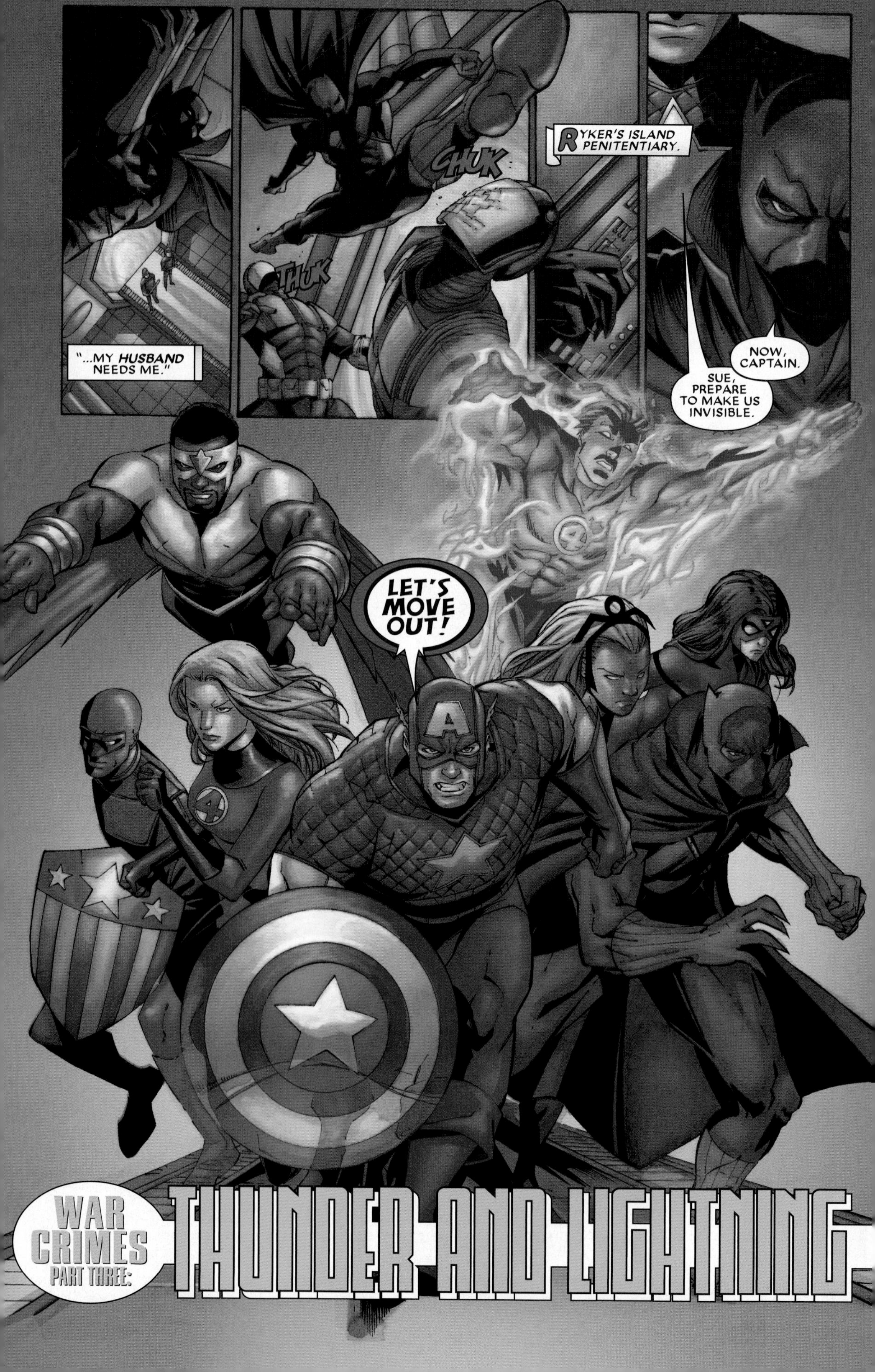
"...MY HUSBAND NEEDS ME."
CHUK
THUK
RYKER'S ISLAND PENITENTIARY.
NOW, CAPTAIN.
SUE, PREPARE TO MAKE US INVISIBLE.
LET'S MOVE OUT!
WAR CRIMES PART THREE:
THUNDER AND LIGHTNING

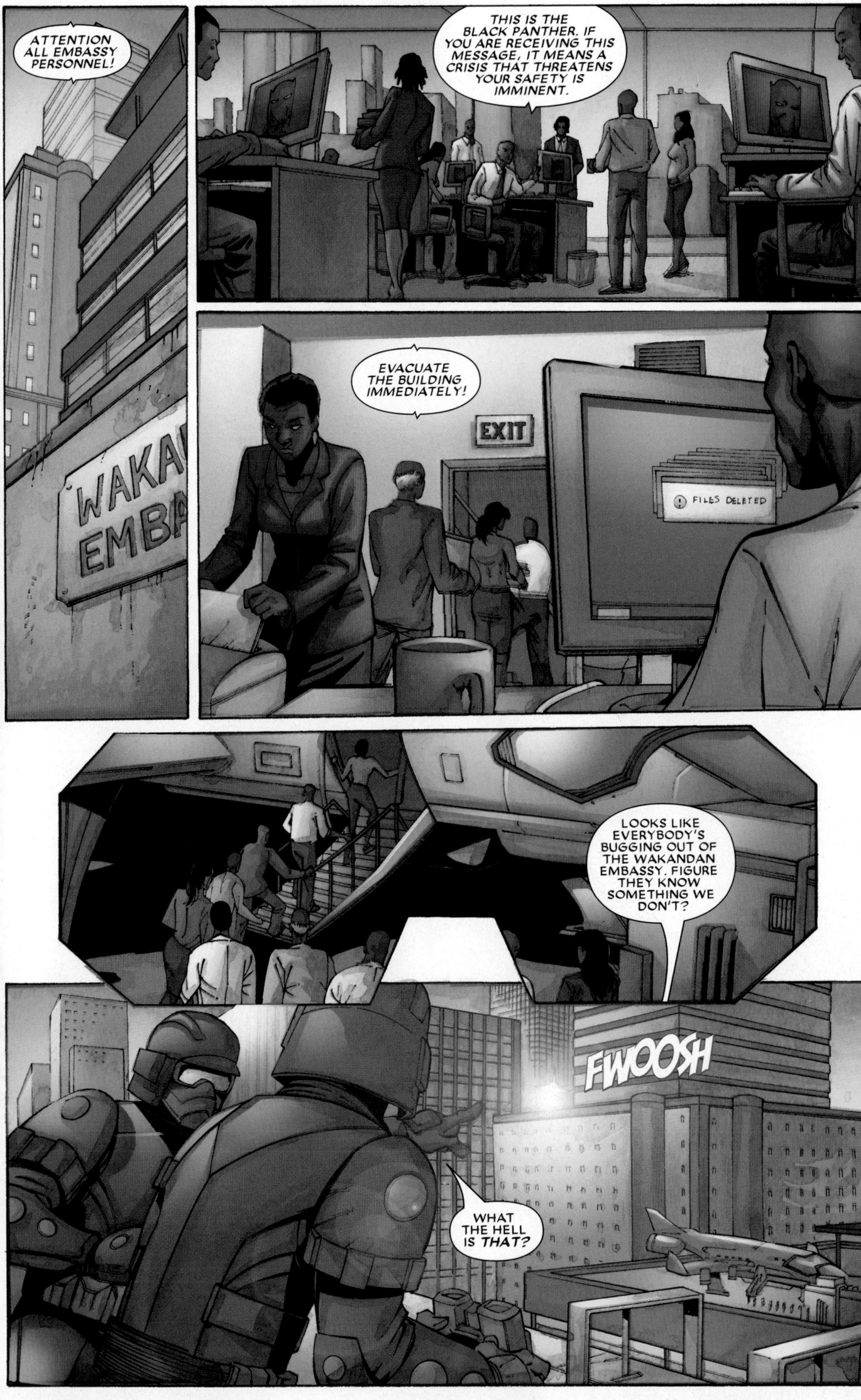
ATTENTION ALL EMBASSY PERSONNEL!
THIS IS THE BLACK PANTHER. IF YOU ARE RECEIVING THIS MESSAGE, IT MEANS A CRISIS THAT THREATENS YOUR SAFETY IS IMMINENT.
WAKA
EMBA
EVACUATE THE BUILDING IMMEDIATELY!
EXIT
FILES DELETED
LOOKS LIKE EVERYBODY'S BUGGING OUT OF THE WAKANDAN EMBASSY. FIGURE THEY KNOW SOMETHING WE DON'T?
FWOOSH
WHAT THE HELL IS *THAT?*

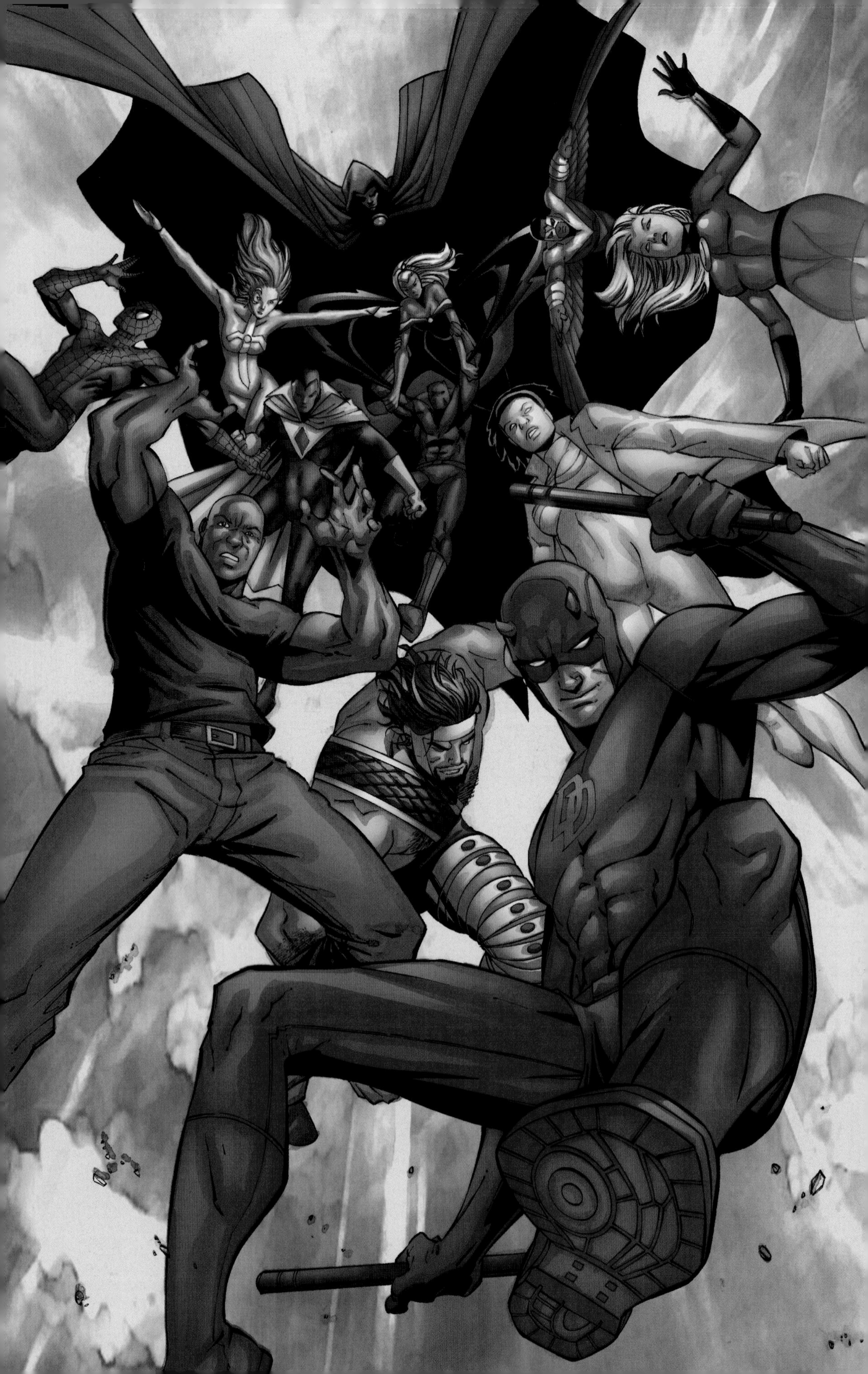

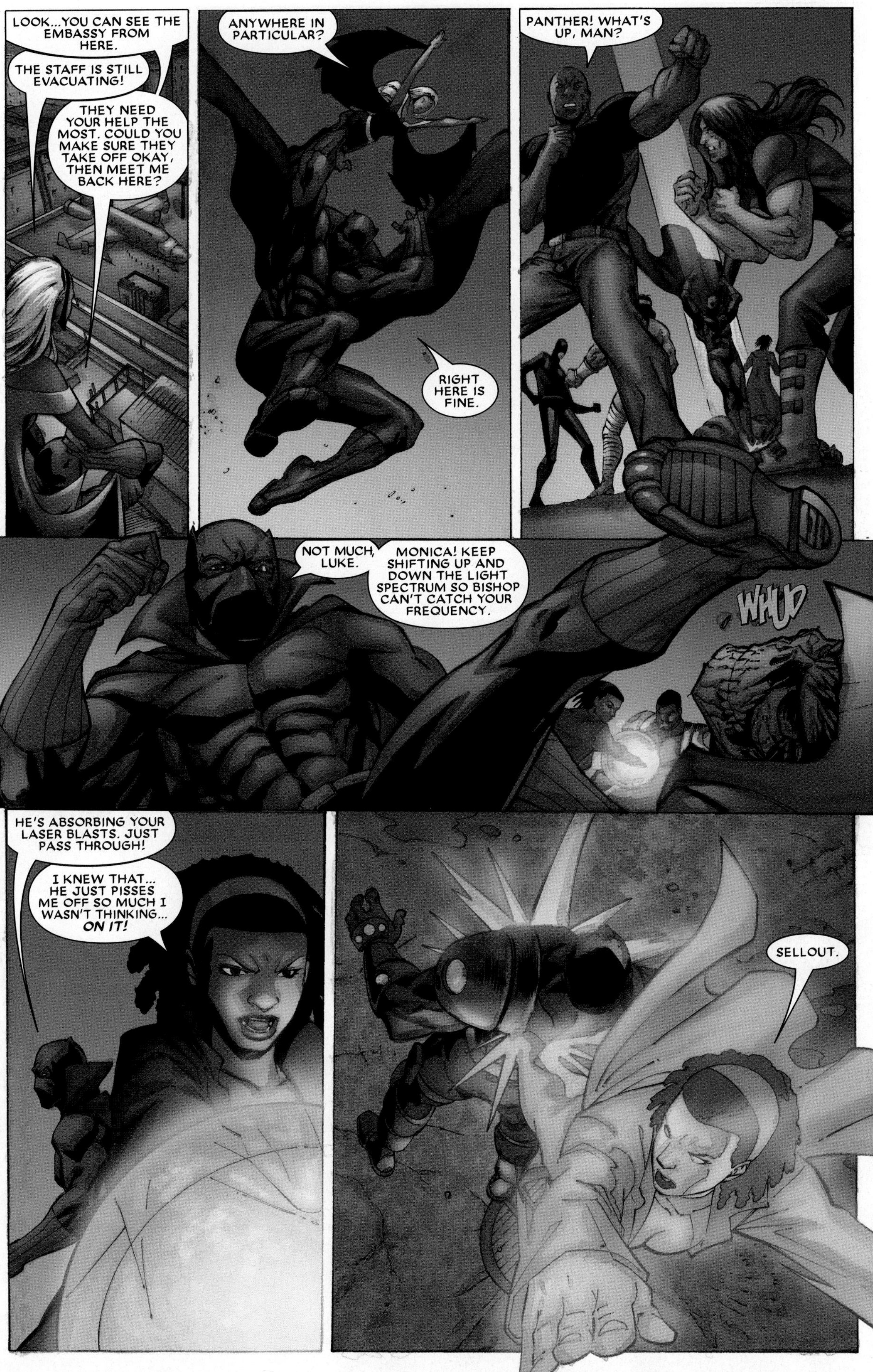
LOOK...YOU CAN SEE THE EMBASSY FROM HERE.
THE STAFF IS STILL EVACUATING!
THEY NEED YOUR HELP THE MOST. COULD YOU MAKE SURE THEY TAKE OFF OKAY, THEN MEET ME BACK HERE?
ANYWHERE IN PARTICULAR?
RIGHT HERE IS FINE.
PANTHER! WHAT'S UP, MAN?
NOT MUCH, LUKE.
MONICA! KEEP SHIFTING UP AND DOWN THE LIGHT SPECTRUM SO BISHOP CAN'T CATCH YOUR FREQUENCY.
WHUD
HE'S ABSORBING YOUR LASER BLASTS. JUST PASS THROUGH!
I KNEW THAT... HE JUST PISSES ME OFF SO MUCH I WASN'T THINKING... ON IT!
SELLOUT.

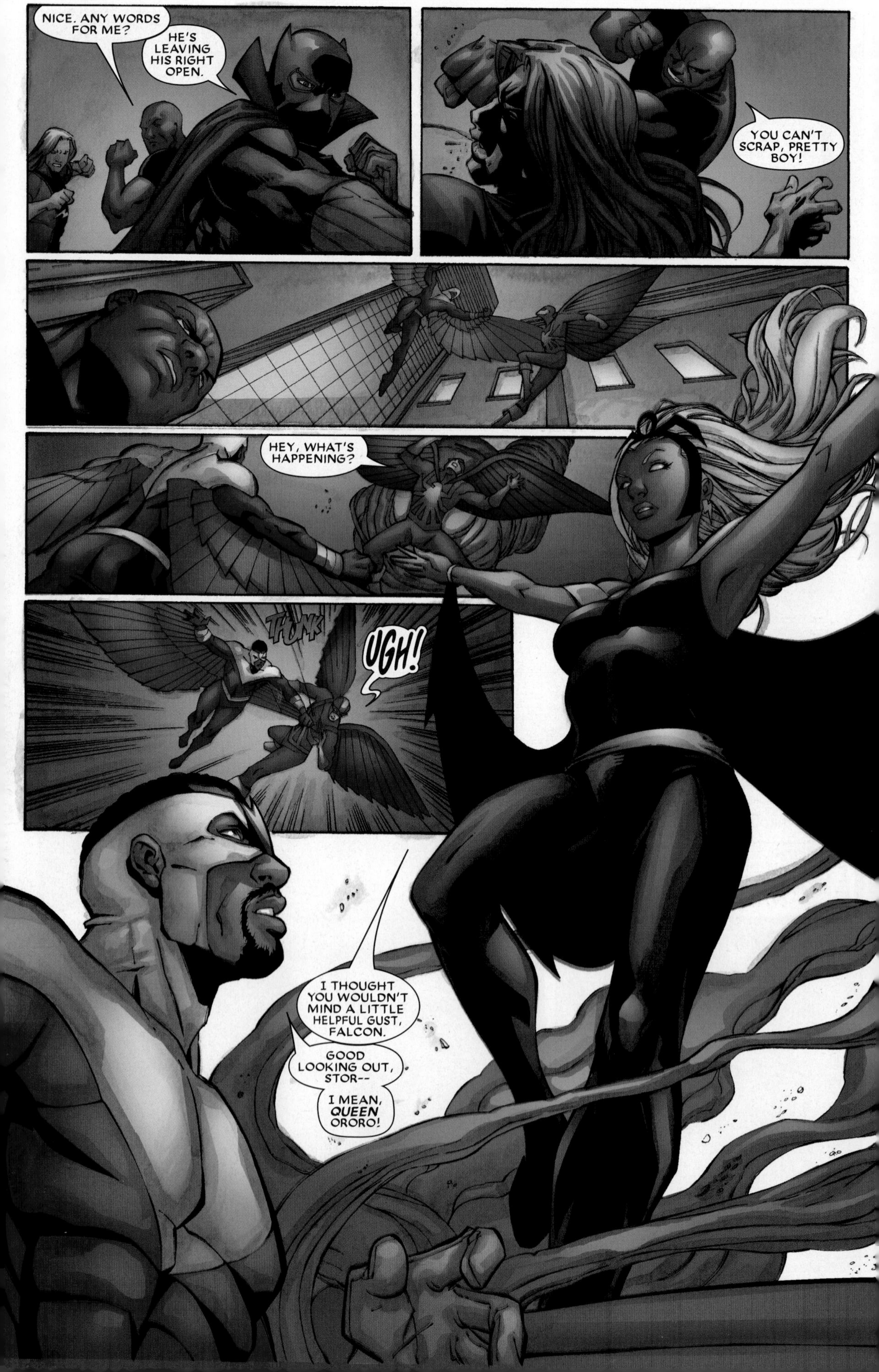
NICE. ANY WORDS FOR ME?
HE'S LEAVING HIS RIGHT OPEN.
YOU CAN'T SCRAP, PRETTY BOY!
HEY, WHAT'S HAPPENING?
THUNK
UGH!
I THOUGHT YOU WOULDN'T MIND A LITTLE HELPFUL GUST, FALCON.
GOOD LOOKING OUT, STOR--
I MEAN, QUEEN ORORO!

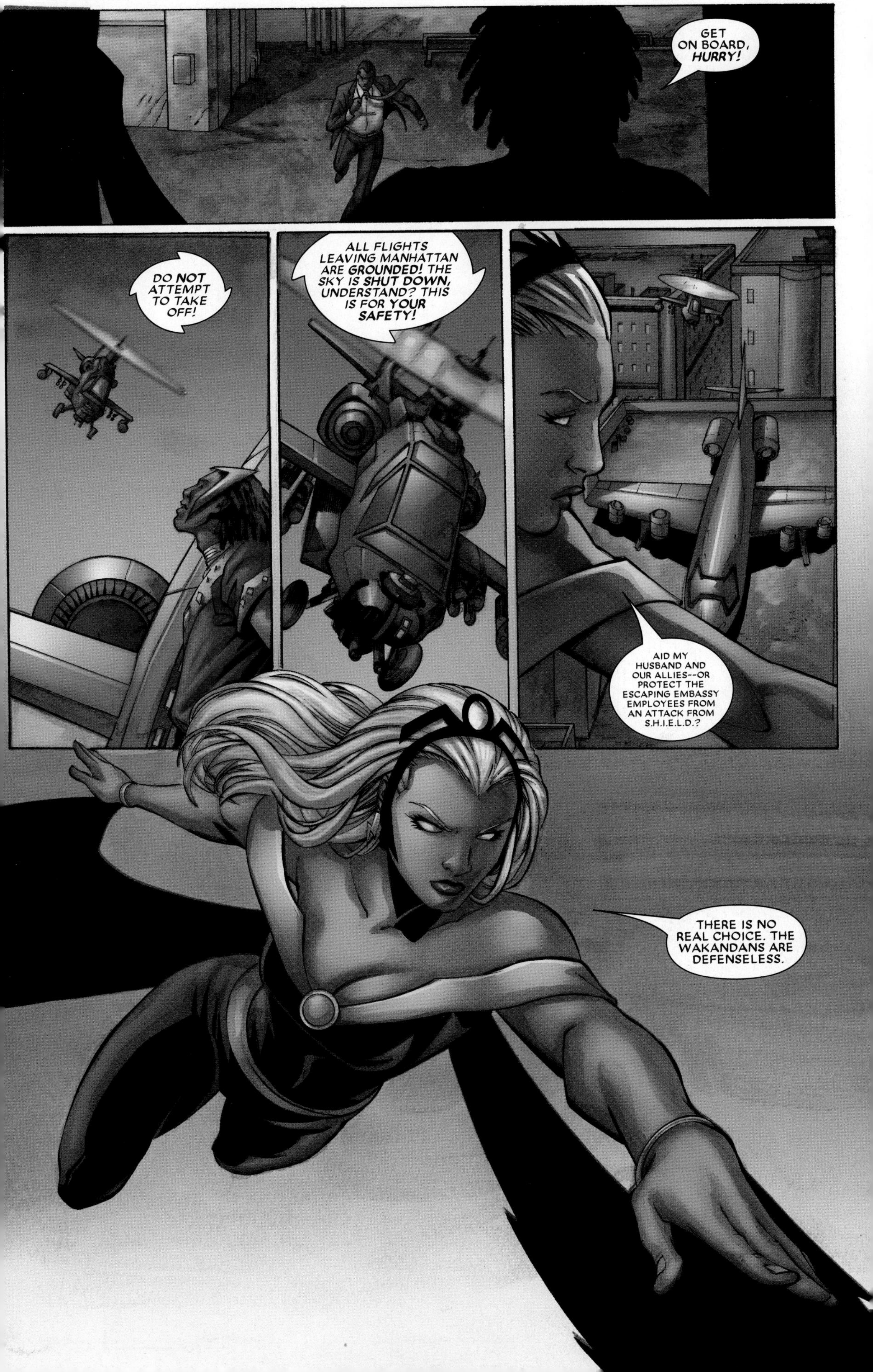
GET ON BOARD, HURRY!
DO NOT ATTEMPT TO TAKE OFF!
ALL FLIGHTS LEAVING MANHATTAN ARE GROUNDED! THE SKY IS SHUT DOWN, UNDERSTAND? THIS IS FOR YOUR SAFETY!
AID MY HUSBAND AND OUR ALLIES--OR PROTECT THE ESCAPING EMBASSY EMPLOYEES FROM AN ATTACK FROM S.H.I.E.L.D.?
THERE IS NO REAL CHOICE. THE WAKANDANS ARE DEFENSELESS.

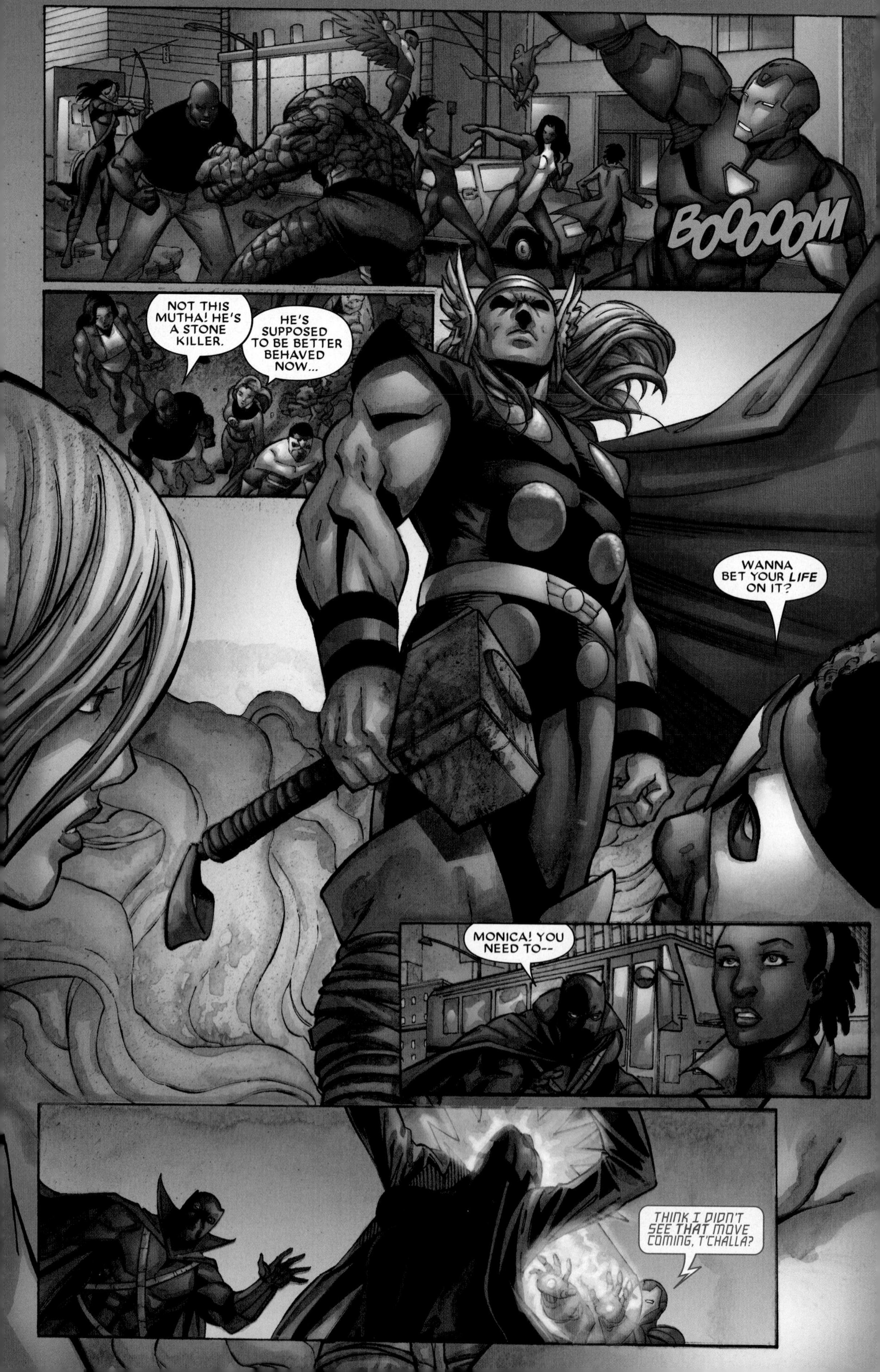
BOOOOOM
NOT THIS MUTHA! HE'S A STONE KILLER.
HE'S SUPPOSED TO BE BETTER BEHAVED NOW...
WANNA BET YOUR LIFE ON IT?
MONICA! YOU NEED TO--
THINK I DIDN'T SEE THAT MOVE COMING, T'CHALLA?

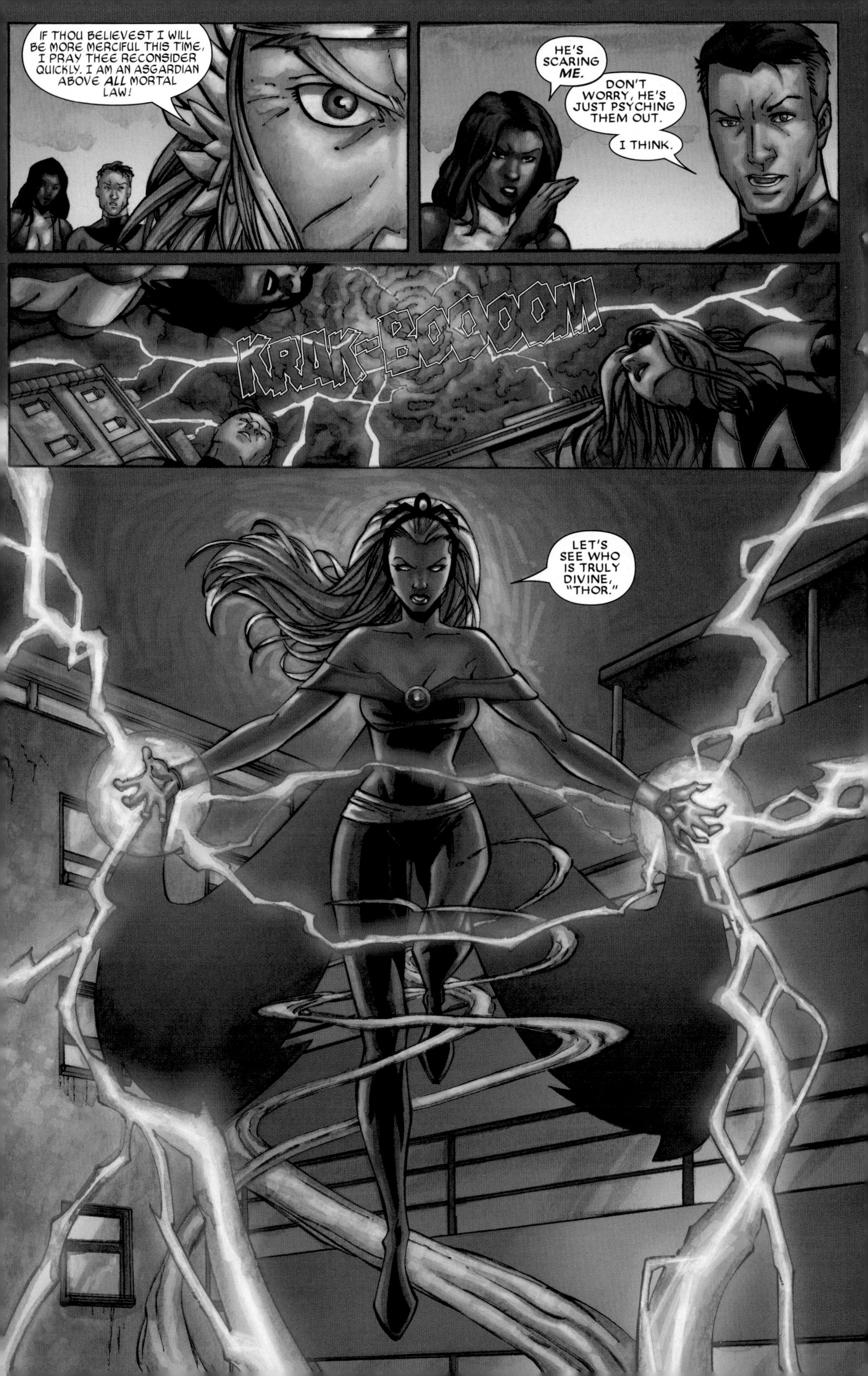
IF THOU BELIEVEST I WILL BE MORE MERCIFUL THIS TIME, I PRAY THEE RECONSIDER QUICKLY. I AM AN ASGARDIAN ABOVE ALL MORTAL LAW!
HE'S SCARING ME.
DON'T WORRY, HE'S JUST PSYCHING THEM OUT.
I THINK.
KRAK-BOOOOM
LET'S SEE WHO IS TRULY DIVINE, "THOR."

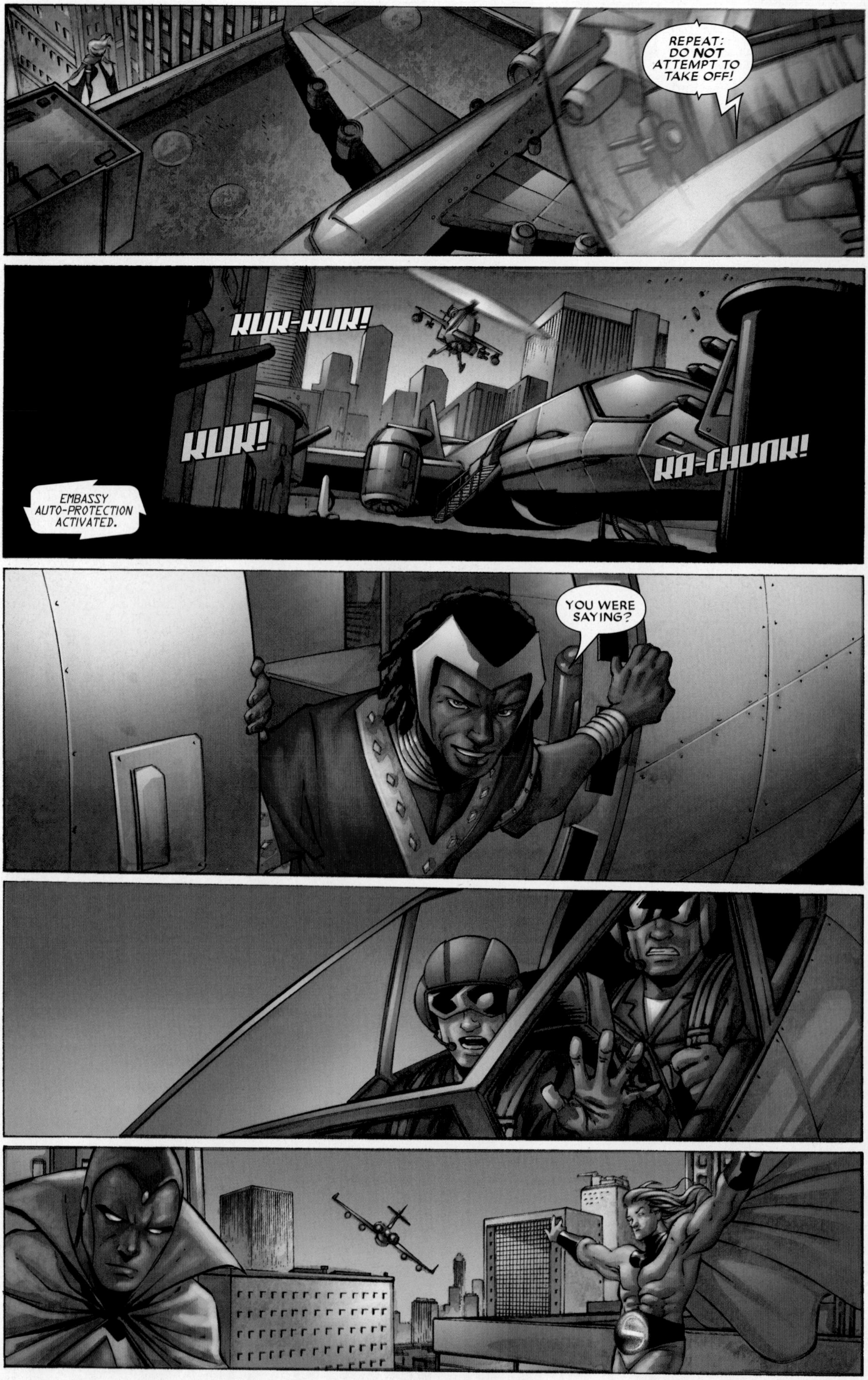
REPEAT: DO NOT ATTEMPT TO TAKE OFF!
KUK-KUK!
KUK!
KA-CHUNK!
EMBASSY AUTO-PROTECTION ACTIVATED.
YOU WERE SAYING?

KER-RAAAAAAASH

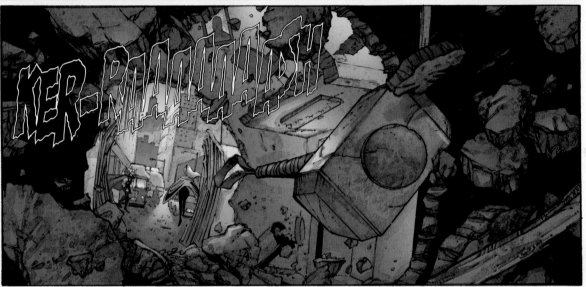

YOU'RE GONNA HAVE TO PAY FOR DAMAGES, YOU KNOW.

DO YOU THINK THIS IS A JOKING MATTER?

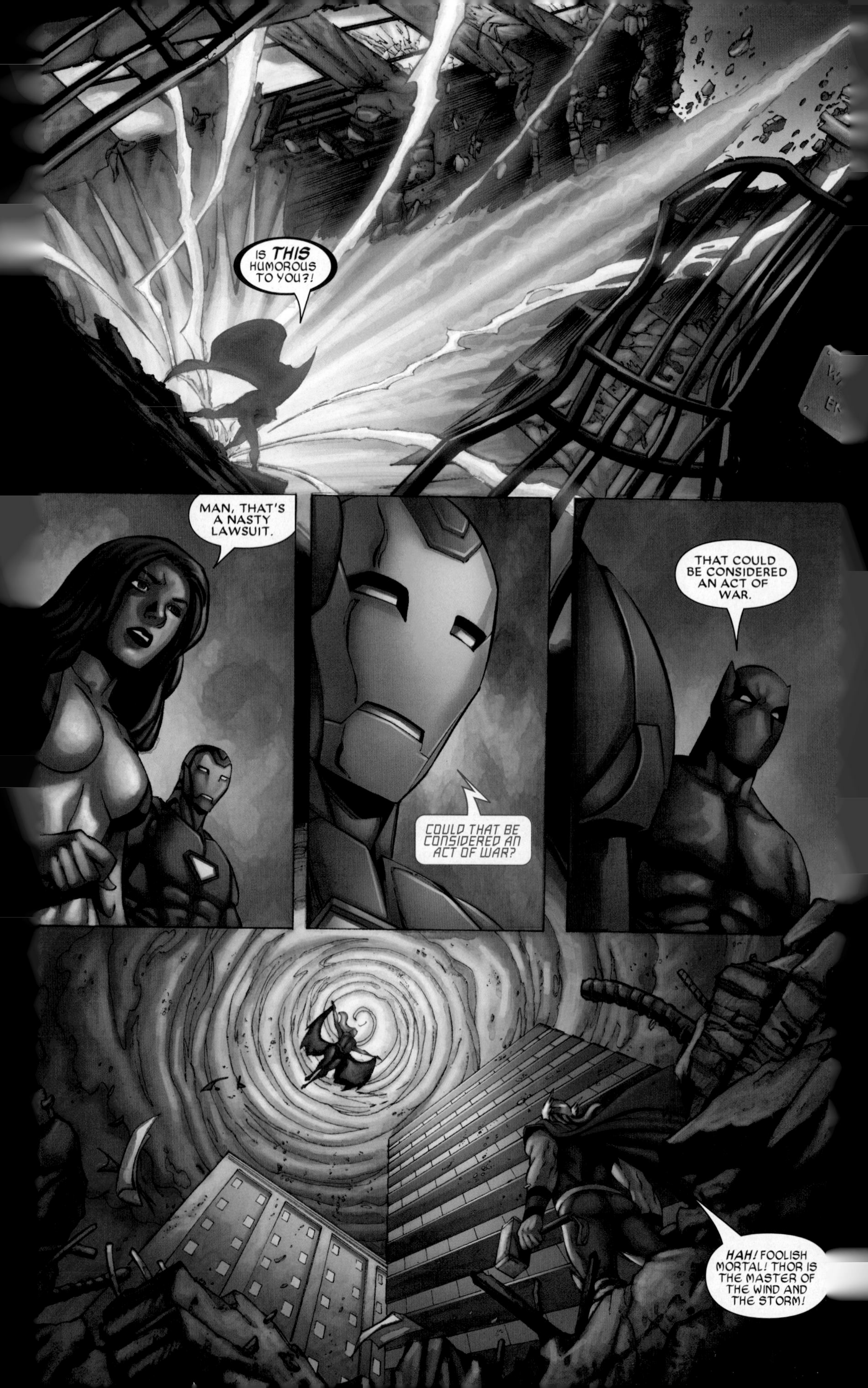
IS THIS HUMOROUS TO YOU?!
MAN, THAT'S A NASTY LAWSUIT.
COULD THAT BE CONSIDERED AN ACT OF WAR?
THAT COULD BE CONSIDERED AN ACT OF WAR.
HAH! FOOLISH MORTAL! THOR IS THE MASTER OF THE WIND AND THE STORM!

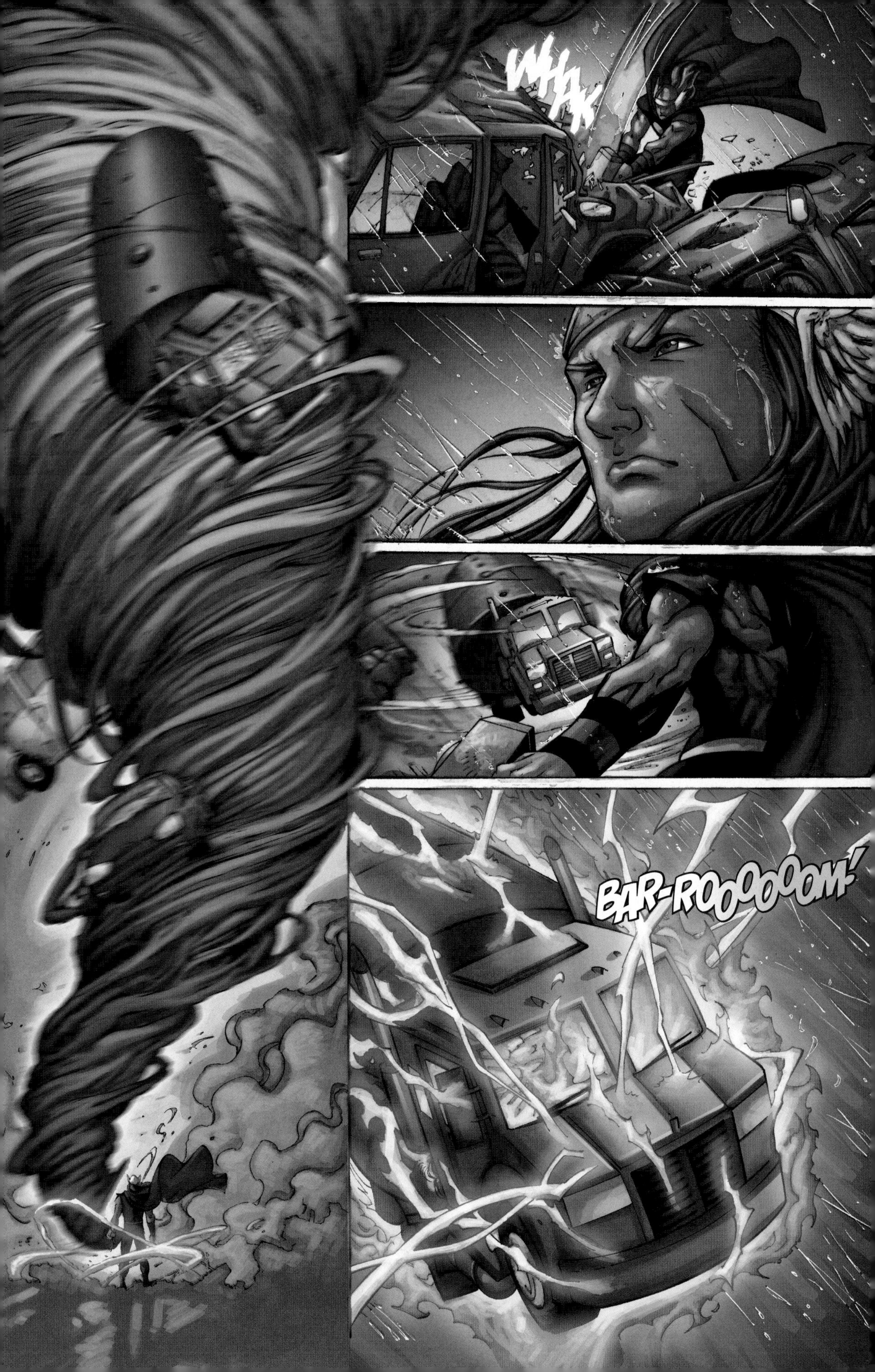
WHAK
BAR-ROOOOOOM!

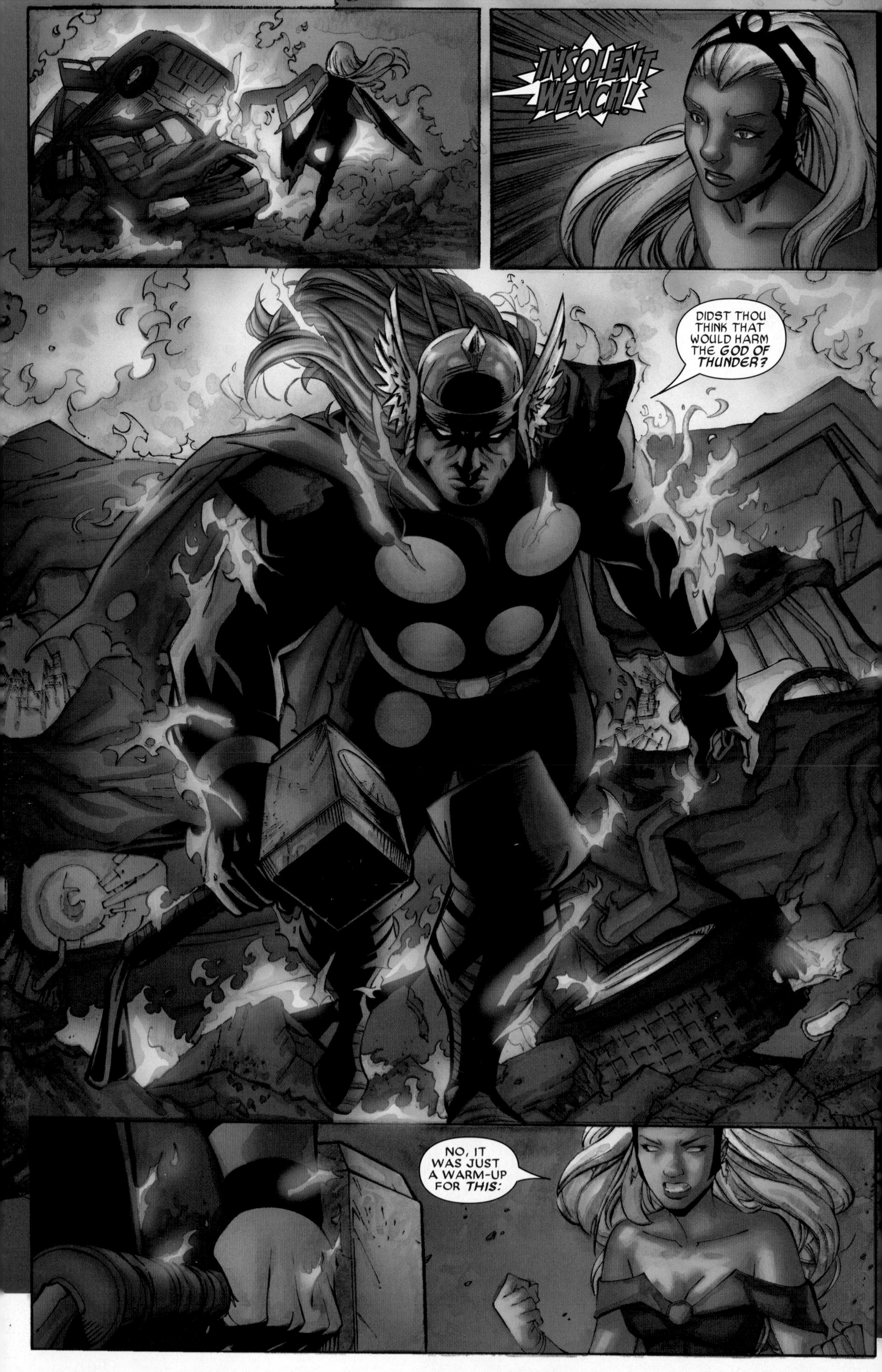
INSOLENT WENCH!
DIDST THOU THINK THAT WOULD HARM THE GOD OF THUNDER?
NO, IT WAS JUST A WARM-UP FOR THIS:

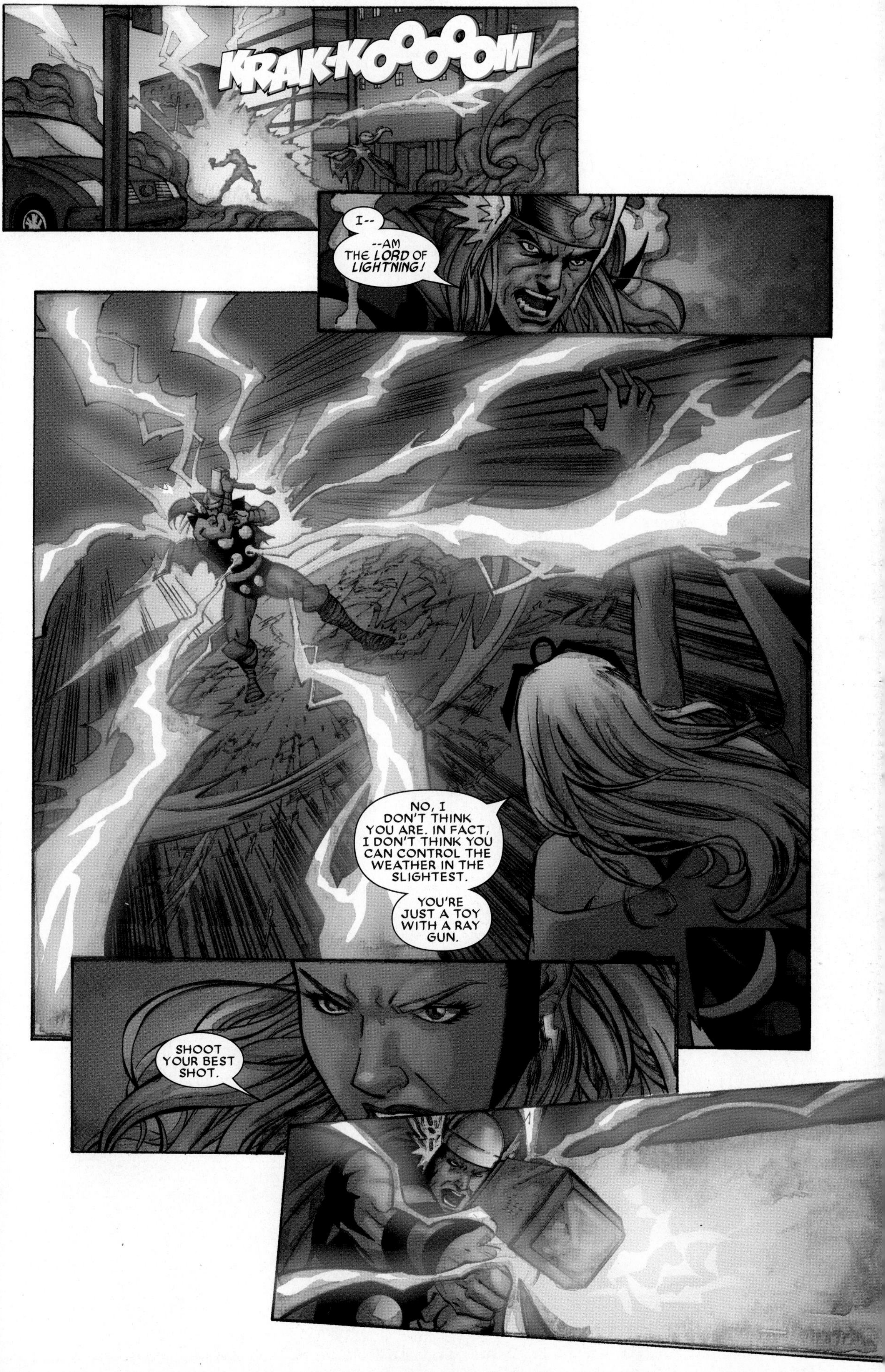
KRAK-KOOOOOOM
I--
--AM THE LORD OF LIGHTNING!
NO, I DON'T THINK YOU ARE. IN FACT, I DON'T THINK YOU CAN CONTROL THE WEATHER IN THE SLIGHTEST.
YOU'RE JUST A TOY WITH A RAY GUN.
SHOOT YOUR BEST SHOT.

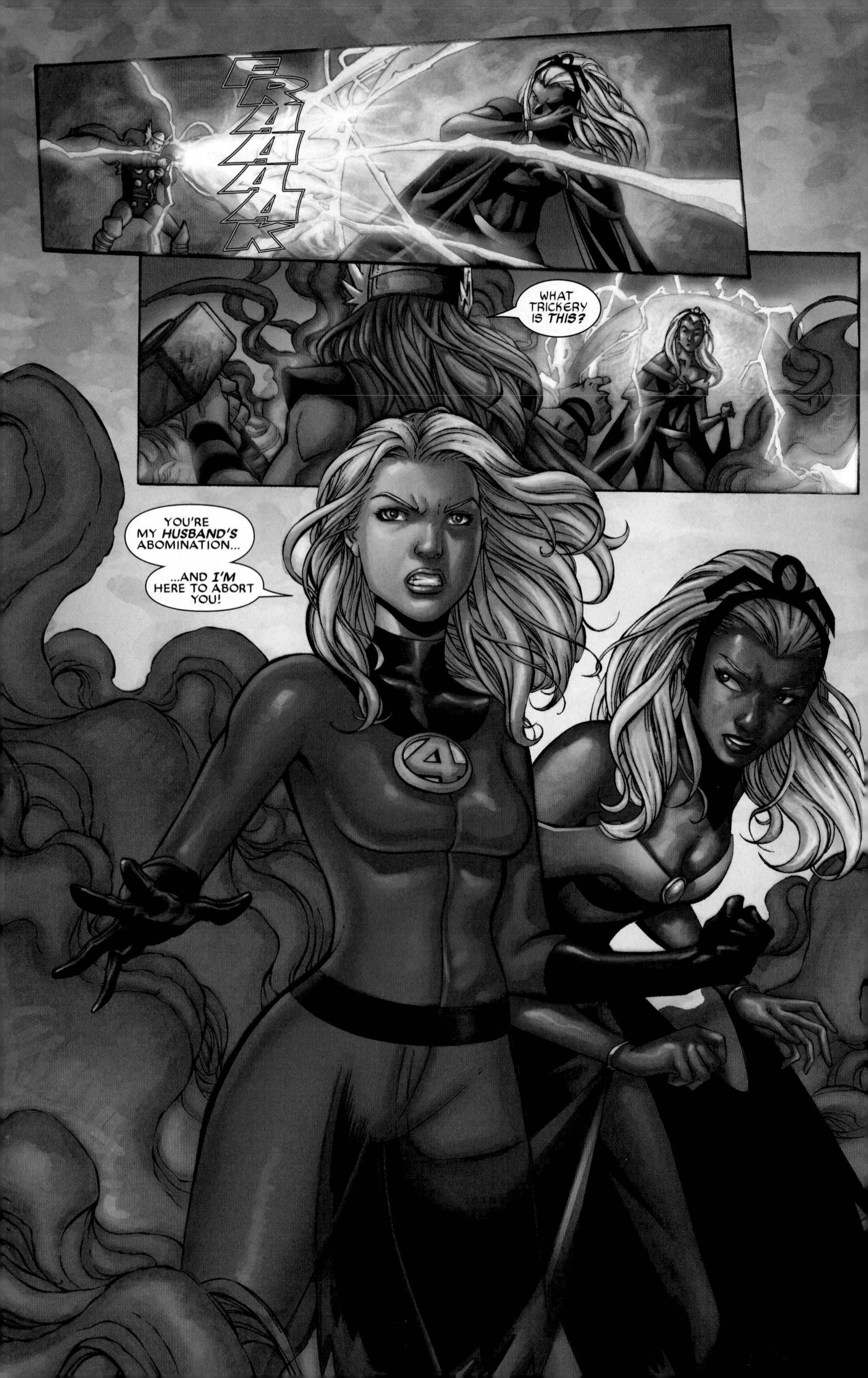
FRAAAAK
WHAT TRICKERY IS THIS?
YOU'RE MY HUSBAND'S ABOMINATION...
...AND I'M HERE TO ABORT YOU!

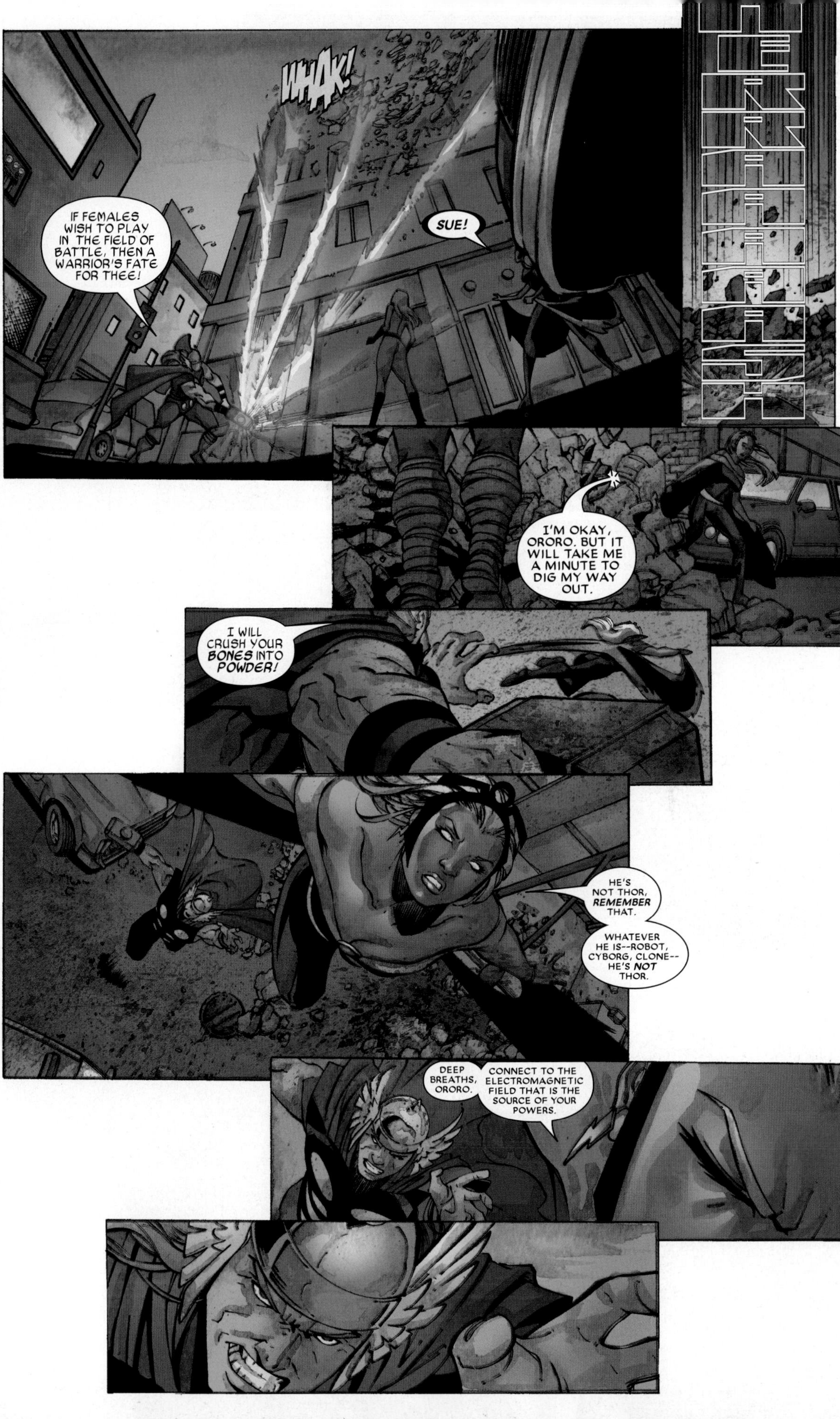
WHAK!
IF FEMALES WISH TO PLAY IN THE FIELD OF BATTLE, THEN A WARRIOR'S FATE FOR THEE!
SUE!
I'M OKAY, ORORO. BUT IT WILL TAKE ME A MINUTE TO DIG MY WAY OUT.
I WILL CRUSH YOUR BONES INTO POWDER!
HE'S NOT THOR, REMEMBER THAT.
WHATEVER HE IS--ROBOT, CYBORG, CLONE--HE'S NOT THOR.
DEEP BREATHS, ORORO.
CONNECT TO THE ELECTROMAGNETIC FIELD THAT IS THE SOURCE OF YOUR POWERS.

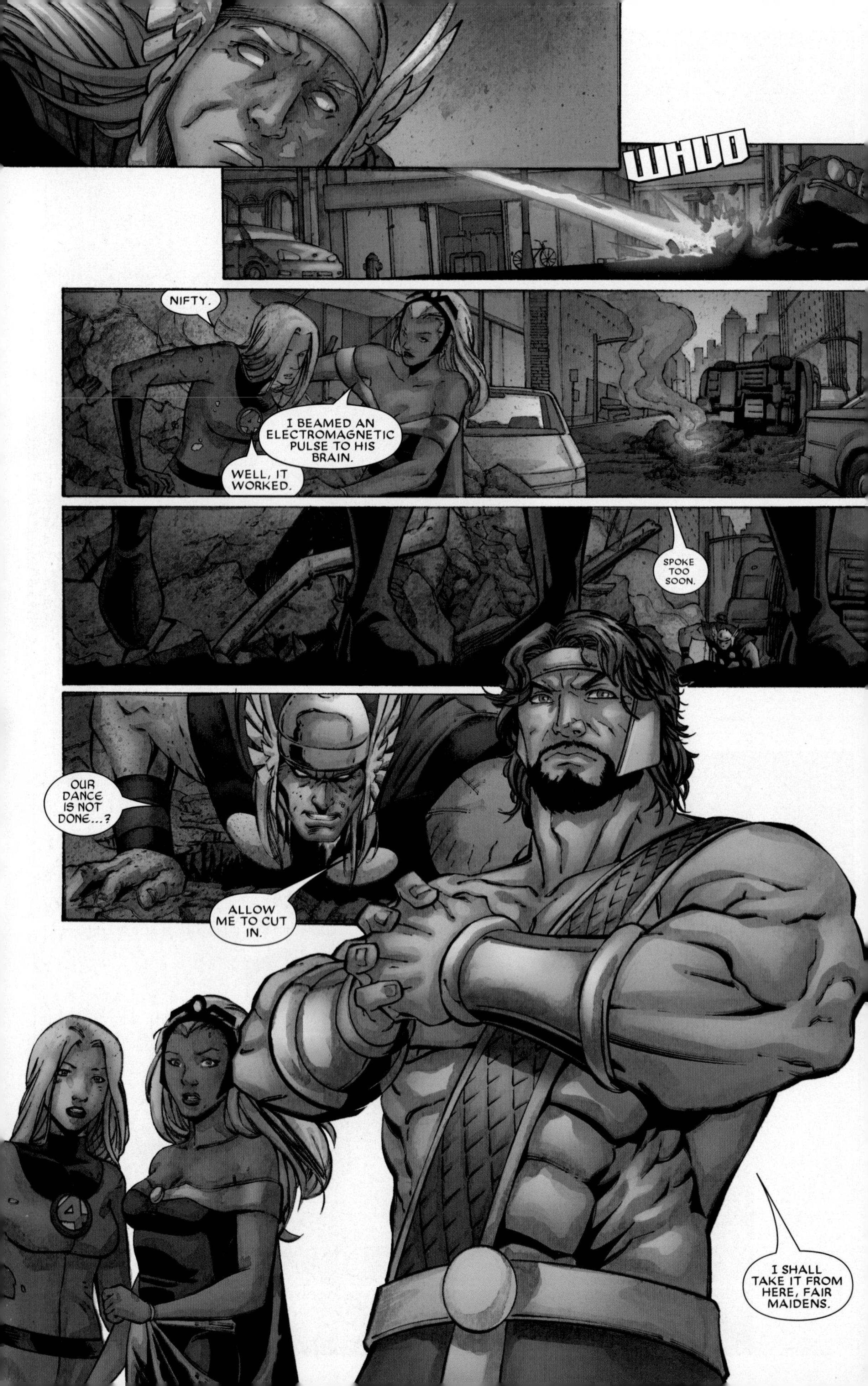
WHUD
NIFTY.
I BEAMED AN ELECTROMAGNETIC PULSE TO HIS BRAIN.
WELL, IT WORKED.
SPOKE TOO SOON.
OUR DANCE IS NOT DONE...?
ALLOW ME TO CUT IN.
I SHALL TAKE IT FROM HERE, FAIR MAIDENS.

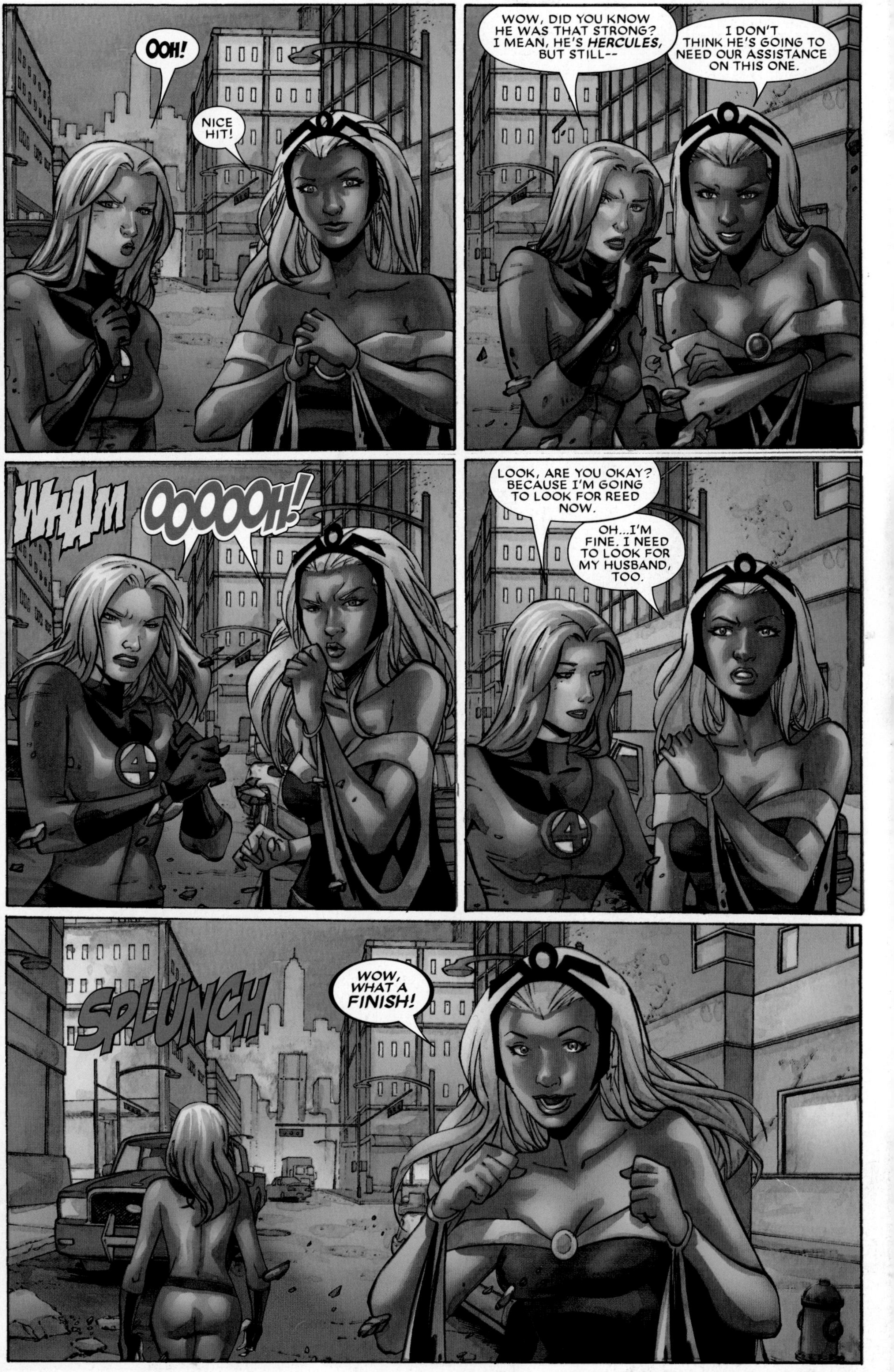
OOH!
NICE HIT!
WOW, DID YOU KNOW HE WAS THAT STRONG? I MEAN, HE'S HERCULES, BUT STILL--
I DON'T THINK HE'S GOING TO NEED OUR ASSISTANCE ON THIS ONE.
WHAM
OOOOOH!
LOOK, ARE YOU OKAY? BECAUSE I'M GOING TO LOOK FOR REED NOW.
OH...I'M FINE. I NEED TO LOOK FOR MY HUSBAND, TOO.
SPLUNCH
WOW, WHAT A FINISH!

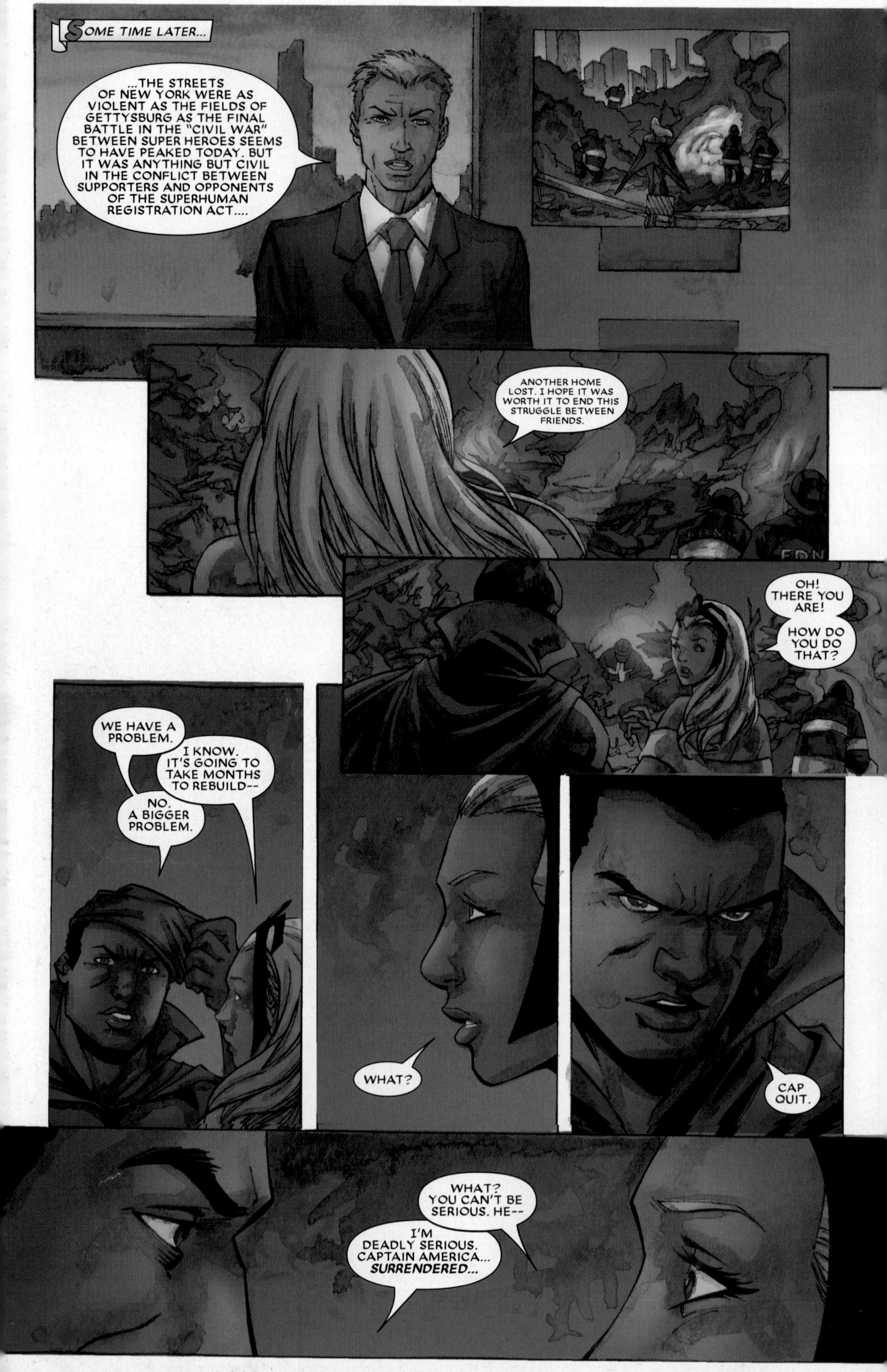
SOME TIME LATER...
...THE STREETS OF NEW YORK WERE AS VIOLENT AS THE FIELDS OF GETTYSBURG AS THE FINAL BATTLE IN THE "CIVIL WAR" BETWEEN SUPER HEROES SEEMS TO HAVE PEAKED TODAY. BUT IT WAS ANYTHING BUT CIVIL IN THE CONFLICT BETWEEN SUPPORTERS AND OPPONENTS OF THE SUPERHUMAN REGISTRATION ACT....
ANOTHER HOME LOST. I HOPE IT WAS WORTH IT TO END THIS STRUGGLE BETWEEN FRIENDS.
OH! THERE YOU ARE!
HOW DO YOU DO THAT?
WE HAVE A PROBLEM.
I KNOW. IT'S GOING TO TAKE MONTHS TO REBUILD--
NO. A BIGGER PROBLEM.
WHAT?
CAP QUIT.
WHAT? YOU CAN'T BE SERIOUS. HE--
I'M DEADLY SERIOUS. CAPTAIN AMERICA... SURRENDERED...

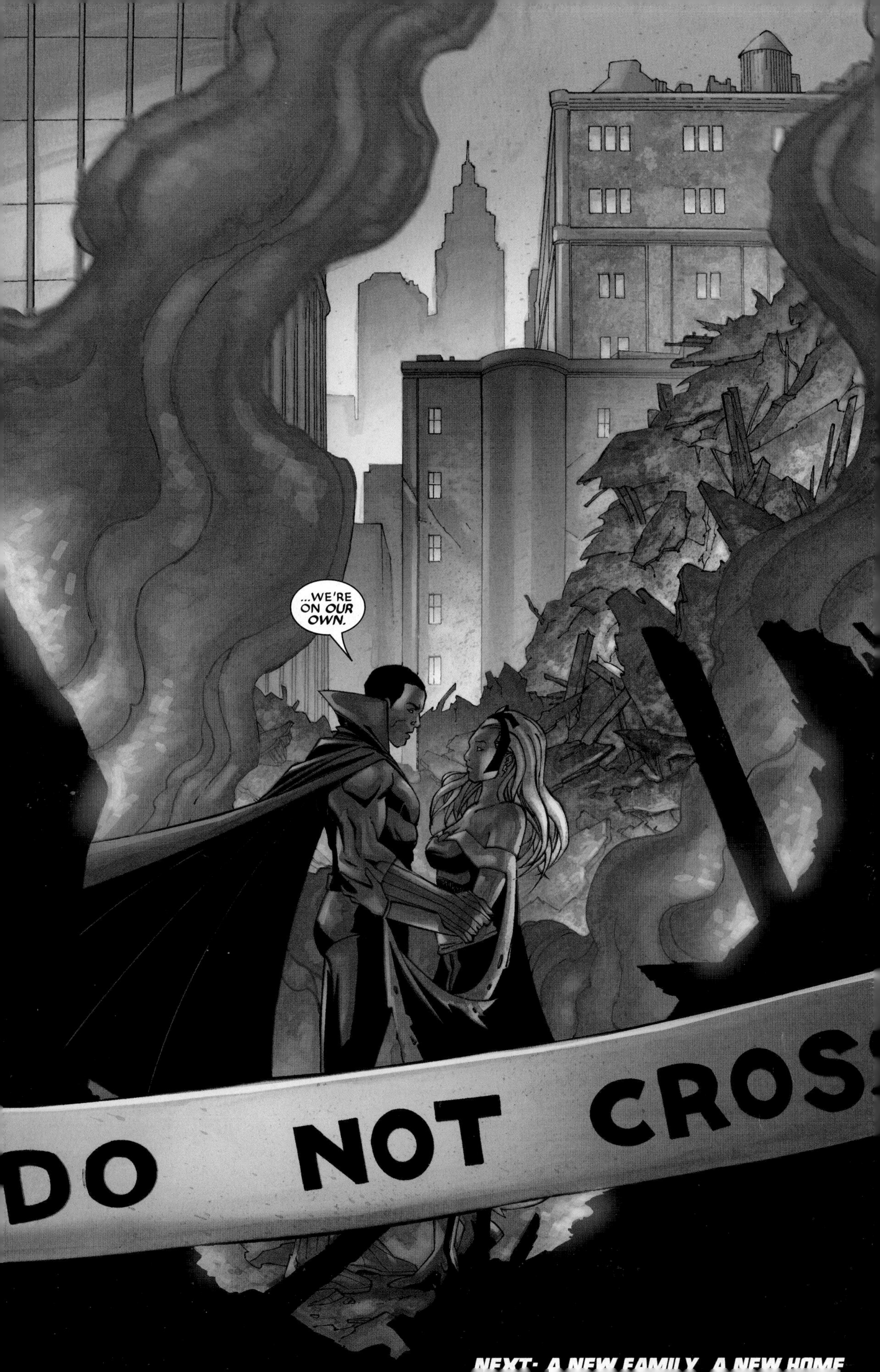
...WE'RE ON OUR OWN.
DO NOT CROSS
NEXT: A NEW FAMILY, A NEW HOME

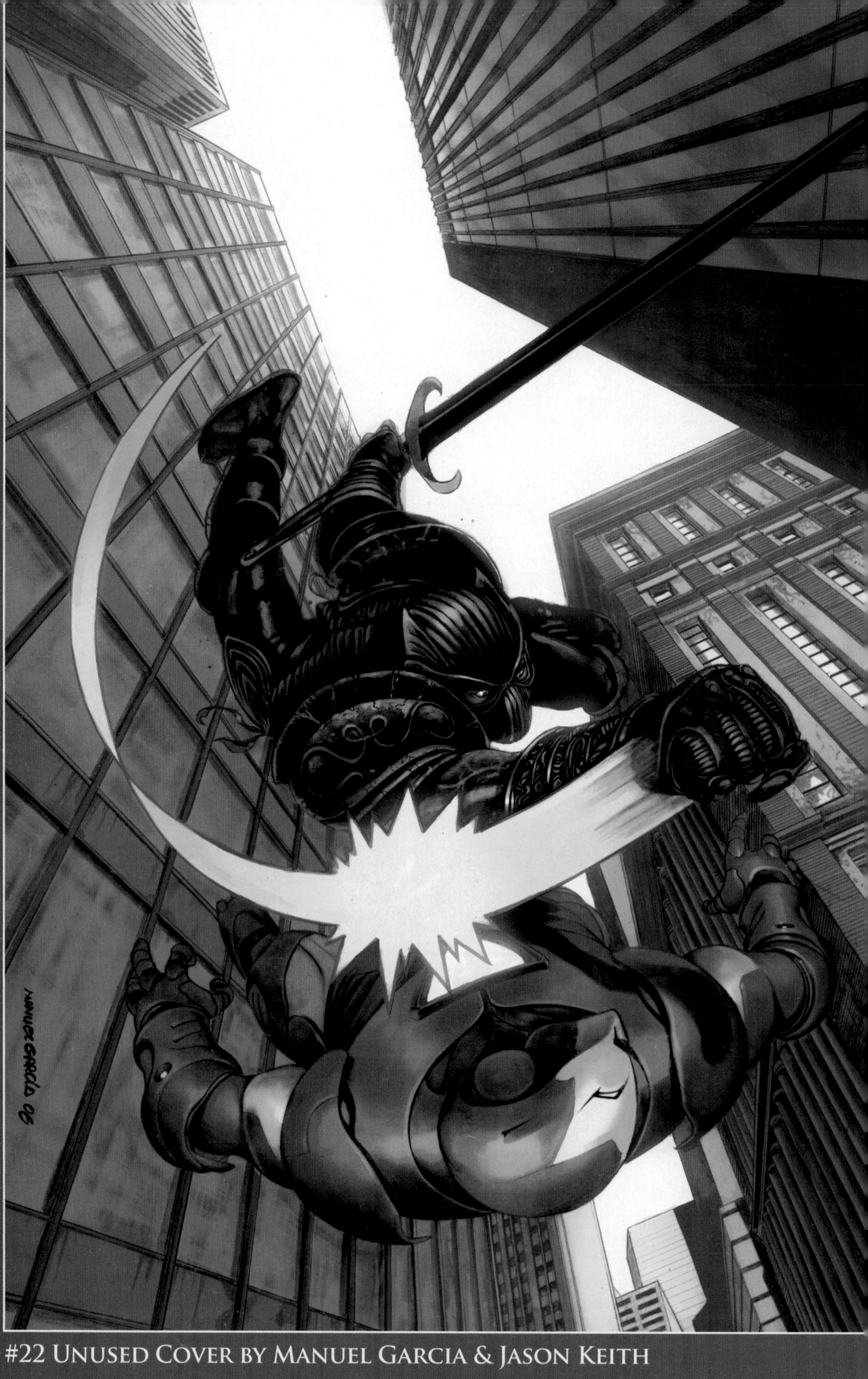

#22 Unused Cover by Manuel Garcia & Jason Keith